American

WOOD TYPE

1828-1900

*notes on the evolution
of decorated and large types
and comments on
related trades of the period*

Rob Roy Kelly

REISSUED BY

Liber Apertus Press

SARATOGA, CALIFORNIA

Reissued April 2010
ISBN 978-0-9785881-7-5

Liber Apertus Press

P.O. Box 261, Saratoga, CA 95071 USA
www.LiberApertus.com
books@LiberApertus.com

First published in 1969 by Van Nostrand Reinhold

ORIGINAL PRODUCTION INFORMATION:

Designed by Rob Roy Kelly.

Type set by Graphic Arts Typographers, Inc.
Printed by Halliday Lithograph Corporation.
Bound by Montauk Book Manufacturing Co., Inc.

ACKNOWLEDGMENTS

A book that is the work of a single person is seldom published, and this one is no exception. I would like to give special thanks to the many students who have assisted me over a period of ten years. I am greatly indebted to the late Roland Baughman, Head of Special Collections, Butler Library, Columbia University, New York for his generous assistance in making available to me materials in the American Typefounders Library. Also, I am indebted to the following persons and organizations for their gracious cooperation and aid.

William Thurman, Superintendent of Printing and Binding, New York Public Library, New York.

James Wells, Custodian, Wing Foundation, Newberry Library, Chicago, Illinois.

Carey S. Bliss, Curator of Rare Books, Henry E. Huntington Library and Art Gallery, San Marino, California.

Dr. James Eckman, Rochester, Minnesota.

Al Puppeteer, Technical Publications, Hamilton Mfg. Co., Two Rivers, Wisconsin.

Dr. Carl Miller, Director, Photographic Division, 3M Company, St. Paul, Minnesota.

Herman Cohen, Chiswick Book Shop, New York.

Willard Morgan and his two sons, Lloyd and Douglas, Morgan Press, Hastings on the Hudson, New York.

Martin Friedman, Director, Walker Art Center, Minneapolis, Minnesota.

Warner K. Morgans, Middletown, New York.

Thompson R. Harlow, Connecticut Historical Society, Hartford, Connecticut.

Thomas Girard, Historical Society of Middletown, Middletown, New York.

Mrs. H. Nichols, Guilford Smith Memorial Library, South Windham, Connecticut.

Edward Graf, Passaic County Historical Society, Paterson, New Jersey.

Jackson Burke, Former Director of Typographical Development, Mergenthaler Linotype Company, New York.

Wayne County Historical Society, Wooster, Ohio.

John Leslie Paper Company, Minneapolis, Minnesota.

Dahl & Curry Typesetting, Inc., Minneapolis, Minnesota.

Colwell Press, Minneapolis, Minnesota.

Kansas City Regional Council for Higher Education, Kansas City, Missouri.

Kansas City Art Institute, Kansas City, Missouri.

Van Nostrand Reinhold Company, New York.

CONTENTS

Rob Roy Kelly created a pioneering work in *American Wood Type* that, forty years on, remains the most comprehensive history of wood type manufacturing.

Kelly's research grew directly out of collecting wood type from local printers for his students to use in their studies at the Minneapolis College of Art & Design. He began gathering the types in the late 1950s and continued adding to the collection over the following decade. Research into the history, manufacture and use of the burgeoning collection started in response to questions that arose from working with his students. The collection grew to consist of nearly 150 faces of various sizes and styles, including examples of the most popular printing types from the nineteenth century. Kelly sold the collection in early 1966, to Dr Bernard Karpel head librarian of The Museum of Modern Art, who in turn sold it to the Harry Ransom Humanities Research Center at The University of Texas at Austin. The collection, now known officially as the Rob Roy Kelly American Wood Type Collection was transferred to the care of the Design Division of the College of Fine Arts in 1993. It remains, as Kelly intended, an active study collection for students and scholars.

Kelly's research was first published in the 1963 issue of *Design Quarterly* (No. 56), followed in 1964 by a limited-edition folio of specimen sheets from his collection, entitled *American Wood Types 1828–1900, Volume One,* and would culminate with the publishing in 1969 of the seminal *American Wood Type, 1828–1900: Notes on the Evolution of Decorated and Large Types and Comments on Related Trades of the Period.* During the 1960s and 1970s, Kelly's published research helped fuel a revival of interest in nineteenth century American printing types, and in doing so, helped preserve a valuable facet of American history. His research also influenced the 1983 Smithsonian exhibition entitled "The Fat and the Lean: American Wood Type in the 19th century" which drew heavily from the Smithsonian's own Morgan Press Type Collection.

While there was a renewed interest in wood type between the publishing of the first edition and the paperback edition of *American Wood Type,* the real growth in interest has occurred in the last 15 years. Since the mid-1990s, wood type has become much more apparent in visual culture and is tied to a broader revived interest in letterpress printing. Testifying to the growing popularity of wood type with a newer generation of printers and typographers, there are a number of ambitious websites focused exclusively on wood type research and discussion: *Woodtyper, End Grain* and *Letterpress Daily*[1] to name but a few. There are also a number of people experimenting with producing wood type, developing new approaches to production with traditional router/pantograph methods, CNC machines and digital laser-cutter processes. Another strong indicator of the interest in wood type was the opening, in 1999, of the Hamilton Wood Type & Printing Museum. Located in the former Hamilton Manufacturing Company factory in Two Rivers, Wisconsin, the Museum is an institution unique for a hands-on approach to its wood type holdings and its collection of working machinery used in all steps of wood type production.

Kelly's work continues to be a vital influence. His astute delineation of the broad outlines of wood type history in nineteenth century America persists as a substantially ac-

curate primary source. It remains the starting point for all current scholarly inquiry, and has inspired researchers and practitioners "to pick up where [Kelly] left off."[2]

The research that I have conducted at The University of Texas at Austin over the past four years has been to expand upon Kelly's original work. In forging new ground, I have focused on developing methods for identifying the manufacturers of previously unattributed type by examining the rough planing patterns found on the back of finished type blocks. The irregularities in patterns between different manufacturers provide a unique ability to specify the production origin of particular type blocks. This has helped expand the information available on nineteenth and twentieth century wood type manufacturing and distribution practices.

Specimen books discovered since Kelly published *American Wood Type* as well as access to the corporate archives of the Hamilton Manufacturing Company, among other sources, have provided the material necessary to correct dates of origin and more precisely name typeface designs. While cataloging the names applied to each typeface design I produced a list of all the names used by all the known manufacturers for any one design and recorded the dates that the design was first shown by each manufacturer. This data more clearly illustrates the time it took a new wood type design to be "adopted" by the original manufacturer's competition. I describe this research in greater detail in an article published by the American Printing History Association.[3]

The Kelly Collection website[4] provides the most current information on all of the items in the collection, not just the types included in Kelly's publications. The site also includes an extensive bibliography of known specimen books from American wood type manufacturers as well as an industry-wide timeline incorporating relevant dates after 1900. The website will be updated as new information comes to light.

Forty years on, Kelly's seminal work remains a giant on whose shoulders we stand. He wrote *American Wood Type* because it needed to be written and in doing so laid the foundation for a new wave of scholarship. For this we can be forever grateful to Mr Kelly.

DAVID SHIELDS
*Associate Professor of Design, The University of Texas at Austin
Design Curator, Rob Roy Kelly American Wood Type Collection*
MARCH 2010

---

1 These sites can be found at www.woodtyper.com, www.end-grain.net and www.letterpress.dwolske.com respectively.

2 Nick Sherman, "Long live Rob Roy Kelly: A dedication and mission statement," *Woodtyper,* entry posted April 8, 2009, http://woodtyper.com/1 .

3 David Shields. "Considering Rob Roy Kelly's American Wood Type Collection." *Printing History,* New Series no. 7 (January 2010): 21–36.

4 www.utexas.edu/cofa/a_ah/rrk/index.php

My first experience with wood type was as a graduate student at Yale University in 1953. The school had just imported some handsome Deberny and Peignot wood types. Nearly everyone has an empathy with fine wood products, and I was no exception. We used the type on a press occasionally, but more often we would ink the blocks individually and hand stamp them. These types proved to be an admirable design tool, and most students worked enthusiastically and produced exciting results.

After graduation, my first job was to set up a graphic design department in a small art school in the Midwest. The advantages of having some wood type were immediately apparent. However, we were not at Yale, and Peignot was out of the question. A brief investigation of prices for wood type manufactured in this country eliminated that source. Someone told me that often old wood type could be found in print shops, where sometimes the owner would give it away or sell it very cheaply.

My initial contact with Victorian wood types was in a loft containing used printing equipment. When the dust had been cleared from the top case and the type exposed, I saw little resemblance between these curved, pointed, and nervous-looking types and the clean Peignot sans serif that was in the back of my mind. Selecting the least offensive faces, I bought these first types and took them into the school. My own curiosity was aroused by these types, but it was really prodded into action by students' questions regarding the name of the faces, how they were made, how old they were, etc.

My problem seemed quite simple and largely one of time. I thought that on my next trip to New York City I should be able to find the answers by visiting the American Type Library in Special Collections at Columbia University. There I found a number of specimen books, but almost no information regarding the history of wood type. Quick trips to other libraries plus letters to individuals and various institutions soon made it clear that little or nothing had ever been written on the subject of wood types.

I accepted the challenge in pure innocence, and spent the next few years collecting types under all kinds of circumstances. A bottle of Scotch was exchanged for two cases of type; long, random trips were made from small town to small town to check print shops; one type was bought to trade off another; printers' relatives were cultivated. There were types for which I would have traded my car, house, or wife, and my reputation as a bore at cocktail parties grew immeasurably during these years, for not that many people were interested in wood type.

My collection grew, however, as did my notes and microfilm records. Then came the awakening: in order to know more about American wood type, it was necessary to learn about American metal types. To study these one had to know European types, as well as eighteenth- and seventeenth-century typefounding. The work did not end there; a knowledge of the related trades, social conditions, business practices, etc. was necessary!

As a result, I find myself now in the curious position of apologizing for having spent only eleven years in preparing this publication. A few years ago, spending this many years to do a simple piece of research would have seemed some form of martyrdom. Perhaps this book is premature—in some respects it undoubtedly is. There are good reasons why there is not a profusion of books on the market which cover nineteenth-century typographical history comprehensively. Sorting and identifying the sheer mass of designs and the polygenetic collection of type faces from Europe and this country is a frightening, if not impossible, undertaking. On the other hand, through a book facts and opinions may be presented which readers may challenge. This process can bring us nearer the truth and, at some later date, provide the documentation that makes accurate history possible.

A book on wood types at this time is important for three principal reasons. One, the wood types are the largest single body of unknown type faces remaining, and represent a major element in the yet-to-be-written history of display types. Two, they are specimens of pure Americana from a period when typefounding was completely dominated by European standards and designs. Three, a large number of these wood types, particularly the semi-ornamented ones, incorporate an artistic flair that can only fascinate both designers who work with the same positive-negative relationships in design and artists who become involved with the same qualities on canvas, such as Arp and Matisse in collages, Stuart Davis and Marca Relli in pigment, or others who specialize in black and white Op Art. My intention is not to encourage a further revival of wood types; my interest is historical, and I believe that nineteenth-century typographical productions can be appreciated without imposing them on current situations.

The history of the Americans as opposed to the English in the printing and typographic trades has largely been ignored in this century. Even the historical works written at the turn of the century by men like Theodore De Vinne and Henry Bullen have received small attention—and De Vinne was a remarkable man. Evidently this problem has existed for a number of years, for in 1907 Bullen commented: "In the old world, too, there has been produced a splendid and interesting literature of our art, dating from the early days of printing to the present, of which American printers know little. We have a De Vinne who has done honor to our art by research and by pen and practice, and there the list ends. We are very wide-awake commercial printers, we have done wonders in perfecting processes for rapid production, for obtaining pleasing effects at small cost; we have polished up our art, scraped off the moss, sharpened our impressions and excelled in all mechanical details; but our art in typography is narrowed to the production of beautiful ephemera, the catalogue, the magazine and its advertising pages to the necessary service of calling custom to the trader." Bullen's comments are still an accurate description of prevalent attitudes in printing and advertising today.

The coverage of related trades, historical sources, and typefounding will undoubtedly be incomplete, since these subjects in themselves each could be a book. My intention has been to pass over whenever possible those aspects which have received adequate treatment in other publications, and to expose the lesser-known details which have had a direct bearing on the evolution of display types and their design.

Seldom can you find a historical blank like the one in the history of wood type, or a profession that has suffered so much from assumptions based on false premises—or to put it more kindly, assumptions based on ignorance. Even by nineteenth-century standards, the wood type business was small and the men connected with it obscure. Although it spanned almost a hundred years, no books have been written on the subject until now, and even in its own day there were few descriptions of wood type written for trade journals. During its period of greatest use, one author prefaced an essay on wood type with the remark: "There is probably no article used by printers the manufacture of which is so little understood."

Then, as now, information was usually inaccurate or contradictory, and frequently would extend only to the life or work of a single man, without regard for predecessors or contemporaries in the field. When one considers the tremendous amount of wood type produced in those years, which may be judged to an extent by what remains, and that wood type and its designs have influenced the evolution of display typography and printing, the men responsible for the type assume an importance heretofore denied them. Though their role was not a major one, Wells, Allen, Cooley, Page, and others made enormous contributions to the printing trades in their day. My intention is to champion their rightful place in the history of American printing.

There were some illustrious metal type experts in the formative period, and although they are somewhat better known than wood type manufacturers, it is still regrettable that they have had such scant attention. The work of Bruce, Connor, White, Hagar, Johnson, and the remarkable family of Starr represents a tremendously rich heritage. As an educator, I have always been puzzled that the almost insignificant amount of history taught in connection with typography in art schools is centered around calligraphy, which is meaningful largely to text letters, that the history of typefounding is restricted to Europe, and that little or nothing is taught on the history of display types, when in truth it is with these that most graduates will work in professional practice.

Perhaps the most difficult task in a book of this sort is to assess the multitude of designs. Although it has been impossible to view every specimen book, I have tried to examine catalogues of the important foundries and to select specimens which seem to be pivotal in the evolution of styles. More details have been given on the typefounders' production up to 1850 for several reasons, one being that there were fewer foundries and with the punch and matrix there were conditions limiting the number of styles introduced in these years. Also, after 1850 the electrotype matrix fantastically increased the number of display styles. The substantial increase in the number of American foundries further complicates study because of the many new specimen books with a corresponding increase in original designs arising from competition.

Although many of the designs shown here may appear overly esoteric to some, they were nevertheless important in the typographic evolution of styles during the period. My inclination is to judge specific type face design on the basis of its application in its own time, rather than to compare the design with acceptable standards for display type today.

Although some nineteenth-century styles have been rejuvenated and reissued under new titles recently (e.g., Memphis, Rockwell, Beton, Ultra Bodoni, Hellenic, Profil, etc.), these styles seldom match in quality the design of plain faces produced by both metal and wood type manufacturers in the nineteenth century. The revivals, for the most part, are unforgivably clumsy in comparison. The ornamental letters, especially those produced in wood, are more than just curiosities, even though their authenticity as typographic forms is dubious. They present a form of artistic expression almost as varied and individualistic as the hand-embellished initial letters of scribes, and this expression is multiplied many times over through the printing and founding technology.

The acceptance of these strange letters as something more than type designs may be better demonstrated in the last twenty years than in their own age. This is clearly shown in the works of contemporary designers who use old letterforms in a spectrum of visual presentations—changing contexts or scale, capitalizing on the pronounced visual qualities, or establishing a period. The results have been both entertaining and striking but, as with other fashions, these letters probably will fade soon into disuse and general obscurity. Before they do so completely, however, my intention is to present a number of pertinent facts concerning their origins, the men who produced them, and the use of them in their own time.   R.R.K.

AMERICAN WOOD TYPE: 1828-1900

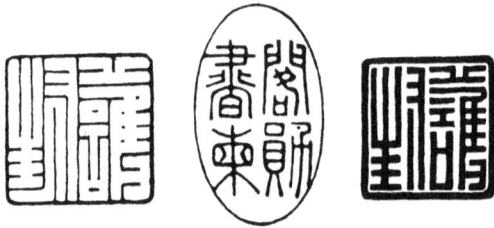

Chinese seals as shown by Thomas Carter in his The Invention of Printing in China and Its Spread Westward.

European playing card from the fifteenth century. Shown by Theodore De Vinne in his The Invention of Printing.

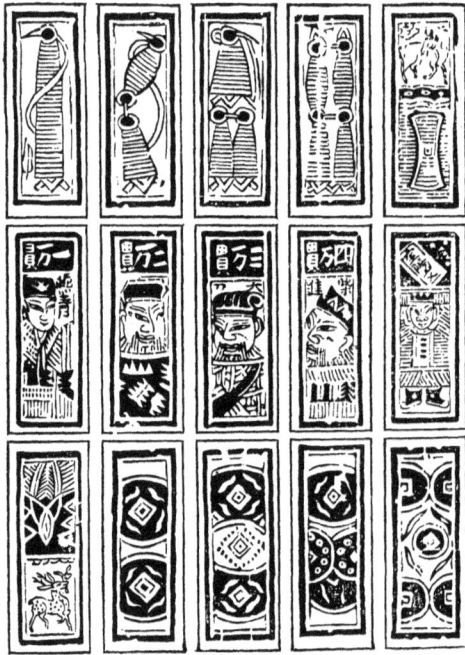

Chinese playing cards printed from wood. Shown by Theodore De Vinne in his The Invention of Printing.

St. Christopher, Germany, 1423. Oldest dated woodcut found in Europe.

*Word symbols of the Uigur Turks, circa 1300. (*The Invention of Printing in China and its Spread Westward, *Carter & Goodrich, 1955.)*

Letter K from the Grotesque Alphabet. Carved in wood circa 1464 and believed to have been done by a French artist. Original size is 3½ x 4⅝ inches. (Jackson & Chatto.)

I. EVOLUTION OF DISPLAY TYPES

The Early Use of Wood in Printing

The history of wood as a printing material has been interwoven into legend as well as fact ever since the inception of the printing arts. Generally, wood has been a prototype medium, and when wood was used originally for letterforms or illustrations, it was almost always supplanted at a later date by an improved material, such as metal, which could be cast, engraved, or etched. Wood preceded other materials simply because it was available in all parts of the world, was comparatively easy to carve, and was capable of receiving and transferring ink exceedingly well by either rubbing or pressing.

It seems logical that printing from raised surfaces on wood may have evolved through the use of seals, stencils, or rubbings, as all three of these processes are extremely ancient. At least two of the techniques, rubbing and printing from seals, include characteristics basic to relief printing: raised printing surfaces and the potential for multiple impressions. Wood, as well as stone, metal, and clay were the principal materials used in these techniques.

While it is not definitely known that seals, rubbings, and stencils originated in China, it is certain that all three were used there at an early date, and on the basis of existing evidence, that there was some continuity from one or more of these processes to block printing. The *Diamond Sutra,* the earliest known wood block print in Chinese history, dates from 868. It was found with an accompanying volume containing identical contents which had been reproduced by the rubbing technique. Even though an earlier block print dating from 770 had been printed in Japan, the *Diamond Sutra* demonstrated such a high degree of refinement that the art of block printing must have been practiced by the Chinese for a number of years previously. Another believed forerunner of the block print in China was a wooden stamp. The image on these stamps was most often that of Buddha and was quite small. Provided with handles to facilitate their use, the stamps must have been similar to the rubber stamps used in offices today.

At about the same time the Chinese began printing pages in books in place of the traditional scrolls, they began producing playing cards printed from wooden blocks. It is interesting, and perhaps even significant that playing cards printed from wooden blocks date among the earliest examples of printing in both the Eastern and Western civilizations, although printing in China occurred several hundred years earlier than printing in Germany, Italy, and France.

The oldest known wood block found in Europe is dated 1423. Depicting St. Christopher, the print has a Latin legend boxed at the bottom which was engraved in conjunction with the illustration, much in the same fashion that pages of the xylographic books were to be printed at a later date.

For the printing of letter symbols, the use of wood again may be traced back to the Eastern civilizations. Thomas Carter, in the *Invention of Printing in China and Its Spread Westward,* describes probably the oldest movable types ever found. These types, word rather than alphabetic symbols carved on wood in the language of the Uigur Turks, date from around 1300. They were found in caves of Tun-Huang by Pelliot. Also reported by Carter are the movable wood types of Wang Chên, which were described by Wang in great detail at the close of his *Book of Agriculture,* written around 1313.

In Europe wooden block books, most frequently religious in content, preceded the invention of movable metal type by many years. It is known that the printing press was used in the printing of these block books, and also that the first oil-based inks came into general use at the same time. Both the press and oil-based printing inks were Western contributions to printing, whereas the concept of movable type and paper came from the East.

The increased demand for block books most assuredly lent impetus to the improved technology and materials that inevitably led to the inventions of Johann Gutenberg. It is the adjustable type mold which is most often attributed to Gutenberg. However, the exact nature of his inventions is unknown both because of the secrecy he imposed concerning his own works and because of the incomplete records from his time. In the nineteenth century, Gutenberg's claims to the honor of having invented movable metal type were hotly contested by supporters of Laurens Coster, a contemporary of Gutenberg, who printed xylographic books in Holland. Coster was said to have arrived at the idea for movable type through cutting out the letters from a single wooden block in order to re-use these same letters for other pages in his books.

Printers from the time of Gutenberg commissioned initial letters carved on wood as well as on metal so that their printed works would retain the ornamented effects of the scribe and rubicator. Books from that period have been described as being comparable in principle to paperback reprint editions today—that is, the first publishers concentrated only on established works, and printing served to make available more copies at lower cost. Also, every effort was made to duplicate the manuscript books so that the new method would be more acceptable to clients. As the printer was beset, however, by technical and cost limitations, he gradually began to drop the older manuscript traditions and build new ones of his own. Initials became smaller; ornamental borders, printer's marks, ornaments, and illustrations were engraved on wood or metal and printed in a single operation with the text.

After the title page was introduced by Peter Schöffer in 1463, and became generally accepted some 12 or 13 years later, it became a focal point for the printer's art. In 1476, Erhard Ratdolt printed the first ornamental title page, which consisted of type with woodcut borders to the sides and at the top of the page. Ratdolt did not immediately repeat this practice in succeeding books, but nevertheless, the idea of the title page was firmly established

At the turn of that century, the styles for title pages ranged from the simple typographical arrangements of Aldus Manutius to title pages that were two-thirds ornamental borders or illustration. At about the same time, printers revived the principle of the xylographic books, with text and illustration carved on a single block, to make title pages. Type could be reversed or interlocked. It could be larger than was possible to cast, or could be integrated with illustration or ornamental effects. This was the period when the reverse, or white-line title pages, initials, and ornamental borders first became popular.

Although it is quite certain that letterforms had been cut on wood, probably as an entire line, or as a word logotype, and used with metal types for many years, not until around the middle of the fifteenth century were records found of letters being carved individually on wood for the larger sizes of type. Frequently, these large wood letters were used to make sand molds for casting types in

De Proprietate Verum, *printed by Wynkyn De Worde, 1495. Letters cut intaglio into an oak block.*

Ornate initials used by Gutenberg in Letters of Indulgence, Mainz, 1455. Probably carved on type metal. Top: 30 line Letters of Indulgence; bottom: 31 line Letters of Indulgence.

Wood cut initials appearing in Chronecken der Sassen, *from the middle of the fifteenth century. Designed by Peter Schoeffer. (Peter Schoeffer of Gernsheim and Mainz, Lehmann Haupt, 1950.)*

metal. Even after the introduction of metal types in the mid-fifteenth century, wood retained an essential role in printing history up to the beginning of the twentieth century, when zinc and copper line and half-tone plates finally replaced wood engravings, and offset printing eliminated the need for large wood types.

Decorated Letters

The earliest letterforms to be engraved on wood or metal by the printer would usually fall into one of two groups: the ornate initials which were patterned after the works of the scribe, or letters too large to cast with the conventional molds, which were used for public notices or occasionally for title pages of books. These large letters were copied after existing styles of cast type, but might include additional flourishes or other modifications resulting from the comparative ease of engraving on wood. These two categories of large and decorated types represent an extremely simple breakdown of what we now refer to as display types. Of course, the use of text types for display is not denied. Text type in italics, all capitals, or arranged with special spacing was the most common means for display until the development of a separate classification called display type.

The evolution leading up to cast display types was relatively slow until the first years of the eighteenth century, when the range of influences became increasingly varied, finally culminating during the nineteenth century in an explosive synthesis of historical revivals, improved technology, increased commercial demand and creative energies. The fanciful letterforms of the penman, the delicacy and flourish of the metal plate engravers and etchers, the tone and fluidity of the lithographic artist—all challenged the competitive instincts of the typefounders and had a profound effect on the design of type forms, particularly the decorated ones.

The earliest decorated letters were large woodcut initials usually cut onto the side-grain of the wood. Because the letters were extremely vulnerable to damage, particularly so with the crude presses of that day, printers soon began to rely on letters engraved on type metal, brass or copper, for longer runs. Wood was used only for the shorter runs. Decorative initials were not cut in complete alphabets, but only the letters required for a specific text. Also, as with ornaments and borders, the printer would often use these ornamental initials for other books or posters, where out of context they often appeared peculiar, if not naïve.

Some of the first known examples of metal initials are those printed by Schöffer in his Psalter of 1457. Lombardic in design, and printed in two colors, they had elaborate filigree tailpieces. After much research it was finally believed that these initials had been printed in a single impression from metal plates and that they had probably been engraved in relief on brass. The two colors in one impression were achieved by making the kernel letter of thin metal which was inked in one color and then nested into a corresponding cavity in the master block which had been inked in another color.

The theory that the initials had been printed from metal was based on the fact that they appeared in numerous books and that they would never have survived the number of impressions known had they been cut in wood. In some editions, since the kernel letter is cracked, but not the main block, the theory that thin metal was used for the inset letter is reinforced. Examining a number of different printings showed that although there was occasional damage to the filigree, it would be repaired for the next printing, probably by soldering.

Although Schöffer's nested technique allowed the printing of complicated initials in two colors with one operation, carving the blocks and making separate impressions for text and initials was both time-consuming and costly, and the technique does not seem to have been adopted by other printers of the period.

After 1600, the extremely large ornamental letters, such as those with filigreed tails and the calligraphic examples of Peter Schöffer, gradually began to disappear. In Germany these large ornamentals lasted for a longer period than elsewhere, perhaps because with their flourishes and tailpieces they were more suited to the angular Gothic letters. They persisted wherever the German Gothics lingered—in Germany, Holland, Northern France, and Spain. Also, as the German books were generally much larger than the ones produced in Italy, they could better accommodate these initials. Teutonic influences in the design of initial letters during the sixteenth century are best exemplified by the letters of Hans Holbein and his Dance of Death alphabet first published in 1530. Usually, initials from this time and place were characterized by pictorial backgrounds as opposed to the abstract arabesques of the Venetians and French.

German and Dutch designers betrayed strong tendencies for the grotesque and genre motifs in ornamental letter design up until well into the nineteenth century. An interesting note on German decorated initials is given by Campbell Dodgson in *Burlington Magazine* (1908): "... Complete alphabets were also produced at this period (second quarter of the fifteenth century), not with the directly practical object of being used in books, but to serve as ornament prints for advertisement of the wood cutter's skill, for the instruction and profit of other craftsmen or, it may be, even for the delight of the collector." Dodgson also noted that during this period there was little or no distinction between the work done in the Low Countries and Germany.

Although printers of Augsburg are reported to have used small metal ornamental initials, Erhard Ratdolt of Venice in 1477 seems to have been the first to make decorative initials regularly for his publications, *Literae Florentes*. These letters were cut in high relief on metal, as it was not practical to cast them in molds at that time. The Venetians favored the small initials, which often had a floral arabesque motif engraved entirely or in part as an outline in order that they might be hand rubicated. There were also the typical dotted designs from this period: a reversed arabesque and letter on a stippled field (white vine pattern).

Even though the Italians had a splendid reputation as designers of ornamental initials and borders, they were soon surpassed by the French, largely because of the works and influence of Geoffroy Tory. After being inspired by the Italian productions, Tory went on to design exquisite initials, borders, and entire books, which were tremendously influential with printers in other parts of Europe.

At about the same time that initial letters were becoming firmly established with printers, and roughly corresponding with the rise of copperplate engraving, writing manuals—small books devoted to instruction in writing—first began to appear around the first quarter of the sixteenth century. The earliest ones came from France and

Two-color initial letter from colophon of the Psalter of 1457.

Initial letter by Erhard Ratdolt.

Large wood cut initial printed by Alaman, 1499.

Spain, and at only a slightly later date from Italy, Germany and Switzerland. The majority of writing manuals were produced through metal-plate processes; however, many of the first ones were illustrated with wood engravings, and during the nineteenth century a great many were reproduced through lithography and a few by steel engravings. Writing masters and engravers were often one and the same. In increasing numbers as time progressed, the manuals allocated space for ornamental letters while the bulk of the book would be used for handwriting styles, flourishes, calligraphic drawings and illustrations showing how to sit, hold the pen, or what tools to use. Beginning in the latter part of the eighteenth century, consideration was given in many of these manuals for the style needs of sign painters and draftsmen, and there were a number of publications directed in entirety to the sign painter.

The writing masters were quite amazing in respect to their daring in the invention and innovation of letterforms, and their works may be viewed as an important transitional stage between the illuminators and typefounders. It was their invention in the field of decorated letters that the writing masters made their greatest contribution to display typography. As in the works of Urbanus Wyss of Zurich in 1549, the typographic styles of the Victorians were anticipated to a surprising degree. Some of the first decorated types of Fournier bore the unmistakable influence of etched and engraved productions of writing masters. Also, the media of engraving and etching included techniques and characteristics which have left their imprint on display types up to this day—shading of the letterform, styles of embellishment, etc.

The ornate letters of the writing master were copiously reproduced by artisans of many crafts other than the typefounder—jewelers, engravers, ceramicists, signpainters, etc.

Shortly after the middle of the sixteenth century, the first copperplate title pages began to appear and they were to soon eclipse the wood and metal relief cuts as the epitome of the printer's art. According to DeVinne, the Italians were the first to practice this art, which was not common in France and Germany during this century. In the seventeenth century copperplate engravings reached a higher refinement in the work of French, German, and Dutch artists, especially Christopher Plantin of Antwerp. For the most part, reflecting baroque and rococo styles, the designs of the engravers either emphasized illustrative motifs such as those of Louis Elzevir, a sixteenth century Dutch publisher, or more commonly, architectural or floral cartouches with the lettering enclosed—all of which were frequently placed on a scroll or tablet incorporated into the main pictorial or decorative theme.

In most instances, the letterforms were secondary to the pictorial aspects of the title page. However, the intaglio title pages exhibited more variations of the letterform than may be found in relief-printed title pages. There were Roman letters opened in the characteristic manner of the engraver, interior shaded Romans, variances in weight of the letter, and finally, the printed reproductions of the penmen's work—fancy and gracefully embellished. From this period up through the eighteenth century, the copperplate engravings for title pages were to maintain their prestigious position with printers and publishers.

Not only did decorated letters change according to time and geography, but many sprang from limitations of

Initial letter by Caxton from The Fifteen O's and other Prayers, *circa 1490.*

Initials by Geoffroy Tory for Robert Estienne, circa 1540.

Alphabet of Death ascribed to Hans Holbein, first used in Basle circa 1530.

Italian initial which shows the influence of Holbein. Giolito, Venice, circa 1550.

printing technology and commercial demands. Crude presses and uneven handmade papers alone were responsible for a number of innovations. The raised thin lines of relief cuts were especially susceptible to damage, and it soon became apparent that the image could be delineated by cutting it *into* the solid areas. Thus, even though reversed, the image would be as easily read and the fragility of the raised thin lines could be eliminated. These "white-line" title pages, borders, and initial letters were used extensively all over Europe. The reverse line title pages were a hallmark of Spanish printing in the sixteenth century.

However, because the crude presses could print only with great difficulty the solid areas, the printer devised a technique for breaking up the solid field with dots creating a characteristic stippled design. This technique, called Criblée, is believed to have originated in Paris. Also, the textural effect of these stippled fields was aesthetically more pleasing in conjunction with the color of types. The dotted or stippled designs were to remain popular with printers for several centuries for the making of ornamental initials and borders.

The first woodcuts used by the printer were open with lines widely spaced. This practice was soon abandoned because of the fragility of these isolated lines. Shading consisting of a number of parallel lines, spaced relatively close to one another, became the most common technique. The lines tended to reinforce each other and at the same time allowed the printer to handle masses without the problems connected with printing solids. Undoubtedly these designs, both typographical and illustrative, evolved from the increased durability of the plate and ease of printing as much as from aesthetic notions.

The outline borders around decorative initials and woodcut illustrations from that period also served a functional purpose since they absorbed the pressure of the press platen as well as protected the cut and insured better printing.

The printer was almost forced to use metal plates even though they were more expensive because of the havoc raised with woodcuts and engravings in printing with the crude presses. Wood borders, ornaments, and illustrations often cracked after only one to ten impressions, which certainly made them a gamble for the artist and printer! Although it is difficult to separate the impressions made from metal from those printed from wood, generally the prints from metal plates demonstrated sharper detail, finer lines, and prints from wood often showed cracks or warpage.

The coarseness of printing associated with wood blocks in the sixteenth century is one of the prime reasons for the rise of engraved copperplate title pages. For many years the printing of wood blocks was to be associated with inferior printing and cheap books.

After 1500, printers began to minimize the use of elaborate initials in many of their editions. This was partly because of changing fashions, but probably more so because of the stiff competition among publishers. Competition was especially evident in Italy where many printing houses had gone bankrupt as early as 1525 because of oversaturation of the markets. Related to competition was the fact that smaller books were cheaper to produce, and the smaller types used reduced the amount of paper required, making books much more economical. The printer eliminated the printing of color by using outline

Page from the fifteenth century xylographic book, Life of St. Meinrat. *Text and illustration were carved on a single wooden block. Actual size, 3⅛ x 5⅞ inches.*

Title page of Aristotle printed by Kalliergi, 1499. Illustrates printer's mark, letterforms, and decorative materials carved on a single block.

Curious titlepiece by Felix Balligault, Paris, 1497. Decorative borders represent seventeen different bits of design. The practice of assembling decorative borders from previous printings to create a new title page was just as common with decorative initials, which were designed for a single book but often used in several publications.

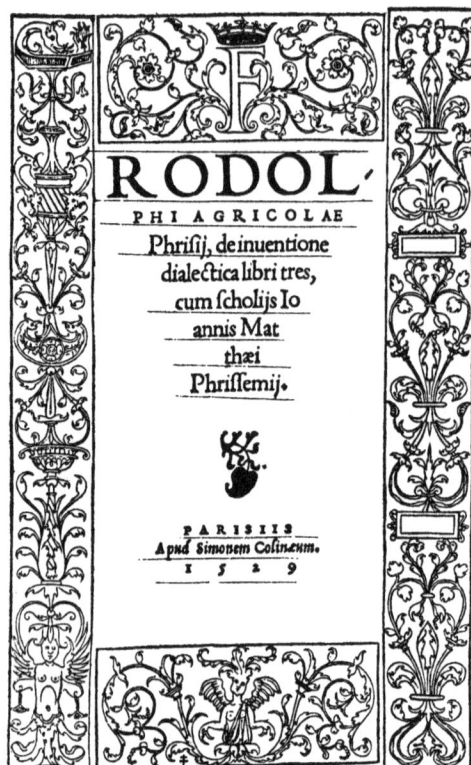

Simon de Colines, Paris, 1529. Pieced title by Geoffroy Tory.

Example of reverse engraving, in which the design is incised into the wood or metal. The practice was most common with decorative borders and initials. Diego de Gumiel, Valencia, 1515.

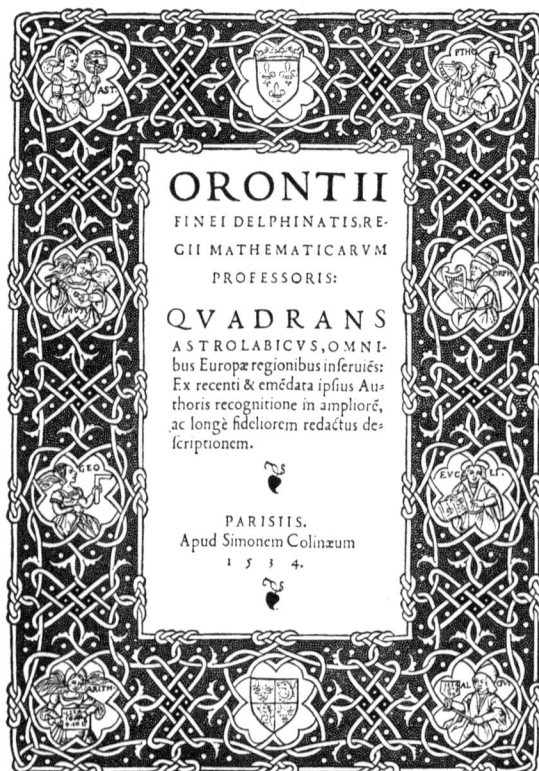

Stippled, or criblée. Simon de Colines, 1534.

As title pages evolved from crude xylographic books through the various styles and techniques concerned with reverse, criblée, and wood and metal engraving, there were corresponding interpretations of decorative elements —first with borders and flowers and eventually with letterforms. The greatest step toward the development of display type came with the design of words or lines of decorative type, and very soon after, the design of complete ornamented alphabets. This advance was first seen on title pages.

Earliest known copperplate title. London, 1545.

Engraved title printed by Balthazar Moretus in the Plantin printing house, Antwerp, 1654.

Baroque copperplate title page by unknown master for Jean de Tournes, Lyons/Geneva, 1602.

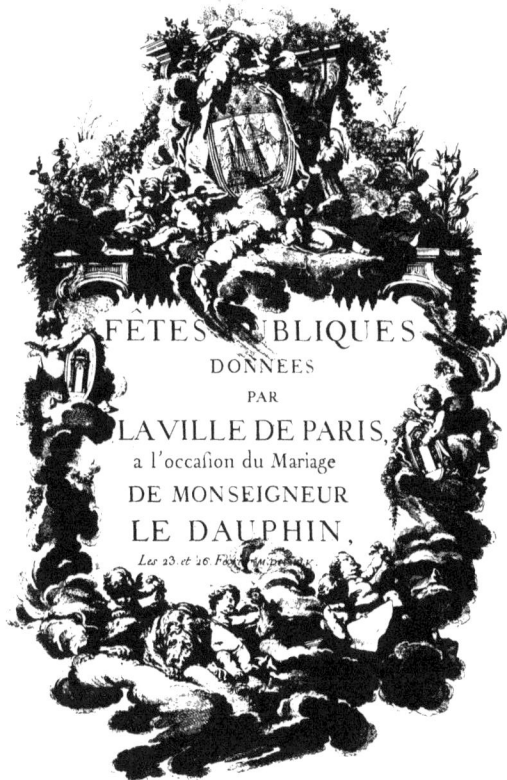

Rococo title engraved on metal by Charles Eisen, 1745.

A curious attempt at an ornamental effect by Caspar Nef in his Kalligraphie, Germany, 1549.

Heading for illustration of Papal Chancery hand, mid-sixteenth century. (Alphabets, Edward F. Strange.)

PANCHRESTO

Decorated capitals from Beaugrand's writing book, Paris, 1604. This was the first French writing book to be printed from copper plates. ("Decorated Letters," by Stanley Morison, in Fleuron VI.)

Urbanus Wyss, Libellus Valde Doctus, elegans & utilis, multa & uaria scribendum literarum genera complectens. Zurich, 1459. In this book, Wyss attempts to show all the different writings used in his lifetime. The plates are carved on wood and framed with decorative pieced wood borders. These plates remarkably anticipate Victorian styles of 300 years later. The broken and bent treatment of the first two specimens was to be used in an identical manner with newer letterforms by English typefounders, and the double-weight Tuscan quality of the third specimen found many interpretations in the nineteenth century.

Engraved letters from the title page of a writing book by Louis Senault. Date of the publication is unknown, but he was active between 1669 and 1680.

Michael Baurenfeind's rococo letters, 1737. (Decorative Alphabets & Initials, Alexander Nesbitt, 1959.)

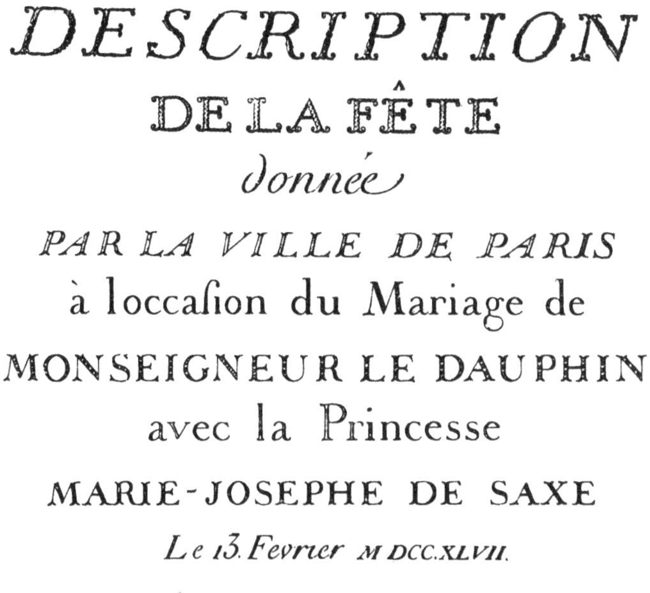

DESCRIPTION
DE LA FÊTE
donnée
PAR LA VILLE DE PARIS
à loccasion du Mariage de
MONSEIGNEUR LE DAUPHIN
avec la Princesse
MARIE-JOSEPHE DE SAXE
Le 13. Fevrier M DCC.XLVII.

Engraved letters from title page by L. LeLorrain, 1747.
(200 Decorative Title-Pages, Alexander Nesbitt, 1964.)

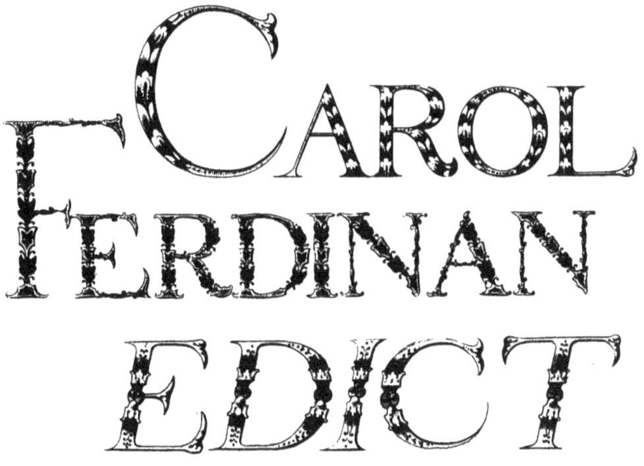

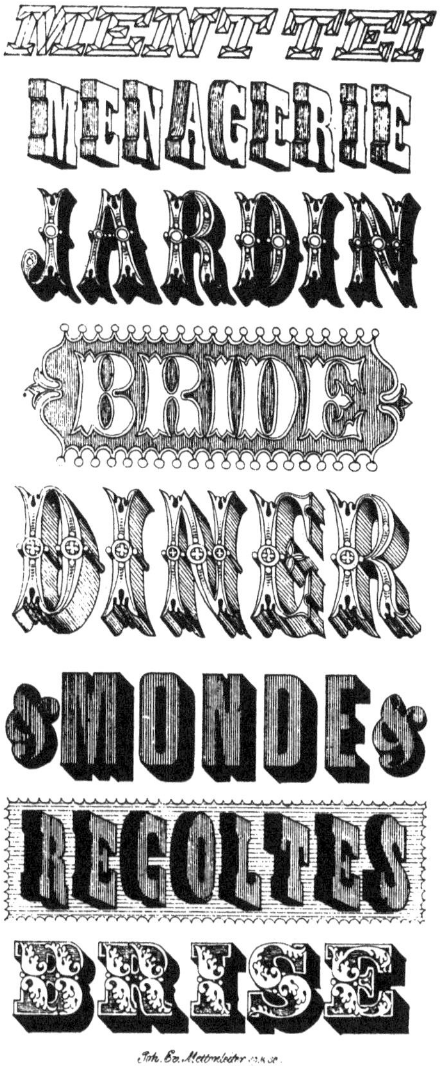

MENT TEI
MENAGERIE
JARDIN
BRIDE
DINER
MONDE
RECOLTES
BRISE

CAROL
FERDINAN
EDICT

Engraved letters from Calligraphia Latina,
(J. G. Schwandner, 1756).

Engraved letters from the writing book of Johann
Evangelist Mettenleiter of Munich. These letters were
copied letter for letter from type specimens shown by
Laurent et DeBerny circa 1837.

EXÉCUTÉES À LA PLUME
par
JEAN MIDOLLE
GRAVÉES SUR PIERRE ET PUBLIÉES
àlaLithographie de F: Emile Simon Fils

Jean Midolle, Strasbourg, 1834-35. Midolle used a
modern display Clarendon some ten years before it was
common to the typefounders, and the shaded interior
treatment of these letters equally predates the typical
Zebra designs of the 1840's. The line shade on the letters
in "lithography of Emile Simmon Fils" convincingly
demonstrates the origin of this device as it was extensively
used by typefounders. In these same specimens, one may
find the prototype for French Clarendons which were not
marketed by founders for another thirty years. Midolle
was also responsible for several grotesque Tuscans—
Romaine, Lapidaire Monstre, etc., which have been
revived with great regularity by publishers of lettering
books ever since.

Outline heading from Gutenberg's first bible of Mainz.

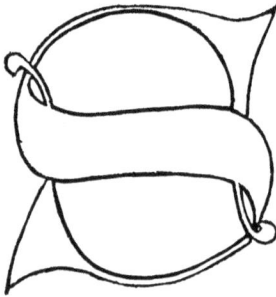

Outline initial used by Holle at Ulm in 1482.

Initial letter from Hypnerotomachia Poliphili *by Aldus Manutius, 1499.*

Sixteenth-century wood cut initial found in the Plantin-Moretus Museum.

initials and ornaments which were to be filled in with color by a professional rubicator at the book owner's expense, or by the owner himself. This practice of outlining initials as a guide for the rubicator is credited to Gunther Zainer, printer of Augsburg, whose first book employing this device was published in 1468. The Venetian printers used these outline letters and ornaments extensively, the style of which was to prevail throughout Europe. The uncolored impressions from these blocks, just as they came from the press, were exceedingly harmonious with the type styles of the day, and books from this period using this device number among the most beautiful ever printed.

It was also common to print a small appropriate lowercase letter (called a director) in the corner of a vacant space left by the printer for the artist to put in the initial letter if he so desired. The outline letter was eventually to become accepted as a decorated letter in its own right. Gutenberg engraved logotypes in the open style and used them as heads, and although it is certain that he intended these to be colored in by hand at a later date, several of his very handsome impressions have come down to us in the unrubicated state.

In the works of Albrecht Dürer we find examples of a Roman open letter—with stems and thicks left open. This was clearly intended to stand of its own accord and can in no way be construed as a guide for rubication. It is not known whether the openings in the letters were included in the drawing of Dürer, or whether they were an independent decision made by the engraver. Metal plate engravers during the seventeenth and eighteenth centuries were prone to open the stems and thicks of the Roman letter in a manner similar to those found in Dürer prints. From opening the letter, it was only a short step to shading the openings with parallel lines to create one of the earliest decorated styles. Examples of these decorative letters can be found on map legends, trade cards, title pages, etc.

Outline letters first began to be used extensively during the sixteenth century, strictly in the context of a decorated letter. One fine example which is quite modern in treatment is shown on a title page from De la Rue's writing book supposedly printed circa 1550, shown by Stanley Morison in *Fleuron VI*. In this title page, outline pointed Gothic and Roman types indicate that their decorative effect was fully recognized. In all respects they were comparable to later models except that they were hand-engraved rather than cast.

Decorated letters were not exclusively produced by the copper engravers even though they may have initiated many new styles. Letterpress printers also showed numerous letters engraved in relief, which, although they lacked the elegance of the intaglio letters, were designed in styles peculiar to them.

While the French showed preference for the lighter, fragile engraved letters, the Germans exhibited a variety of bolder letters which could be printed in conjunction with cast type and woodcut illustrations. An excellent example of these letters, shown by Theodore De Vinne in his book *Title Pages as Seen by a Printer,* is the title page from *Dissertatio Qua Simul Artis Typographicae,* printed by Gleditsch circa 1710. Both the rustic or tree trunk letters and the ornamented Roman lowercase in this example were to find additional exploitation in the following century. De Vinne comments that although the Germans were the first to ornament Roman type, they found

1515
RHINOCERVS
ÆD

Letters taken from a plate engraved on wood for Albrecht Dürer, 1515.

Alphabet de dissemblables sortes de lettres :
En vers Alexandrins

PAR.
Iaques de la Rue escriuain,
Auec priuilége, duRoy.
A Paris Rue S. Jaques deuant le Plessis.

Outline Gothic and Roman carved on wood for title page of De la Rue's writing book which was published in Paris circa 1550. ("Decorated Types," by Stanley Morison, in Fleuron VI.)

DE
GERMANIÆ MIRACVLO
OPTIMO, MAXIMO,
TYPIS
literarum,
EARVMQVE DIFFERENTIIS,
DISSERTATIO,
QVA SIMVL
ARTIS TYPOGRAPHICÆ
VNIVERSAM RATIONEM EXPLICAT
PAVLVS PATER, PP.

Excerpt from title page of Germaniae Miraculo Optimo, Maximo, Typis Literarum, *printed in Leipzig, 1710, by Gleditsch.*

it unsatisfactory in combination with the pointed Gothics used for text. It remained for the Italians, Spanish, and French to capitalize on the decorated Romans for display.

Although ornamental types may have been used in the seventeenth century, examples are rarely found. It is certain, however, that typefounders experimented with casting decorative letters at an early date. De Vinne briefly discusses a curious ornamented type used by Guillaume Le Rouge of Paris, 1512, in an edition of *Lucan*. It has an upright italic lowercase; capitals were made quite large in proportion to the lowercase, extending below the line as well as above, and printed with the lowercase centered on the vertical height. These capitals had some Tuscan treatment of the serifs, a median ornament (a short horizontal bar through the center of the stems). With a capping bar on the "A," they closely resembled manuscript initials. De Vinne further states, "the new type was not approved (by other printers), and soon went out of use."

Stanley Morison in his article on "Decorated Types," *Fleuron VI,* speculates that a curious ornamented face found in Blageart's *La Devineresse,* Paris, 1680, may be the oldest known cast decorated type. The ornamental letters from *La Devineresse* are found used as heads with the text as well as on the title page. It would be interesting to make a close examination of these letters to see if they were cast, and if cast, if they were modified by hand engraving. The style suggests that this could have been done easily. It is of interest that this same decorative device was used by Palatino in *Lettera di bolle Apostoliche,* a book of papal Chancery-hand dating from the mid-sixteenth century in Italy.

In casting ornamental types the typefounder encountered many difficulties, among which were the fragility of punches plus the not so small problem of getting lead into the detailing during the casting process. It was not until the nineteenth century when lead was forced into molds under pressure that the casting of ornamental types became a practical venture.

By early eighteenth century the intaglio and hand-engraved relief letters had gained favor in the trade, and it was logical that the typefounder could realize a potential market if he could find a means for successfully casting decorated letters. One of the oldest known cast decorated types is Union Pearl, which was found in England. Even though the original matrices still exist and were found in Grover's inventory (James and Thomas Grover, English typefoundry established in 1674), exactly when and by whom the face was first designed is a mystery. The type, dated circa 1690 in a single newspaper advertisement, appears to be closely related to the work of seventeenth-century writing masters on the Continent. Harry Carter and Christopher Ricks in the notes at the back of their 1961 edition of Edward Rowe Mores' *A Dissertation upon English Typographical Founders* do mention that the matrices for Union Pearl were struck with the letters upside down, and if fitted into English molds, they would produce type with the nick at the back, which was normal in France. The footnote suggests that the matrices were made to fit a French mold, and mentions that some similar matrices belonged to Nicholls and that perhaps Nicholls' French molds descended to Grover. It seems strange that no historian has yet advanced the thought that perhaps the Union Pearl matrices were designed and made in France and exported to England. They were evidently made to fit

Büchdruckerey,

Marci Annei Lucanipoeta:

COMEDIE.

Lettera di bolle Apostoliche.

The Most Ancient English Type

a French type mold, and their design appears consistent with writing styles then popular on the Continent.

Fournier *le jeune,* during the first half of the eighteenth century, was the first typefounder to be successful in the casting of decorated types—successful in the sense that his decorated faces were not only handsome but were also accepted by other founders and printers. Fournier had studied drawing under J.B.G. Colson, miniaturist and watercolor painter, and this background must certainly have contributed to his success later as a designer of letters and ornaments. Also, Fournier's first decorated types confirm the influences of the metal plate engravers and etchers.

However, it should be noted that preceding the decorative ornaments and types of Fournier, there had been a long tradition of printer's flowers and decorative borders which had evolved over several centuries. Eastern arabesques had come into Italy via the trade routes from Persia, and the Muslim decorative calligraphy had come into Europe with the Moors. Many of these motifs had been refined by the book binders, and printers had been using similar designs as book ornaments since the mid-sixteenth century. Fournier, a brilliant and original designer in his own right, was to draw from the historical sources to produce a combination of ornamental flowers, borders, and decorated types which surpassed anything done in decorative printing with cast types up to his time.

Fournier *le jeune* showed his most important specimens in the *Manuel Typographique* of 1764, which included not only his own decorated types, but also specimens borrowed from Fournier *l'aîné,* Cappon, Herissant, and Breitkopf of Leipzig. The *lettres ornées* shown by Fournier in this specimen had been cut in nine styles between 1749 and 1766 and ranged from 6 to 44 points. Later he added designs up to 84 and 108 points. His ornate designs had been inspired (according to D. B. Updike) by the works of vignettists such as Cochin, Eisen, and St. Aubin.

Fournier's designs fall roughly into two categories: floriated designs and tooled designs. The latter style was a formalized version of the tooled letters popularized by metalplate engravers, or an imitation of the engravers' letters by printers who had handtooled existing types. The tooled Romans became popular with the trade, and are representative of decorated letters in the last quarter of that century. Also, in principle, they carried over into the nineteenth century almost as strongly—adapted to the Fat Face designs, as well as to most new styles as they came onto the markets.

Fournier's designs became popular, and even though never adopted by the Imprimérie Royale, they were borrowed by other typefounders, notably Gando in Paris, Rosart of Haarlem, and several provincial typefounders. The floriated letters of Fournier were, however, but a brief experiment that ended with his own productions and those of his immediate followers. (Deberny and Peignot did revive a Fournier face in 1913 under the name "Fournier," which has had limited use since that time.)

Two styles shown by Fournier in his 1764 specimens deserve special attention: the tooled Roman (a conventional Roman with an inline stress to the left) and a tooled Roman Italic in several sizes with floriated serifs. The nature of the latter device further confirms what the inline tooling suggests—that these decorated types could have been made from previously designed punches, and were made to compete with the letterforms of the metal-

Typographical ornaments in Fournier le jeune's Modeles des Characteres, 1742.

de Gros-canon.

GB
SE

Moyennes de fonte.

NI

The floriated and tooled Romans of Fournier, which are highly suggestive of reworked punches.

MODÈLES
de quelques Lettres de deux points
ORNÉES.

de Nompareille.
ABCDEFGHIJKLM

de Petit-texte.
ABCDEGH
NOPRST.U

de Petit-romain.
ABCDEFGI
BLMNOPQ

de Philoſophie.
ABCDEFG
HIJLMNO

de Cicéro.
ABCDE

de Saint-auguſtin.
FGHK
JMLN

M M initiales.

Fournier le jeune's decorated types from his Manuel Typographique, 1764.

ROSART

JACQUES FRANÇOIS ROSART.

MATTHIAS ROSART.

ENSCHEDE.

VEUVE DECELLIER

Decorated letters cut by Rosart which followed both in time and style those of Fournier.

E R

R

P P P

G Q

D G B H

A series of decorated letters which were made by engraving directly on cast, solid faced types. This collection is at the University Press, Cambridge University. ("Decorated Types," by Stanley Morison, in Fleuron VI.)

BURY

Ornamented, S. & C. Stephenson, 1796.

plate engravers. There is small difference other than hardness of metal between engraving type metal and engraving a punch. Enterprising printers of that time were not ignorant of the practice of adding distinction to a line of type by hand engraving types that were already cast. The Cambridge University Press still has a number of decorative faces which had been engraved from solid-faced cast types. The variety of these designs, and their similarity to Fournier's letters as well as to other decorated types used in the last quarter of the century, are strong evidence as to what was possible through modifying a conventional Roman punch.

In America the documentation of re-engraving a tempered punch can be verified from two sources—David Bruce, Jr. and Joseph Warren Phinney. While employed at the Boston Type & Stereotype Foundry in 1828, Bruce improved upon some discarded punches, and later in the century, Phinney recut some punches of a heavy Runic to create the popular light style of that face. It would be interesting to know how many designs for decorated faces from the eighteenth century were the result of punches refurbished to oblige new fashions. The period most pertinent to this practice would fall between 1745 and 1800, even though similar designs were marketed in numbers up to 1840. The role of refurbished punches in the evolution of display types seems to have been largely ignored as a distinct phase in the development of ornamental types.

French styles soon spread to Holland, and the Dutch decorated types were then carried across the channel to England around 1780. Strikes or punches for decorated faces imported from the Continent were used for the earliest productions in England. Many of these designs, suggestive of designs accomplished by the previously described process of modified punches, went up to eight and ten line pica in size. One style which is representative of these designs is a face shown by S. & C. Stephenson in 1796, an 8-line Roman identified only as Ornamental, with a reversed serpentine line centered inside the thicks and oval dots in the loops of the serpentine line (this type closely resembles the "G" shown in hand-tooled types included in the collection of Cambridge University).

In the period just preceding the nineteenth century, there was a continuation of the designs made popular by the metal engraver—the shaded, tooled, and embellished Romans. Many of the designs coming from France were script italic, or semi-italic, which reflect the influence of the penman. In addition to this influence, Morison points out that the *lettres fleuragées* developed by the goldsmiths and jewelers in France had been based on the ornamental capitals of Nicholas du Val (1650) and Claude Auguste Berey (1670). There can be little question that the origins of the decorated letters are more rooted in the works of French writing masters, artisans, and typefounders than in any other single source.

The English were prompt in the design of new decorative faces once the designs imported from Holland and France began to gain favor. Perhaps one of the most renowned of these new designs was that of Richard Austin, called Fry's Ornamented and cut in 1796. It combined two of the most common devices of the day—tooling and the pearl. The result was a handsome and dignified display letter.

In these same years, a pronounced shading on many of the ornamental Romans became more evident, with either a right or left emphasis. Occasionally the oblique was used to add an illusion of dimension to the letter. This device, gradually exaggerated into a style which was adapted to the new Fat Faces, was extremely popular between 1800 and 1840.

Somewhat different from the English styles were decorated letters produced by Pierre Didot *l'aîné* near the end of the eighteenth century. Characteristic Didot letters were Roman, slightly condensed with modern serifs. The thicks were ornamented on the interior with finely engraved embellishments. The matrices still survive in the inventory of the Enschédé foundry. While these designs were in the French tradition, they did not extend into the next period. In this respect, they suffered the same fate as Fournier's decorated types. It is believed that these Roman designs failed because the conventional weights of Roman did not work as well for ornamentation as did the newer Fat Face Romans then coming onto the scene. Fat Face Romans in the ornamental styles were to be exceedingly prominent during the first 40 years of the nineteenth century.

A minor, but characteristic grouping of letters pertinent to Victorian typography may be found in the historiated types; i.e., letterforms decorated with natural forms such as fruits, vines, people, animals, or architectural motifs. These types may be fairly ascribed to the long tradition of illuminated and engraved initials, the designs for the majority of which are believed to have come from Germany and France. Victorian historiated letters differed most from tradition in that the embellishment was *inside* the letterform, as compared to the initials from historical sources which usually had a simple Roman or Gothic letter *surrounded* by, or interwoven with natural forms.

The distinctive mark of the nineteenth-century historiated letters was the use of the modern Fat Faces for the basic letterform—Roman, Antique and Gothic, and the fact that most were eight line or larger. They reflect qualities associated with relief engraving, parallel lines used for shading, and an overall textural color. German and Dutch founders produced the most elaborate and sometimes grotesque designs. Some floral faces marketed by Bower & Bacon in England during the 1830's are typical of English productions. French styles were frequently ornamented with floral or architectural motifs without the heaviness of the German designs. The French, as in other decorative branches of the trade, led all other founders in the design and production of these letters.

Historiated faces were common to the first years of the nineteenth century, and occasionally would show up after mid-century. They diminished in importance, however, as type founders gained confidence and moved to other modes of decoration. Also, economic factors connected with their high susceptibility to damage and their cost to produce must have contributed to their general decline.

An important nineteenth-century letterform, the Tuscan, with its host of variations, comprised one of the major categories of letters from the period. Nicolette Gray dates the important period of Tuscans as being between 1815 and 1875—beginning the period with the first English Tuscan which was shown by Figgins' foundry in 1815. She defines the Victorian Tuscan as "a letter the face of which may be left plain (black or white) or decorated. The form of the letter may be bifurcated or curled at the terminals, and in the center of the stem it may be enlarged or broken. Finally, it may have a shadow, either outline, black or shaded. The shadow is, however, for color or

BIBLIOTHECA
MOGUNTINA
LIBRIS
SÆCULO PRIMO TYPOGRAPHICO
MOGUNTIÆ
IMPRESSIS INSTRUCTA,

Excerpt from title page of Würdtwein's Bibliotheca *printed in Augsburg, 1787. Ornamented letters look as though they may have been tooled from existing types or cast from modified punches.*

TYPOGRAPHY.

Canon Ornamented, Caslon, 1816. These decorated letters could have been made from modified punches.

VINCENT FIGGINS.

Representative of designs which may have been cast from retooled punches. Figgins, 1824.

ABCDHFGIJKL
ABCDEFGHIJKL

Tooled Roman. Richard Austin, 1788. Bottom line: Fry's Ornamented by Austin, circa 1796.

ABC
ABCDEFGH
ABCDEFGHIJ

Decorative letters, circa 1800, by Didot l'aîné.

Historiated letters (complete alphabets but usually without figures). Wood & Sharwood, London, circa 1838.

Representative of early nineteenth century French ornamental letters in the large sizes.

Representative of the grotesque designs that originated in Germany and Holland during the early nineteenth century.

emphasis, not to give solidity. The idea does not include the solid and illusionistic letters, which form a distinct and unmistakable category of their own."

In his article, *Decorated Types,* Fleuron VI, Morison illustrates a stone inscription by Furius Dionysios Filocalus of Rome made during the fourth century which shows a pronounced Tuscan treatment of serifs—bifurcated and curly-cued into decorative terminals. Nicolette Gray surmises that these fishtail serifs originated with the Greeks, and that their use became common in Rome during the third century. This treatment of serifs was given amplification by scribes, and in succeeding centuries became transformed into an identifiable and separate body of letterforms. Some of the Tuscan's best interpretations were accomplished by Italian illuminators and engravers during the sixteenth and seventeenth centuries. After 1800 Tuscans were imported into England, presumably from France, and here they multiplied fantastically in form and number. The original Tuscan models had been designed as ornate initials, but as revived by the typefounder, they were made into complete alphabets, frequently without lowercase or numerals. Also, the design properties of the Tuscan—bifurcated and trifurcated serifs, bulging medians, etc.—were adapted to new letterforms as they came onto the scene, and entirely new families of Tuscans were created in this manner during the century. Americans were responsible for a great number of innovations in the drawing, or contour, of Tuscans. On the other hand, European typefounders stayed with their historical sources and the conventional surface embellishment in their production of Tuscans.

As many of the Tuscan styles appear to be unique in design, that is, nonderivative, they are extremely difficult to classify. Usually they have to be grouped separately. This is especially true for designs coming from Europe; because many of the American Tuscans were influenced by Gothics or Antiques they can be classified differently. At the same time that the Dutch, German, and French typefounders were entering into the design and manufacture of decorated types on an expanded scale, three letterform inventions took place in England within the span of a few years which were to add great impetus to the entire field of display typography. Fat Face Romans, Antiques, and Gothics brought in a new era for the typefounder; they were neither decorated, nor always large, but their consistently dark color was exactly what commercial interests of that day were looking for to better publicize their wares. The popularity of the Fat Faces with job printers was almost immediate. Additionally, they were soon adapted to the many decorative devices which had preceded them, such as outline, shade, and historiated.

The first advertising Fat Face was based on a Roman, and the model now most often associated with this style was the result of a gradual process of fattening the Roman letter, which came into full-fledged form sometime after 1810. Edward Rowe Mores describes a first step in the evolution as beginning with Thomas Cottrell and his large Roman letters shown in 1766. Then during the next 50 years the contrast between thicks and thins gradually became greater. However, since none of these letters reached the extremities of contrast of later designs, Nicolette Gray refers to them as a transitional style, which finally disappeared by 1815.

Circa 1810, the design we now know as Fat Face Roman

INTEGRACVMR

Fragment from original Damasine *inscription on stone, circa 380, signed* Furius Dionysios Filocalus. *("Decorated Letters," by Stanley Morison, in* Fleuron VI.*)*

DIF

Engraved facsimiles of illuminators' art from the Sforziada, *1490.*

P

Tuscan initial used by Fenzo of Venice in 1758.

PETITS GENRE

Lithographic engraving of a Tuscan by Jean Midolle. Taken from title page of Oeuvres de Jean Midolle: Ecritures Modernes *1834-35.*

RAN

Nineteenth century Tuscan. Italian Tuscan, Thorowgood, 1825.

TYE

Popular French Tuscan widely used in America as well as Europe in the early years of the nineteenth century.

first began to appear as a fashionable type in the printing of public notices and small bills. Nicolette Gray mentions that the change from the transitional designs to the undoubted Fat Face must have been abrupt. Even though there are no known specimens, Robert Thorne, successor to Thomas Cottrell, is regarded as the originator of the Fat Face. A. F. Johnson writes that the popularity of Fat Faces began to wane within a short time, and that their revival in England was brought on through extensive use of the design in America and Germany during the 1820's. During this same period, the Fat Face Roman included an Italic, Backslope, Open, and Shade, as well as some ornamental styles.

Nicolette Gray describes the Antique, or Egyptian: "it is normally, but not necessarily, even-line and it has unbracketed slab serifs. By virtue of both these characteristics it is a heavy letter, and so has a formal advantage over the classical." She goes on to say that the principle of the slab serif may be traced back to the fifteenth-century Roman letters, where it had been employed on capital letters. However, it is unlikely that there is continuity between these early uses of slab serif and the models of the nineteenth century. It seems reasonably well established that Antique styles came to the typefounder from the sign painter, possibly from his three-dimensional letters used for building or business identification. Antique was first shown by Figgins in 1815 in four sizes with no lowercase—5 and 4 lines, 22 and 12 points. In 1821, Thorowgood specimens did include lowercase and a titling Antique with tooling (emphasis to the left). Americans were showing the Antiques during the early 1820's, apparently some 4 or 5 years before the Germans, who showed them circa 1830, according to A. F. Johnson. The American designs, which seem to be slightly heavier than the Figgins styles, were to become even heavier with wood type. The Albany Foundry of Richard Starr shows a Tooled Antique with lowercase (emphasis to the right) and an Italic Antique without lowercase. Also shown was an interesting Antique Outlined including a lowercase, a design which differed from a similar face first seen in the specimens of Figgins in 1833 in that all serifs were unbracketed. It is not known if the Figgins design had a lowercase. Antique Open and Shade, patterned after the same styles of Roman that preceded, soon became representative letters of the era.

Gothic, or sans-serif, was no exception to the rule, and like Antique, its origins predate by several centuries its first showing by typefounders. Greeks often used a sans-serif style of lettering, and there are many examples of Roman letters minus their serifs which have distinct Gothic qualities but which retain the thick and thin relationships of the parent letterform. James Mosley in his article, "The Nymph and the Grot: The Revival of the Sanserif Letter" (Typographica 12) shows many fine examples of Gothic which precede the first specimen of the founder—that of William Caslon IV in 1816. Several of these examples, the architectural drawings of Sir John Soane in 1791, engraved Gothic titling on a silver cup designed by John Flaxman in 1805–1806, and engraved lettering for the title page of Thomas Hope's *Household Furniture* from 1807, all illustrate a full-blown even-lined Gothic very much like the designs to be issued by the founders during the 1840's.

Caslon's specimen, a medium-weight full-faced Gothic letter, was shown once more by Blake Garnett in 1819,

TYPE

Transitional Roman. Fry & Steele, 1807.

GRAVING

Transitional Roman Open Shade. Caslon, 1808.

CUMBE

Transitional Roman Tooled. Caslon, 1816.

MA

Full Face Roman. Edmund Fry, 1816.

An

Full Face Roman Italic, Caslon, 1821.

Aucti

Full Face Roman Backslope. Figgins, 1821.

BRIG

Roman Open Shade. Thorowgood, 1821.

ABCDEFGH
Catilina,

Full Face Roman Tooled. Caslon, 1832.

MANKI

Antique. From first known specimens as published by Figgins, 1815.

THOR
bourn

Antique. Thorowgood, 1821.

ABCDEFG
speculators

Antique Italic. Caslon, 1825.

ABCDEF
ABCDEF

Antique, Antique Italic. Caslon, 1832.

ABCDEFGHIJK COMMERCIAL

Antique Outline. Blake & Stephenson, circa 1833.

W CASLON JUNR

Gothic. First specimen of Gothic shown by a typefounder. William Caslon IV, 1816.

TO BE SOLD

Gothic. Figgins, 1832.

CANTER

Gothic. Thorowgood, 1834.

FREE SHED MOR

Gothics. Johnson & Smith, 1834.

LECTURES AT THE ANTIQUE

Gothic Outline. Blake & Stephenson, circa 1833.

before being replaced by a heavy, condensed Gothic by Figgins in 1832. Thorowgood showed a somewhat more condensed style in 1834, and in the same year, Johnson & Smith of Philadelphia showed three styles of the heavy Gothics—a condensed Gothic with a lowercase, and a full-faced Gothic in both plain and ornamented. Most certainly these last three designs were cut on wood.

The lighter styles were kept alive through these years by some small outline Gothics first shown in 1833 by Figgins, and Stephenson & Blake. In 1836, Robb & Ecklin of Philadelphia brought out a well-executed condensed Gothic in two sizes without lowercase. Nicolette Gray shows this same design for Wilson in 1843. During the late 1830's and all through the 1840's, Gothics multiplied in styles—both plain and commercial, and equaled the Antiques and Romans in popularity with the trades.

Postscription, or Poster Types

The typefounder first became concerned with the need for larger sizes of type during the sixteenth century. Modeled after the existing Roman, Black Letter, or pointed Gothic designs, these first letters of unusual size were engraved in wood or type metal as logotypes and displayed on title pages of the large books then fashionable in some parts of Europe, and for large posting notices. Records preserved in the files of the Plantin-Moretus Museum describe the manufacture of a font of large Roman type by van den Keere, a sixteenth-century Flemish punch-cutter. Undoubtedly, his procedures were representative of the practice from that period. He drew and engraved the letters on pear wood, after which he hired a carpenter to cut them apart and to align the font. The models were then used to make an impression in sand, and the designs were cast in type metal. The faces were fused to metal bodies or fastened to wood blocks and planed from the bottom to a proper height for printing. Also during the sixteenth century, Christopher Plantin of the same foundry engraved large letters on boxwood and cast the faces in sand. The type bodies were then fused with the type through the use of a special mold. During the latter part of the fifteenth century examples of identical initials or borders printed in scattered locations at approximately the same time indicate that some method of casting duplicates had been devised.

Since this process reached a considerable degree of refinement in the sixteenth century, it is believed that printers had borrowed sand-casting techniques from the goldsmiths and other jewelry artisans. The duplicating processes were to become an important factor in the dissemination of typographic styles in the Western world, and it appears in light of recent evidence that stereotyping was used both earlier and more extensively than heretofore believed.

The practice of duplicating initial letters and decorative pieces was firmly established early in the sixteenth century. The common method was to press the original engraving—engraved on either wood or metal—into moist sand and cast in brass or type metal. These earliest duplicate plates may be identified today by a characteristic concavity at the center of the larger cuts, or by nail heads used to attach the plate to the block, which often are revealed in the impression. Stereotyping was essential to the decorative side of printing as a means for making duplicate ornaments and borders, and for making letters in metal larger than those which could be cast in molds.

ABC
DEF
GHK
LMO
RVX
YZÆ

abcde
æ&œ

La Plus Grande Romaine. *Letters cast in sand from wooden pattern letters cut in 1565 by Hendryck van den Keere.*

In 1740, Gessner described the sand-casting process: "The ingredients of casting sand are fine sand, to which is added calcinated baking-oven glue, the redder the glue the better. This mixture is finely pulverized and passed through a fine meshed sieve. Thereupon the mixture is placed upon a level board. The center is hollowed out and good beer is poured into the cavity—much or little according to the amount of sand used. This (the sand and beer) is well stirred with a wooden spatula. When, through the pouring of this beer, the mixture begins to steam, the mass must be well mixed in order that every single particle of sand is moistened. Then the sand is formed into a heap. Gradually and very carefully a little of it is taken up with the wooden spatula, making sure to separate the wet globules which stick together. When it is too dry it breaks easily in the casting operation; if it is too wet, it does not cave in when casting but cakes and falls out of the casting tray. By moistening it with spirits of ammonia it produces a clean cast. The type is placed on the flat sand or form-board. When a letter cut in wood or type high is to be reproduced, then straight boards or furniture must be placed around the form board and the letter placed so that it protrudes high enough to give the thickness of the cast desired. Then the face of the type is cleaned with a brush and the casting tray is placed over it, held down firmly with the left hand, to avoid shifting.

"Thereupon the type is dusted by means of a dauber filled with coal dust; then the moist sand is loosely poured upon it until the casting tray is filled up. At first it is gently pressed down and afterward harder pressure is exerted until the casting tray is firmly packed full. Thereupon the casting tray is evenly and gently raised. Should the type adhere to the sand, a tap on the tray with a knife will cause it to separate. The overflow of the sand is pared off at both sides of the tray with a knife so that this excess sand does not drop from the cast in the tray onto the type. The sand is delicately cut out so that the type metal may flow without difficulty. By permitting the form to dry somewhat it flows much more easily. The form or figure is blackened with a candle having a good flame and is then placed on a level tray itself in such a manner that the side of the figure is situated below. In order that the flow of the type metal may pass over the board and well over the figure, place two boards in a hand vise and then pour the type metal in. When the metal is melted, roll a piece of paper together and stick it into the metal. If the paper chars, the metal is satisfactory; if a flame appears, the metal is too hot."*

Essentially the sand-casting process used by Thomas Cottrell in England during the early 1860's was the one described by Gessner. Cottrell, whose large letters ranged up to 12 lines, is said to have been the first to cast letters of such bulk. At the same time, Caslon was casting letters no larger than 5 lines. After Cottrell's specimens, Isaac Moore (manager for Fry and Pine) cast 10-line letters in 1770, Fry & Wilson cast some 12 line in 1785-86, Caslon some 19 line in 1785 and Thorne, successor to Cottrell, showed 19 line in 1794. Mention is made that after Cottrell produced his first large specimens, Caslon began to make the large types with "beautifully finished" brass patterns (Caslon Circular, Vol. III, No. 10, July 1877). However, it is thought that the use of brass matrices may

*Christian Friedrich Gessner, *Die so noethig als nuetzliche Buchdruckerkunst,* Leipzig, 1740.

have begun with Cottrell, as he is listed in Mortimer's *Universal Director* of 1763 as the inventor of "a new method of cutting Letters in brass for monumental and other inscriptions." ("English Vernacular," James Mosley, *Motif,* Winter 1963-64, p. 18.)

In 1810, William Caslon IV introduced an invention that was an improvement on the sand-casting processes. He is said to have used a stencil plate of considerable thickness as a matrix, which was faced with another plate fastened by rivets. This matrix was built up along the edges to form only the face and perhaps a thin shoulder. A. F. Johnson states that these faces were cast and mounted on wood blocks, reducing both the amount of type metal required and the weight of the letters. This new method of casting large types was described by Hansard (extravagantly described, according to T. B. Reed) as the "greatest improvement in the art of letter-founding that has taken place in modern times." The pierced matrix system, called Sanspareil, was popular with most English typefounders of that day. The Thorowgood specimen book for 1821 showed Roman in sizes up to 24 lines. Identified as "Cast in mould and matrix," these types were undoubtedly cast with the Sanspareil process.

It is doubtful if American typefounders ever cast metal types any larger than those of the English since large letters were available at low cost after the invention of mass-produced wood type in 1828. Before that date, Americans used hand-engraved brass matrices.

David Bruce, Jr. learned the typefounders' trade in his father's foundry as an engraver of these brass matrices. It is an interesting coincidence that Fournier *le jeune* had also learned the founders' trade in the family shop in the production of large types. D. B. Updike describes how Fournier engraved punches for capital letters known as *grosses et moyennes de fonte,* which were of a size previously supplied only in type cut on wood. The brass matrices used by American founders seldom were larger than 15 line, although occasionally 20-line matrices were cut. Even after the invention of mass-produced wood type the brass matrix remained in limited use, as some printers felt that metal types printed more evenly than wood on calendared and card stocks. The brass matrix finally disappeared after the perfection of the electrotype matrix at mid-century.

One reference to what *may* have been at least similar to, if not the same as Caslon's Sanspareil process, was found in the opening pages of the 1828 specimen book of the Boston Type & Stereotype Foundry, which informed its clientele: "Large Letters and cuts (are) cast in moulds and Matrixes, on metal bodies, and with the exactness of small letters." These specimens included a 20-line Roman, but the majority of the types were in the 6- to 8-line range.

The first type specimen book published in America was that of Binny & Ronaldson of Philadelphia in 1812. Although the largest type shown here was 7-line Pica Roman, the frontice page assured the trade that larger sizes would soon be available. In 1815, George & David Bruce showed no ornamental or large letters, and in 1824 they included a 10-line Antique, 8-line Antique Outlined, and some large 16-line ornamented lottery figures; in 1826, the Albany Type Foundry showed a 10-line Antique and 14-line Roman; and the previously mentioned Boston Type Foundry with its 20-line Roman in 1828 was manufacturing the largest types made in this country before the invention of mass-produced wood type.

*Initial from a work printed by David Sartorius, 1582. The four black points in the corners are the heads of nails showing in the impression. (*A New History of Stereotyping, *George A. Kubler.)*

Twelve Lines Pica.

Specimen printed from 12 line letters sand cast by Thomas Cottrell, circa 1765.

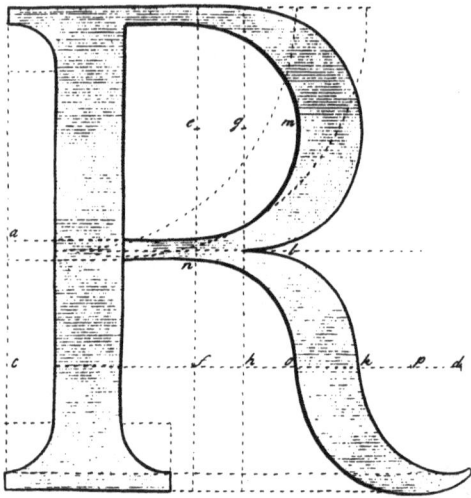

From Geometrical Construction to form the Twenty-four Letters of the Alphabet, *George Bickham, Jr., circa 1755. It is said that Caslon III followed closely the letter models provided by Bickham in the design of the large letters cast by the Caslon foundry during the second half of the eighteenth century. (*Alphabets, *edited by R. S. Hutchings.)*

Eleven line letters cast by Caslon III, circa 1764.

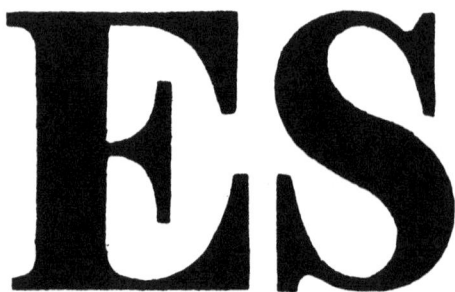

Ten line letters cast by Fry & Steele, 1808. (Reduced.)

After the first wood types came onto the market in 1828, it was only a short time before they were being sold by the typefounders. The 1834 catalogue of Johnson & Smith stated on the price list: "Most of the six line and larger types are cut on wood." The White, Hagar & Company price list for 1835 announced that the 16-line and larger types were cut on wood, and both Connor & Cooke and Robb & Ecklin in 1836 on their price lists said that designs 6-line and over were cut on wood. None of these larger types was identified as being wood at the place of specimen showing, but carried the information *only* in small type at the front of the catalogue, usually on the price list.

There are numerous examples of specimens shown by founders being identical to those shown by wood type manufacturers—except that the wood type catalogues are dated earlier than those of the founder. Johnson & Smith in 1841 illustrated several pages of large ornamental types, with a selection that had been shown by Nesbitt in 1838. At least once an 8-line Tuscan was set in the same word with identical spacing as in the Nesbitt specimen. There are other examples: Hagar in 1850 repeated a showing of an ornamental design shown by Wells & Webb in 1849, Alexander Robb in 1844 illustrated designs taken literally from the Nesbitt catalogue of 1838.

It would seem, however, that a practical means did exist of duplicating a wood design in metal. Wells & Webb in 1840 advertised on their price page that some 15 to 20 ornamental styles, ranging from 4 to 12 lines, could be had in metal if the customer desired. In 1859, James Connor advertised that Page's wood types, from 3- to 5-line, could be had on copper-faced metal.

Although most of the large letters were made of wood, there is one recorded instance of a large display letter originating as a metal type face. This was National, in five sizes ranging from 36 points to 10-line picas, engraved by Julius Herriet, Senior, for the L. Johnson & Company circa 1855. The design, the first to be patented by the foundry, was a Gothic with reversed stars in the upper third of the letter and undulating stripes covering the remaining letter. Revived as a patriotic face during the Civil War, the style could print in either one or two colors. Interestingly enough, this letter was never cut in wood.

It would seem that during these years, the American printers enjoyed a considerable advantage over their European counterparts in the marketing of large letters, because of the durability, tremendous number of styles, lighter weight, and lower cost of mass-produced wood types.

Adorinam Chandler, listed as a New York typefounder in 1820, but in subsequent years as a stereotyper, published in 1822, *A Specimen of Ornamental Types and Embellishments.* In the "notice" he advised the trade: "The ornamental types exhibited in this specimen are cast in stereotype plates, and the letters separately fixed to wooden bottoms. A great quantity of this kind of job type has been in use for three years past, and those who have tried it, speak decidedly in its favour. Printers are left to judge for themselves, whether it is not a saving to buy this, instead of giving forty-two cents per pound for type metal. It is warranted to last as long as any job type cast in the United States. It will be made up in founts to suit purchasers, at eighteen cents per letter."

James Connor, a prominent nineteenth-century American

typefounder, was to describe at a later date how as a young man operating a stereotype house in New York City sometime between 1828 and 1830, he took an old set of stereotype plates and cut an alphabet from them of 16-line Antique—which seemed to be in great demand at that time for large posters. Making additional stereotypes from the alphabet, he blocked them on wood and sold them to the trade with great success.

What appears to be a similar method to the one employed by Connor and Chandler was advertised by Eduard Hanel of Berlin in an 1841 edition of the journal, *Buchdruckerkunst, Schriftgiesserei.* Under the heading of "Samples of Poster Letters," he showed a sizable number of plain and ornamented styles which were advertised as being mounted on either metal or wood according to the customer's wishes. The firm was identified as a letter die-casting, etching, and type company. Almost certainly the letters were stereotypes mounted on wood, especially when the letters were extremely decorative.

There are some old types in both the Robinson-Pforzheimer collection at the New York Public Library and in Special Collections at Columbia University which appear to have been manufactured by the stereotype process, and which seem very practical for printing. They consist of metal plates—shoulder and letter, nailed to wooden blocks. Richness of detail, which was the style of the day, could be accomplished with comparative ease by stereotyping, whereas it presented great difficulty with the Sanspareil matrix of Caslon or the brass matrix of the American typefounder. It is not known why stereotyping of large letters did not find an even more widespread use than it did, but De Vinne wrote: "while the cost of metal is less, the cost of labor is more, and the practice was soon discontinued."

There were innumerable patents throughout the century relating to more economical means for producing large types. One of the more unusual ones was for Galvanized Wood Type, patented by M. Duval of Paris. This invention was described as follows in *Inland Printer* during 1888: "In the larger sizes of display type it is possible, through the use of a galvano-plastic bath, to coat the face of the (wood) type with a coating of copper. A special patented process allows only the face to be coated. Under these circumstances, the letter preserves the lightness of wood but attains the qualities of metal type. The galvanized copper also protects fine detail and serifs." It was also mentioned that the same process might be applied equally as well to wood engravings.

The Printing Times and Lithographer for October, 1879, announced an invention by Peter Gfroerer of Terre Haute, Indiana: a type face with the sides and body made of wood, veneered with rubber or analogous material. In effect, this invention was similar to what we call linoleum blocks today. The main advantage of the letters, which were cut in the facing material, was that their resiliency resulted in more even printing. Unevenness in pressure from worn types, improper makeready, etc., were countered; and there was a substantial reduction in the amount of ink required. This, in turn, eliminated the problem of flooding the smaller types when enough ink was used to cover the large type adequately.

Another method which apparently found some application in the manufacture of large, and especially, ornamental letters and typographic ornaments, was the polytype process. This technique was invented in 1784 by

Franz Ignaz Joseph Hoffmann, a native of Alsace who settled in Paris. The process was closely related to stereotyping except that for the latter, liquid metal was poured into a matrix taken from the original block or form. For polytype, liquid metal was poured onto a sheet of paper or into a cardboard frame; when the metal had cooled to a doughlike consistency, a weighted matrix was dropped from a height into the metal, after which the resulting cast relief was trimmed and mounted for printing. For relatively small items, such as ornamental letters, ornaments and woodcuts, the polytype process was believed to be superior to stereotyping because duplicates could be made more rapidly and shoulders could be depressed more deeply than with stereotyping. (A note at the bottom of a page from a Laurent et Derberny type specimen book, circa 1874, states: "Nota. La Collection se continue sur six Grandeurs Supérieures, voir les lettres d'Affiches Polytypées.")

Some brass poster types were discussed in the 1871 Ringwalt *American Encyclopedia of Printing.* Invented by Herr Pappelbaum, these types were described as being almost as cheap as wood types, accurate in body, height, lining, and width, and not affected by moisture or atmospheric changes.

However, the founder was plagued with a multitude of problems in casting large types. The metal was difficult to keep in a liquid state for pouring. Frequently it would cool unevenly and produce concave surfaces. (One method to overcome this problem was to place a red-hot iron in the core of the letter during pouring, but this procedure was not always successful.) Because most printers found the cost of the large letters prohibitive, they would rent the larger sizes. In addition, the large types tended to be brittle and highly susceptible to damage. Weight was another problem. Since a 10-line capital M would weigh a pound, one can imagine the tremendous storage and shipping difficulties associated with a font of type of this size cast in solid form. Later in the century, typefounders experimented with casting letters on arches to reduce the weight and amount of metal, but the economy was pushed too far, and the slender arches often broke in locking-up.

Wood Type

As previously stated, the use of wood in printing and as a material for making type had been known for hundreds of years before the nineteenth century. In America, with the expansion of commercial printing in the first years of the nineteenth century, it was almost inevitable that someone would perfect a process for cheaply producing the large letters so much in demand for broadsides. Wood was a logical material because of its ready availability, lightness, and known printing qualities.

Darius Wells of New York City, who finally found the means for mass producing wood letters in 1827, published the first known wood type catalogue in March, 1828. Wells introduced a basic invention, the lateral router, which in combination with the pantograph added by George Leavenworth in 1834, constituted the essential machinery for making end-cut wood types. In 1880, J. D. Hamilton of Two Rivers, Wisconsin, perfected a veneer type which he was able to sell for less than half the price of end wood types. William H. Page and George Setchell, in 1887, patented and manufactured a die-stamped type which, though limited in sizes and styles, was superior to veneer and sold for the same price.

A celluloid-faced wood type was marketed in New York City around 1885, and this type, along with end-cut, die-stamped, and veneer types, represented the four principal kinds of large wood letters manufactured between 1827 and 1900.

In the preface to his first wood type catalogue, Darius Wells made the following remarks:

1. "The cost of metal types of the sizes here offered, especially the larger, precludes their use, except by a few who are extensively engaged in job printing. This objection is now completely obviated, as the prices of those offered, are less than one half those of the Founders.

2. "In point of durability, they possess the same advantage over metal types, that wood cuts do over stereotype ones. Besides, they are incomparably less liable to damage by carelessness and accidents.

3. "These types are prepared with a machine, which gives them a perfectly even surface, and renders their height exact and uniform, while large metal types are more or less concave on the face, arising from the unequal cooling of the metal when cast.

4. "The difference in the value of the material, after the types are thrown aside, is greatly overbalanced by the fact, that the interest on the cost of a metal fount, would in less than seven years pay for a wood fount equal in size and beauty, and more durable.

5. "The perplexity and loss arising from the breaking of metal types through the centre, as well as of the descending and kerned letters, is completely obviated by my wood letter. This advantage, all printers, especially those at a distance from foundries, will know how to appreciate. The subscriber is enabled to state from experience, that the use of wood types when carefully prepared in the manner of those in this specimen, are in no respect objectionable; that they are more convenient in many respects, are more durable, and cost only from one quarter to one half those of metal.

Time was to prove Wells' observations correct, and it appears that not only was he successful in the wood type venture from the beginning, but in the preface to his 1840 catalogue he was able to remark, "Having in the year 1827, originally established the business of Wood Letter Cutting, it is with no small satisfaction that he (Wells) views the great improvement in Job Printing that has in consequence taken place. For want of large type, no larger posting bills than of medium size were then printed, and these exhibiting but a lean variety; while the metal type cost so much as to limit their use to a very few establishments. The manufacture of Wood Type formed a new era in job printing; and the use of them, although at first opposed by a strong prejudice, has now become general; and the universal satisfaction they have given, attests the high estimation in which they are held. In regard to their cheapness and durability, no argument is now necessary."

European Wood Types

It is not known to what extent mass production of wood type flourished in Europe during the same time it was manufactured in America. However, it is believed that Americans dominated the European markets as well as their own after 1870. There are a number of European wood type manufacturers identified through specimen books: Dubosc of Paris in 1865; Eglington of London,

who supplied wood types to the Caslon foundry around 1870; Miller & Richard of London and Edinburgh, who advertised in a specimen book circa 1865, "Miller & Richard, Typefounders Brass Rule & Manufacturers, Wood Letter Cutters;" Day & Collins who also made type for Caslon & Company. One listing was found in the catalogue for the Grand Exposition of 1851 by a R. Fairbairn of R. 37 Gate, Cambridge Street & Hackney Road. On the basis of examining as many of these specimens as possible, there seemed to be little, or no relationship between American and European designs. Wood type manufacturers in the United States did borrow many ornamental designs from European typefounders in the period between 1828 and 1850, but after that date, they devised most of their own styles, which were far superior in design and execution to wood types produced abroad in the same years.

Sold THE HER Mount Form MEN edition has FRENCH Auction sale

Wood types shown by Miller & Richards in their 1865 specimens.

HORN
HINZE
Baku
ACTION
KEHL
ODE
AM
E

GAE
RAI
TRA
PE
JOB
Choisy
CORPS
SIRE

Poster types shown by Eduard Haenel, Berlin, 1841-43. These impressions were probably made from metal-faced types; however, they are representative of styles then popular in Germany.

Wood types by Dubosc, Paris, 1865. Forty-five pages of wood letters in this specimen.

Darius Wells (1800-1875).

The Wells factory located in Paterson, New Jersey, as it appeared in 1867 just before it was destroyed by fire.

Any narrative describing an industry must, of necessity, emphasize the life and works of the men connected with its founding, growth, and practices. It is unfortunate that more information is not available about the wood type industry, but the business was a minor one, the men obscure, and the records incomplete.

Darius Wells

The founder of the industry, Darius Wells, was born in Kingsborough, New York, on April 26, 1800, the son of James Wells, a Connecticut veteran of the Revolutionary War. James Wells died when Darius was eleven, and at this time, Darius was apprenticed to a William Childs, a printer of Johnstown, New York, who published the *Montgomery Republican*. Wells was released from his apprenticeship at 17 or 18 years of age, and in 1819 he married Almira Waters.

In 1822 he moved to Amsterdam, New York, where, in conjunction with Childs, he founded the town's first newspaper, the *Mohawk Herald*. Records are vague as to whether William Childs or Asa Childs went to Amsterdam with Wells. Since an Asa Childs, four years later, went to New York City with Wells, it would seem likely that Asa and not William (who has been named in some references as Wells' associate in Amsterdam) was a partner in the newspaper at Amsterdam. In 1826 Childs and Wells established a small printing shop at 194 Greenwich Street, in New York City. Asa Childs was to die very shortly after this move, and afterwards it is conceivable that Wells entered into another partnership with a printer named John C. Johnson. Darius Wells' obituary in the *Typographic Messenger,* signed "B," (perhaps Henry Lewis Bullen) does not mention the Childs and Wells partnership, but does describe the formation of a Johnson and Wells partnership, shortly after which Johnson died. The *New York City Directory* for 1826, however, does not show a Johnson and Wells but does list Childs and Wells. Additionally, John C. Johnson, printer, is listed for that same year, but is indicated as deceased in the following directory. It is entirely possible, therefore, that Wells may have entered into two partnerships in 1826, and that in both instances the partner had died.

Wells continued to operate a small jobbing shop, and during these years became interested in making wooden letters. His first experiments were done while he was confined to his home during a period of convalescence from a serious illness. These early experiments were most notable from the standpoint that Wells worked on end grain of the wood after the manner of wood engravers, rather than one side grain, which was customary for printers then who carved large letters for their own use. Because there is at least one documented example of a font of wood type entirely hand carved and stamped on the bottom "D. Wells, N.Y.," it seems likely that for a period of time Wells did carve wood type by hand for the market.

There is an account of how Wells and David Bruce, Jr., joined together for the purpose of finding a method for mass producing large wood types. The article rather humorously describes the dissolving of their partnership, "but having more brains to project than to prosecute the business, they were soon compelled to discontinue it." However, in spite of the problems, it was during this partnership that Wells invented the lateral router, the invention that was to make practical the mass production of wood types.

In March of 1828, Wells issued his first catalogue of wood type specimens from the back room of George Long's Book Store at 161 Broadway. This event marked the beginnings of the American wood type industry. At that time, Wells listed himself in the New York directory as "D. Wells, letter-cutter." There is not a listing for Wells for the years 1829 and 1830, and at present it is not possible to ascertain the significance of his absence from the city directory for that year. In 1831, his name was again included, this time as a "type-cutter." Wells organized the company of D. Wells & Company in 1835 with Thomas Vermilyea, V. Riggs, and others as partners in the enterprise.

In 1839, Wells took in Ebenezer Russell Webb, an employee of several years, as a full partner. The company, known as Wells & Webb, established a plant on Water Street in Paterson, New Jersey. E. R. Webb oversaw the Paterson mill while Wells operated the New York City offices. The plant in Paterson produced wood type, reglet, printer's furniture, and engraver's wood, while the business operations were conducted from the New York offices. Wells & Webb moved from 38 Ann Street, in 1842, to the corner of Fulton and Dutch Streets, where they opened the first general printer's warehouse in America. They carried anything the printer might need in new and used equipment. During these same years, they commissioned the Bruce and Connor typefoundries to cast metal types exclusively for their use. For the most part, these metal types were probably ornamental faces based on original or popular styles of wood type produced by Wells and Webb.

In this same year, 1842, Webb took over the New York office and Wells moved to Paterson. As Wells & Webb expanded their business, they moved their Paterson quarters further down the river to an old building which they enlarged several times. Although Wells decided to sell his interest in the business to Webb in 1854, he continued to manage the Paterson plant until 1856, when he finally withdrew from the wood type business altogether. Abraham Lincoln appointed Darius Wells as postmaster of Paterson in 1861, a position he was to hold for the next 13 years. His health suddenly began to fail in 1874, and in November of that year he was confined to his quarters. He died on May 27, 1875.

William Leavenworth

The next man to enter the wood type business after Darius Wells was William Leavenworth, who also made a solid contribution to the mechanical end of the trade by introducing the pantograph, which, combined with the router, formed the basic machinery for making all end-cut wood types throughout the century.

William Leavenworth was born on November 10, 1799, at Canaan, New York. His early life was spent working with his father in Barrington and West Stockbridge, Massachusetts. During 1833 and 1834, he lived in Syracuse, New York, with his brother Elias, who at a later date was to become Secretary to the State of New York. While in Syracuse, Leavenworth engraved and published a map of the two villages of Lodi and Syracuse. It has been reported by De Vinne and others that Leavenworth adapted the pantograph to the router at this same time, around 1834. One account states that Leavenworth and a man named A. R. Gillmore were working together when this machinery was perfected. However, it has been impossible to find any additional information on Gillmore, or on how Leavenworth happened to become interested in the wood type business.

William Leavenworth had married a Mary Debow of Allentown, New Jersey, in 1830. After completing his improved machinery for making wood type, he moved to Allentown where he and his father-in-law went into the business of wood type manufacture. The one surviving specimen book of Leavenworth's type is now housed in the New York Public Library. The cover advertises "Leavenworth's Patent Wood Type . . . manufactured by J. M. Debow of Allentown, New Jersey." Even though the legend "Patent" appears at the bottom of each specimen page, no records of a patent registration have been found.

An article in the *Allentown Messenger* during 1904, which describes the history of an old factory building located nearby, includes the following information: "In 1836 the place came into the possession of William Leavenworth, who then made alterations for conducting a wood type manufactory. Under the supervision of Ebenezer R. Webb the business prospered for a few years, but was finally abandoned." The company closed down when Webb became a partner of Wells in 1839, and the new firm of Wells and Webb took over the inventory of the Leavenworth manufactory. No doubt it was in this manner that Wells obtained possession of the combined router pantograph machinery. Up until 1839 he had probably manufactured wood type by a more cumbersome process using only the router.

Elias Leavenworth was to describe his brother William as abounding in enterprise, enthusiasm, and genius. Also, oversanguine and hopeful, William Leavenworth was said to be more intent on the object to be accomplished than on its pecuniary results. In the family genealogy Elias wrote that William was a man of great ingenuity, a fine mechanical genius, a splendid penman, a fine engraver, and indeed a man capable of anything requiring ingenuity, mechanical skill, or taste. This would account for the novel letter designs produced by the Leavenworth manufactory during the few years of its operation. William Leavenworth should be rated along side of William Page, as a fine designer of original letters for wood type. The last found notice regarding William Leavenworth relates to a patent applied for on April 18, 1839, for a means of propelling canal boats. It would appear that he spent the remainder of his life in Allentown, where he died on May 6, 1860, of consumption. The combined pantograph and router were to be invented all over again by Edwin Allen in 1836. As far as can be determined, there was never any connection between Allen and Leavenworth, and it is believed that their inventions were arrived at independently.

Edwin Allen

Edwin Allen was born in Windham, Connecticut, on March 27, 1811, and with a twin brother, he was the youngest son of Amos D. Allen, a cabinet maker who had settled in Windham during 1800. In addition to the cabinet shops, the family cultivated a small farm lying on the west banks of the Shetucket River. Allen lived on this farm until he was old enough to become an apprentice in his father's factory. Allen was more interested in ma-

Edwin Allen (1811-1891).

The Tontine building at the corner of Wall and Water Streets in New York City. It was from this establishment that George Nesbitt sold Allen's wood type.

The type mill built by Edwin Allen in 1852 on the fulling ponds above South Windham, Connecticut. This photograph is believed to have been taken around 1900, when Charles Tubbs was operating the mill. (Courtesy of the Guilford Smith Memorial Library, South Windham, Connecticut.)

chinery than wood working, but since his father's wish was law, he dutifully fulfilled his apprenticeship as a cabinet maker.

His interests in machinery were not completely denied during these years, because he had the opportunity of studying his father's machinery. As new machines were brought into the shops, he learned about mechanical improvements. During the years with his father he was to make numerous improvements on existing machinery in the factory. He also invented new equipment for doing work that had previously been done by hand.

In 1835 Allen left home and joined a brother who was a cabinet maker in Norwich, Connecticut. The new employment was brief, for in the fall of 1836 his brother's factory was destroyed by fire. Thrown out of work by the calamity, he leisurely combed the town of Norwich for a new job. Eventually he came to the office of the *Norwich Courier,* then owned by John Dunham. Never having been exposed to a printing plant, he was curious about its operation, and in particular, about the machinery used in printing.

The owner politely received Allen and showed him through the entire plant. A font of wood type caught his eye; it was 9-line Antique, was coarsely cut, and had various imperfections. He asked many questions about wood type, how it was made, its cost, and so on—all of which Dunham answered the best he could. After returning to his rooms, Allen was greatly occupied with ideas on the manufacture of wood type. In three days he constructed a machine for making wood type and cut his first samples. This first machine was operated by foot power, probably some treadle device.

With the encouragement of local printers, he returned to Windham and set up a shop for the production of wood type. His first quarters were in an out-building owned by Smith, Winchester & Company of South Windham, and power was conveyed across the highway by an underground shaft. This would indicate that steam power was substituted for the foot treadle. He improved his machinery, increased his repertory of patterns, and by March of 1837 was producing such quantities of wood type that it became imperative that he find new markets.

New York City was the most obvious place to begin. Boxing up samples to show, Allen embarked by packet for the city. He first approached the typefounders, who either rebuffed him or showed little interest. Next he began visiting individual printing houses and, in a matter of time, entered the offices of George F. Nesbitt. Nesbitt received him, examined his samples, and after a long discussion, suggested an arrangement whereby Allen would manufacture the type and Nesbitt would sell it under the name of the George F. Nesbitt Company.

Allen returned to Windham where he added to his styles, and generally extended his facilities. By 1840 he was to move from the Smith, Winchester & Company building to a steam-powered plant on his father's homestead where he employed twelve workmen and manufactured type cases and galleys in addition to wood types. It is not known how these items were marketed as they were never mentioned in the Nesbitt catalogues. He is reported to have been very secretive about his operations in these years. The "No Admittance" signs he ordered tacked on all the doors to his factory were strictly enforced.

Without any apparent reasons Allen's business began to fail in the late 1840's. During this time, he is believed to have concentrated his efforts on manufacturing and selling his "Allen's Educational Tables," which had been patented in 1849. The last listing by Nesbitt of Allen's wood types is found in the 1850–51 (this would cover the year 1849) *Mercantile Union Business Directory* and the New England Type Foundry of Hobart and Robbins for 1851.

In 1852 Allen moved to the fulling ponds above South Windham where he constructed a new mill using water power. Shortly after the building was completed, the entire works were sold to John Gaines Cooley, a printer in Norwich, Connecticut. This mill continued as a wood type manufactory for 11 years more under Cooley, who then sold it to Guilford Smith. Smith attempted to establish a felt mill, but because of the Civil War and its attendant problems of receiving raw materials and reaching markets, the business never really prospered. In 1878 Smith leased the mill to Charles Tubbs and his partners, who manufactured wood type at this location until Tubbs' death in 1903. To residents of South Windham, the building, which no longer exists, was always the "old type mill," and the road leading up to it was known as "type road." Today, this street is marked with a modern metal street sign reading "Type Road," which is probably the only monument or marker standing to commemorate the wood type industry in America.

Edwin Allen is thought to have moved to Glastonbury, Connecticut, where he engaged in the clock-making business. There are patents for veneering and clock calendars registered in his name during these years which would tend to support this supposition. At a later date, Allen moved to Newark, New Jersey, and carried on his clock business for a brief period of time. In Newark, George F. Nesbitt, who was well aware of Allen's genius with machinery, retained Allen to develop a machine for producing stamped envelopes. Nesbitt had just received the first government contract for the production of these envelopes, the existing machinery for which was both cumbersome and unreliable. Allen built the most successful machinery of the time for turning out stamped envelopes about 1860 or 1861, and after completing the basic machine for Nesbitt, he returned to Norwich as a machinist. In 1865 Allen formed the Allen Manufacturing Company with Mr. John Turner and General W. G. Ely as partners, to manufacture the new Allen Rotary Envelope machines which were to be used for the company's eventual manufacture of envelopes. In 1866 Allen took out new patents on envelope-making machinery, and in 1867–68 (patents both years) patented the Allen Rotary Printing Press. In 1869, the company ceased to do any printing, but concentrated on the manufacture of envelope-making machinery. Evidently because of poor management, the company came into bad times and in 1873 was finally sold to Lester & Wasley, a firm renowned in later years for its contribution to the envelope business. In the same year after Allen sold out his interests in the envelope business, he purchased the exclusive rights to manufacture John G. Preist's card and printing press. He was to patent several improvements on this press, but gave up the venture in a few years.

In 1876 Allen formed the Allen Spool and Printing Company, which was first located in Norwich. The new company was made a joint-stock operation in 1879 with a capital of $15,000, half of which Allen had put up.

In New England at this time there were a number of firms manufacturing thread, and Allen's company was established to furnish the thread people with wooden spools. Their manufacture was described in the *Norwich Bulletin* of January 21, 1881; "...the blanks from which spools are turned having been made by rounding a stick, boring it and cutting them off, are poured into a hopper like corn at the grist mill, whence they are fed automatically. The spools then made are poured into the hopper of the printing machine where they are fed automatically at the rate of 100,000 per day, both ends being printed in two colors, the letters being raised, or in other words, the surrounding surface being depressed. One fourteen-year-old boy can tend five such machines at a time." This machinery was another invention by Allen. In 1884, the plant was destroyed by fire, and it is not clear whether it was rebuilt in Norwich or not; but in 1888, the firm was reorganized with a capital of $30,000 and 40 employees, and moved to Mystic, Connecticut.

Edwin Allen was an exceptionally gifted man as far as machines were concerned, but in business he was not nearly so skillful. His financial success with the Allen Spool & Printing Company, and the fact that he died a wealthy man should probably be attributed to the sagacity of his partners. Allen seems to have been a man whose interest was working with machinery, so single-mindedly that he could be easily victimized in business matters. This is well demonstrated by Allen's failure after he made wood type for Nesbitt. It is believed that his selling his mill in 1852, when the wood type business was expanding, and when Page was yet to make his fortune in the same endeavor, might be traced to exploitation by Nesbitt, who was reputed to be honest but shrewd in financial dealings. More amazingly, Allen must have felt little or no rancor toward Nesbitt, as he was to enter into the envelope machinery contract with him less than 10 years after his wood type business failed.

Allen's patents over a 30-year period illustrate the versatility of his interests as well as of his abilities. In addition to the items already mentioned, he had patents for stone carving, veneer polishing, clock calendars, paper feeder improvements, a gunstock machine, a door lock, a printing press, an envelope gummer, a hearse, a printer's chase, a wood plane, and a circular saw. The rotary printing press patented by Allen in 1867–68, which was developed for printing envelopes, was written up in the *Inland Printer* 20 years after his first patent because of the originality of the concept behind its construction. With all his inventions, Allen made a considerable contribution to the printing arts—more so than he has been given credit for to this date. Edwin Allen died in Mystic, Connecticut, on January 4, 1891.

William and Samuel Day

Two brothers, William T. and Samuel D. Day, who had worked for Allen in Connecticut, were to embark in the wood type business in Fredricksburg, Ohio, in 1845. Using an old blind horse for power, a cut-off saw, a revolving power-burr, and a planer, they began in a small way the manufacture of wood type. They cut and prepared the local woods, apple and dogwood for the small types, maple and cherry for the larger ones. William, who was an expert engraver and finisher, was responsible for the wood cutting and preparations. Samuel's activities during the cutting of the wood might be described as filling a wagon with the finished type, hitching up the blind horse,

This building was erected by the Day brothers circa 1852 as a wood type manufactory. At this time they employed about twenty-five workmen, and they were the only manufacturers of wood type west of the Allegheny Mountains. In 1856 the building was converted into a day school for boys and was known as the Fredricksburg Academy.

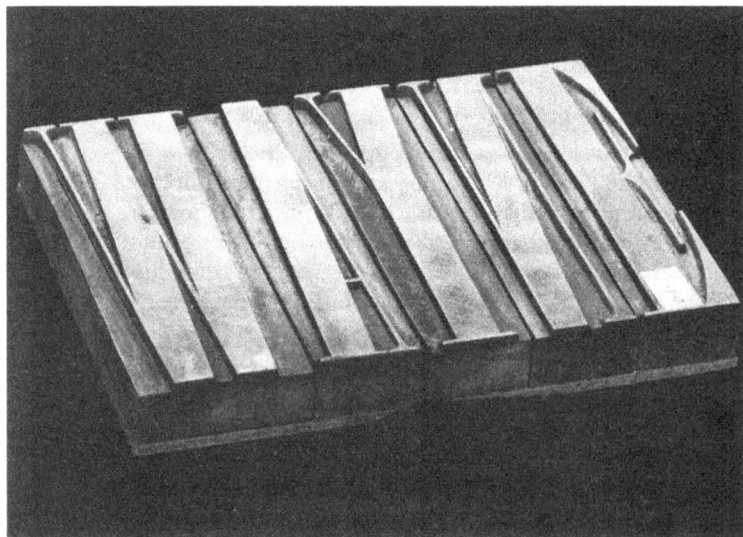

Specimens of wood type from the Day manufactory which were entered into the collections of the Wayne County Historical Society. (Courtesy of the Wayne County Historical Society, Wooster, Ohio.)

and setting out through the small towns in the surrounding regions to peddle the type. *A Census of Manufacturing* for 1850 indicates that the W.T. & S.D. Day & Company had a capital investment of $1000, planks valued at $100, one horse for power, and three male employees. The average monthly cost of labor was $60, and the annual product value was $2,500.

The types were priced considerably below what the Eastern manufacturers were asking, but even so, the Days did well enough so that in 1852 they were able to put up a new building in Fredricksburg where they employed 25 to 30 men. It is thought that the Days never engaged in the manufacture of any goods other than wood type, such as printers' furniture, etc. Along with the new facilities in Fredricksburg, W.T. & S.D. Day & Company opened outlets in Chicago with J. P. Rounds. Probably most of the wood type used in the Midwest during these years came from the Day manufactory.

Late in 1855 the Day Company's employees started a strike over higher wages, which was to become a bitter contest. A third Day, James, who had joined the company, was directly responsible for the working force. He laid down the final ultimatum that on a given day and hour, if the strikers had not returned to work, they would be laid off. The men did not return, and the shop was closed. The Day brothers, having sensed this possibility from the beginning, had already made arrangements with the authorities of the Ohio State Penitentiary at Columbus to open a wood type manufactory to be operated by convict labor within the prison walls. After obtaining a good shop within the prison they secured all the labor they needed at the State's price of 50 to 60 cents a day per man. Some of the workmen who had not struck went along as foremen. Of the strikers, Edwin Ferry, an expert trimmer and engraver, his brother Thomas Ferry, John McNulty, and M.S. Richards embarked in the wood type business at another location in Fredricksburg. The company at this time is thought to have been named "The Fredricksburg Type and Engraving Company." In a catalogue in the Newbury Library of Chicago, there is a D. Knox & Company of Fredricksburg listed for 1858. It is believed that David Knox represented the capital necessary to set up the manufactory, which was the firm made up of the strikers. It is possible that, lacking sufficient capital, the strikers could have taken in financial backing after they had set up the original organization. However, the new company was unable to compete with the Days and their convict labor, and finally the bursting of a mill-dam on Salt Creek caused a flood that washed away their factory, just when the company was facing bankruptcy. No further efforts were made to re-establish wood type manufacturing in Fredricksburg.

In Columbus, Ohio, W.T., J.R., & S.D. Day Company continued to market the wood type produced in the prison workshops through 1857, when a fire in the penitentiary destroyed the machinery. Wood type manufacture in the prison ceased at this point. In the January issue of *Rounds' Monthly Printer's Cabinet* for 1858, there was an announcement to the effect that W.T. & S.D. Day & Company were the successors to the J.D. Foster & Company, manufacturers of printing presses, of Cincinnati, Ohio. The announcement further stated that the manufacture of wood type would be continued.

There is some confusion as to where each Day brother was after the take-over of the Foster Company. The Columbus Directories show that William T. Day stayed in Columbus and advertised as a type and press maker until 1862, but there was no further reference to the Day brothers. From this, it would appear that the brothers never left Columbus even though the Foster firm was located in Cincinnati. Also, the directories indicate that the younger brother, James, was included in the company during the years when convict labor was used. Apparently he left the company after the prison fire because the name of the company reverted from W.T., J.R. & S.D. Day Company to W.T. & S.D. Day & Company when the Foster concern was purchased.

There is an interesting story connected with the Day enterprise which has probably never been told in its entirety before. In the mid-forties, the Merritt Players, a traveling troupe under the direction of Issac Merritt, came to Fredricksburg, and stayed because of a lack of finances. Merritt, accompanied by his wife and child, and desperate for work, was to take a position in the Day brothers' wood type manufactory. Being an inventive fellow, he made a number of improvements in the factory's machinery, which added materially to their wood type output. He also conceived of a new machine for making wood type which he began to perfect. Altogether, Merritt worked for the Days approximately 2 years, during which time he was made sales distributor but never a partner. Then about 1849, after accumulating enough wood type, Merritt left town with a horse and wagon full of wood type, all belonging to the Days. In the next town he sold everything: horse, wagon, and type; he is then believed to have moved to Baltimore, where he gained employment in a machine shop.

By this type, Merritt had patented his wood type machine, and George Zieber, a would-be capitalist from Boston, paid him $3,000 for the Massachusetts rights to the type-carving machinery. Zieber rented a space in a Boston machine shop and brought Merritt along to demonstrate the machine to prospective buyers. As the wood type machine was not exactly a flourishing item on the market, Merritt was soon distracted by new ideas. The machine shop, owned by Orson Phelps, specialized in the repair of sewing machines.

On examining a Lerow & Blodgett sewing machine, Merritt was certain that a better mechanism could be constructed. When Phelps told Merritt that if he could invent a better machine he would make more money in a year than he could with the carving machine in 50 years, Merritt agreed to form a new company with Zieber and Phelps to manufacture sewing machines. Zieber would put up $40, Merritt his inventiveness, and Phelps his machinist's skill. Merritt, in fact, was Issac Merritt Singer, the man who patented the Singer Sewing Machine. Singer never returned to Fredricksburg, but to his credit, some years later he did make good to the Day brothers the loss incurred when he absconded with their horse, wagon, and type.

The building built as a manufactory by the Day brothers was to stand for many years. After the wood type works had been moved to Columbus, the former manufactory was to house the Fredricksburg Academy until 1866. When a new owner purchased the building during this century, he found great quantities of wood type stored there. Although the type was discarded, a few specimens had been previously catalogued into the collections of the Wayne County Historical Society. They are listed under

"Samuel Day, wood type, 1848" in the catalogue.

Horatio and Jeremiah C. Bill

Two more Connecticut brothers were next engaged in the wood type business, Horatio N. and Jeremiah C. Bill. They, too, had been employed at South Windham, Connecticut, by Edwin Allen—under whose auspices they had learned the business. No doubt they also copied his machinery when setting up their own manufactory.

In or about 1850, the brothers established their own manufactory in Lebannon, Connecticut. The following year they moved to Willimantic, where they set up their business in the basement of Mill No. 3, then owned by the American Linen Company. The quarters would suggest that the company was not large. Some wood types, stamped on the side with a S.B.S., are believed to have been manufactured by the Bill brothers between 1850 and 1853. There is a catalogue for 1853 which identifies the company as Bill, Stark & Company. Although nothing is known about Stark, it is conceivable that he, along with another man whose initial was S, financed the company when it was originally founded, and that the third party withdrew in 1852 or 1853 when the company became Bill, Stark & Company. After Stark dropped from the company in late 1853 or early 1854, the business was known as H. & J. Bill until it failed late in 1854. The equipment was purchased by William Page in 1856.

Horatio Bill had a son, Arthur, who, with a Mr. Hall, founded a commercial printing company in Willimantic in 1847. Hall & Bill published a newspaper, the *Journal,* handled the community printing needs, and did a great deal of label printing for the mills. Horatio was to work for his son until his death in 1892.

Jeremiah was listed in the Willimantic City Directory as a teacher in Normal School, carpenter, florist, and finally, in 1898, as a cucumber grower. In 1902 he worked at the Hall & Bill Printing Company. It is believed that his mind began to wander, and in 1903 he was committed to Coventry, in Norwich, Connecticut, where he died in 1906.

Wood type manufactured by the Bill brothers was of good quality. They exhibited their wooden types at the New York World's Fair of 1853, where their specimens were destroyed by the fire which ravaged the Crystal Palace. The Bill, Stark & Company catalogue for the same year showed mostly the standard faces and contained only a few ornamented styles.

Their competition for the market in the New York City vicinity was Wells & Webb, George Nesbitt & Company until 1852, and John G. Cooley, who succeeded Nesbitt. There are few clues as to why the company lasted such a short time. One can only conclude that the Bill brothers lacked the business acumen or capital to reinforce their abilities as wood type makers. In fact, neither Horatio or Jeremiah was to enter business on his own account after the wood type company failed.

John Gaines Cooley

John Gaines Cooley was born in East Hartford, Connecticut, on January 30, 1819. He attended the local schools until he was sixteen, then went to work for Samuel C. Starr, a bookseller in Norwich, Connecticut. In 1837 he apprenticed to John Dunham, owner of the *Norwich Courier,* to learn the printing trade. At the completion of his apprenticeship, he published the *Total Abstinence,* the first temperance paper in Connecticut. It was a short-lived publication, and he followed it in the next year with the *Spectator.* A paper of the same name had been published in Norwich nearly 15 years earlier, but no relation between it and Cooley's publication is known.

In 1843, the *Spectator* was superseded by the *Reporter,* which came out weekly. This paper lasted longer than any of Cooley's previous publishing ventures, even though it was described as being published under "various conditions." He was a spirited reporter, and was frequently involved in controversial situations, not to mention one lawsuit for slander in 1847. It was said of him by his contemporaries that he was a writer of marked individuality who was strong in his convictions, that he was absolutely fearless in the matter of publishing a paper, and that nothing could dismay him when he considered himself right.

During these same years, Cooley operated a successful job shop in conjunction with his publishing, and although the date when he ceased to publish the *Reporter* is unknown, he was still bringing it out in 1847. Around 1852, he founded the *Examiner,* a religious paper with several local clergymen as editors. Also in 1852 he purchased the wood type manufactory of Edwin Allen in South Windham, Connecticut. Since, however, several printings exist with a Norwich date line attributed to Cooley in 1853, he is believed to have maintained his job shop in Norwich for at least one more year before moving the entire operation to South Windham. In 1858 John Cooley published the *Wood Letter Advertiser* in South Windham. No copies are known to exist, but it was listed in the library catalogue of the *New York Typothetae* of 1896 and was announced in the *Printers' Monthly Bulletin* for June of 1858. On the basis of the wording in the *Printers' Monthly,* it would appear that Cooley listed his firm simply as J. G. Cooley, South Windham, Connecticut.

In 1859 John Cooley went into partnership with Robert Lindsay, a typefounder, with whom he established the John G. Cooley & Company at No. 1 Spruce Street in the old *Tribune* building in New York City. A printer's warehouse was combined with the wood and metal type, and the business prospered from the beginning. Cooley continued to manufacture type in South Windham until around 1863, after which he moved his entire business to New York. The company then expanded from 1 Spruce Street to include 3,5,7, and 8 Spruce Street, and if Cooley's advertisements can be interpreted correctly, wood type played less and less of a role in his business as the printers' equipment and supplies became more prominent. Also, Cooley's instinct for publishing had not completely died with his new success in New York, for in 1863 he published the *Typographic Arts.* The publication, however, was short-lived.

In 1864, the partnership with Robert Lindsay was broken off for unknown reasons. Bullen wrote the following about the business conducted by Lindsay and Cooley during their partnership, "they made metal type and sold wood type from a location at the northeast corner of Gold and Fulton Streets. They were price-cutters and copied the successful designs of their competitors." In 1865 John Cooley took his son into the business with him, and John G. Cooley, Jr. ran the printer's materials while his father was responsible for the wood type.

Cooley's next partner was to be Samuel Theodore Dauchy, a merchant dealing in hardware. He became associated in 1866 with the company which was then known as Cooley & Dauchy. In addition to the printer's warehouse, the partners engaged in the relatively new business of advertising agents. Cooley's many contacts in the publishing profession proved useful to him in the placing of advertisements. Many years later, Bullen, who criticized the business procedures of Cooley during his years as an agent, charged, "Cooley has the unenviable distinction of originating the plan of paying for advertising space with type . . . at first wood type, and afterward with metal type. All the concerns which dealt with publishers by paying for space with types, etc., made money. It was a good plan for them, but a bad one for the printer. Printers are generally wiser today, and the business is not active though not dead. If it were worthwhile uncovering it, an interesting tale of the unethical business could be told."

Sometime in late 1868 or early 1869, there was a fire that destroyed the business offices. Cooley became sick and physicians advised him to go to the country for recuperation and leisure. The New York City Directory for 1870-71 (would be the year 1869) listed John G. Cooley as "nervine," and his son, John, Jr., as selling patent medicines. The wood type part of the business was sold to William H. Page of Norwich, Connecticut, and his interest in the printer's warehouse and advertising agency was bought out by S. T. Dauchy. Both transactions took place in 1869. By 1870 Cooley had moved to Franklin, Connecticut, where for $50,000 he acquired 250 acres of land and built a handsome house called "Middle Hills." In the next few years he led the leisurely life of a country gentleman, and his health improved considerably. In 1874 he was publicly to propose turning "Middle Hill" into a home for indigent and disabled printers. He expected them to work as much as they were able, and in return, he would feed and clothe them, and give them a decent burial. Since he could not take everyone who would apply, he would give preference to those who had attained editorial work after a regular apprenticeship. His proposal was received somewhat skeptically. Questioned more than criticized, it was never put into practice.

In 1875, Cooley went back to publishing in Norwich, where he brought out a newspaper called *Plain Folks.* After the first few issues he discontinued the publication, and in July of 1876, published *Cooley's Weekly.* Selling for 50 cents a year, it was so successful that it carried over into the twentieth century. In 1880 John Cooley, Jr. took over the publishing of *Cooley's Weekly* after a stroke partially paralyzed his father. In 1888, after selling the paper, Cooley retired to his Franklin home where he was to remain until his death. While an invalid, he read the entire Bible through 18 times and the New Testament 70 times. He wrote literally thousands of letters to friends during these years, but was never again active in business or publishing.

It is difficult to assess just what kind of man John G. Cooley was, although some traits are recorded and others are apparent. There is unanimity among those who knew him that he had an infectious sense of humor. Bullen said that he was a thorn in the side of his competitors, albeit a humorous one. From the content of several publications that he initiated and the papers on Biblical or temperance matters that he published in papers other than his own, one learns of his dedication in terms of moral issues. Although not a hypocrite, he appears to have been a shrewd business man who seldom lost money on any venture in which he had an interest. He seemed to have lacked the artistic taste or sense of perfection associated with Page, and the mechanical abilities of Allen, Wells, or Morgans. The remarkable number of publications put out by Cooley in his lifetime might possibly reflect his egotism, but there are no references to his vanity, or to his being a difficult man to work with other than as a competitor. His entry into advertising during the infancy of the field, when "advertising agent" was an ugly name to printers and typefounders, would indicate both progressiveness in light of the future growth of advertising and courage of conviction. John Gaines Cooley died in Sheltering Arms, a nursing home in Norwich, Connecticut, on April 7, 1909.

Cooley's "Middle Hill" home which was built in 1869 and now stands on the edge of Highway 32 between Willimantic and Norwich.

William Hamilton Page, 1829-1906.

Ebenezer R. Webb

In 1854, Ebenezer Webb took over Wells' interest in his business, which then continued under the firm name of E. R. Webb & Company. Beginning in 1859, the company practically monopolized the business of preparing engraver's wood during the golden age of wood engraving in America. This side of the business—the finishing of engraver's wood—was carried on in New York City; the manufacture of wood type and other printer's goods was done at the Paterson plant. In 1862, E. R. Webb bought out his partners, Guy Wells, William Havens, and William Titterton, after which the company became E. R. Webb. It continued as such until Webb's death in 1864.

Very little is known of Webb's life except that he was born in the western part of New York State about 1812. As a young man he worked as a printer. The first reference to his connection with the wood type business is that he was a foreman in the Allentown manufactory of Leavenworth. There is mention of the fact that George Bruce, the typefounder, bought out Leavenworth's interest and sold it to Webb on exceedingly generous terms. This made possible the partnership between Wells and Webb in 1839. In 1863, Webb contracted a bleeding of the lungs which eventually resulted in death on June 22, 1864. He was buried in Stamford, Connecticut.

William H. Page

William Hamilton Page was born in Tilton, New Hampshire, on March 14, 1829. He was raised on a small farm situated in the Connecticut River Valley. At the age of fourteen, he left home to begin an apprenticeship at the shop of a printer in Bradford, Vermont. Here he served two years learning the trade, and then moved on to Newbury, the next town up the river. In 1846 he moved back to New Hampshire as a resident of Haverhill. Then after a time at Concord, capital of the state, he moved to Boston. Beginning in 1850, he worked for two years as foreman for the *Spy* in Worcester, Massachusetts. From there he went to New York City, where, while employed at the *Tribune,* then owned and edited by Horace Greeley, he worked through the Pierce Presidential campaign of 1852. From New York he went to Norwich, Connecticut, to work for Edmund Clarence Stedman of the *Norwich Tribune,* and in February of 1855, he joined John Cooley in South Windham, Connecticut, where he was first introduced to wood type manufacturing.

His initial job was as a wood type finisher. As neither Cooley nor his foreman had "practical" knowledge of wood type making, Page had to depend entirely on his own judgment. He had a sound knowledge of printing, had tried wood engraving with moderate success previously, and had some experience with machinery and tools. It was readily apparent to Page that considerable improvement could be made in the manufacture of wood types.

In the fall of 1856 he purchased the equipment of the defunct H. & J. Bill & Company and, in partnership with a James Bassett, founded Page & Bassett. In October of 1857, the company moved its works to Greeneville, a suburb of Norwich. Sometime in late 1858 or early 1859, Bassett, for one reason or another, withdrew from the firm and Page took Samuel Mowry as a new partner. Little is known of Mowry other than that he had been the founder of the Mowry Axle Company which was located in Greeneville, and that the business dealings of Mowry and his sons were to be intertwined with those of Page for the next 50 years.

The new company was known as Page & Company of Greeneville, Connecticut. Mowry's capital made possible the new facilities required to expand the business, which was soon housed in a multi-storied factory built on the banks of the Shetucket River. Forty to fifty employees worked here, and seventeen wood type cutting machines were in operation. A catalogue published in 1859 illustrates an extensive new line of styles, and the great skill employed in cutting these faces. In this year Page entered into an arrangement with James Connor's Sons, a prominent New York City typefounding firm, which was to distribute his type and show the Page designs in the *Typographic Messenger* for the next 20 years. During the Civil War, Page perfected his machinery and consolidated his markets so that his firm rose to be the chief producer of wood type in the country. In 1869 the wood type business of Cooley & Dauchy was purchased by William Page and incorporated into his already flourishing William H. Page & Company. Shortly after this purchase, an article in the *Norwich Bulletin* noted that the employees of Page had gone on a piece work basis, under which system workmen made as much in 9 hours as they had under the old 10-hour day and fixed wage.

Also during the Civil War, Page had hired women because of the manpower shortage, and finding them so adept at many operations in the manufacture of wood type, he continued to hire women regularly until the business was sold in 1891. Up until 1872, Page had concentrated on wooden products—types, borders, tint blocks, and bleachers' stamps; in 1872 he started advertising printers' goods, including country presses, card cutters, mitering machines, and inks.

After Samuel Mowry retired from the firm in 1876, the company was reorganized as the William H. Page Wood Type Company, and moved one-half mile to Norwich, Connecticut. During this period, Page was active in exploring an overseas market, for which the company began to exhibit wood type in the international expositions. The Page company was awarded medals at the Paris Exposition of 1878, at the International Exposition of 1880 at Sidney, and at the Melbourne Exposition of 1881. There is one existing catalogue issued by a Sidney dealer for Page's wood types from these years.

In 1879, William Page first published his *Page's Wood Type Album,* a publication carrying news of the trade, advertisements, and examples of new styles of wood type and borders. It was patterned after the newsletters which had been published for many years by the typefounders—*The Typographic Messenger* of James Connor, *The Typographic Advertiser* of L. Johnson, and *Printer's Monthly Bulletin* published by the Boston Type Foundry. Cooley had attempted to establish two such wood type publications earlier, the *Wood Letter Advertiser,* and The *Typographic Arts,* but neither lasted more than one or two issues.

In the 1880's George Case Setchell was brought into Page's company. Their combined work led to the successful production of the die-cut types in 1887. However, the Page Company was feeling the effects of competition with the Hamilton Manufacturing Company of Two Rivers, Wisconsin. In 1888, a Norwich Board of Trade Directory showed the Page Company as having a capital stock of $10,000, 40 employees, an annual gross of $45,000, and

labor costs of $18,000 per annum. This was down somewhat from 1869, and when the company was finally sold to Hamilton in 1891, there were only 30 employees.

In 1889, George Setchell had sold his share in the business as well as his patent rights to S. T. Dauchy of Dauchy & Company. In the following year, Dauchy was president of the William H. Page Wood Type Company and William Page was listed as Treasurer. After the sale of the company to Hamilton, all equipment and stocks were moved to Two Rivers, and as part of the selling arrangements, William Page was to become a stockholder in the Hamilton company. If Page did actually move west to Two Rivers, he did not stay long as he was soon involved in new business ventures back on the East Coast.

William Page had patented a small steam heater around 1879, and it is believed that in this same year he founded the Page Steam Heating Company in Norwich. James D. and William C. Mowry and I. M. Johnson were his partners. He registered a patent for a steam radiator in 1882, at which date or soon thereafter he founded or helped to establish the Combination Company, a steam heating equipment supply firm. During these years, Page maintained an active role in the two steam heating concerns as well as in his wood type business. In or about 1894, Page organized the Victor Steam Heating Company in Norwich, but withdrew shortly afterwards to establish the W. H. Page Boiler Company. In Plainfield, he founded yet another boiler-making industry. He purchased the Exter Radiator Company of New York City in 1900, and finally founded the New England Boiler Company in Mystic, Connecticut, in 1905 which he moved to New London in 1906. At the time of his death 3 months later, he was scouting a new location for his boiler company in Norwich, Connecticut. William Page was a self-educated man with a broad range of interests that he cultivated throughout his life. One of his interests was painting. By today's standards, he was a better-than-average "Sunday painter," and his landscapes are said to have graced many Connecticut homes. He was active in community affairs, especially so during his residency in Norwich. His ornamental gardens were one of the sights of Norwich. As a businessman, he appears to have had a rare combination of shrewdness and imagination backed by a great deal of physical energy. His continued aim for perfection in all matters that captured his interest should be admired. This perfection is well demonstrated in the surviving specimen books issued by his company, and his originality is confirmed by the number of inventions registered in his name. His company, catalogues, designs, and business procedures can be considered representative of the era. A remarkable individual, Page was capable, charming, and generous to a degree not always found in the commercial world of that period. William Hamilton Page died while a resident of Mystic, Connecticut, on May 6, 1906.

Heber Wells

After the death of Ebenezer Webb in 1864, the complete inventory of his wood type business was bought from his estate by Heber Wells, the youngest son of Darius, along with Alexander Vanderburgh and Henry Low for $9,250. The new firm went under the name of Vanderburgh, Wells & Company. Low died in 1865, but his widow, Mary Low, retained his interest in the company. In 1867, a fire burned the Paterson factory to the ground. A new three story brick building 106 feet by 30 feet was constructed on the site by the owner, Samuel Pope, who leased the property to Vanderburgh, Wells & Company. After the fire, all the wood type-making machinery was moved to New York, where it occupied three full floors at the company's location on Dutch and Fulton Street; the wood type operation in New York at this time required 14 workmen. In 1887 Mary Low withdrew from the partnership, and the business continued under Vanderburgh and Wells until 1890, when Alexander Vanderburgh also withdrew. Heber Wells continued the business under his own name after moving to 8 Spruce Street. In 1898 the entire works were sold to the Hamilton Manufacturing Company of Two Rivers, Wisconsin.

William T. Morgans

Perhaps the least known of all men connected with the manufacture of wood type is William T. Morgans. Born in Bethel, New York, on July 2, 1843, Morgans was the son of Eleazer Morgans, supervisor of Callicoon, Sullivan County, and a merchant of Youngsville. William was an exceedingly bright pupil, who in addition to being one of the best scholars in the district school, learned to speak, read, and write fluent German and French under the direction of Professor Oudet, a tutor retained by Eleazer Morgans to instruct his children. Morgans exhibited inventiveness and dexterity with machinery at an early age. At 15 years old, he was conducting a watch repair business in Youngsville. He also designed and built a wooden printing press which was used for a number of years to print the Jeffersonville *Record*.

In 1862, William T. Morgans enlisted as a private in the 143rd Regiment, which was recruited from Sullivan County. Though slight of build, he became a valiant soldier who was promoted to Lieutenant by the end of the war. After the war, he returned to Youngsville, where, in quick succession, he married and founded a newspaper. The name of the publication is unknown, but it is remembered for its articles regarding the conduct of local men during the Civil War.

Shortly after this, he moved to Liberty, New York, where he founded the Liberty *Register*. During these years, William became a skillful printer. His naturally inventive mind soon had him involved with improving printing machinery. One of his first patented inventions was the Hercules Jobbing Press, which was manufactured and sold extensively. He also invented and patented a type-setting device, in 1870, which was never marketed. Sometime in the next few years, William perfected machinery for cutting wood type. There are no records of this machine's having been patented; however, several accounts describe Morgans' equipment as being of his own invention.

After the *Register,* he enlisted the financial support of George Young, a wealthy industrialist from Ellenville, and founded the Young & Morgans Manufacturing Company in Napanoch, Ulster County. This was in 1876, and the company prospered until it was destroyed by fire in 1880. At the suggestion of Senator Madden, the businessmen in Middletown, New York, asked that the new plant be built in their town, and work on it began in July of 1880. As George Young had extensive holdings in Ellenville, and had no desire to involve himself in the Middletown plant, he sold his interest in the company to H. K. Wilcox of Middletown, who had for the previous 11 years served in the United States Internal Revenue Col-

Heber Wells (1835-19—?).

William T. Morgans (1843-1882) immediately following the Civil War.

lector's Office for the Middletown district. The firm became the Morgans & Wilcox Manufacturing Company, which with an entirely new manufacturing complex, produced wood type, type cases, cabinets, paper-cutters, and other printers' supplies.

The July 28, 1880, edition of the *Middletown Daily Press* described the proposed Morgans & Wilcox Manufacturing Company: "The plan of the buildings shows one hundred feet on Wisner Avenue with two L's 30 x 70 feet extending back parallel with North Street and at right angles to the main part on Wisner Avenue, with space of fifty feet between the two. The main part will be of brick two stories and fireproof, and the L's of wood and one story. The machinery will be in these parts, which being open on both sides and low will be well lighted and adapted to running machinery and handling heavy articles. They chose a location near the railroad with the purpose of putting in a switch for convenience in handling lumber, etc., of which they will use great quantities." It also mentioned that the new company would employ from 70 to 80 workmen.

At this time, William T. Morgans, an ambitious young man of 36, devoted himself to his new enterprise with great vigor. His career was cut short by pneumonia on April 14, 1882. He had been stricken some 3 days previously, and had appeared to be recovering when a sudden relapse ended in his death. His interest in the company remained in his widow's hands. The Directory of the New York, Ontario, Western Railway for 1888 showed William G. Slauson as President, Robert Cochran, Secretary and Treasurer, and Floyd W. Morgans, son of William T., as Clerk. The company was highly successful, and Bullen was to rank it third-largest of its kind in America during the late eighties. The wood type part of the business was sold to the Hamilton Manufacturing Company about 1899. The title page of the Hamilton catalogue for 1899–1900 listed Hamilton as the successor to the Morgans & Wilcox Manufacturing Company, and informed customers that the Middletown offices were being kept open as a convenience for Eastern markets.

Only the printers' supply business was purchased by Hamilton, as Floyd W. Morgans bought out the Slauson interests in the 1920's. Floyd Morgans' son, Warner, conducted a manufacturing business under the family name through World War II.

Little was known of William T. Morgans during his lifetime. There are no references to either him or his work by Bullen or De Vinne, who were the most avid chroniclers of printing data in that period. It is evident that Morgans was an exceptional man: sensitive, tremendously energetic, and a mechanical genius. Many speculations may be made about what else he may have contributed to the printing trades had his life not been cut short.

Charles Tubbs

Charles Tubbs of South Windham, Connecticut, with two partners, John W. Martin and George L. Keyes, leased the old Allen mill from Guilford Smith in 1878 to manufacture wood type. The three men had all worked for William Page previous to this venture. In fact, Charles Tubbs had begun working with Page in 1860. The new firm was called the American Wood Type Company.

In 1883 the two partners sold out their interests to Tubbs, who continued the company under its old name until after the turn of the century. During the 1880's the company employed 17 hands and had patterns for 200 styles of type, most of which were believed to have been borrowed from William Page. Tubbs' factory was operated by water power from the Pigeon Swamp fulling ponds, and it was said that when the water was low, Tubbs waited for rain with a great deal more patience than his customers. His types were of good quality, however.

A woman still living in South Windham said that she could remember as a little girl seeing Tubbs go to work each morning. One of the reasons she could remember him so well was that he walked in a doubled-over position as a result of an injury to his back suffered in an elevator accident when he was a young man. Around 1902, the name of the firm was changed to Tubbs & Company. After Charles Tubbs' death in 1903, the business was moved to Ludington, Michigan, where the name became the Tubbs Manufacturing Company. In 1905 a large modern plant was completed in Ludington that manufactured a complete line of wooden goods for the printing trades. According to an announcement in the June issue of *Inland Printer* in 1907, the Tubbs Manufacturing Company, which was becoming a strong competitor of Hamilton, was opening salesrooms and a warehouse in New York City, as well as offices in London, England, and other foreign cities. The Hamilton Manufacturing Company purchased Tubbs Manufacturing Company in or about 1918.

James Edward Hamilton

James Edward Hamilton was born on May 19, 1852 in Two Rivers, Wisconsin, a small lumbering town on the shore of Lake Michigan. His maternal grandfather was a descendant in the sixth generation of Simon Huntington, born in Norwich, England, who sailed to America with that party of emigrants that established Norwich, Connecticut; but he died from small-pox before landfall. His son, Simon, born in England in 1629, was only four years of age when he came to America. He lived to be one of the pillars of new Norwich, a leader in the church and in the State of Connecticut.

Henry Carter Hamilton, father of J. E. Hamilton, was of Scotch-Irish extraction. Having come to Two Rivers to work as a druggist in Hezekiah Huntington ("Deacon") Smith's store, Henry soon met his employer's daughter, Diantha, who at eighteen had just returned to Two Rivers from finishing school. Their courtship culminated in Henry Hamilton's marriage into the Smith family, after which he became involved in a number of business ventures. These proved to be unsuccessful in spite of the assistance of the Deacon, whose large holdings gave him considerable influence in the community. Against the Deacon's wishes, his son-in-law entered into politics. When Henry Hamilton was elected to the state legislature in 1857, Deacon Smith cut off his ties with the family businesses. The Hamilton family then moved to Waucousta, now known as Greenbush, where Hamilton entered into partnership with another man in the grist mill business. After the Civil War broke out, Hamilton enlisted as a First Lieutenant and Quartermaster in the 21st Wisconsin Volunteer Infantry. He died on April 4, 1864, at Nashville, Tennessee.

Hamilton's family lived for a time in Two Rivers, but eventually decided to move to Lockport, New York, where Henry Hamilton's two brothers lived. Mrs. Hamilton saw to it that James Edward was able to complete two years of education at Lockport Union High School. These were the last years of his formal education. As he became, in turn, newsboy, water carrier in a rock quarry, and a cash boy in a local dry goods store, he was a breadwinner at fourteen. In 1868, the Hamilton family moved back to Two Rivers. Hamilton worked as tender of a clothespin lathe, a job secured for him by Deacon Smith. During the two years at this job, he spent a great deal of time as a volunteer helper in the boiler room where he acquired considerable knowledge of engineering.

In 1872, one of the Lockport uncles, Horace Hamilton, opened a brick factory in Two Rivers, and gave his nephew the opportunity of testing his new-found knowledge of steam-powered machinery as operator of the stationary steam engine. The business languished for 2 years and folded, but Edward Hamilton retained use of the brickyard engine room and steam engine to start his own business. He manufactured bric-a-brac and other odds and ends of furniture that might be constructed or ornamented with the scroll-saw work in vogue at that time. The small market for these products was soon saturated. However, the knowledge that Hamilton gained from this venture helped make him successful with wood type at a later date. In 1873, Hamilton began working for various contractors as a pile-driver engineer on the Sturgeon Bay Canal. After several years he was finally to return to wood working as a piece worker in a chair factory. At this time he succumbed to the "tales" sifting back from the gold

J. E. Hamilton (1852-1940).

The house where J. E. Hamilton lived at the time he made his first wood types.

"Grand Ball," the first veneer wood type made by Hamilton.

strikes in the Black Hills, and in 1887 made the journey there with 12 or 13 other Two Rivers residents. The experience, financially unsuccessful as well as hazardous, fostered his determination to settle down and make good at home.

He returned to his old job in the chair factory until one day, Mr. Lyman Nash, publisher of the *Two Rivers Chronicle,* asked him to help with a printing emergency. Without having the required type, Nash had accepted a job for some large dance posters. Since it was too late to order new type, he turned to Hamilton, whom he thought might be able to improvise some wood type for the job.

Hamilton sketched out on paper a crude outline of the words, "Grand Ball at Turner Hall" in more or less Gothic capitals. With the approval of Nash, he transferred the design to a thin sheet of hardwood and, with a foot-power scroll saw, cut out the outlines which he then mounted on a block of softer wood. The surface was sandpapered and polished and the underside planed approximately type high. The finished work was a single piece, with the letters reversed (incised into the surface) so as to print white letters on a black ground. The job printed well and marked J. E. Hamilton's beginning in the wood type business.

He was to experiment further with the scroll saw and the veneer letters. Finally he sent a number of them to George and Henry Hamilton, his brothers, who were proprietors of the *Becker County Record* in Detroit, Minnesota. Finding that the type printed well, the brothers sent back some small wrappers which could be affixed to samples of type to be mailed out as "feelers" to the market. The wrappers read, "This is a sample of Holly Wood Type. If you are interested, write J. E. Hamilton, Two Rivers Wisconsin for further particulars." The first order resulting from the advertising was a $2.50 order from the *Green Bay Gazette.* Hamilton gave up his job in the chair factory to devote full time to the wood type enterprise.

Then twenty-eight, he took a second bold step in marrying Etta Shove, the village school teacher. Orders began to come in, and Mrs. Hamilton became bookkeeper and cashier as well as wife and mother. Their first child, Grace, was born a year after the marriage. It was not long before Hamilton realized he needed additional capital. In 1881, he sold one-half interest in his business to Max Katz for $1,600. A small barnlike wood type factory was built with the new capital, and twenty workmen were employed by the new company—now called Hamilton & Katz.

The business prospered. Hamilton attributed his success to the construction of new machinery to make wood type. For the first 2 years, only wood type was manufactured, but then Hamilton realized that other wood products that he could manufacture easily were needed by print shops. Therefore, he was soon marketing furniture and reglet, which was followed by a display chart with movable letters for advertising purposes. During this period he became familiar with printing shops. Finding most of them disorderly and dirty work areas, he became convinced that he could economically develop a line of wooden goods to improve the lot of the printer. In 1887, Katz sold his interests in the company to a William Baker of Springfield, Illinois. As Baker viewed his purchase mostly as an investment from which he could draw profits, he was not interested in putting up capital to expand the firm.

However, the Hamilton Company grew at a tremendous rate because of Hamilton's improvements in printers'

A photograph taken circa 1882, shortly after this manufactory was built by Hamilton & Katz. (Courtesy of the Hamilton Mfg. Co. Archives.)

An engraving of the new plant built by the Hamilton Mfg. Co. in 1891 at Two Rivers, Wisconsin. This plant represented one of the most modern factories in the country at that time.

furniture, as well as the company's reasonable prices. Since most of the Hamilton products were wood, the company employed some of the most skillful cabinet makers in the country during the last 12 years of the century. The Polhemus cabinets that Hamilton introduced in 1888 brought about a beneficial reform in composing room equipment throughout the country. The Polhemus cabinets replaced the old Eagle cabinets that had been a favorite with printers. The Eagle cabinet, a product of the Wells family, had been manufactured at the Paterson plant. In a few years the cabinet part of Hamilton's business was expanded. Catalogues from that time illustrate roll-top desks in several models, office wall cabinets, a great variety of type cabinets, as well as composing tables and racks.

In 1889, Hamilton was able to raise enough capital to buy out Baker's interest in the company, which was incorporated as the Hamilton Mfg. Co. on January 1, 1889. The new firm had an authorized capital of $50,000 and paid-in capital of $30,000. The original incorporators were James E. Hamilton—131 shares, Walter C. Luse—17 shares, J. P. Hamilton—18½ shares, W. C. Clark—19½ shares, William Richards—86½ shares, and L. J. Nash—27½ shares. J. E. Hamilton was elected president of the company, an office he held until 1920.

In 1891 a new factory was built at Two Rivers. The plant was described in the *Inland Printer* during 1891 as, ". . . a new factory building 40 x 100 feet, to be built and used for type purposes. This will be connected to a brick fireproof office building 30 x 38 feet, a new warehouse and finishing department 40 x 100 feet and three stories high. The machines of the entire plant will be driven by an improved Corliss engine of 250 horsepower, located directly between the two factory buildings. The plant will be lighted by electricity under the Edison incandescent system, generated by its own dynamos. It will be protected against fire by a complete system of sprinklers and steam fire pumps connected by hydrants with all parts of the works, and heated by the Sturtevant hot air blast system. The works are situated on lots having several hundred feet of river frontage which are docked and capable of floating the largest vessels to the factory door. Taken as a whole, this plant will constitute the most complete one in the country for the manufacture of printer's wooden goods." The company employed about 150 people at the time the new plant was completed.

J. E. Hamilton was an astute, aggressive businessman and had in common with Allen, Wells, Morgans, and Page an inherent knack for working with machinery. He attributed most of his success to developing machines that would do the job effectively and economically. In time he became a civic leader in his home town, Two Rivers, Wisconsin, and during his lifetime bestowed many gifts on individuals and the community. James Edward Hamilton died in Two Rivers, on May 7, 1940.

After blemished areas such as the dark wood at top center are removed, letters will be incised in this slab of polished hard maple.

Preparation of the Wood

The preparation of wood for wood type was generally the same as that used for most wood engraving done in the nineteenth century. Cherry, apple, dogwood, pine, boxwood, mahogany, holly, and maple were preferred woods. The use of cherry and apple was limited, as the size of the trees did not allow large enough blocks of wood to be taken from them. Pine was readily obtainable in any size or quantity, but its use was most often restricted to short runs. The wood, soft and easily shaped, wore down rapidly and was highly susceptible to damage.

Mahogany and Turkish boxwood, which had been used for type during the first 10 or 15 years of type manufacture, were costly and less available because they had to be imported. Occasionally, when a customer wanted a particularly durable font of wood type, he would specify either boxwood or mahogany. Hard maple, a close-grained wood which was abundant throughout the Northeast and many of the central states, was the most extensively used for making wood type. The maple timber was often cut in the winter months so that the wood would freeze and stay frozen for some time, since when the sap had not run, the wood remained clear.

To prepare the wood for end-cut and die-stamped types, slabs slightly more than type high were cut cross-grain from the end of the log. The slabs were then cut in half and stacked so that air could circulate freely. Several companies used different means for curing the wood. The Hamilton Manufacturing Company cut its wood in the winter to be cured (for 2 years) of its own accord. Page would steam the wood before stacking it to be cured, and again, for a period of 2 years. Page also introduced kilns, or "steam-dry houses," as they were called in his 1878 catalogue, to speed up the drying; the time for curing wood was therefore reduced to one year. A mechanical device brought the cured slabs down to type high and gave them a first finish. A mixture of linseed oil and pumice applied by hand gave them a high finish, and coats of lacquer or varnish, alternated with light sandings, furnished the final finish. Shellac was often used as a final finish on types in the earlier years of wood type manufacture. Irregularities in slabs, such as knots and dark wood forming the center, were removed by a saw in order that as large a piece of unblemished wood as possible would be directed to the machine operator for cutting type. The finished wood type was soaked in oil for a period of time before wrapping and shipping.

Veneer faces, cut from thin sheets of holly wood, were frequently advertised as Holly Wood Type. The body of the type was made from pine and required little or no finishing. Wood used in Celluloid type was usually a soft wood such as pine, which required no special preparation other than facing with celluloid.

Manufacturers recommended cleaning type with benzine and soft rags, which would improve the type by hardening and smoothing it. Type was also commonly cleaned with lye and water. Manufacturers claimed that this procedure would not deteriorate wood letters if they were not allowed to soak.

End-Cut Types

Wood type was first mass produced by the end-cut method, the only process to survive into the twentieth century. The type is cut on the end-grain of the wood after the manner of wood engravers. Leavenworth is an exception, as it is known that he regularly engraved on the side grain of wood. First the design is cut from a pattern by a pantograph process and the excess wood removed with a powered router.

For a time, Wells carved wood types by hand, and sold

them to other printers. Horace Carr, in 1924, described a font of hand-carved type discovered after a fire in the *Leader* printing plant in Cleveland. The type was an ornate Roman Tuscan stamped with a steel punch on the bottom with the legend "WELLS, NY." Of particular interest was the fact that the shoulders of the type had been removed by a horizontal saw cut, and that the sides of the letter had been split down to meet the cut so that superfluous wood was effectively eliminated. The method used indicated that the type predated the invention of the router.

De Vinne describes the early work of Wells in his *Plain Printing Types:* "The work of preparing blocks was done entirely by hand; the tools most used were the ordinary saw and slide-plane. Model letters were drawn for all the characters on cardboard, which was then neatly cut to serve for patterns; and with this method, a new pattern was required for each size of type. When the outline of the patterns had been traced by pencil on the surface of the block, a graver was used to cut a wide furrow near the penciled line. This done, the counters and shoulders were cut away by chisels and gouges. Finishing was done with gravers and fine files." At about this same time, 1827, another New York printer by the name of John Lomax is reported to have cut types on side-grain wood for use in his own printing shop. He evidently enjoyed some repute as a designer of fine wood letters. However, since Lomax made no attempt to establish himself in the field, it remained for Darius Wells to pursue a practical means for manufacturing wood type.

David Bruce, Jr. and Wells worked together on constructing the necessary equipment for a brief period, during which Wells perfected the first router. As Bruce is known to have joined the Boston Type and Stereotype Foundry in 1828, both Bruce's partnership with Wells and the invention of the router must have taken place immediately preceding Bruce's 2-year stint in Boston. In later years, Royle (of John Royle & Sons) described Wells' first router: "supported from the ceiling by wooden braces and iron straps, of slow speed and limited capacity; but it saved much hand labor, and served a useful purpose." De Vinne describes the router, "a flat-faced and half-round steel bit, made to rotate at high speed. The bit is suspended vertically over the wood to be cut, by attachments made for raising it or depressing it at will. The block of wood to be made into type is firmly fastened under the router, and the operator moves the cutter spindle around the pattern until every part of the counter and shoulder are removed." Since Wells' first router was stationary, and the block moved around the bit, the equipment described by De Vinne represents an improved machine. Wells' invention, not having been patented, was quickly adapted to other branches of the printing trade. It was particularly useful in stereotyping, where it provided a speedy means for clearing shoulders and negative spaces within the characteristically shallow plates. It was also excellent for routing out unwanted areas in wood engravings. Today, the routing machine is a basic tool for many trades other than printing: wood-working or milling, machine tooling, and others.

In 1834 the pantographic principle was adapted to the router by George Leavenworth of New York State, and independently, by Edwin Allen in 1836. Neither Allen nor Leavenworth attempted to patent their use of the pantograph for working wood type. De Vinne provides

An impression made from the letters hand engraved on wood by Darius Wells sometime before 1828.

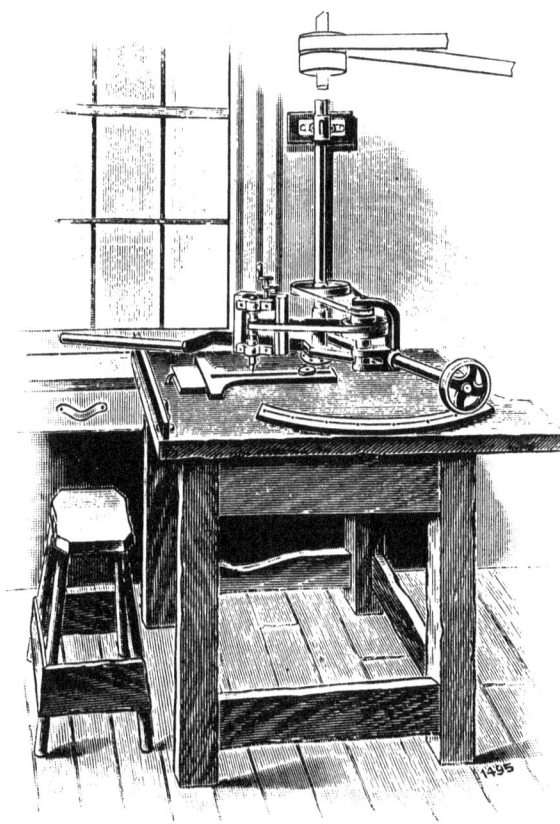

The routing machine used by E. R. Webb & Company circa 1857. It represents a machine better than the original router invented by Darius Wells in that the router bit was no longer stationary but could be moved around the letter or piece being routed.

The rough wood slabs are stacked carefully so that the air may circulate freely around all surfaces and in this manner the wood is cured preparatory to surfacing and cutting it into type.

Wood type is surfaced by hand with oil and pumice. The process was usually repeated several times until the wood became beautifully polished and took on a slight oil patina.

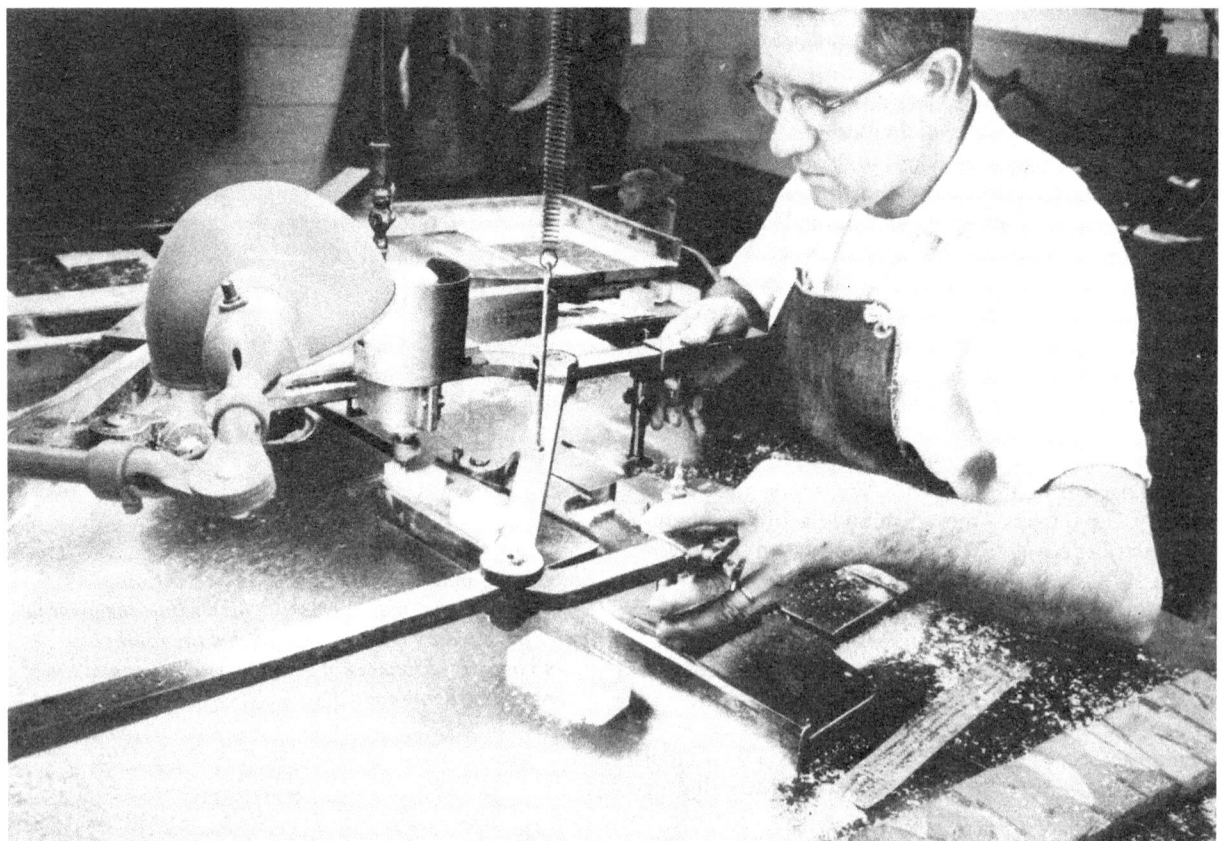

The operator incises the letter on the polished wood through the pantograph and routing machinery. While the tracing needle follows the outlines of the pattern, the router is cutting the design according to a predetermined size.

Wooden slabs are run through a gauge to ensure a perfect type-high block preparatory to engraving.

After the type came from the pantograph, skilled engravers hand-finished it, corrected any irregularities in cutting and put in the acute angles such as counters of the capital A, N, M, W, etc.

the best description of the combination machinery: "The pantograph is a strongly jointed and adjustable open framework of wrought iron and steel, rhomboidal as to shape. When put to work, it is suspended about eight inches over a flat metal table. It has five short projections extending toward this table; some of them are the extreme angles of the framework. Two of these four projections at opposite extremities reach the table; and serve as rests to steady the action of the machine; one of the four projections is a guiding rod, or feeler, which follows the outline of the pattern letter beneath it (which is practically an enlarged type in high relief), and accurately communicates every deviation of motion in a reduced proportion to the router. The fifth projection is near the center of the framework and carries the router, which is suspended over the block to be cut and can be raised or lowered at will. The router, driven by steam, rotates at unusual speed; fourteen thousand revolutions a minute is a common rate. Each movement of the operator's hand in guiding the index around the pattern letter is followed by a corresponding exactness of movement in the router that cuts the block. The type is often made in as short a time as one could trace the outlines of the pattern by pencil, and it is cut more accurately than a type made by hand. When it leaves the pantograph it is nearly finished; an exacter angling of the corners by the graver is nearly all the additional work required."

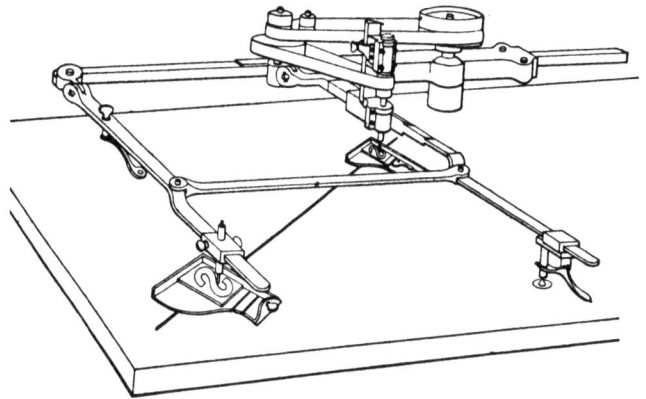

At later dates, William Page, William Morgans, and J. E. Hamilton all modified this machinery to suit their own purposes. How much variety there was between the machinery of the respective manufacturers is not known, but each man built his own equipment. In 1872, it was reported that Page's cutters cost approximately $1,000 each to build. One improvement in his machines was an increase from 12,000 revolutions to 18,000 revolutions per minute, which allowed twice as much work to be accomplished. On these improved pantograph machines, the spindles were so accurately fitted that they would run a half day on one drop of oil without becoming hot. The spindles ran in cast-iron bearings, as nothing else would stand the test, and only the best sperm oil could be used. The principles of Page's machinery had been borrowed from Edwin Allen—both because Page had purchased the equipment of the Bill brothers (who after having worked for Allen had copied his designs for their own cutters), and because Page had bought equipment from J. G. Cooley (who when he succeeded to Allen's business, had acquired Allen's machinery).

Allen had made several improvements on his original machine within a year or two of its invention. In 1838 the Nesbitt catalogue advertised: "The superiority of the types in the accompanying specimen, over all others heretofore manufactured, exists in their having been got up by machinery; the blocks are in the first place dressed by machinery, which gives them a uniformity in height never before possessed by wood types; they are then cut by machinery in such a manner as to make every type a correct facsimile of the other as much as though they were metal types and cast in a matrix. They are cut deeper than any wood or metal types now or heretofore in use, and the hairlines instead of being cut straight down are given a gentle increase in thickness so as to add strength to that part of the letter; an improvement never before applied to the manufacture of wood type." It is thought that this increase in hairlines was achieved through the introduction of a tapered bit.

The cardboard patterns used by Wells were soon replaced by sheet-brass ones. Then came cast brass patterns with elevated edges which when pressed into the wood both marked and engraved the outlines of each letter. Both Leavenworth and Allen used wood patterns, but those used by Leavenworth were grooved. Allen used the raised version, which in time was adopted by all wood type manufacturers. The raised pattern was so similar to the manufactured article that it was possible to buy a font of a competitor's type and, with a small amount of hand finishing, to use it as a pantograph pattern.

A description of Page's procedures affords a good insight into the methods used by most manufacturers in the preparation of patterns. The designs for letters were drawn on white wood (probably basswood) boards approximately ½ inch thick, and most plain letters were on boards 24 inches high. Ornamental letters were made on 12-inch boards. From these, a half-length pattern was cut by machine; that is, a 12-inch from the 24-inch boards and a 6-inch from the 12-inch. For extended designs, a 3-inch pattern was cut from the 6-inch size. From these four sizes of patterns, any size letter, from 2-line pica to 120-line pica, could be made.

During a recent visit to the wood type department of the Hamilton Manufacturing Company, I saw patterns made from precise drawings on paper which were traced on fine-grained plywood. The plywood patterns were cut out with a conventional jig-saw and glued to a block. The drawings on paper were filed as master patterns. Workmen informed me that occasionally the wooden patterns had to be replaced because of wear on the sides of the letter from the rubbing of the tracing needle. Their patterns were quite large in relationship to the size letters being cut on the pantograph, because any imperfections in the pattern were reduced proportionately when a smaller size of type was cut.

All end-cut types require a hand finishing: burrs are trimmed off and the acute angles such as counters of capital A, M, or N are graved out with a hand tool.

A curious practice of the end-cut type manufacturers may be found in their use of patterns in such a manner that several styles could be produced from a single pattern. This was accomplished by engraving an elaborate pattern and then either eliminating elements from one cutting to

the next, or routing out—for example, an Outlined could be made into an Open through routing the interior of the letterform. This practice seems to have come into being about mid-century, but was used most often in the 1880's when competition among the wood type producers was at its zenith.

Patent No. 265,623. Patent drawing by V. M. Moreau for a machine for cutting wood type. Patented October 10, 1882.

Die-Cut Types

In 1852 a Mr. J. McCreary of Chesterville, Ohio, filed for a patent on an improvement in the making of wood type. His remarks to introduce his application illustrate that the idea, if not the machinery, for die-cut type was already existent at this early date. His description states, "I make a die by using a suitable piece of steel or other metal of sufficient strength and solidity. I face one side and then engrave or stamp upon this face the desired letter, figure, or device to the proper depth. I then prepare a piece of wood by cutting it at right angles with the grain and facing it upon one of the ends and making it in all other respects of the appropriate size and shape. I then place the die with its face upon the treated end of the piece of wood and apply power sufficient to make the required impression. The die is removed, and any little elevation upon the sides of the piece of wood that may have been produced by the pressure is removed by the use of any convenient cutting instrument. I then saturate the end of the wood with linseed oil, or some similar oil which prevents the condensed wood from swelling when any cleansing fluid may be applied for the removal of ink from its face. For the purpose of facilitating the operation of making the impressions by means of dies, as above described, I use a screw press...."

McCreary's invention hinged on a mechanical device that fed a blank of wood into the machine in such a manner that with each pull of a lever, a new section of wood moved under the die.

The reverse action of the lever stamped the wood. McCreary claimed that the press could be worked at 20 to 30 strokes of the lever per minute. In this manner the wood blank was produced with a number of impressions,

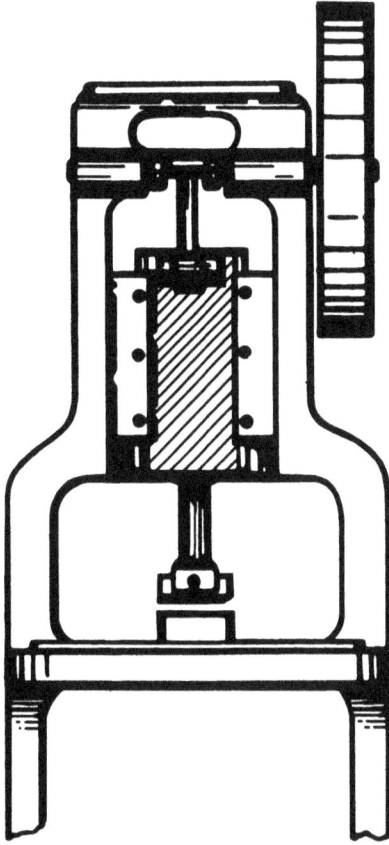

A drawing taken from patent papers of William H. Page which illustrates the press used to make die-cut types.

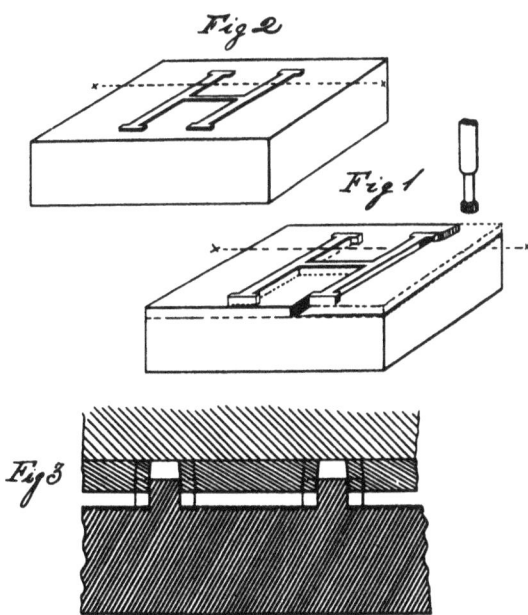

Patent No. 387,527. Submitted by Mortimer Merrit. Patent filed on August 7, 1888.

which were then separated by a fine buzz saw in another operation. He further suggested that it was possible to make a single die with six to eight letters when type from 4 to 6 lines was being made. If more pressure was needed, steam power could be used which would also increase the rate of production. At the end of the patent application, McCreary explains, "I do not claim the use of a press and dies for the purpose of manufacturing wood type." This would seem to reflect that there was a general use of dies in manufacturing at that time, such as for forming leather, papier-mâché, or wood decorations found on furniture of the period.

McCreary's patent application nevertheless did accurately describe many aspects of die-cut types as manufactured by William Page, in 1887. As the lower price of veneer types cut into the markets of William Page, who was manufacturing end-cut types exclusively, Page had the needed incentive to pursue quickly and diligently some new process for meeting the price competition. He and George Setchell were to perfect the process for successful die-stamping of wood types between 1887 and 1890. The William H. Page Wood Type Company announced "New Process Wood Type" in 1890: "This type is made of solid rock maple, finished exactly the same in every respect as our well known machine-cut wood type. The only difference being that the face is cut on the wood by dies, by Wm. H. Page's new patent process instead of the expensive pantograph machine method. Wood borders and ornaments have been made by this new method for nearly ten years, but it is only lately that the invention of machinery had made it possible to apply it to the making of wood type. The face of the New Process Type is much more perfect and clear cut than was possible to produce by the old method, as the dies now finish each letter without any hand trimming."

This method of manufacturing produced a face superior to the veneer, which could be sold for only a fraction of a cent more. Its greatest disadvantage was that it required a new die for each size. Page brought out an entirely new line of styles with the new process, which by 1890 included 17 different faces ranging from 3 to 15 lines. The price list indicated sizes from 2 through 16 lines. Although this catalogue is dated 1890, the new process type had been distributed since 1887 on a testing basis. After announcing their invention in October of 1887, Page and Setchell had made such improvements and adjustments that they doubled the capacity of their earlier machinery by December of the same year. Page was to take out nine domestic and four foreign patents on machines for making die-cut types. In a contemporary account, the working of the machine was described, "Wood of the proper size is fed into a machine in strips about fifteen inches long, and by a mechanism somewhat resembling that of a type revolving press is stamped in the places which should be low, leaving the face of the letters in high relief. This is done with incredible rapidity."

These machines could stamp out 100,000 small letters per day or 3,000 of the large letters. The production in a single hour was nearly as great as the output of an entire shop in 3 days by the old method of router and pantograph. The *Norwich Bulletin* was to say of the invention, "This is one of the most important inventions of the age, and one that will make a tremendous change in the product and prices of wood type all over the world." Although somewhat exaggerated in importance, the invention had

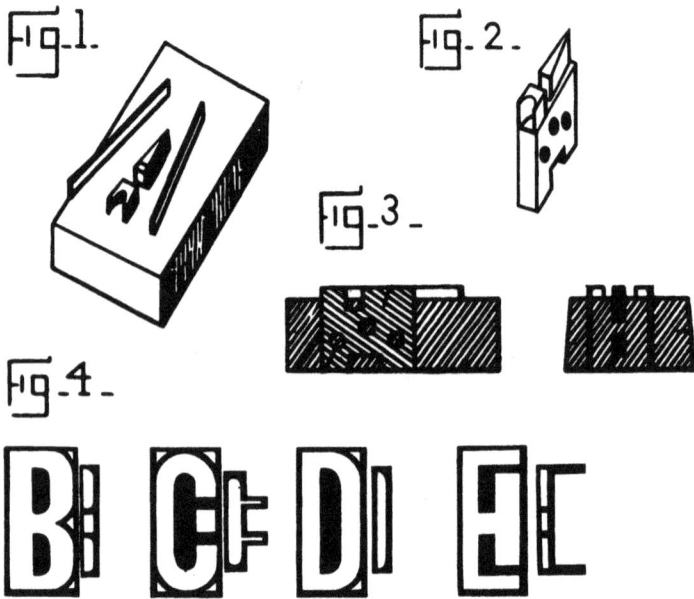

Fig.1.

Fig.2.

Fig.3.

Fig.4.

Patent No. 375,008. Submitted by G. C. Setchell for Wm. H. Page Wood Type Company. The diagram illustrates the metal counter punch and how it was used. Figure 1 shows the die with steel edges and center punch in position. Figure 2 shows center punch detail. Figure 3 shows a cross-section with punch in position. Figure 4 shows some of the other counter punches. The router was used to remove the excess wood. By punching the two sides of the A, the router could be used at right angles to the cut made by the die; thus, the sharp corners were quickly made, and the die accounted for sharp corners so there was no need for hand finishing of the type. Patent filed December 20, 1887.

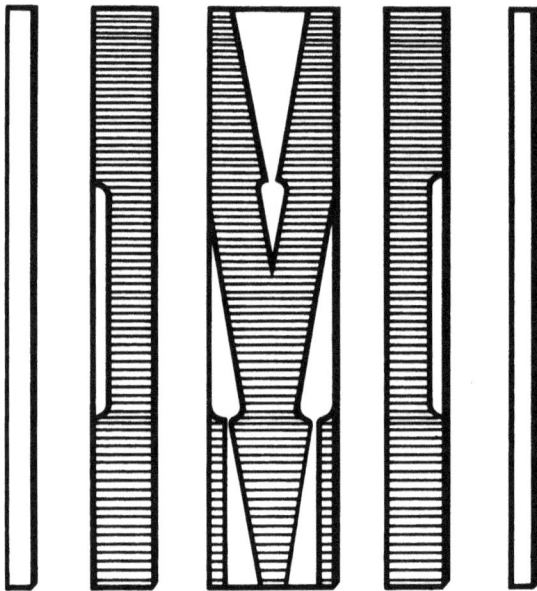

Patent No. 402,850. Submitted by William H. Page and G. C. Setchell. The diagram illustrates the sectional die and, in particular, the additional depressing die. This allowed for smooth shoulders on some letters and in other instances defined the edge of the letter; it also separated one letter from another in the stamping process (they often stamped several letters at a time, or stamped several letters on one block and separated the letters with a fine saw). The dies described are the two on either end. Patent filed May 7, 1889.

great potential. Even Page must have hoped for greater appreciation and results from his invention, as he was to write in the preface of his 1890 specimen book, "In smaller sizes this new type will take the place of the metal letter as it is very much cheaper and much easier to handle."

Even though the types produced by stamping were superior products, the invention had two serious handicaps. One problem was the market. Even with the older machine processes it was possible for all wood type manufacturers to overproduce. With the speed and ease of the stamping process, Page could not sell as quickly as he could manufacture. The second problem was that a separate die was needed for each size and style, and these dies were expensive and time consuming to make. It is difficult to know how refined the stamping press became, or whether it was ever operated by steam power. A patent drawing illustrated a simple cam-shaft press which appeared possible to run either by hand or steam power. As noted in Page's introduction of the new process type, his company had experience with wood stamping through the introduction in 1879 of molded ornamental borders, in many respects a more successful venture than the stamped types. The borders were designed so that less pressure was required than that needed for types. Thus a number of technical problems resulting from subjecting the wood to tremendous pressures were eliminated. This experience probably contributed a great deal to the eventual success of the Page Company in solving the problems of die-stamping wood letters.

The specific difficulties connected with the manufacture of die-cut types can be demonstrated through an examination of the successive inventions. In December of 1887, George Setchell patented in the name of the Wm. H. Page Wood Type Company a die which was more economical than the solid die, yet retained its advantages. The Setchell die was formed by outlining the letter on a wood blank with the pantograph and a fine cutter; steel ribs were then forced into the recessed lines and a steel punch conforming to the counter of the letter was placed in the trimmed-out counter. Walls were constructed around the entire block so that after type metal was poured into the contained space the metal ribs and counter punch were firmly secured. When the metal had cooled and the walls had been removed, the punch was ready for use. The raised ribs and center punch corresponded to the recessed areas of the finished type. Excess wood was cut away by the conventional pantograph and router. The removal of this excess wood was fast and accurate since the die was formed from the recessed lines originally cut with the pantograph pattern. The time saved by eliminating hand finishing of acute angles and square corners was the chief advantage of this procedure.

The types, cut on oversize blanks, were trimmed after the letters were formed, as the pressure used was sufficient to leave an irregular surface on the sides through the crushing of the wood fibers. Within 2 years this difficulty was eliminated by a new mold which depressed the entire shoulder. Also, a new device for securing the die in the machine allowed the die to finish the face and shoulder without damage to the sides of the blank. Since no hand finishing was necessary the type was ready for printing immediately after an oil treatment. Another significant improvement was made by tapering the pointed sections of the die—for example, the part necessary to form counters, like the triangular counter of the capital A. Previously, these sections of the die were subject to bending and breaking under pressure. The tapering strengthened the die without interfering in forming the letter.

One of the more ingenious variations of the die process was the sectional die patented by Setchell in 1889. The letter dies were divided into basic sections, such as stems, and bowls, which then assembled to form an entire letter. Because the curved die used for one side of the capital O could also be used for one side of the capital C, G, and so on, the work required to tool the dies as well as the number of dies were greatly reduced (by one third, Page claimed). Also, the sectional dies were easier to make since the individual sections offered the tool-maker easy access to the interior of the faces. The sides could be removed, and the sharp corners that presented difficult and time-consuming work in making the solid die were executed with a minimum of effort. Since in his patent application Page specifically stated that he was not claiming sectional dies as his invention, it would seem that there were other patents.

There is a patent dated August 7, 1888, filed by M. G. Merritt of Springfield, Massachusetts, that describes the following use of the die. A metal die of the letter is impressed on the wood so that the letter is left in slight relief. A standard lateral router is used to remove the excess wood from the counters and shoulders. The block is then subjected to the metal die once more in order to compress the wood on the face and thus to increase the wood's density. Consequently, the wood becomes more durable and less susceptible to warpage or damage. This same patent lists the advantages of this process over letters formed entirely by dies: "The above-described process of manufacturing wood type provides for the production thereof in such a way that such die pressure as is requisite to the proper finishing and hardening of the face of the letter can be effected without working against the said great resistance of the block to such a great degree of reduction, and the type retains its form and is not likely to warp. Wood types have heretofore been made by the formation of the letters thereon by die pressing the letter and then removing a portion of the face of the block surrounding said outline; but type blocks so treated have to be subjected to such great pressure to depress the surface around the letter that the so made does not retain its proper form, and great inconvience results therefrom; and furthermore, presses of great power have to be employed in their manufacture."

Almost certainly the idea of using dies in making wood type was widespread, because there was hedging in patent applications by patentees who disclaimed the basic principles in their inventions. It is difficult to know today just how many manufacturers actually employed the die stamping process, or some variation of it. William H. Page Wood Type Company and its successors, Hamilton Manufacturing Company, are the only concerns known to the author that actually marketed a die-cut type. Apparently there were two distinctly different applications of the die. The first one was to stamp only difficult counters and acute angles and then to finish the type with conventional tools. This application of the die was probably used in conjunction with established letter styles. The second use of the die—stamping the entire letter—had designs that were unique to this process. It is interesting that the letterforms illustrated in the patent papers

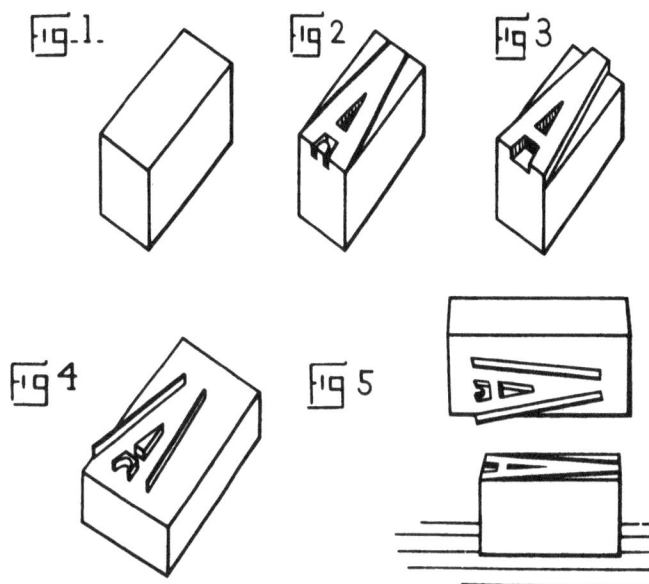

Patent No. 389,112. Submitted by G. C. Setchell for the William H. Page Wood Type Company. Figure 1 is the wood blank. Figure 2 shows the stamped letter, Figure 3 the completed letter, and Figure 4 the die. Figure 5 illustrates the blank and die coming together. The most important aspect of this patent is found in the metal bars which outline the letter and the metal counter punches. By having to depress only the outline of the letter, the problem of warpage caused by extreme pressures was reduced. Excess wood was removed by the router. Patent filed September 4, 1888.

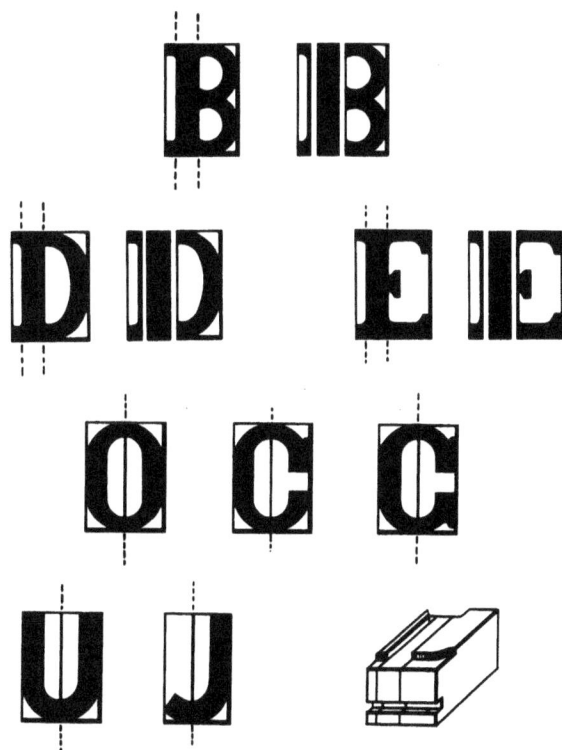

Patent No. 402,852. Submitted by William H. Page. The diagram shows the principle of the sectional die. It points up the interchangeability of parts: one die might serve to form the stem of the E, F, L, K, etc., or one section might be used to form the side of the O, C, G, etc. Mr. Page estimated that this type of die reduced by one third the cost and time of making steel dies. Patent filed May 7, 1889.

of Page and Setchell bear no relation to the 17 styles of die-cut type that they issued between 1887 and 1891. The actual types are stamped, "Patented, Dec. 20, 1887," and the letters of the stamp are raised from the surface of the shoulder. This confirms that the letters were incised into steel dies and stamped into the wood under great pressure. However, the patent papers of December 20, 1887, show that only the outline of the letter was stamped and that the shoulders were removed by routing machinery.

The die-cut types which have survived and which have had considerable use have a slight splintering or peeling on the sides, usually not affecting the face of the letter. Die-cut types that have had less extensive use are in practically the same condition as at the time of their manufacture.

Die-cut types may be readily distinguished from end-cut ones by the shallow depth from face to shoulder, which is usually one third to one half as deep as that for end-cut types. The stamped ornamental borders were extremely shallow, even when compared to the die-cut types. When the Hamilton Company purchased the Page works in 1891, it continued to produce the die-cut types, and advertised them as "the cheapest ever made." The last known advertisement, or mention of die-cut types for sale, was in a 1906 Hamilton catalogue.

Veneer Types

Veneer type was introduced to the trade in 1880 by J. E. Hamilton of Two Rivers, Wisconsin. No other company is believed to have produced wood type by this process. The letters were cut from sheets of holly wood approximately 1/16 inch thick with a scroll-saw and mounted on

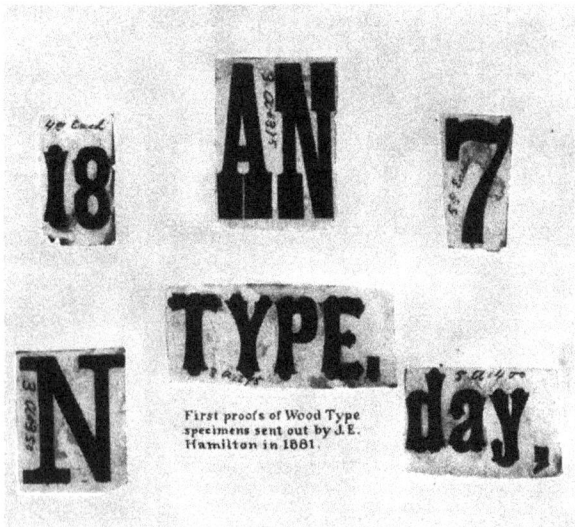

Specimens from Hamilton's first veneer types in 1881.

pine blocks with a special glue. This method for making wood type was so economical compared to the one for end-cut types that veneer could be marketed for one half the price of the wood type being sold by other manufacturers. Initially, a new pattern was neeeded for each size, and only the plain-faced types could be produced by this process. However, in 1887, Hamilton and Baker announced in the preface to their specimen book, "During the past year we have doubled our facilities for the manufacture of wood type, borders and Printers' wood material, having added new machinery and devised many new methods of manufacture, enabling us to turn out much better goods than formerly." The specimens in this catalogue showed great improvement in cutting techniques. The use of one number for each series of designs would seem to indicate that the pantograph had been combined with the scroll-saw.

Veneer type printed quite well, but lacked the preciseness of the end-cut types; the edges of the letter would splinter, and pointed or fine serifs damaged easily. However, veneer type easily satisfied the needs of the country printers. Hamilton guaranteed that the glue would hold under all reasonable conditions. The letters and blocks in some of the surviving types have separated. Usually this happened when the type had been stored over a long period of time in damp quarters.

Veneer types were, for the most part, discontinued in 1889. In the larger sizes of type, 100 lines or more, the company frequently used the veneer process since there was believed to be less warpage with the veneer than with end-cut type in the larger sizes. It was somewhat ironic that Hamilton was able to establish his company through selling low-priced veneer types to the considerable detriment of his competitors selling end-cut wood types. Then when he had consolidated his share of the market he switched to the manufacture of end-cut types, and eliminated all effective competition within 15 years through purchasing the other manufactories. And after this, he raised his prices!

Celluloid or Enameled Wood Type

Information regarding the persons and manufacturing processes connected with the manufacture of celluloid types has been exceedingly difficult to uncover. In advertisements and specimen books, the National Printers' Materials Company is the one listed manufacturing concern, and its product was labeled "Enameled Wood Type." The New York City Directory shows this company as listed from 1887 to 1895, when it was dropped. The Celluloid Stereotype Company, listed for the same address as the National Printers' Materials Company, is first found in the directory of 1885. After 1887, when new quarters were built, both firms continued to be listed at the same address.

An announcement in *The American Bookmaker* of 1886, states, "The New York Celluloid Stereotype company has just leased a building on Front Street, and will remove to it on or about May 1. It will take this opportunity to increase its facilities also. Celluloid wood type is a growing feature of this business." In this same advertisement, a testimonial from the *Brooklyn Eagle* says, "We have used celluloid wood type in our poster department for three years, and can testify to its superior printing qualities." This would indicate that celluloid types had been manufactured since 1883 by this same company, but perhaps before 1885 under another company name. Bullen mentions a Celluloid Wood Type Company located in New York during the late 1880's. Whether or not this was another firm is not known. While the National Printers' Materials Company advertised only "Enameled Wood Types," the Golding Press Company advertised in The *Inland Printer* of 1887 as the sole agent for Celluloid Wood Type.

An examination of some celluloid faced types in the Morgan Press collection of wood types revealed that there were two distinct methods used to face the wood letters. In one, the celluloid was attached to the block by dovetail grooves. The celluloid letters appear to have been formed by the stereotype process with an additional ⅛-inch thick shoulder, probably manufactured in strips of letters. The strip had a molded triangular wedge on the under side which was slid into a corresponding groove in the wood body. Possibly some adhesive supplemented the locking device of wedge and groove. By this process, a number of letters could be made as a single unit. Then the letters would be cut apart, finished on the sides, and used. The completed letter retained a thin celluloid shoulder.

The second process was based on fusing celluloid and wood. A sheet of celluloid was placed over a block of porous wood and subjected to heat of about 250 degrees and pressure (600 pounds) for 2 or 3 minutes. A fusion took place which produced a smooth surface and impregnated the wood to a depth of approximately ⅛ inch. The letters were then produced by conventional wood type cutting machinery. They may be distinguished from celluloid types made by the first process only by the fact that the face was celluloid and the shoulder was wood.

These types were described as having the advantages of an accurately made hard maple or mahogany end-wood letter, but with a durable ivory-like face that did not absorb ink. Celluloid made an extremely good printing surface, which is well demonstrated by its use in stereotype work where it could give more than 100,000 impressions, as compared to 30,000 from an ordinary plate. Bullen commented that correctly made celluloid type was equal to metal. He could not understand why the process was abandoned in such a short time unless, perhaps, the wrong men were behind the company.

A patent was issued to John Stevens and William Wood of Newark, New Jersey, in October, 1885, for a process that they described as laminating celluloid to wood, and that they labeled "enameling." This patent provides the first reference to a celluloid product being enameled. Some of the celluloid types found today have reticulated surfaces, much like old linoleum; others seem to be in their original condition except for wear from normal use. The cause for the reticulation in some faces, whether from different materials used, or from improper storage or use, is not known. Also, some types appear to be a yellowish color while others are white; again this could indicate two different materials, two manufacturing processes, or different storage conditions.

Of the specimens of enameled type found today, there have been none over 24 lines even though the enameled type catalogues advertised sizes up to 110 lines. This lack might suggest that celluloid facing may have deteriorated more quickly in the larger sizes. On the basis of available information, it would seem reasonable to assume that the manufacture of celluloid types spanned a period of little more than 12 to 15 years.

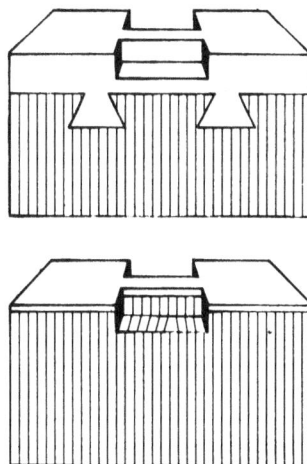

Two methods for applying celluloid to wood in the making of enameled wood types. The top drawing illustrates what was probably a stereotype process—a number of letters cast in a strip with a dove-tail on the bottom which interlocked with a corresponding groove in the wood block. The bottom drawing shows the celluloid pressed into the wood with heat under pressure.

REVISED PRICE LIST,

May 1st 1890.

Subject to Special Discounts on large orders.

Lines Pica	Class A Cents	Class B Cents	Class C Cents	Class D Cents	Class E Cents	Class F Cents	Class G Cents	Class H Cents
2	6	6	6	6	10	14	16	24
3	6	6	6	6	12	16	18	24
4	6	6	6	6	12	16	18	24
5	8	6	6	6	14	16	20	24
6	10	6	6	8	16	18	22	24
7	10	8	8	8	16	20	24	26
8	12	8	8	8	18	20	26	28
9	14	10	8	10	20	22	28	30
10	16	10	8	10	22	24	30	32
12	18	10	10	10	24	26	32	34
14	20	12	10	12	26	28	34	36
15	22	14	10	12	28	30	36	38
16	24	14	12	14	30	32	38	40
18	26	16	12	14	32	34	40	44
20	28	18	14	16	34	36	42	48
22	30	20	16	18	36	38	44	50
24	32	22	16	20	40	40	46	52
25	34	24	18	22	42	42	48	54
26	36	26	18	24	44	44	50	56
28	38	28	20	26	46	46	52	60
30	40	30	20	28	48	48	54	62
32	42	32	22	30	50	50	56	64
36	44	34	24	32	52	54	58	68
40	48	36	28	34	54	56	60	72
45		38	32	36	56	60	62	76
50		40	36	40	60	64	64	82
55		44	40	44	64	68	68	90
60		50	44	48	68	72	76	94
65		56	48	52	76	80	82	100
72		60	52	56	80	84	90	106
80		64	56	60	88	92	100	112
90		68	60	66	96	100	110	120
100		74	64	80	100	110	120	130
110		80	68	86	108	120	130	140
120		90	72	96	120	130	140	150

On all Sizes larger than 120 Line, Special prices will be given.

Prices of our "New Process" Wood Type shown in another book are still lower than those quoted above.

SCALE OF FONTS.

3A Capitals 75 Letters	3a L. Case. 65 Letters	4A Capitals 106 Letters	4a L Case 90 Letters	5A Capitals 120 Letters	5a L. Case. 104 Letters
A....3	a....3	A....4	a....4	A. .5	a....5
B....2	b....2	B....3	b....3	B....3	b....3
C....2	c....2	C....3	c....4	C....4	c....4
D....2	d....2	D....3	d....3	D....4	d....4
E....4	e....4	E....5	e....5	E....6	e....6
F....2	f....2	F....3	f....3	F....3	f....3
G....2	g....2	G....3	g....3	G....3	g....3
H....2	h....2	H....3	h....3	H....4	h....4
I....4	i....3	I....4	i....4	I....5	i....5
J....2	j....1	J....3	j....2	J....3	j....2
K....1	k....1	K....2	k....2	K....2	k....2
L....4	l....4	L....5	l....5	L....6	l....6
M....2	m....2	M....3	m....3	M....4	m....4
N....3	n....3	N....4	n....4	N....5	n....5
O....3	o....3	O....4	o....4	O....5	o....5
P....2	p....2	P....3	p....3	P....3	p....3
Q....1	q....1	Q....2	q....2	Q....2	q....2
R....3	r....3	R....4	r....4	R....5	r....5
S....4	s....4	S....5	s....5	S....6	s....6
T....4	t....4	T....4	t....5	T....5	t....5
U....2	u....2	U....3	u....3	U....4	u....4
V....2	v....2	V....3	v....3	V....3	v....3
W....2	w....2	W....3	w....3	W....3	w....3
X....1	x....1	X....2	x....2	X....2	x....2
Y....2	y....2	Y....3	y....3	Y....3	y....3
Z....1	z....1	Z....2	z....2	Z....2	z....2
&....1	fi....1	&....2	fi....1	&....2	fi....1
!....2	fl....1	!....3	fl....1	!....3	fl....1
.....3	ff....1	4	ff....1	1	ff....1
-....2	-....1	-....1	-....1	-....2	ffi....1
,....2	ffi....1	,....2	ffi — 1	,....2	
!....1		!....2		!....2	
;....1		;....2		;....4	
,....3		,....4		,....2	

Figures,   1 2 3 4 5 6 7 8 9 0 $

No. of each, .. 3 .. 2 .. 2 .. 2 .. 2 .. 2 .. 2 .. 2 .. 2 .. 5 .. 1 ... 2

The first wood types advertised by Darius Wells in 1828 were sold by the letter. The price was governed by size and additional specifications. For example, the letter could be in-lined on one side or shaded for a slightly increased cost. The customer was asked how many of each letter he desired, or how many letter A's, which would determine the number of other letters, much in the same manner as metal types were sold. As early as 1838, George Nesbitt had divided the styles distributed by his firm into nine categories, each of which represented a different price, ranging from 5 to 48 cents.

This method of pricing was adopted by all wood type manufacturers throughout the century, and categories were usually labeled as "plain," "ornamented," etc. Later they were designated by alphabetic symbols—Class N, O, etc. The Wells & Webb catalogue price list gave font schemes, 3A—74 letters, 3a—64 letters, 4A—106 letters, 4a—90 letters, 5A—120 letters, and 5a—104 letters. Thereafter, all manufacturers gave some variation of these font schemes. A figure font consisted of 26 characters, but all letters or figures could be ordered in any quantity. Sorts could be purchased, or substitutions made to suit any purpose. For jobs requiring large letters, the printer would often purchase only the necessary type.

An interesting deviation from the American system is found in the catalogue of William Eglington, an English wood type manufacturer in 1870. He sold by the dozen characters, which he advertised as, "made in founts from five and a half dozen upwards."

American manufacturers sold ornamental borders by the foot. Corners were individually priced, and ornaments, banners, logotypes, etc., by the unit. Most specimen books listed type sizes ranging from 2 through 100 lines. Expanded letters usually began at 2 lines, and the condensed letters were made from 4 lines and up. The 1892 Hamilton *Large Wood Type* catalogue, showing sizes up to 120 lines, announced in its preface that the larger sizes were impractical to show, but that the company did make type in two and three sheet sizes. Every catalogue reminded the customer that wood type would be made to *any* size desired by the printer. The majority of very large types, in fact, were custom made, and hand engraved—as the pantograph was impractical on sizes over 120 lines. The *Norwich Bulletin* for September 23, 1871, reported an order to the William Page Company from Detroit for wood type that required 160 feet of lumber for each letter. Later in life, William Page described this order for type in two colors as being the largest wood type he ever made. Each letter was in nine blocks, 29 by 42 inches in size for each color. The blocks were placed on the floor, where Page proceeded to "survey" them in his stocking feet. They were then routed and finished (these letters would have been 7 feet 3 inches by 10 feet 6 inches). Page said that the larger types were drawn by hand and routed on a machine built especially for that purpose, but did not describe how the equipment differed from a conventional router. Although die-cut types were manufactured to maximum size of 18 lines, the styles were advertised as being available in larger sizes as they could be cut by the pantograph and router method.

A number of companies stamped an imprint on their capital A's. The following excerpt from a Page publication explains, "knowing that considerable wood type is continually being sold for our own make, which it is not, we hereby continue to caution all printers to bear in mind this one fact; we stamp our name on A's of each and every font of type manufactured by us, so that none need to be deceived, and thus fail to get a 'warranted' article." Not all manufacturers however, would imprint the lower-case letters. Several, most particularly the Hamilton Company in its first years, would use a paper slip attached to the type to identify the company. Since these paper slips were usually lost in a short time, the type is impossible to identify today.

German fonts were commonly stamped on the capital C, the reason for which is unexplained. Some of the type manufactured by Darius Wells was stamped on the bottom, "D. Wells, New York." This is the only type stamped on the bottom which has come to my attention. End-cut types were usually stamped on the sides, and die-cut types on the shoulder. If dates can be associated with specific imprints, they can be helpful in deciding when a particular type was produced. As some imprints, however, were in continued use after the status of a company had changed, this system of dating is not entirely reliable. Companies known to have used an imprint are "D. Wells & Co.", J. G. Cooley, William Page, Hamilton Manufacturing Company, American Wood Type, Heber Wells, Morgans & Wilcox Manufacturing Company, Tubbs Manufacturing Company, Vanderburgh, Wells & Company, and Bill, Stark & Company.

Diversification

It was apparent almost from the beginning that the wood type manufacturer would need to expand his operations if he hoped to build a substantial business. This was due mainly to his ability to overproduce and saturate markets quickly. The first firm to enlarge its business to include more diversified services and products was Wells and Webb in 1842 when it opened its Printers' General Warehouse on the corner of Fulton and Gold streets in New York City. In addition to wood type, the firm sold printers' furniture, type cabinets, reglet, etc.

Wells and Webb were agents for R. Hoe & Company, A. B. Taylor & Co., Worrall & Co., F. J. Austin, A. Ramage and Adams & Co.—all press manufacturers. They dealt in newspaper, book, and job types at regular foundry prices, carried several lines of job presses, and advertised second hand printing materials. Also, they advised the trade that they would furnish, on order, heads for newspapers and magazines, fancy lines for show bills in two or more colors, as well as the usual services of providing stamps and stereotype blocking. The Wells' company was to continue this tradition up to the last decade of the nineteenth century when the company was absorbed by Hamilton Mfg. Co.

J. G. Cooley was to establish a similar outlet for printers in 1859, and additionally expanded into the advertising business which was in its embryonic stages at that time. As early as 1859, William Page also served as an agent for leading typefoundries and advertised metal types at the founders' prices. By 1879, Page had expanded his line to include a variety of printers' needs such as mitering machines, card cutters, presses, etc.

Both Hamilton and Morgans & Wilcox were to build extensive outlets for printers' materials, perhaps some of the largest in the country during their time. Henry Lewis Bullen listed Morgans & Wilcox as third largest distributor of printers' materials in the United States during the late 1880's, and Hamilton Mfg. Co. was the largest manu-

Page & Co., Greeneville, Conn. Believed to have been in use between 1857 and 1859.

Wm. H. Page & Co., Greeneville, Conn. In use in 1859 (so stated in catalogue).

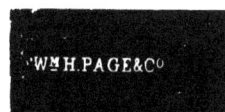

Wm. H. Page & Co. In use in 1870 (so stated in catalogue).

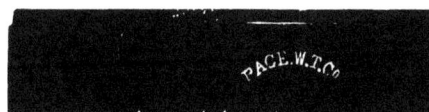

Page W. T. Co. In use between 1876 and 1891.

J. G. Cooley, New York. In use between 1859 and 1868.

V. W. & Co. 18 Dutch's Street, New York. In use between 1864 and 1867.

Vanderburgh, Wells & Co., New York. In use between 1867 and 1890.

M. & W. Mfg. Co., Middletown, N.Y. In use after 1881.

61

Hamilton Mfg. Co., Chicago, Ill., and Two Rivers, Wisc. In use between 1889 and 1891.

The Hamilton Mfg. Co., Two Rivers, Wisc. Unknown.

Hamilton, Two Rivers, Wisc. After 1891.

American W. T. Co., South Windham, Conn. Believed to have been in use after 1883.

American Wood Type Co. Unknown. (It appears there were several American Wood Type Companies, and it is not clear to what company this imprint and the one below may be attached. Those that include South Windham undoubtedly refer to the one founded by Mr. Charles Tubbs in 1878, reorganized in 1883, and continued until around 1900, when it is believed to have been called Tubbs & Co. In 1903 it was moved to Ludington, Mich., and called Tubbs Mfg. Co. There is an American Wood Type Company operating today on Long Island.)

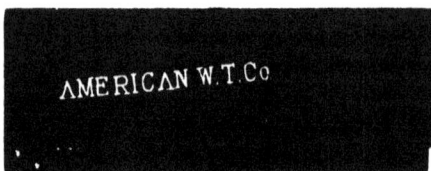

American Wood Type Co. Unknown.

facturer of wooden printers' goods at the end of the century.

In 1887, The National Printers' Materials Company in New York City dealt successfully in new and used equipment for printers in addition to manufacturing enameled wood types. In combination with the Celluloid Stereotype Company of the same address the company conducted an extensive business in celluloid stereotyping. These types were advertised as being more durable than metal ones, and as weighing 50 to 90 percent less.

There is some reference to Edwin Allen's producing type cabinets and cases, but it is not believed that the business was significant because Nesbitt, Allen's distributor, never made mention of these goods in any of the known specimen books. Leavenworth, the Day brothers, the Bill Brothers and Tubbs are not known to have engaged in any additional manufacturing or distributing operations other than wood type, and a limited amount of wooden goods such as reglet, composing sticks, etc.

Also manufactured and distributed by wood type manufacturers were several unusual items. A Wells & Webb catalogue for 1849 carried the conventional printers' supplies, but included in the list were book ends and candle sticks. William H. Page Wood Type Company advertised in its 1879 *Album*: "Setchell's / Parlor Dominos / Match by Color as well as Numbers / Sample box sent by mail on receipt of 50¢." Hamilton & Baker were promoting the sale in 1887 of an interchangeable Sunday School Chart. A device similar in operation to that used on theater marquees today, it had a wooden frame, 6 feet high, with grooved horizontal slats to take individual letters. The letters, silver on a black background, could "easily be read across the largest room." The kit sold for $8 with letters included. In 1849, Edwin Allen patented and sold "Allen's Educational Tables," which consisted of a shallow open box with horizontal and vertical grooves that allowed small wooden letters, locked into grooves, to be slid into any arrangement or combination of letters.

An 1840 Wells & Webb specimen book contained 10 pages showing metal stereotypes of wood engravings, which were patterned after trade cuts then being sold by typefounders. This was the only instance of finding these items in a wood type catalogue. Every producer of wood type advertised stereotype blocking, custom engraved logotypes, or bleachers' stamps. Also all the manufacturers were prepared to supply engravers' wood to the trade. In 1860 E. R. Webb & Company almost monopolized the preparation and sale of engravers' wood. Boxwood imported from the West Indies and Turkey and the domestic hard maple were the most desirable woods for these engravings. Page advertised in 1872, "Boxwood, Maple, Mahogany and Pine prepared for wood engravers, Mahogany and Cherry blocking for stereotypers." Tubbs advertised that he would produce custom ordered fancy labels.

Another specialized product of the wood type manufacturer was the tint block. Tint blocks were used for printing envelopes or decorative backgrounds upon which additional printing was laid. Probably tint block printing was one forerunner of the present safety papers, and if not as effective, at least dedicated to the same purpose. This was achieved by printing an exceedingly fine pattern in areas on which a signature or sum might be superimposed by either printing or writing. Any attempt to alter the overprinting would necessarily disfigure the fine pat-

Tubbs & Co. Believed to be in use circa 1900.

Tubbs Mfg. Co., Ludington, Mich. In use after 1903.

SETCHELL'S
Parlor Dominos.
Match by Colors as well as Numbers.
SAMPLE BOX SENT BY MAIL
ON RECEIPT OF 50 CENTS.

THE WM. H. PAGE WOOD TYPE CO.,
NORWICH, CONN.

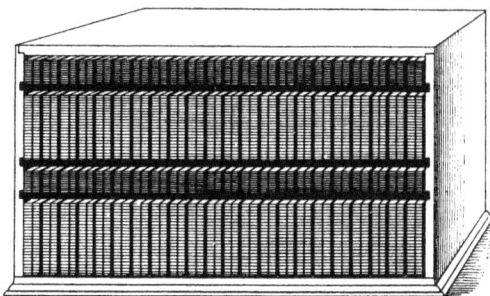

Wood type manufacturers also produced related wood products for the printing trade. Wooden quoins, furniture and reglet were the most common items.

tern and reveal the tampering. Lithographers and metal plate engravers also did work similar to that accomplished by the tint block. It would seem that the Page Company engaged in the manufacture of these blocks to a greater extent that any other wood type manufacturer. An account at that time describes the William Page operation: "There are also several machines for the preparation of various other styles of wood-cutting, a most successful feature being the elegance achieved in the cutting of tint blocks for envelopes and other purposes. The lines on these blocks are cut so exceedingly fine and delicate that it becomes a matter of wonder that it is possible to print from them without the ink at once filling the surface of the block; yet some of the choicest specimens of presswork that we are familiar with have been done from these same wooden blocks." (The Great Industries of the United States, Hartford, Connecticut, 1873, "Wood Type", pp 1265-71.)

Distribution

Typefounders provided a substantial outlet for goods produced by wood type manufacturers. The type sold through these channels seldom was marketed under the name of the manufacturer, but rather it was advertised under the name of the typefounder. In 1845 the Boston Type & Stereotype Foundry was the first to list wood type as a separate item on its price list. George Bruce in 1848 was the first to include a wood type font scheme on the price-list page.

As the century progressed, the demand for large sizes of type increased so much that the typefounder found it impractical to compete with wood type manufacturers in the field of large types. A letter from Bill, Stark & Company in 1853 to George Bruce reveals what was probably a customary arrangement between wood type manufacturers and founders: "Our terms at wholesale are ½ discounted from our list price, quarterly settlement and three months credit or 3% off for cash."

There is no known instance of an American typefounder entering into wood type manufacture. The typefounder L. Johnson of Philadelphia was to handle the entire line of Wells & Webb in 1846, issuing a type specimen with his own cover and firm name. The cover of the 1849 Wells & Webb catalogue announced that Messrs. George Bruce & Co., John T. White, W. Hagar, James Connor & Son, New York; Messrs. L. Johnson, A. Robb, L. Pelouze, Philadelphia; Boston Type & Stereotype Foundry, Dickinson Foundry, Holmes & Curtis, Boston; F. Lucas, Baltimore; N. Lyman, Buffalo; and C. T. Palsgrave, Montreal, were agents handling wood type for Wells & Webb. The 1850 specimens of Boston Type & Stereotype Foundry showed a number of wood type designs by George F. Nesbitt.

Initially, the founders would identify wood types only on the price list, but later, founders would label and intersperse wood types with the metal faces. During the 1880's and afterwards, it was a regular practice for the wood type designs to be gathered into one section which would be at the back of the founder's specimen book.

In 1857 Page & Bassett sent samples of their types to S. P. Rounds of Chicago. In *Rounds' Printers' Cabinet* for November of 1857, the type was described, "In all our experience in the business, we have never met with wood type more true in body, cut more accurately or with better face." The same article indicated that Rounds would be a

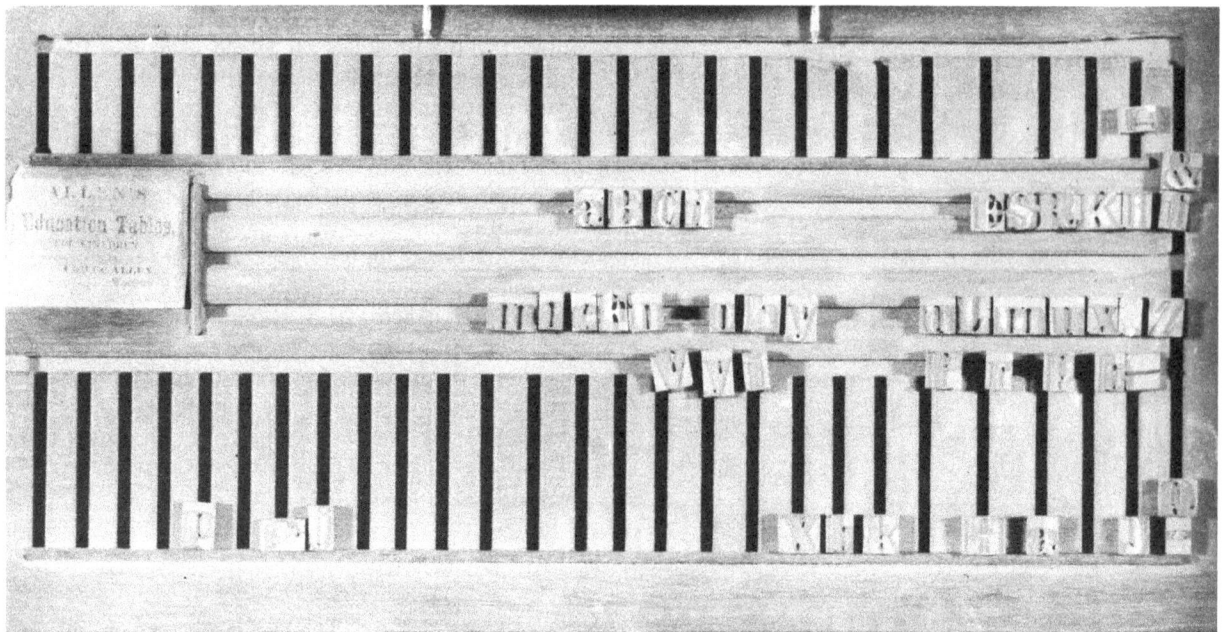

Educational tables patented by Edwin Allen in 1849 and marketed by him for the next few years. This label indicates that these tables were eventually manufactured by Edwin's brother, Lewis. (Courtesy of the Connecticut State Historical Society, Hartford, Connecticut.)

Poster stick made of wood with brass-lined ends, iron knee and screw clamp. It came in sizes ranging from 16 to 42 inches long.

Standard American large wood type cabinet.

dealer for the Page & Bassett Company. Page also began to distribute through James Connor's Sons in 1859, after which his designs were shown regularly in Connor's *Typographic Messenger* for many years.

Dauchy & Company of New York City issued a complete catalogue of Page's types in 1872, and Shniedwend & Lee of Chicago were to do the same in 1883. D. Knox & Company of Fredricksburg, Ohio, listed a dealer in Dubuque, Iowa, in 1858, Gillmore & Corr, Printers. In addition to outlets provided through typefounders, several wood type firms maintained distribution offices in key cities throughout the country. In this manner they could furnish delivery on short notice, and since competition was fierce in the latter part of the century, service was a factor in the success of a manufacturer. Hamilton established offices at 259 Dearborn Street in Chicago during 1889, and in New York City in 1891. W. T. & S. D. Day & Company maintained offices in Chicago during the early 1850's. S. P. Rounds, who handled their type, advertised it as "quite a large percentage below New York prices." In an 1890 catalogue, Page reminded the trade that his company maintained a complete stock in San Francisco and Chicago to serve its customers better. He had already established a New York City office located at 61 Beekman Street in 1882. The Tubbs Manufacturing Company carried an announcement to the trade in the *Inland Printer* during 1907 that it had opened offices in New York City at 536—38 Pearl Street, with warehouses in England and other foreign countries.

In 1878, the Page Wood Type Company announced in the preface to its current specimen book, "The entire world is our market." They had opened a dealership in Sidney, Australia, in 1878, and had outlets in Europe. Edward Hamilton, who also had outlets on the Continent, made several trips abroad for the express purpose of exploring new markets. It is believed that great quantities of wood type were sold abroad in the last quarter of the century.

Competition

Wide diversification of products and services offered by most wood type firms may be traced in part to the fact that during much of the century there was only a limited market for wood types. With a capacity for producing 10 fonts when he could sell only one, the wood type manufacturer had the one alternative of expanding into related fields, wooden printers' goods being the one most commonly exploited. Sometime during the 1860's, William Page facetiously commented, "a canvasser traveling from Maine to Texas could not dispose of enough wood type to pay his whiskey bills."

Between 1827 and 1880 there were seldom more than two or three wood type manufactories in operation at any one time, and in the 1880's there were six. Competition was so intense that by 1900 only two survived from the six. In the first years of wood type manufacturing, Nesbitt and Wells were bitter competitors. The preface pages of their specimen books bristled with remarks blasting each other's claim to superior products. A specimen styling in the 1859 Page catalogue stated, "Beware of traveling botch type makers who use these specimens to sell their work by." It is thought that this remark was directed against the Day brothers of Fredricksburg, who peddled their type from a wagon as they traveled from town to town.

THREE LINE CLARENDON LIGHT FACE.—10 A, 10 a, $12.00.

Beware of traveling botch TYPE MAKERS, WHO use these specimens to sell their work by. 1859.

THREE LINE IONIC.—10 A, 10 a, $12.00.

EXCELSIOR WOODEN Type Manufactory, Wm. H. Page & Co. Greeneville, Ct. 1859.

The most intense contest was probably the one between Hamilton and Page beginning about 1885. In 1874, Page had boasted in a circular that his company was producing seven-eighths of all the wood type manufactured in America. Hamilton & Baker 12 years later stated that they were the largest single producers of wood type. This change had come about mostly because of the difference in price between end-cut and veneer type, and to a lesser extent, because of the expanding market in the Midwest, which was more accessible to Hamilton. It is interesting to note that Hamilton kept his prices for veneer and end-cut, which he produced regularly after 1888, to one-half the prices of the William H. Page Wood Type Company. Then after his purchase of the Page concern in 1891, Hamilton doubled his prices.

Printers' Review in 1888 was to comment, "Wood type is an important item in the equipment of every large printing office, and of late years competition has so reduced the price that it has come into quite general use." Three years later, the *Inland Printer* reported, "Until

The Hamilton Mfg. Co. exhibit which was entered in the Columbian Exhibition of 1893. This exhibit won a gold medal, and a duplicate of it was purchased by the Inland Printer. *(Courtesy of the Hamilton Mfg. Co. Archives.)*

recent years the prices for this material (wood type) were so excessive that the poster printing business was confined to a few large houses who had fortunes invested in wood type; but strong competition among the manufacturers has resulted in new methods of manufacture and today wood type is selling at about one third the price received for it ten years ago." The price war between the Hamilton and Page companies weakened the entire industry and contributed to the Hamilton Manufacturing Company's absorbing every major wood type producer in the country by 1906—except for the Tubbs Manufacturing Company, which was not purchased until 1918.

Wood Type Specimen Books

An examination of remaining wood type catalogues reveals the activities and accomplishment of the industry throughout its brief history in a manner no amount of words can do. Darius Wells' first specimen book was most humble in terms of size. It had a brown wrapper, and was printed on one side of the page in black. The overall effect was one of simplicity and directness.

Ten years later, the Nesbitt specimens reveal how much the industry had grown. One cannot help but be impressed by the intricacy of detail and volume of styles. Volume was to be the keynote for wood type manufacturers through Wells & Webb, Knox, and Page. During the 1870's, William Page was to publish several specimen books with hard covers, exquisite press work, and color printing. During the 1880's, a period of financial stress for the trades, conditions were reflected by catalogues which had returned to being printed only in black. Styles were jammed onto the page—sometimes two columns to a page. Covers were soft, and there was printing on both sides of the page.

Specimen books printed in the last years of the century, and afterwards, progressively grew thinner, and the variety of styles decreased, especially after 1900. The decline in the importance of wood type was clearly obvious. The author has yet to find a wood type specimen book which showed complete alphabets, but this is understandable because of the scale of most wood letters. This partial display creates barriers to research, as it is virtually impossible to determine differences between cuttings of the same design by various companies. The number of catalogues available for study is comparatively small in relationship to the number which must have been printed between 1828 and 1900. Some specimens seem to have survived because of the striking qualities associated with large types, colored printing, and hard covers, and as a consequence the types have been preserved as curiosities if not for historical value.

Many wood type catalogues, like the metal type specimen books, have been mutilated through the practice of customers' cutting a design out of the book to send it to the manufacturer to indicate what was wanted. This would make the customer's book incomplete, and it is conceivable that after not too many such depredations he was requesting a new catalogue. On the price page of most catalogues, the manufacturer carried an admonition to the users that such a practice was unnecessary, and that to order by name or number would be sufficient.

As the number of wood type styles increased, so did the cost of publishing the specimen books; this was partially a result of a predicament to which every type manufacturer contributed by adding to the already voluminous

MAY
band

Darius Wells, 1828.

8 Line Pica Tuscan Shaded.

HOUSE

8 Line Pica Antique Shaded.

HOUSE

G. F. NESBITT.   NEW-YORK

Nesbitt, 1838.

Ten and Six line Roman Extended.

ME
ine
12345

D. WELLS & Co. NEW-YORK.

Wells & Webb, 1840.

number of designs in use. This problem was met in several ways. Some dealers issued new catalogues every year, supplementing them with broadsides. A number of William Page catalogues after 1870 solicited advertising from related printing trades to defray the cost of publishing. In 1879, William Page began issuing every three months a small pamphlet called *Page's Wood Type Album*. It was the stated purpose of this publication to not only show new designs and changes in prices, but to furnish news about the industry and to inform the buying public regarding changes of policy within the firm. It is thought the *Album* continued to be published until 1881. John Cooley who had published the *Wood Letter Advertiser* in 1858, published *The Typographic Arts* in 1863. Both of these papers were devoted to largely the same ends as Page's *Album*.

During these years, several typefounders had regularly published similar trade papers. Many of the wood type catalogues carried announcement pages, or circular letters. These pages often mentioned new facilities, awards won by their products, or changes of policy. Also, they often reflected competitive conditions or the economic situation which prevailed at that time. Many of the statements have to be weighed carefully before being accepted at face value, since the manufacturers were not above exaggerating their own abilities and products. These pages, however, have proved very useful, not only for the general information, but because they are usually signed and dated.

Of the surviving catalogues, several stand out for either historical reasons, or because of the artistic merit connected with their publication. Of the former, Darius Wells' first and only surviving specimen book is of especial importance. The book is an oblong quarto, 8 by 13 inches, with a stained brown cover and contains 20 specimens (Bullen counted 7 styles and 21 sizes.) of Roman, Italic, Antique, Backslope, and shaded letters, the sizes running from 7 to 20 lines, and the prices going from 8 cents to 28 cents per character. The Nesbitt catalogue of Allen's types published in 1838 is the next catalogue after that of Darius Wells. It has the most extensive showing of Allen's wood types (to the author's knowledge), and is particularly good for ornamental letters from that period. *Leavenworth's Patent Wood Types sold by J. M. Debow,* published sometime after 1836, is the only known catalogue for Leavenworth. Many of the styles are unique, and for this reason the catalogue is of special interest. This book is in the New York Public Library.

The Wells & Webb specimens for 1840, 1849, and 1854 are important because many new styles were introduced to the trades through these catalogues. Several of these, Antique and Gothic Tuscan, Gothic Expanded, and others, are believed to be original creations by the company. The specimen book of John G. Cooley, published circa 1860 (listed as 1850 by the Newberry Library in Chicago), is the only known specimen of Cooley's types. If the book is examined, it should be kept in mind that the condition of the catalogue is poor and that there are some specimen pages from Vanderburgh, Wells & Company mixed in with the Cooley specimens. The catalogue for the D. Knox & Company of Fredericksburg, Ohio, is the only known copy from this company, and is important because it is thought to contain many specimens from the Day brothers manufactory, for which there is no known catalogue. The small 14-page catalogue, which was the first issued by J. E. Hamilton in 1881, is interesting from the standpoint of seeing the first styles of this company.

The quarterly issues of William Page's *Wood Type Album* from 1879–81 have value in that they show new styles as they were introduced to the market. Perhaps the finest German types cut in wood were all included in his 1870 specimens of exclusively German types.

The catalogue put out by the National Printers' Materials Company in 1887 probably contained its most extensive showing of styles. One catalogue important both for its historical and aesthetic considerations is the *Chromatic Wood Types* printed by William Page in 1874. It is perhaps the most expensive specimen book printed by a wood type manufacturer—$10,000 for 1000 copies. The catalogue consists of approximately 175 pages, is 13¾ by 18 inches, and is printed in several colors. The catalogue card file in Special Collections, Columbia University, describes this catalogue as being the most beautiful wood type catalogue ever printed.

Another exceedingly handsome specimen book which has not had proper attention is the *Large Wood Types* published by Hamilton Mfg. Co. in 1892. Measuring 14¼ by 20 inches, it is easily the largest wood type specimen of the century. It was printed in a number of colors and showed types up to 120 lines, and it was hard-bound.

Perhaps the most unusual and notable specimen book was printed in 1906 by the Hamilton Company. Its preface explains, "It has long been our aim to compile a wood type catalogue embracing all the type and border designs which we have in our possession. These patterns comprise not only all the regular and special patterns made by us during the twenty-five years we have been in business, but also embrace the complete wood type patterns of the William H. Page Wood Type Company, Morgans and Wilcox Manufacturing Company, and Vanderburgh, Wells & Company (later Heber Wells). It has been almost an endless task to arrange this reference catalogue, comprising all of the above mentioned material, and the specimens shown in this catalogue comprise everything of value that has been turned out in the way of wood type designs during the past fifty years. Necessarily, owing to the great bulk of material, we are only able to show a single size of each design, and these are shown in a uniform size, so that a comparison of the different patterns will be an easy matter. It is often difficult in matching up wood type to tell from just what particular pattern the original type was cut; but with the aid of these specimen lines, each showing a considerable number of characters, identification will be easily accomplished, and errors and misunderstandings avoided.

"It is not our intention to publish this catalogue for general distribution, but merely for reference purposes; therefore only a very limited number are published, and it is not our intention to have any of these books leave our hands permanently."

As one would expect, this specimen book is invaluable for the identification of wood types. The tragic sequel to this special publication was that later, in keeping with a company policy of clearing out any equipment not being used to make room for new machinery or manufacturing operations, Hamilton destroyed *all* patterns dating back to Darius Wells. Now the only means for collecting the old designs in complete fonts is to locate actual types and to proof them.

Debow, c. 1837.

Cooley, 1859.

Hartford

LUSTER

FIRE!

BILL, STARK & CO.   WILLIMANTIC, CT.

Bill, Stark & Co., 1853.

Numb!

Bud

Wm. H. Page, German specimens, 1870.

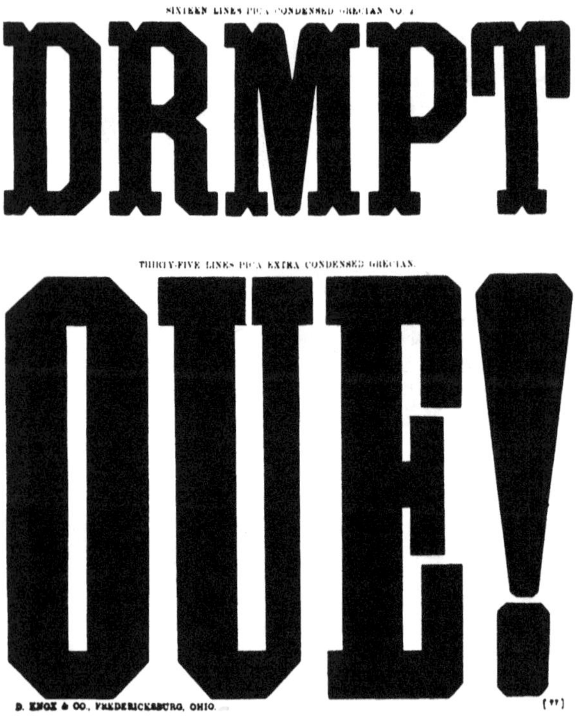

DRMPT

QUE!

D. KNOX & CO., FREDERICKSBURG, OHIO.   [99]

D. Knox, 1858.

The WM. H. PAGE WOOD TYPE Co.,
NORWICH. CONN.

Six Line No. 110.   Class C. 5 Cents.

Established

Ten Line No. 110.   C. 9 Cents.

Surface

Fifteen Line No. 110.   C. 11 Cents.

Tare

Border No. 221. $1,00 per foot.

22

Wm. H. Page, Page's Wood Type Album, 1879.

Wood Type, Manufactured by Wm. H. Page & Co., Greeneville, Conn.

All Type and Borders, shown in this Book, have a name or number printed over it, by which it may be ordered, and therefore the page need not be mutilated by cutting out specimen lines, &c. to order by.

6 Line Egyptian Ornamented   D   7 Cents

Court District
SHORE LINE

8 Line Egyptian Ornamented   D   9 Cents

Demented
ISTHMUS

10 Line Egyptian Ornamented   D   11 Cents

REDER

12 Line Egyptian Ornamented   D   13 Cents

LIMES

15 Line Egyptian Ornamented   D   16 Cents

ROSE

20 Line Egyptian Ornamented   D   19 Cents

SEN

25 Line Egyptian Ornamented   D   23 Cents

TN

In ordering, leave out no part of the name or number printed over the line. The price for all sizes will be found in the Price List. All Letters made any size desired.

Printed with WADE'S INKS. from H. D. Wade & Co., 50 Ann St., New York.

Wm. H. Page, 1872.

---

89   THE WM. H. PAGE WOOD TYPE CO.

Four Line 512.   Class N

NEW PROCESS TYPE

Ten Line 512.   N

HORNED
Pine 45

Wm. H. Page, die cut specimens, 1890.

Specimens of Wood Type manufactured by The Hamilton Manufacturing Co., Two Rivers, Wis.

N

Hamilton, Large Wood Types, 1892.

Specimens of Wood Type Designs manufactured by The Hamilton Mfg. Co.

No. 3010   Class N   Morgan & Wilcox Mfg. Co.'s Skeleton Antique   6 Line, 8c per Letter

RENAGS damersh 2456

No. 4127   Class N   Wm. H. Page Co.'s Antique Skeleton   6 Line, 8c per Letter

RENADGS damers 2456

No. 4055   Class N   The Hamilton Mfg. Co.'s Special Antique Skeleton   6 Line, 8c per Letter

RENASTU 234567

No. 4071   Class N   The Hamilton Mfg. Co.'s Special Antique Skeleton   6 Line, 8c per Letter

REANST 2456

No. 3020   Class O   Heber Wells Skeleton Antique No. 1   6 Line, 8c per Letter

REN dae 256

No. 250   Class O   Wm. H. Page Co.'s No. 52   6 Line, 8c per Letter

REN dan 26

No. 3020   Class O   Morgan & Wilcox Mfg. Co.'s Geometric Light Face Condensed   6 Line, 8c per Letter

RENAS dame 2356

No. 3021   Class O   Morgan & Wilcox Mfg. Co.'s Geometric Light Face   6 Line, 8c per Letter

REN dan 16

All Type shown can be made in any size desired. Caps, Lower Case and Figures where shown. For prices of all sizes see Page 1.

Hamilton, 1906.

Traditionally there has been an attitude that American type manufacturers had only imitated European fashions in the nineteenth century—a notion often fostered by Europeans but readily accepted by Americans! A review of works by early American metal and wood type producers would indicate that they made more substantial contributions to typographic styles than has been supposed. This is particularly so in the field of refining or modifying existing designs. In this respect our typefounders were responsible for some important and handsome faces, and for a few peculiarly American designs which were never exported.

Although there has been little question regarding the leadership of American typefounders in the field after 1870, the period before this date has not had the deserved recognition of its importance to the development of display typography.

The contributions of the wood type industry to nineteenth-century American typefounding and printing are both concrete and substantial. First, wood type manufacturers made available the larger sizes of display types which were so widely used throughout the era. Although the typefounder cast types up to 24 lines, these were overly expensive and somewhat impractical to produce. After wood types were regularly marketed, the typefounders seldom cast any styles over 8 lines, so that wood types had the field of large type to themselves. The Nesbitt catalogue for 1838 showed 225 styles and sizes, plus several ornamental borders; the Wells & Webb catalogue of 1840 showed only slightly less than Nesbitt—a remarkable number of ornamental and large types for that day.

Second, wood type manufacturers introduced many European styles into this country. Even the most cursory examination of wood and metal specimen books from the 1830's and 1840's conclusively demonstrates this point. Many of the German perspectives, historiated styles, French Shaded designs, and all large Backslope Roman, Antique, and Gothic faces were sold only by the wood type manufacturers. Third, the processes and materials connected with the manufacture of wood type allowed the ornamentation of existing styles to a degree which was impractical for the typefounders to duplicate. The wood type manufacturer's freedom to outline, shade, double outline or otherwise embellish these styles permitted wood type catalogues to carry many designs that never showed in the typefounder's specimens. Occasionally, innovations by wood type designers were borrowed by the founders who cast these same designs in metal.

Fourth, many of the variations of solid faced letters, such as condensed and expanded, and particularly all those shades in between, came from the designs of wood type manufacturers, and some were adopted by the typefounders.

There were several designs cut in wood which were original with the wood type manufacturers. A few of these original productions were borrowed by the founders and included in their own repertory of metal types, notably Antique and Gothic Tuscans. Perhaps just as important as these original designs is the fact that wood type producers were responsible for the design of many lowercase fonts. This was particularly true for ornamental styles, as many of these did not have a lowercase. In Europe, it did not seem to be a regular practice for founders to include a lowercase, or figures, with their ornamental faces. Conversely, it was exceptional to find a design without a lower-

case in an American wood type specimen book. In the seventies and eighties, wood type catalogues showed lowercase for even the most extreme designs.

Lastly, cheapness and availability of wood types allowed their inclusion in shops of any size and at any location. Because of this widespread distribution, wood types played a significant role in all poster printing throughout the United States between 1828 and 1900. An examination of European ephemera from the 1860's on through the century illustrates that a considerable number of American wood types were also being used abroad during these years.

The artists who created the new styles in the early years are not generally known, although Darius Wells had a reputation as a fine draftsman of letters before he entered the wood type business. Edwin Allen was more interested in the mechanical than the artistic aspects of the trade. William Leavenworth, because of his known artistic bent, is thought to have created several original styles of type. Also, he is credited (along with a man named A. R. Gillmore) with changing letterforms from a full face to Condensed, Extra Condensed, and Double Extra Condensed (*Rounds' Monthly Printers' Cabinet*, Vol. I, No. 4, May 1857, "Wood Type"). Wells & Webb, Edwin Allen, and William Leavenworth were the only men making wood type in these first years of wood type manufacture, and the author's opinion is that the new designs were being produced mainly by Wells and Leavenworth.

Nesbitt and Allen seemed to have been more interested in keeping up with new styles than in creating them. They made this announcement in 1841 to the trade, "Having made arrangements to receive all the additions made to the assortment of types in the old country, printers can be supplied with new styles almost daily." Edwin Allen, after sealing his contract with George Nesbitt, was said to have hurried back to South Windham to set up his factory, where he introduced into wood the popular styles found in English and French as well as American specimen books. Since these specimen books seldom showed complete alphabets in the larger sizes, many of the wood copies most certainly varied from the originals because of improvisation by the American pattern makers in the instances where there were no models.

The one surviving specimen book of William Leavenworth, issued during the mid 1830's, included some unique wood type designs. Condensed and Italic styles of Roman, Antique, and Gothic had curious slitlike counters, and were composed in tight arrangements, creating a not unpleasant effect in a word or line of type. The hooks on the lowercase Roman letters were offset on the body so that they aligned with the hook of the adjoining letter—as if for a script. These letters were the only ones of their kind shown during the century by wood type manufacturers. There were also symmetrical Gothics: curvilinear letters based on circles, and an unusual cornered Gothic Full Face which appears to be based on a French design.

It is doubtful if John Cooley initiated any new designs during the 16 years he produced wood type. Labeled a "stealer of designs" by Bullen, he was an astute businessman, whose real love was publishing. Although there are new showings in his one existing catalogue, it is not known whether or not they were original with him. Charles Tubbs is said by a contemporary to have borrowed most of his letter styles from William Page, and there is nothing in his catalogues to suggest otherwise.

There are no known surviving catalogues of the W. T. & S. D. Day & Company. The only clue to their productions is in the one specimen book of D. Knox & Company in 1858. Since employees from the Day manufactory later worked with Knox, it is felt that they probably recut those faces which had been successful for the Day concern. There are a number of design innovations in the catalogue which are peculiar only to Knox, or perhaps, the Day Company. There are versions of semi-ornamented and ornamental Grecian, a curious treatment of Clarendon, and a number of semi-ornamental styles which show marked individuality of design.

Hamilton is thought to have followed styles already established, as he was mainly interested in the mechanical and business side of wood type manufacturing. Also, because his company expanded into areas of printing furniture and other new lines, he gradually became removed from direct involvement in wood type. In the last decade of the nineteenth century, the Hamilton Company paid royalties to cut and market in wood the new metal styles of the typefounders.

It appears that Heber Wells did not attempt to introduce many new styles, but contented himself with advertising established faces. Because there are, however, a few ornamented and semi-ornamented designs in his 1877 specimen book which are shown only by his company, he did market some exclusive styles.

Of all the men connected with the wood type industry, William Page is the one known with the most outstanding talent for designing letterforms and borders. Not only are his letter patents proof that he engaged in designing, but also there are records of his work in this field by contemporaries. For example, William E. Loy wrote for the *Inland Printer* on "Designers and Engravers of Type" in 1899: "The chief events in the career of William H. Page are so intimately connected with the development of the manufacture of wood type in America that a history of his life may be taken as the history of wood type making... besides being a designer of letters and a practical printer."

Page was among the first to realize the value of producing original works, or of incorporating some degree of originality into his design. Scarcely 3 years after entering the business he was to show a number of faces reflecting his own taste in decoration—particularly some checkered Tuscans and ornamented Gothics. In the 1860's he began to patent a number of German designs, and during the 1870's he patented a number of ornamental and chromatic styles. The title page of his 1874 specimen book states that all the designs with the exception of two or three are original with him. This specimen book, 1000 copies of which cost $10,000 to produce, has been rightfully acclaimed as containing the most superb wood type specimens ever printed. Many wood borders manufactured by Page, especially those after his invention of stamping patterns into wood, are undoubtedly of his own design since they were never shown or produced by any company other than Hamilton after he purchased the Page Company. Page also had a large number of chromatic borders in the famous specimen book of 1874. The design of these wooden borders appears to have been an art distinct from that of the typefounder.

The sensibilities of William Page for the artistic in fields other than letter and border designs found expression in designing ornamental gardens and in painting. He had experimented with wood engraving with what he described as "fair" success, and brought 12 years' experience in practical printing to the making of wood type. He was certainly the most prolific and best-recognized artist of the wood type industry in the nineteenth century.

During the 1860's, when American typefounders adopted the new French fashions of lighter styles, wood type manufacturers created original designs to an even greater extent than before. A number of their styles from this period never found translation into metal, and many of those designs copied after metal types found their greatest range of interpretations and finest rendering in wood. Near the end of the century, beginning in the 1880's, the wood type producers returned to the typefounder as a source of designs. The many popular metal types—those of Post, De Vinne, Bradley, Jenson, Pabst, Ben Franklin, and others—were cut in wood.

CHROMATIC SPECIMENS FROM THE WM. H. PAGE WOOD TYPE CO. GREENEVILLE, NORWICH, CONN.

Manufactured by Wm. H. Page & Co.

KINGDOM
MOUND
SIZE

HIDE
bctnf
GOTHS
ABCDE
HAT
ROSE
HOUSE

Wood type manufacturers were quick to realize that any modification of one letter could be applied equally to another one. Devices such as Outline, Outlined, Shade, etc., plus the condensing and expanding of solid-faced types, were adapted to the older styles, and to the new ones as they came onto the market. The multiplicity of designs from the nineteenth century can be attributed in large degree to the many adaptations of a single idea.

Innovations on the Wood Letters and Related Items

Especially for the wood type designs, any device successful with one style would usually be equally as successful with another. Devices such as Outline, Outlined, Tooled, Shade, etc. or any specific decorative motif could be applied to new designs as they came onto the market. The result of this practice has added considerable confusion to the identification of type faces because designs created at the end of the century would be treated with devices characteristic of the earliest years; e.g., the blending of the new letterform with older devices would tend to make a design appear older than it really was.

Documentation of the wood type manufacturer's abilities over those of the founder in experimenting with new styles or in copying designs appeared often in the preface to the wood type specimen books. Darius Wells stated in 1828, in the first wood type specimen book ever published, "Those wishing any particular size or proportion of type, different from any in this Specimen, have only to draw one letter, and forward it on, and they can have a fount made perfectly agreeing with the specimen sent." Also, he was to remark that customers could have any style with Shade or "opening the letter on one side" for a small additional cost.

Ten years later, George Nesbitt was to make an even more remarkable offer, "...and should any of his patrons wish a fount of type, a specimen of which is not herein exhibited, no matter if it should be of an entirely new drawing, and never before cut, they have only to draw one letter correctly, and the rest of the alphabet shall be designed, and a fount cut and delivered without any additional charge for getting out the pattern; and should they not give good satisfaction on delivery, they can be returned." Other wood type producers continued to advertise in the vein of Wells and Nesbitt throughout most of the century. If patterns could be made at no charge, cost obviously was a negligible factor for any wood type manufacturer wanting to introduce new designs. These conditions allowed more freedom for experimentation than had been known by any producers of type, wood or metal, up to that time. Not only did the wood type manufacturer embellish, and invent new styles, but in time he was to market a variety of decorative pieces such as ornaments, dashes, borders, and logotypes.

The practice of reversing a type face on a decorative or solid ground begun in the 1820's was perhaps first done on a small scale such as for check figures, but very quickly found a broader application as a decorated letter. Nicolette Gray states that Reverses probably originated in England or Germany during the late 1830's (although reversed check figures are common before that date). The Nesbitt catalogue showed one paled Reverse in 1838, and several other similar styles in 1841, which are definitely European in origin. The Paled Reverses—with a thin white line between letters and usually a pointed top and bottom on each letter field—are characteristic of the earliest reversed designs. They are believed to have been designed in this manner consciously to avoid problems of alignment in make-up and printing.

After the common use of European Reverses during the 1830's and 1840's, there seemed to be a lull before the American styles came onto the market in numbers. In 1879, Page announced that nearly all types among its specimens could be ordered in the reverse styles. At this time, the paling had disappeared, and all letter styles were American. Page offered more in the way of reversed styles than any other wood type company, except Hamilton after he bought the Page Company.

The majority of these designs were simply a letter reversed on a block. These blocks butted against one another, and either end of the line was capped with a choice of ornamental pieces. Each font included a variety of type-high spacing materials, and the printer would often use wax to seal the spaces between letters to assure an even printing of the field. A variation of the Reverse, first introduced by Page, was called Streamers. It was similar to the Reverse but differed in that the letters were type-high on an oversized block—top and bottom. There would also be a type-high line at top and bottom of the block which in a word or line composition created an outline panel around the letters. Streamers were also capped at either end with an ornamental piece. Somewhat later in the century, some Reverses were marketed that were designed so that each letter and its field would stand separate from the next. Usually the letter bodies had either an oval, a circular, or some decorative shape (shapes would be type-high but mounted on a squared body to facilitate make-up). The Reverses were fashionable up until the last decade of the century, and then gradually disappeared. Solid, blank reverse panels were also marketed, which the printer could assemble to a proper size, print in color, and then overprint in black with conventional wood types. A number of the earliest Reverses were designed to be printed in more than one color. Page was to show a large number of the Chromatic Reverses during the 1870's and 1880's.

Chromatic types, type faces made to print in two or more colors, were advertised by Nesbitt in 1838. Appearing quite regularly in the founders' specimen books (notably those of Bruce and Hagar) during the 1840's and 1850's, most of these designs were done in a manner that allowed the printer to use the letter in one color as well as in two. Once more William Page dominated the production of this particular style of type in both wood and metal. His efforts culminated in the previously mentioned specimen book of 1874, which was devoted entirely to Chromatic Types. Many of these handsome styles, designed so that one color would overlap another and thus create a third color, demanded the ultimate in careful workmanship, both in manufacturing and printing. The Chromatics were printed from separate blocks; and in their manufacture, one pantograph setting had to be used for cutting both blocks, because otherwise it was impossible to achieve the perfect register needed to assure a fine printing. Chromatics, which lent themselves to the prevailing styles of colored bill printing that began in America during the 1840's and lasted throughout the century, are representative of the finest work produced by wood type manufacturers at any time in their history.

Wooden borders were manufactured by wood type producers at an early date, the first being in the specimens of George F. Nesbitt in his 1838 catalogue. The first wood borders were patterned after European styles, one of the most typical of that period being variations on the Greek Fret. However, borders were not shown in great numbers until the Page catalogue of 1859. It is thought that these designs, the majority of which were shown as borders around specimen pages, were original to Page. Most of the borders were based on a vine or floral motif.

Reverse shown by Nesbitt, 1838. Same reverse shown in Paris by De Berny in the thirties, and in England during the next decade.

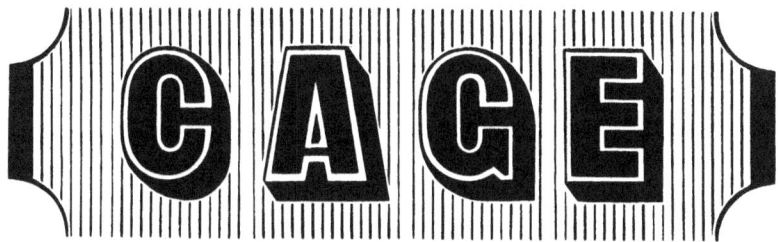

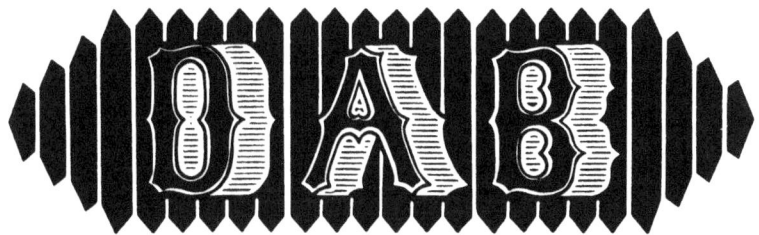

Reverses with ornamental caps shown by William Page, 1879.

Hamilton, 1892.

Reverses and Streamers designed in units and cut by Page before 1891.

No. 3236—Class P   Morgans & Wilcox Mfg. Co.'s Eclipse

No. 3237—Class P   Morgans & Wilcox Mfg. Co.'s Scranton

No. 381—Class P   Wm. H. Page Co.'s Block Streamer No. 7

In about 1879, William Page perfected a means for stamping ornamental borders, probably with steel dies and hydraulic pressure. As these borders had shallow counters, the designs were quite intricate and often geometric. The borders were manufactured in great quantities. The printer could purchase a variety of corner pieces which would be interchangeable with different borders. There is no evidence that any other wood type company produced these stamped ornamental borders except Page (and Hamilton after his purchase of the Page Company). End-cut borders continued to be produced even though the stamped designs were more economical. Wood borders ranged in size from ¼ inch to 3 inches in width.

Sometime during the 1870's, it became fairly common to find a variety of wooden ornaments, arrows, hands, stars, etc. In 1872, Page showed one full page of hands in two styles and various sizes. Ornaments appear to have become common somewhat later. In the 1890 Page catalogue of die-cut types, there were a number of wood ornaments. Hamilton was to show perhaps sixty such ornaments during the 1890's. A peculiar ornament shown by Hamilton, and perhaps produced by Page also, was the quarter or half rounds. These were very intricate circular designs which were manufactured as either half or quarter units. Assembled units (4 quarters) that came to the author's attention averaged about 6 to 8 inches in diameter. Another item sold by wood type houses around 1880 were catch words—"of, the, in, office of," etc. These were very convenient for the printer in composing lines where he wanted to reduce copy in order to keep the type as large as possible. Near the end of the century, Hamilton advertised "Perpetual Calendar" sets cut in wood. They consisted of figures, logotypes for the months, and other decorative materials for printing calendars. Vanderburgh, Wells & Company during the 1870's showed a number of bag ornaments: shocks of wheat, scythes, banners, and other related stock cuts.

American wood type manufacturers cut many wood letters in foreign languages—both for export and for domestic use. Hebrew, Greek, and German types were cut mostly for use in this country, but Russian, Chinese, and Burmese were manufactured for export only.

Connor had begun to cast German in metal about the middle of the century. Page, who followed soon after with wood types, began to patent his German styles in 1866. In 1870 he published a handsome small catalogue exclusively of German faces. Hamilton was to devote a large portion of his first specimen book to German types. An old printer told the author that in North Dakota just before 1900, there were more German newspapers than English, which reflects the great migration of German speaking people to the United States from the mid-nineteenth century on through the homesteading period. Hebrew types were distributed mostly in the large Eastern cities, and even today, one may find examples of these types still in use in New York, Philadelphia, and Boston.

The *Norwich Bulletin* for January 2, 1875, gives the following account of an order received by the William Page Company: "(They) received an order from China for wood type to be cut in Chinese characters. They are to represent Sunday School hymns, Scriptures, etc., and will be used by Christian missionaries. Page had made up an assortment for this work five years ago, and this order arises from that work. The people of Norwich are

Twelve line Pica Grecian Border, Nesbitt, 1838.

Seven Line Pica Grecian Border. 2 colors. 16 cts.

Nesbitt, 1841.

SIX LINES PICA GRECIAN BORDER

SIXTEEN LINES PICA GRECIAN BORDER No. 2

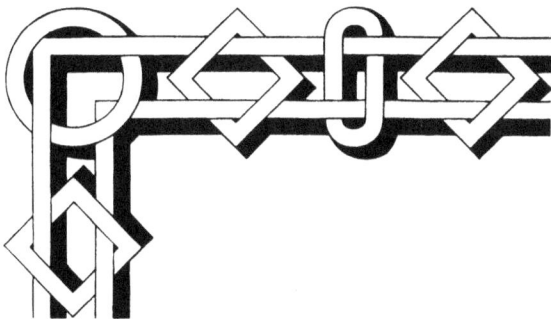

Wells & Webb, 1854.

SIX LINES PICA GRECIAN BORDER.

SIX LINES PICA BORDER No. 2.

Bill, Stark & Co., 1853.

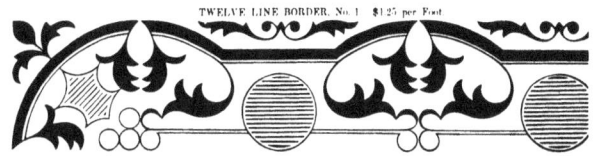

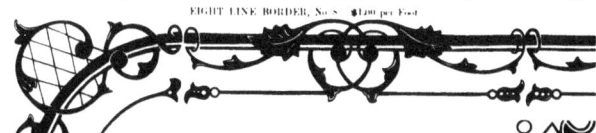

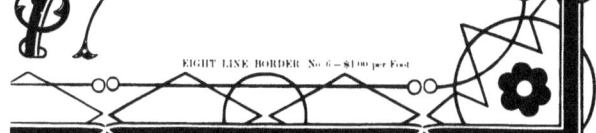

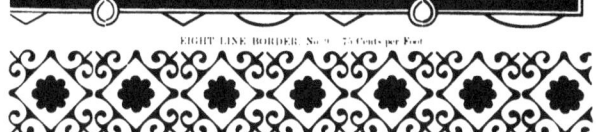

TWELVE LINE BORDER, No. 1 $1.25 per Foot

TEN LINE BORDER No. 5 — $1.25 per Foot

TEN LINE BORDER No. 4 $1.25 per Foot

EIGHT LINE BORDER, No. 8 $1.00 per Foot

EIGHT LINE BORDER No. 6 — $1.00 per Foot

EIGHT LINE BORDER No. 9   75 Cents per Foot

Routed borders shown by William Page, 1859.

Cooley, 1859.

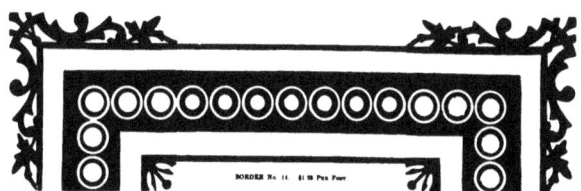

National Printers' Materials, 1887.

Routed borders shown by Hamilton in 1906, but believed to have been designed by William Page.

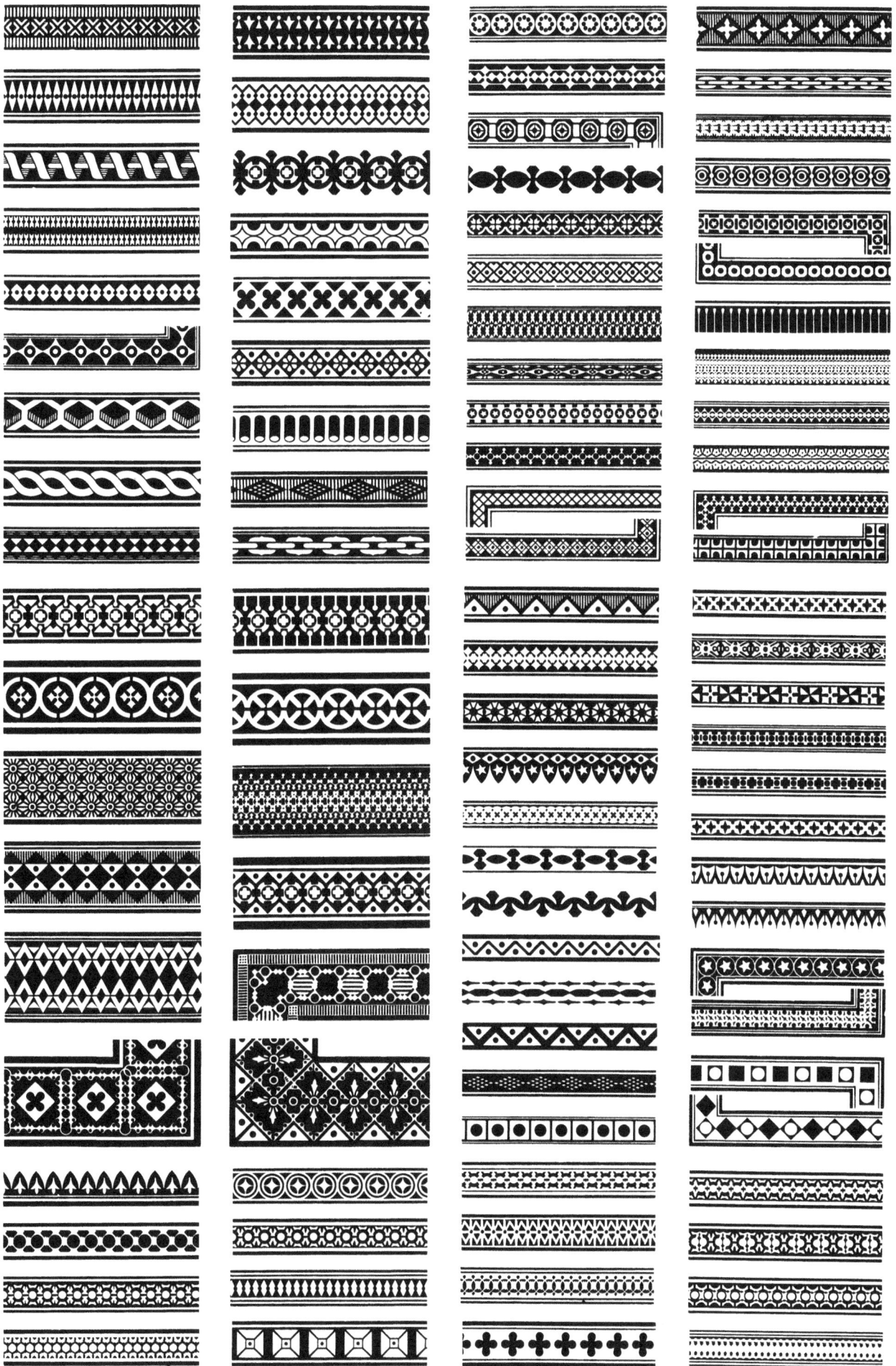

Die-stamped borders by Page.

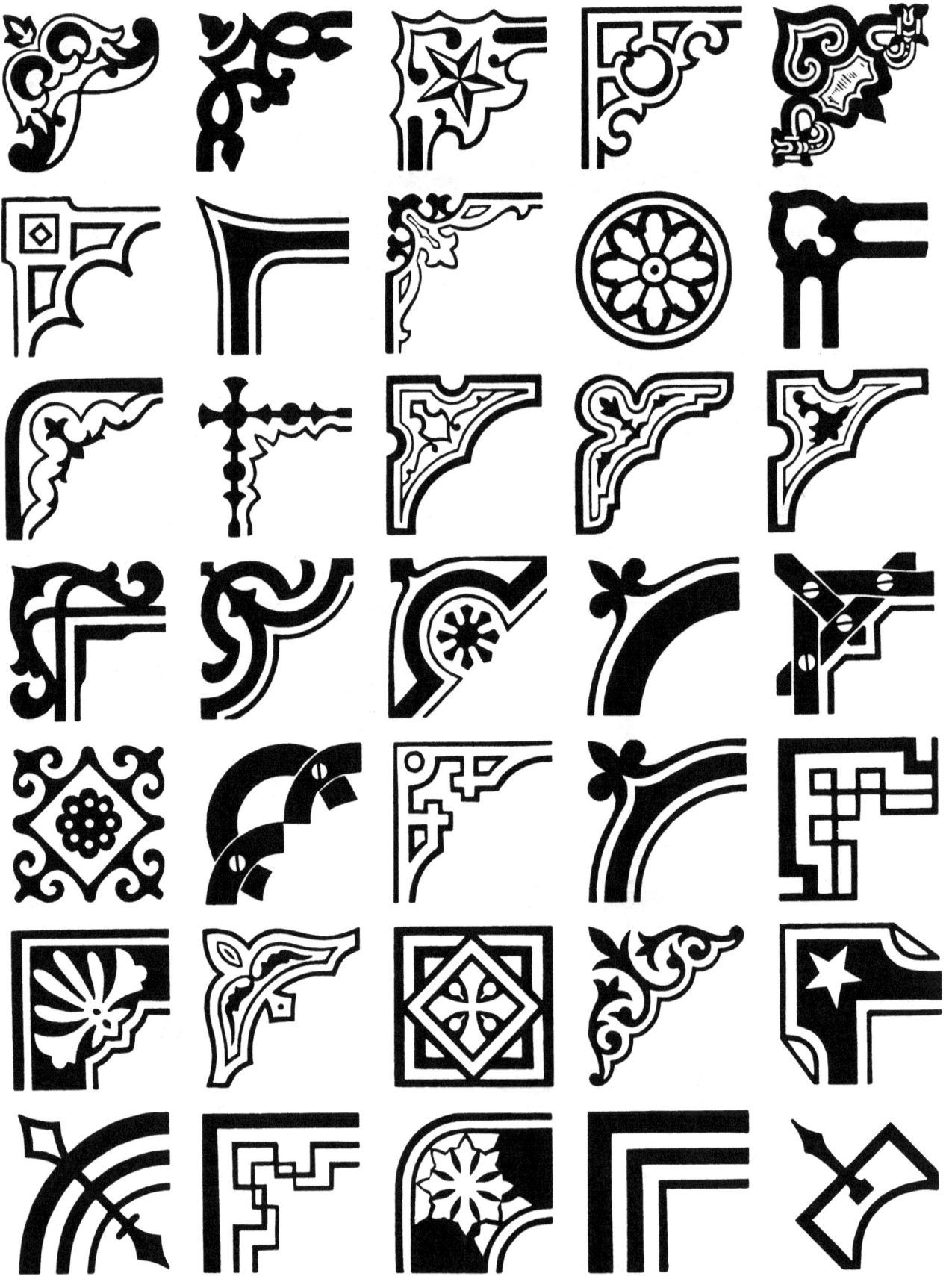

Ornamental corners, Hamilton, 1906.

Ornamental tailpiece, Hamilton, 1906.

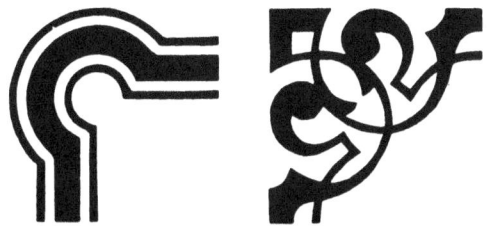

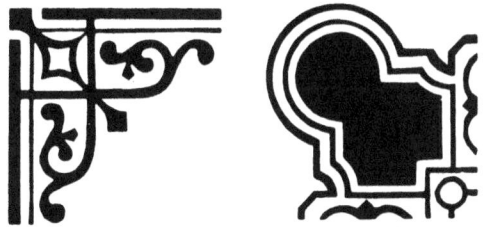

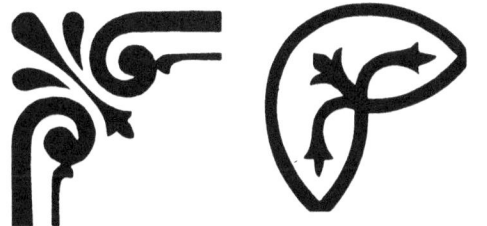

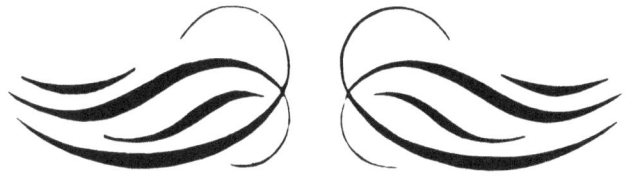

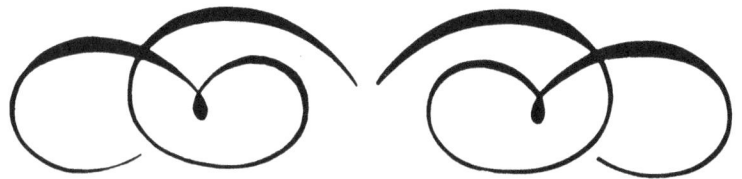

Wood flourishes, Hamilton, 1906.

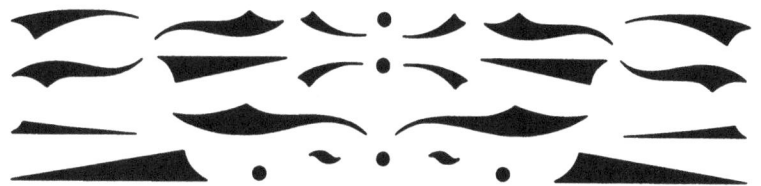

Wood pointers, Hamilton, 1906.

Seven Line Space Ornaments. 402   403

401

407

409

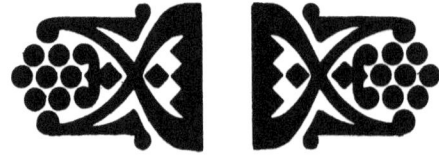

408

400

Eight Line Space Ornaments.   405

Die-cut wood ornaments shown by Page, 1890.

Wood ornaments shown by Hamilton in his 1906 specimens.

Custom-made monograms, any size, all companies.

Quarter rounds, Hamilton, 1892.

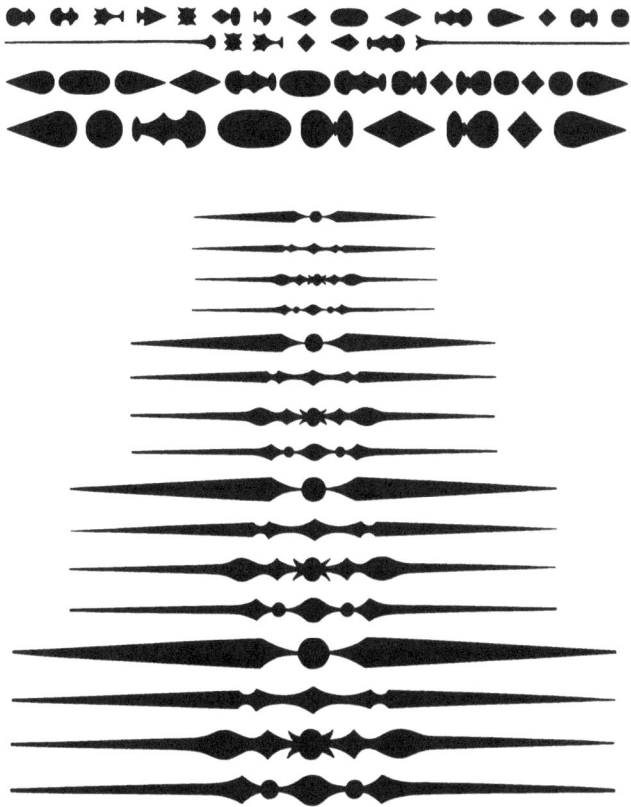

Extension dashes and dashes, Hamilton, 1892.

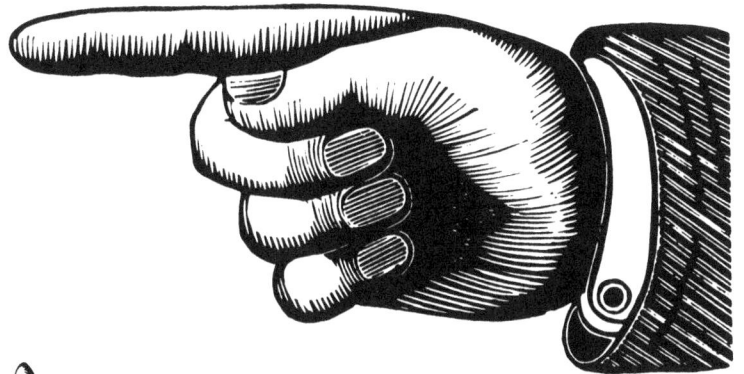

Hands, Wm. H. Page, 1872.

Stars, Hamilton, 1892.

Bag ornament and logotypes, Vanderburgh & Wells, 1877.

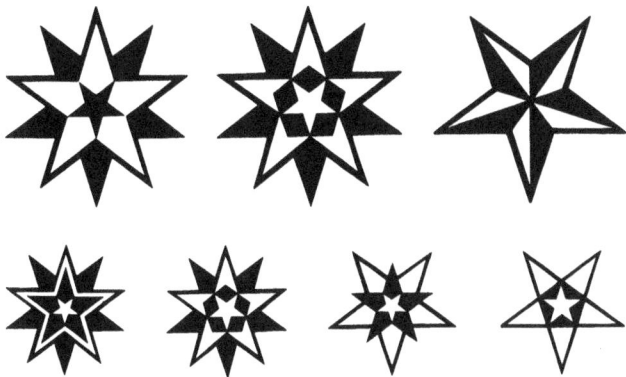

Catch-words, Hamilton, 1892.

Prozeßboes

Composite Condensed (German). Page, 1870.

℧ΨΔΣ

Greek. Hamilton, 1906.

מוצבאגבה

Hebrew. Hamilton, 1906.

Burmese. Hamilton, 1906 (Page design).

RENAS dane 25
Antique Condensed, Hamilton

RENA dane 25
Antique Condensed, Page

RENS dane 25
Antique Condensed, Heber Wells

RENS dan 25
Antique Condensed, Morgan & Wilcox

Shown here are four specimens of the same design by four different companies. It can easily be seen how variations in cutting a design between different companies added to the typographical confusion.

Wm. H. Page Co.'s No. 93

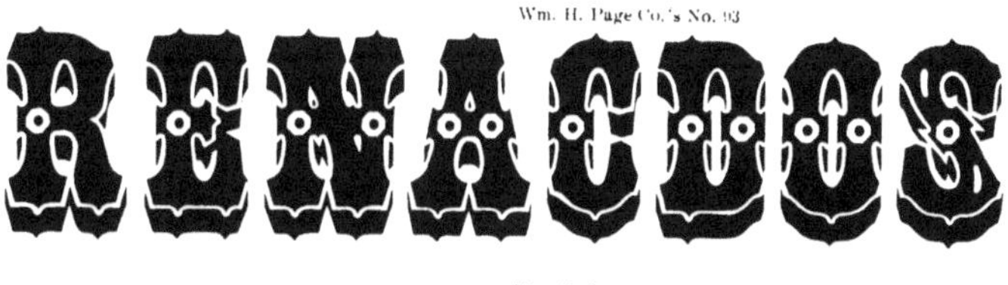

RENACDOS

Wm. H. Page Co.'s No. 96

RENACDOS

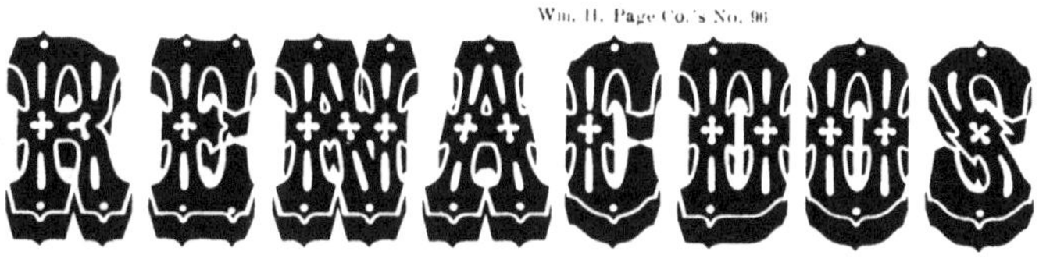

Wm. H. Page Co.'s 'Renaissance' No. 1

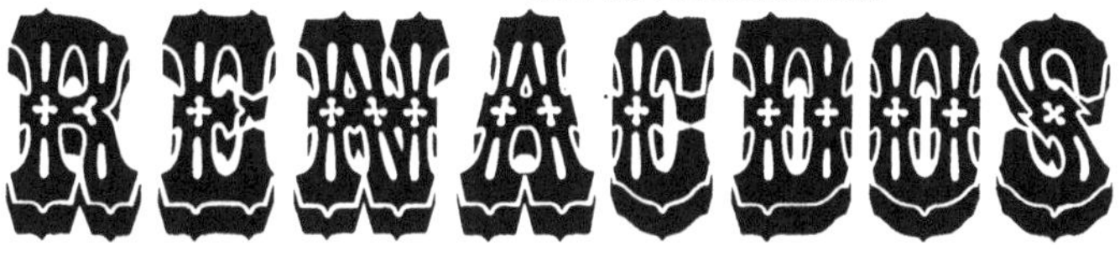

RENACDOS

Throughout the era, but especially near the end of the century, it was a fairly common practice to make one pattern in such a manner that several styles could be cut from a single pattern-block. In the instance shown here, three styles are cut from a single pattern.

Shading on the interior of the letterform remained popular until the 1850's and then gradually disappeared. The use of shading had carried over from the eighteenth-century engravers, and in all probability it came into disfavor because of the inherent fragility of so many fine lines.

Dimensional letters were exceedingly popular during the first half of the century, and a few of the more common means for creating an illusion of dimension are shown here.

85

Roman

Antique

Gothic

Aetna

Clarendon Full Face

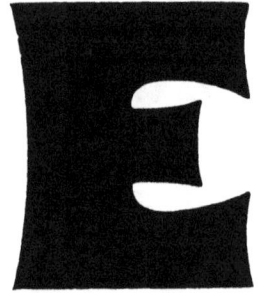

Concave Tuscan

Old Style

Antique Tuscan

Teutonic

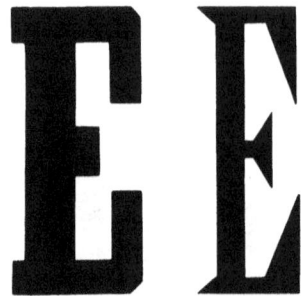

Grecian X Condensed; Latin X Condensed

Bevel

invited to visit the plant and view these Chinese letters."
The Burmese faces shown by Hamilton in its 1906 cata-
logue are known to have been originally cut by the Page
Company.

Titling

It was in the titling of type faces that the wood type
manufacturers' practices differed most from those of the
typefounder. This difference provides an excellent guide
to the evolution of styles, classifications, and families of
all type faces produced in the nineteenth century. Lacking the flexibility of sizes inherent to the wood types,
the metal types, particularly the ornamental ones, were
titled with a number and a size. In the earliest years, the
customer could order by size only—Two Line English
Ornamental, for example, which would be quite a difference from the Two Line Pica Ornamental design. As the
founder increased his repertory, there would be a number
after "Ornamental"—Double Paragon Ornamental No. 6,
Canon Ornamental No. 6, etc.—which would designate
two sizes of the same design. However, since the number-
ing system was peculiar to one company, the same design
would be titled under a different number by another founder. As new designs were added, a new number would be
assigned and, as the number of sizes increased for a given
design, sequential numbers would be used.

With wood type, since size was simply a matter of the
customer's choice, up to the late 1870's a name was assigned to each face. All the wood type manufacturers used
the same names. There were a few exceptions—notably
some ornamental styles and the semi-ornamental faces.
Also, because of the ease of making patterns, the wood
type manufacturers marketed variations in a design much
more quickly than typefounders. The most common
device was either to condense or expand a letter. Wood
type manufacturers devised a system of Condensed, Extra
Condensed, Double Extra Condensed, Treble Extra Condensed and Extended and Expanded. This system was
never used as consistently or to the same degree by the
typefounders as it was by wood type producers.

Another very useful peculiarity of wood type titling
was that the name of the parent letterform was consistently
employed in the titles of the derivative designs—e.g.,
Antique Tuscan, Gothic Tuscan, Clarendon Italian. Wood
types as well carried the title of the parent family in the
modifications of Light Face, Extended, and Full Face,
whereas the founder was likely to assign an unrelated
name to each style of the same design.

One of the most outstanding consistencies of the wood
types is found in the title of Antique. The same face was
first called Antique by the English, but later labeled
Egyptian so that today either name is used. American
typefounders used the two names interchangeably, but
wood type manufacturers retained the name Antique in
every instance. There was a totally separate design called
Egyptian, which was marketed in the 1870's by wood type
distributors.

*The top row shows the primary faces of Roman, Antique,
and Gothic. Letters directly under each face represent the
main secondary designs which, in turn, frequently were
basic letterforms for additional families of type. This
chart is not complete but indicates in a small way the
derivative nature of many nineteenth-century wood type
designs.*

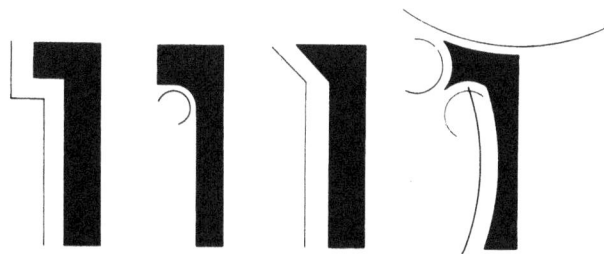

Antique

Clarendon

Latin / Antique Tuscan

Tuscans

*Chart illustrating how a variety of letter styles derived
from a basic Antique.*

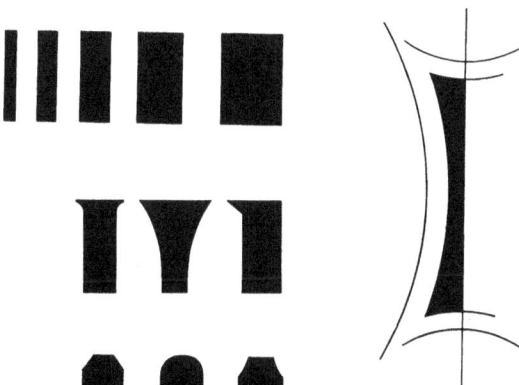

*Chart illustrating how a variety of letter styles derived
from a basic Gothic.
Series, pulling corners into points, cornering, Gothic
Tuscans.*

Solid, or plain faced. No interior decoration; contours usually regular.

Italic. Letter slanted to the right. Almost any style could be italicized.

Backslope. Letter slanted to the left. Referred to as "Contra Italic" by Nicolette Gray. This style probably began in England with the Fat Face Romans. American wood type manufacturers cut Gothic, Antique, and Roman Backslope during the first half of the century, and there were only a very few styles of backslope issued by the founder. Most notable were some small Romans by L. Johnson, small Ornamentals, Bulletin script and Grotesque Italian.

Ornamented. Refers to an interior embellishment of the letterform.

Semi-Ornamented. Identified through ambivalent figure / ground relationships in the counters or spaces between letters and the letterforms themselves.

European Tuscans. Frequently have interior embellishment, and the letterforms are based on Tuscans modelled after decorated initials from manuscripts. The designs are usually not derivative.

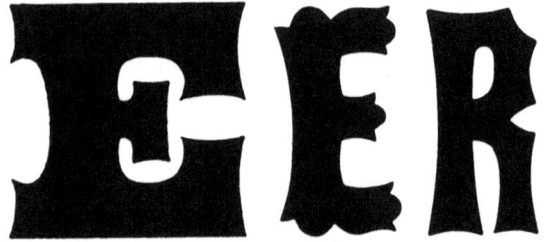

American Tuscans. Letters have Tuscan characteristics but are often derived from a primary face and in many instances are cut in a series or related to other similar designs.

Historiated. Most often a primary Fat Face with interior motifs based on nature—landscapes, people, animals, fruits or flowers, etc., but may use architectural motifs, tools, etc.

Perspective. The letterform is drawn in perspective— slanted, lying flat, etc. Most often associated with German styles, but a few came from England.

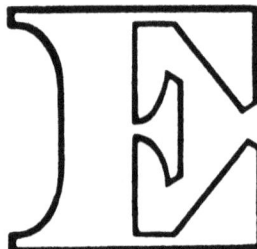

Outline. A single line delineates the letterform.

Modulated Outline. Weight of the outline changes to create the illusion of slight relief.

Outlined, Rimmed or Fluted. A solid face with an outline which creates a white line inline.

Double Outlined. Parallel lines defining the letter, the outside line usually being the heavier.

Tooled. A single line cut parallel to one side of the letter—either right or left. A device used a great deal with the Roman letter in the eighteenth century. It was carried over to the nineteenth century and applied to a great variety of type styles.

Open Shade. An outline letter with a solid shade—usually emphasis to the right.

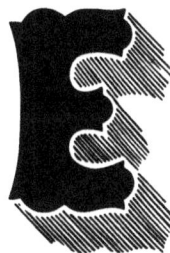

Outlined with Shade. An outlined letter with the addition of a solid shade. The resulting white inline is even more pronounced than in the Outlined styles.

Solid Faced with Open Shade. Letter is solid and shade is outline.

Meridian Shade. Either an open- or solid-faced style, with shade vertical and sometimes at the top of the letter.

Line Shade. The effect is similar to the Tooled, but the line is outside the letterform, whereas in the Tooled it is within.

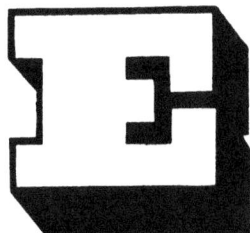

Ray Shade. A shade formed by parallel lines. Often combined with other styles of ornamentation. Most common in the 1840's.

Interior Shading. Inside of the letterform embellished with parallel lines—vertical, horizontal, diagonal, and sometimes graduated.

Chromatic. Letters designed in two blocks to print in two colors.

Reverse. Letter reversed in solid block. Line is terminated at either end with ornamental caps.

Paled Reverse. Designed to print with fine white lines running vertically. It is believed that the design was made to eliminate problems of alignment of the solid bodies, and printing of same.

Streamer. Similar to the Reverse in that the type is on an oversize body, but differs in that the letterform and a line at top and bottom of the block will print, thus creating an outline panel with type inside.

The wood type titling system began to break down in the 1870's and 1880's because of the fiercely competitive marketing conditions. New styles were pirated and given different names to create an illusion of bringing out new designs. The April, 1879, volume of *Page's Wood Type Album* carried a notice to the trade which announced, "hereafter we shall adopt numbers to designate our type instead of names, which after all have no particular meaning." This statement is not entirely true since the designs tended to lose their identity because of the difficulty of associating a design with a number. For example, many people today have reacted against the substitution of digits for prefix names in telephone numbers. However, with the number of metal and wood type producers then operating in America and the multitude of designs on the market, there were real problems for both the customer and the manufacturer in the matter of ordering. *Ringwalt's Encyclopaedia of Printing,* published in 1871, noted, "There are now made in the United States more than two hundred radically different styles of job letter, besides about the same number which receive the common name of Ornamented, though each differs from the other. Including size and style, the variety of metal job letter now in use far exceeds two thousand, exclusive of Scripts which number more than a hundred. Among the two hundred styles which have been called radically different, many differ as widely within themselves as from other distinct families (reference to Light Face, Extended, Condensed, etc.). . . . This is independent of wood type, which varies as much in style as metal type, and by scope it affords in size, may be extended to more than twenty thousand distinct alphabets."

The importance of the wood type titling system should not be underestimated. The partial dissolution of it in the late 1870's does not alter its effectiveness since all the basic styles had been previously designed. Because most of the display types of the typefounder can be classified under the wood type system, a common terminology can be developed. Only the Tuscan and Ornamental designs, which seem difficult to classify or describe as groups, are best handled on an individual basis.

However, Nicolette Gray has done an excellent job of grouping the Tuscans by period according to such design characteristics as median bulges, trifurcated or bifurcated serifs, etc. (*XIXth Century Ornamented Type Types and Title Pages,* Nicolette Gray, "Analysis of Variations of the Tuscans," p. 103.)

Classifications

The fantastic volume of type designs from the nineteenth century made classifying these designs into some semblance of order very difficult. As just mentioned, part of the confusion springs from the typefounders not titling their designs within a common system as did the wood type manufacturers. To the uninitiated, the typographic output of the nineteenth century appears a mass of unrelated designs. However, there was more of an evolutionary continuity to the development of styles than has been supposed.

In the group of solid faced types, a tremendous number of these designs can be classed as either primary faces: Roman, Antique, and Gothic, or secondary styles, which are derivative from the primary ones. A Gothic which is either Outlined, Cornered, Ornamented, Expanded, or Condensed, is still basically a Gothic, and by extending

As a design became popular, the number of variations on it increased. By the 1840's, all primary and many secondary faces were cut in a "series." By the 1880's, this series included almost all the variations shown above.

First Row: Roman XXX Condensed, XX Condensed, X Condensed, Condensed, Roman, and Extended.

Second Row: Antique XXX Condensed, XX Condensed, XX Condensed No. 1, X Condensed, Condensed, Antique, Special, and Extended.

Third Row: Gothic XXX Condensed, XX Condensed, X Condensed, Condensed, Gothic, Expanded, and Extended.

this same reasoning to Roman and Antique, one can account for the lineage of the majority of display designs from the period. Tuscans, especially the European models, have to be handled as a separate category, because many of these designs do represent independent inventions. These can be considered according to design characteristics such as serifs, notches, bulges, etc.

Display types from the period are generally broken down into the following categories: Ornamented, Semi-Ornamented, Plain Faces, Texts, Scripts, and Ornaments and Borders. Occasionally there are problems separating the Semi-Ornamented from the Plain Faces, and an arbitrary judgment will have to be made. A third category of grouping would be the "series" (as it pertains to wood types). This refers to the various degrees of Extending and Condensing or changing the weight of a single design. By the 1840's, all primary faces of Antique, Roman, and Gothic were cut in additional styles of Condensed, X Condensed, XX Condensed, Extended, and some were cut as Light Face. The condensing and expanding of type designs has been attributed to Americans more than to Europeans, and there is strong evidence that many of these variations sprang from the wood type producers. In most wood type specimens after the middle of the century, particularly in the 1870's and afterwards, all of the primary, and several of the secondary faces, were cut in a series of six to eight weights or styles. No specimen book of the founders during these same years ever showed an equal number of variations on a single style.

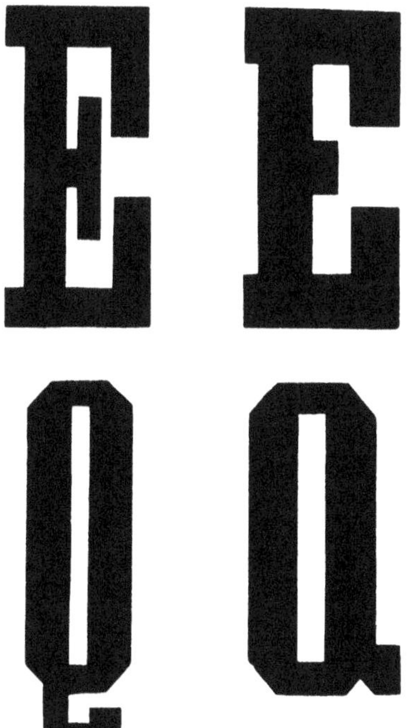

A serif on the middle arm of the E and hanging tail on the Q are characteristic of the older designs. Examples on the right show the modifications which were most commonly used after 1850.

1828 Through 1849

This period in American printing history was the beginning of the rapid expansion of printing and all its related trades into an industry which reached immense proportions by the end of the century. At this time foreign machinery and workmen trained abroad were essential to the American industry, for Americans were just beginning to advance their own ideas and inventions. The first presses, such as those of Ramage, Wells, Treadwell, Smith, and Adams, were the most common printing machinery found in the American printing shops. Bruce, Starr, Lothian, and a few other men were designing and cutting the first type styles to originate in this country.

While there were a tremendous number of inventions in the printing trades during this period, there were a few key improvements in the development of typographic styles. The introduction of the gelatin rollers greatly facilitated the printing of elaborate ornamental types; the improved presses later in the period, especially those of Hoe, Taylor, Gordon, and others, not only increased production but resulted in a higher quality of work. Also important were the pump-injection devices used in casting type (the invention of David Bruce, Jr.). The electrotype matrix by Thomas Starr in the forties lead to the proliferation of all type designs; and there were corresponding refinements in the making of ink and paper.

In 1850, Joel Munsell of upstate New York was to describe the trades as then being divided into three categories: newspaper, card and jobbing, and book publishing —the latter being dominant. New York was the largest printing center of the time. Philadelphia and Boston were also primary centers for the printing trades, and small shops were profusely scattered throughout the countryside. Many of the foreign craftsmen located in New York, Boston, and Philadelphia constituted a sizable element of the skilled labor required for the practice of the trade. Competent workmen could make $9 to $15 a week, and almost all work was piece work. In the printing centers, workmen were scaled into three groups: two thirders (apprentices after 2 years), country printers, and city printers, who received the highest wages for their labor. In these years, "subbers" constituted a large part of the work force. As most of the composition was done on a piece-work basis, employers would hire these part-time compositors according to the work load demanded. Early each morning the subbers would gather outside the newspaper and publishing houses to compete for work with other "subbers." If the price of composition became too high, the printers could practice the simple expedient of placing advertisements under a ficticious name or the name of a competitor to announce great amounts of work or high wages then being paid in the city. The rush of compositors into the city would immediately drive prices down, since competition increased according to the number of men seeking work. It is small wonder that the strike of typographers in the succeeding period did not take place at this time!

During the 1840's the first poster houses were established in Boston and New York City for the printing of broadsides. The fact that specialized printers like this could successfully operate reflects the general growth of printing during these years.

Men working on improved or automatic equipment (power presses or paper-making machinery) were forced to work in absolute secrecy to prevent the tradesmen who feared being replaced by machinery from destroying the new inventions. In several instances, equipment was actually destroyed by fire at the hands of the workers.

The great era of printing expansion began at about the same time that the first wood type specimen book was printed—the one issued by Darius Wells in March of 1828, in New York City. There were 10 years between the first Wells' publication and the next surviving specimen book, which was that of Allen's types brought out by George F. Nesbitt in 1838. What developments took place in this 10-year interim can only be surmised, but when Wells formed Wells & Company in 1835, he undoubtedly gained additional capital from his new partners which permitted him to expand his operations. Leavenworth began manufacturing wood type circa 1834; Allen began to manufacture his types in 1836. Between 1835 and 1849 the competition between the three wood type manufacturers must have been a spur to the production of new styles.

The main design emphasis in this period was on Fat Face versions of the primary families and Ornamental styles. Secondary styles or first modifications of primary faces were first shown. The styling for the most part was heavy and boxy. Tooled Antiques, which were an extension of the Tooled Romans dating back into the previous century, were popular. Specimen books of both metal and wood type manufacturers included the large Roman and Antique Open Shades of the English founders. The same ornamental treatment as previously applied to the Roman and Antiques was extended to the heavy Gothics shortly after they were first introduced in the thirties. Backslopes in the large display sizes were restricted to the wood type producers, and were in greatest evidence in this period. Romans, the basic letterform for Ornamental designs, were extensively applied in these years although they gradually disappeared from specimen books afterwards. The large Inside-Shaded Ornamentals of French, German, and English origin, with floral or other decorative motifs, plus a few of the European Tuscans, were shown regularly in all specimen books.

During the entire century, but particularly during this first period, the refinement of letters cut in wood was considerably greater than that found in the same designs produced by the typefounders. The ease of shaping wood was undoubtedly a factor governing the superior manner in which the plain faces—both capitals and lowercase— were executed by wood type manufacturers.

At the beginning, the design sources were almost all European, and the use of Shades was a dominating treatment of the letterform. Open, Ray, Half, Line, Meridian, and combinations or variations of these Shades prevailed in quantities not duplicated in any other period. During the second half of the era the American wood type manufacturers marketed in advance of the founders designs based on the older devices of Shade, Outline, etc., and the new letter styles as they became fashionable (e.g., the Clarendons, American Tuscans).

The Antiques

Wood type Antique is a slab-serif letter, unbracketed and, in most instances, with a serif that is nearly equal in weight to the stem. The serif is heavier than the stem in French Antique, Egyptian Antique, and some of the Specials; it is lighter than in Antique, Antique Light Face, and Extended Antique. Mowry Antique, cut by William

MENTAL
manifest
MENTAL
MENTAL

Wells, 1828.

BDE
abcd

HAN
hast

HED

Nesbitt, 1838.

Page, has a heavy bottom serif and a light top serif.

The principal derivative faces of Antique are Clarendon, Antique Tuscan, Grecian, Latin, French Egyptian Antique, Aldine, Columbian, Ionic, and French Clarendon. Antique and its secondary designs, as well as Ornamental Antiques and its secondary face, constitute a major portion of the nineteenth-century typographic styles.

The first Antiques shown by Darius Wells included an Antique Backslope that may have originated with him. Nicolette Gray has shown no such style on her design charts for English founders, and American typefounders demonstrated very little partiality for the Backslope styles. To the author's knowledge, the only Backslopes produced by American founders were a few sizes of Roman cut by Richard Starr for Johnson of Philadelphia, the Bulletin scripts originating with David Bruce, Jr., Italian by Connor, some European perspectives which were imported, and an occasional Backslope Gothic later in the century. In contrast to the typefounders, wood type manufacturers marketed a great number of Backslope designs up until 1850, and only occasionally after that date. Darius Wells also showed an Antique Italic without lowercase, and an Antique with lowercase and figures. Italic Antique was shown by Nesbitt in his 1838 specimens. Wells' Antique was considerably heavier with more pronounced shading than the original Antique by Figgins in 1815.

Ten years after Darius Wells' first specimen book, George Nesbitt dispayed an amazing variety of Antiques. His specimens included Antique Condensed with lowercase and Antique Extra Condensed without lowercase—the latter was shown 2 years later by Wells and Webb; Antique No. 2 which was a sightly expanded design was introduced with a lowercase; Antique Italic had a lowercase; Ornamental styles of Double Outlined Antique with vertical interior shading; Antique Condensed with Ray Shade, Antique Outlined Shade; and an Antique Italic Line Shade—each had a lowercase. Both Antique and Condensed were exhibited as Outlined, but neither had a lowercase; Antique Condensed Tooled was a new showing and did not include a lowercase.

The Clarendon-like Outlined Antiques originating with Figgins in 1821 and produced by American typefounders as early as 1828 at the Boston foundry did not show up in the specimens of wood type manufacturers. It is difficult to understand the reason for this omission.

Perhaps the most significant innovation in the Antiques during these years was Antique Expanded, complete with lowercase and figures as shown by Nesbitt in 1838. Nicolette Gray credits the design to the Americans around 1841. Elihu White of New York City showed a metal version of Egyptian Expanded Outline Shade in 1839, but this design looked more Roman than Antique, largely because of the extremely thin serifs. It certainly lacked the authority of the Nesbitt specimens!

The wood type version of Antique Expanded did not show up in the founders' specimens regularly for another 10 or 12 years. In 1851 the first specimens issued by the founders were those of the Boston Type Foundry, which had no lowercase. Hagar expanded the series in 1854 to four sizes with a lowercase. There had been an Antique Expanded Tooled first shown by White in 1849. More like the wood letter version, this design was to turn up regularly for the next 15 years.

The sequence of Antique Expanded in this country followed the initial showing by Nesbitt in wood in 1838 and

12 LINE PICA ANTIQUE NO. 2

HED hum

10 LINE PICA ANTIQUE ITALIC

PHIR court

14 LINE PICA ANTIQUE, LINE & SHADE

IDE

12 LINE PICA ITALIAN

HOLD

2 LINE ANTIQUE EXTENDED

AMERICA scienticomk

Nesbitt, 1838.

metal specimens of Open Shade by White in 1839, Tooled by White in 1849, and the Boston Type Foundry in 1851. The latter appears to be the model for the one produced by Shanks in England during the 1880's, which in turn was the basis for the types of this design used in the twentieth century. The Antiques shown by Wells and Webb in 1840, and in particular the Condensed styles, were designed with a block emphasis to the curvilinear letters. It is believed that this practice became common as a means of more evenly spacing letters and to allow more compact composition. The practice was adapted to Gothic as well as to Antique.

In 1849, Wells and Webb brought forth an Antique X Condensed in a Double Outline and an Outline, neither with a lowercase. Both interpretations were in keeping with the trend toward the lighter styles of display of that era. Another new design appearing to have been cut in wood first is Antique Tuscan, first shown in capitals only in the 1849 Wells & Webb specimens. Antique Tuscan lowercase first appeared in the Wells & Webb 1854 catalogue. The design, a modification of the Antique, was achieved though substituting curved for straight lines and extending the corners of all serifs into fine points, which gave it its Tuscan qualities. This face was soon shown by all wood type manufacturers. In 1859 the range was shown by Page as Condensed, X Condensed, XX Condensed, and Extended. Later, there was one cutting of a Light Face Extra Condensed. All had lowercase. Hagar and Connor had shown a large size of Antique Tuscan in 1850. In both instances, it would seem that either metal stereotypes of the wood type or wood specimens were used. Antique Outlined, Outline, and Condensed Line Shade, which were exhibited in the early 1850's in both wood and metal specimens, appeared to be popular with the trade. Antique Tuscan was engraved in steel for the typefounders (probably the Boston Type & Stereotype Foundry in the 1850's) by Samuel Sawyer Kilburn in five sizes: Pica, Great Primer, Two Line Small Pica, Two Line English, and a Six Line. Dickinson listed all five sizes in 1867, and MacKellar the first four sizes in 1868 (the label of "L. Johnson & Company" at the bottom of the page would indicate that the specimen had been set up at least a year earlier), but as Kilburn had died in 1864, these can not be the first listings. Even though Antique Tuscan was common to the wood type manufacturer and occasional to the typefounder in the 1850's, the face was not to become really popular in metal until the 1860's, after which it found increased use for the next 40 years.

One of the first styles to be adapted by the typefounder was the Antique Tuscan Condensed with a line shade shown by L. Johnson in 1853. Antique Tuscans were called "Antique Pointed" by many founders and the Extended styles "Broadgauge." If the amount of use a type may be put to can be criteria for judging its importance, Antique Tuscan would have to rank as an important American type face, despite its questionable typographic qualities. The design has been practically unknown to Europeans, although a modern face called Duo was designed by A. Finsterer for Klingspor in 1954. While not an exact duplication of the Antique Tuscans, the treatment of serifs is similar. The differences occur mostly in the design of round letters, where Antique Tuscans had an angular pointed treatment, and where Duo has a smooth contour.

Nicolette Gray identifies two English designs as Grecian—

94

one is the same as the design called Grecian in America—a letter approximately the weight and style of Antique X Condensed, straight lines substituted for curved lines, serifs angled and square counters. It is this design which in later years was accepted as Grecian. The other design was a small, outlined and shaded Tuscan-like letter called Grecian Outline and was issued by Thorowgood circa 1844. Nicolette Gray attributes the origins of Grecian (first example) to English typefounders during the early 1840's.

The American founder L. Johnson first showed Grecian in two sizes in his 1841 specimens (the design was an Extra Condensed style), and the first wood type catalogue to show this design was that of Wells and Webb in 1846, a catalogue produced especially for the Johnson foundry. In the 1849 Wells and Webb catalogue, Grecian was shown in Condensed, Extra Condensed, and two Grecian X Condensed Open styles. There was no lowercase for any of these styles.

The Grecian Open, quite popular with American founders for a number of years, originated in Europe. Grecian was first introduced as a Condensed style and was not produced Full Face until 1859 by Page. Lowercase for all Grecians was more common in the period around 1870, even though there are occasional examples of lowercase at earlier dates—Wells and Webb included a wider style of Grecian which was correspondingly lighter in weight. Like most other similar designs produced up to the time of the heavy, full-faced Grecian as shown by Cooley and Page circa 1860, these styles were awkwardly designed.

Grecian was to have few ornamental interpretations during the century. Knox probably showed more than any other wood type manufacturer. However, Grecian was one of the significant poster faces of the century.

The Grotesque Italian of Caslon, which had found such favor with American typefounders, had only limited showings as a wood letter. After 1850 it almost disappeared from wood type specimen books. Nesbitt illustrated a solid faced with Shade Open, which was perhaps one of the most novel interpretations of this design. Italian Open Shade was produced in limited quantities by both wood and metal type manufacturers between the 1830's and 1850's.

Nesbitt exhibited an Antique Extra Condensed in 1838 with the letterform broken at the middle and bent to the left. Antique Broken Grotesque Open Shade was shown as a metal type in a 22-point size by Connor in 1859, the design for which had probably been imported from Europe. This same treatment of the Roman Extra Condensed is also illustrated, which is similar to the Zig-Zag credited to Figgins in England circa 1845, except that the Zig-Zag breaks to the right and the American bends to the left.

Nesbitt labeled an unusual French design that he showed Condensed Cornered. It was distinguished by the diagonal cutting of serif corners, and on letters such as A, M, N, and V there was a characteristic Grecian treatment of the letter endings not having serifs. Another version of this design, which might have been exclusive with Nesbitt, was an Italicized and outlined style called Antique Italic Rounded. In America these designs did not show up at any time afterwards in any wood or metal specimen books, even though Europeans, especially the French, showed the design, and several variations on it, for a number of years.

All of the English styles of Antique Open Shade, Outlined, etc., were shown regularly by all wood type manufacturers.

10 LINE PICA ANTIQUE OPEN SHADED

HIDE

bctnf

12 LINE PICA ANTIQUE ITALIC OPEN SHADE

TE

hul

12 LINE PICA ANTIQUE OPEN

HAT

12 LINE PICA ANTIQUE OPEN CONDENSED

HAND

14 LINE PICA ANTIQUE CONDENSED OPEN, NO. 2

CANE

Nesbitt, 1838.

MANE
hasten

D. WELLS & CO.   NEW-YORK.

16 LINE PICA EXTRA CONDENSED ANTIQUE

WINTER
streamlet

14 LINE PICA ANTIQUE SHADED NO. 2

BIRD
hand

D. WELLS & CO.   NEW-YORK.

12 LINE EXTRA CONDENSED ANTIQUE OPEN

DEMOCRAT

12 LINE ANTIQUE ORNAMENTED

DAN

Wells & Webb, 1840.

The Solid Shades, first shown by Nesbitt in 1838, and considerably expanded by Wells & Webb in 1840, appear to have been extremely popular in these years. The device was applied to Antique, Gothic, Roman, and the Condensed styles of the same faces; occasionally there would be a lowercase shown for these designs. Nesbitt, and Wells and Webb both showed a few of the German styles of Antique Perspective, but by mid-century these designs had disappeared from the specimen books of wood type manufacturers.

Antique Double Outlined with a half ray and half solid shade, usually with a double outline, were first shown by Wells & Webb in 1840, even though the same device had been applied to Gothic in their 1840 catalogue. A number of ornamented Antiques from Nesbitt and Wells and Webb were very likely innovations by these two companies. The same designs were never cast in metal, except for Nesbitt's Amalgamation Shaded, an Antique Shade with the letter divided horizontally through the center. The top half of the letter was open with the shade solid, and the bottom half had the reverse. The design was shown in a 24-point size by John White in 1849. There are several Ray Shades, and letters with an interior shading—vertical, horizontal, and diagonal, which are thought to have been done only in wood, even though these devices were popular with typefounders in America and in Europe in the 1840's.

Nesbitt showed a few Antique and Roman faces with a diamond cross hatch or diagonal stripes which are identified as French Lined or Diamond. These were borrowed from the specimens of Laurent et Derberny issued in Paris during 1835 and 1837. Nesbitt also exhibited three ornamental Antiques based on designs issued by Bower & Bacon circa 1830. These incorporated thistle, rose, and acanthus motifs. Two somewhat similar faces were shown in 1840 by Wells and Webb, who, with Nesbitt, were the only manufacturers to exhibit these faces in wood.

18 LINE PICA ANTIQUE CONDENSED CORNERED

BA

10 LINE ANTIQUE ITALIC ROUNDED OPENED

PHR

Nesbitt, 1838.

10 LINE PICA TUSCAN ANTIQUE

SINCE

Wells & Webb, 1849.

15 LINE ANTIQUE TUSCAN CONDENSED

HEM!

24 LINE ANTIQUE TUSCAN EXTRA CONDENSED

RUM

20 LINE ANTIQUE TUSCAN DOUBLE EXTRA CONDENSED

MOHGCD

3 LINE ANTIQUE TUSCAN EXTENDED

FIRES!

14 LINE ANTIQUE TUSCAN CONDENSED, LIGHT SHADE

SOBIER

Page, 1859.

20 LINE PICA EXTRA CONDENSED ANTIQUE OPEN NO. 2

LINES

16 LINE PICA EXTRA CONDENSED ANTIQUE OPEN

TOBINS

Wells & Webb, 1849.

14 LINE PICA EXTRA CONDENSED PERSPECTIVE

GERMA

10 LINE PICA ANTIQUE AMALGAMATION SHADED

ABD

10 LINE PICA ANTIQUE FRENCH DIAMOND AND SHADED

BADE

8 LINE PICA ANTIQUE, ROSE ORNAMENTAL

HORS

8 LINE PICA ANTIQUE, TULIP ORNAMENTAL

TYPE

8 LINE PICA ANTIQUE, THISTLE ORNAMENTAL

STOK

Nesbitt, 1838.

10 LINE ANTIQUE OAK LEAF ORNAMENTED

HONE

Wells & Webb, 1840.

12 LINE ANTIQUE SHADE NO. 2   12 LINE ANTIQUE SHADE NO. 3

EW EW

Debow, c. 1837.

MARBLE

Wells & Webb, 1849.

30 LINE PICA EXTRA CONDENSED GRECIAN

GOVE

12 LINE PICA CONDENSED GRECIAN

SCORIGE

6 LINE PICA GRECIAN SHADE NO. 1

Monument Washington

Wells & Webb, 1846 (Johnson & Smith specimens).

15 LINE PICA ANTIQUE GROTESQUE, CONDENSED

FEAB

12 LINE PICA ITALIAN OPEN SHADED

HOD

Nesbitt, 1838.

The Romans

In the 1828 specimen, Wells showed the usual Fat Face Roman with both Italic and Backslope, all with lowercase. While the Blackslope Roman in display sizes had been cut in England by Figgins as early as 1815 (called Contra Italic by Nicolette Gray), it was not produced in the large sizes by Americans other than by Darius Wells in this first catalogue, and by Leavenworth, who designed a curious version. The Roman Condensed and Extra Condensed were to be seen first in the 1838 Nesbitt catalogue, with the Condensed but not the Extra Condensed in an Italic. All three styles had lowercase and figures.

During the 1840's the lighter, condensed styles of Roman gradually replaced the more squat Fat Face Romans in popularity, and in the following decade the condensing was carried to even greater extremes. There was a considerable variance in the cutting of Romans during these early years, but in essence all designs except those of Leavenworth were patterned after the English models. Nesbitt did show a Roman Extended with lowercase and figures in 1838, a design which was to be imitated by other wood type manufacturers in succeeding years. Of most interest in this showing is the lowercase, since American founders did not show a lowercase and none is listed by Nicolette Gray until the one by Thorowgood in 1842 and by Figgins in 1847.

All of the common English styles of Open Shade, and the heavily embellished French Ornamented Romans are exhibited in wood. Nesbitt showed a Roman and an exceedingly handsome Roman Condensed Outlined complete with lowercase and figures. It is believed that both designs originated in wood, as founders here or abroad never showed the same design. Also shown were two Roman Extended faces, with shading on the interior, which surely was done only by Nesbitt. The Open Shade was applied to the same Roman Extended. Roman and Roman Condensed were given the same Outlined Shade treatment that had been applied to Antique and Gothic, and were first shown in the Wells & Webb book of specimens for 1840, which also marked the first showing by wood type manufacturers of the Roman Light Face and lowercase, a design to be further expanded in the next decade.

The Romans exhibited by Leavenworth were probably the most unusual ever designed in America; the Condensed and Italic styles were shown by Wells & Webb in their 1840 catalogue, and then disappeared. A new design for Roman Condensed was introduced by Wells and Webb in 1849, with the counter slightly more open and the letterform taller than those previously shown. The 1849 Wells and Webb specimens did not show any Roman Condensed or Extra Condensed Italics, and all the Italic styles of Gothic and Antique were also deleted from succeeding specimens. It is thought that this disappearance of Italics was caused by the difficulties attendant on composing the inclined type bodies. Only occasionally were new Italic designs in wood introduced during the balance of the century.

An interesting omission from wood type specimen books in these years was the Roman Double Shade, extremely popular with all American typefounders before mid-century. There is no explanation for this shading device never being adapted to wood, although the principle was applied to a curious half Ray Shade combined with a solid shade on Antique and Gothic during the late 1830's and throughout the 1850's.

18 LINE PICA

BED man

15 LINE PICA, ITALIC

LET hand

12 LINE PICA, BACKSLOPE

Adams

Wells, 1828.

8 LINE PICA ROMAN CONDENSED

ADBCFE modelbac

12 LINE PICA ROMAN EXTRA CONDENSED

GUILFOR vidence

Nesbitt, 1838.

10 LINE PICA ROMAN CONDENSED SHADED

TRENT

7 LINE ROMAN SHADED NO. 2

RESTON

Wells & Webb, 1840.

8 LINE PICA ITALIC, CONDENSED

REPUBLIC enthusiad

2 LINE EXTENDED

ABCDEIMO abcdehikln

15 LINE PICA ROMAN EXTRA CONDENSED SHADED

ADMIRE mechani

4 LINE PICA EXTENDED SHADE

TEA

4 LINE PICA EXTENDED ORNAMENTED SHADE

TEA

Nesbitt, 1838.

10 LINE PICA, LINE SHADED

HOPE

Wells, 1828.

6 LINE ROMAN OPENED

ORNSEA

12 LINE PICA ROMAN GROTESQUE

10 LINE PICA ROMAN OPEN SHADED

TIRE

Nesbitt, 1838.

6 LINE PICA ROMAN, LIGHT FACE

REND bread

Wells & Webb, 1840.

16 LINE ROMAN LIGHT FACE OPEN SHADE

MN h a

10 LINE CLOSE CONDENSED ROMAN

MERIT human
$25787£

Debow, c. 1837.

16 AND 12 LINE CLOSE ITALIC

MAY
hour
2758
MUAV

16, 12 AND 6 LINE CONDENSED BACKSLOPE

USE
hen
RIOT
SHEFFIELD
burrington
13456789

LEAVENWORTH'S   PATENT.

Debow, c. 1837.

The Gothics

In 1834 Johnson and Smith introduced through their metal type specimens the first heavy, or Full Face Gothics shown in America in two styles of Gothic and Gothic Condensed. Gothic was also shown in two ornamental styles—Open Shade and Open Shade with a tooled treatment of the shade. It is not known whether or not these designs originated with a typefounder, but it is thought they were either wood, or made from wooden models. After these first few clumsy examples only a few years passed before the wood type manufacturers were showing a range of Gothics: Gothic Condensed, X, XX Condensed, Extended, Italic, Backslope, Light Face, and Ornamental Gothics, and all these designs had reached a high level of refinement as compared to the initial specimens of Johnson and Smith, and most had a lowercase. Typefounders never showed the Fat Face Gothics extensively, and no styles at all in small sizes which would tend to reinforce the idea that the earliest specimens in the larger sizes were probably wood. Gothics in all their styles were extremely popular with the wood type trade, and constituted one of the major display types used in poster printing in this era. The important styles of Gothic common to this particular period were Gothic (Full Face), Condensed, Italic and Backslope, all with a lowercase except the Gothic. The Gothic lowercase was first shown by Wells and Webb in 1849. Nicolette Gray does not list an English founder showing a lowercase for the Full Face Gothics until Miller and Richard in 1887. Nesbitt in his 1838 catalogue showed Gothic Condensed, Italic and Backslope (the last two styles were Condensed); additionally, he showed a Gothic Condensed and Backslope in Outline, the former with a lowercase. Neither of these two designs ever appeared in the specimens of the typefounders. Also included were a Gothic Condensed Double Outlined with Ray Shade, and Gothic Condensed Outlined with Shade; neither had a lowercase. There were several Gothic Condensed styles with both shade and interior shading. Nesbitt was the first in this country to show an extensive number of ornamental interpretations of Gothic and Antique, particularly the Ray Shades. In his 1838 specimens he included a Gothic Condensed Outlined Ray Shade which he titled Gothic Shade Ray. Another style of Gothic with Ray Shade enclosed by a line was exhibited. Nesbitt also illustrated a Tooled Gothic called Gothic Open No. 2 without lowercase which was not repeated in any other specimen books. A metal version of Tooled Gothic Condensed was shown by Robb and Ecklin in 1836 and was shown again by Johnson and Smith in 1841, but both differed substantially from the design of Nesbitt—tooling was to the left on Nesbitt and to the right on the others. An unusual Gothic dimensional letter called Octagon with several decorative treatments of cross-hatching or dots, plus one Perspective Gothic and a Gothic Round Outlined filled out a large assortment of plain and ornamental Gothics in the Nesbitt catalogue. Gothic Round Condensed in a variety of styles was to be a popular face with both metal and wood type producers throughout the second half of the century. The first English styles of Gothic Round Condensed, dated from the mid-1840's and attributed to Caslon, were a Tooled and Ornamented design. Although the American showings predate the English ones, the exact origin of this design is unknown.

Wells and Webb in 1840 introduced a curious Gothic based on the weight distribution of the grotesque Italians.

12 LINE PICA GOTHIC CONDENSED

6 LINE PICA GOTHIC

4 LINE GOTHIC SHADED

4 LINE GOTHIC SHADED OPEN

Johnson & Smith, 1834.

12 LINE PICA ROMAN GOTHIC COND.

Nesbitt, 1838. The relationship between the Nesbitt specimen and that of Johnson and Smith is obvious. However, the slit counter of the lowercase b, a and u are most like the designs of Leavenworth, and it is believed that Leavenworth made his first wood types in 1834.

12 LINE PICA ITALIC GOTHIC CONDENSED

RUNTE
mothers

10 LINE PICA GOTHIC CONDENSED BACK SLOPE

LEBANON
huminster

10 LINE PICA GOTHIC

HORN

14 LINE PICA GOTHIC OPEN NO. 2

ART

18 LINE PICA GOTHIC CONDENSED SHADED

HUM

Nesbitt, 1838.

18 LINE PICA GOTHIC CONDENSED OUTLINE

RAG
mutc

18 LINE GOTHIC CONDENSED BACK SLOPE OUTLINE

RAN

20 LINE PICA GOTHIC CONDENSED, MERIDIAN OPEN SHADE

STEM

20 LINE PICA GOTHIC, OPEN SHADED

MA

Nesbitt, 1838.

As strange-appearing as it was, a somewhat similar but heavier version of this design was marketed by Hamilton in the 1880's, and very successfully.

Wells and Webb gave one showing of a Gothic Round Outlined in a full face style and in this more extended version, it is a strangely limp looking design. The instability was created by substituting curves for angles in the counters. In a few years the practice was to restore the angles where appropriate, and reserve the curved or rounded effects for the terminals. However, the face by Wells and Webb is unusual, and clearly reveals the groping connected with the production of new designs.

Wells and Webb in 1840 presented a Gothic Extended without a lowercase but with figures. A light style of this Gothic Extended had been engraved as a logotype for the title page of the specimen book. It is thought by the author that these showings were the first for this design, and that it did originate as a wood type. The first lowercase for Gothic Extended was not shown until 1850 by Nesbitt in the specimens of the New England Type Foundry, and only occasionally throughout the rest of the century was Gothic Extended shown with a lowercase.

Leavenworth's specimens circa 1837 show the most interesting variations on the Gothic letterform. The Gothic Close Condensed is typical of his designs, but there is a Full Faced Gothic which is cornered; on curvilinear letters straight lines have been substituted for the outside curves, much like the Grecian designs. This design does not show up again until the 1880's, and then in the Condensed styles. Also, there was a very full faced Gothic employing circles to delineate the round letters. There are some Gothic Meridian Open Shades distinguished by the vertical rather than diagonal shade as well as a Gothic Meridian Outlined with Shade. Both of these designs are carried by Wells and Webb in 1840 who are believed to have used Leavenworth's patterns for this showing, and by Nesbitt who probably imitated the Leavenworth designs.

The 1849 Wells and Webb specimens included an interesting Gothic Extra Condensed Outline, and as the line was heavier than that usually found, it gave another color quality to these letters. Essentially the same treatment was given to the Antique Extra Condensed in the Wells 1840 catalogue, but it was quite different from the examples in the Nesbitt catalogue.

Gothic Tuscan Condensed first appeared in the 1849 Wells and Webb catalogue as a solid faced and an Outlined style, neither with a lowercase. This design, destined to be characteristic of American display typography during the century, was again American in origin and created first in wood. The design occasionally had a lowercase. There were a few ornamental versions other than the Outline and some embellished styles by William Page in 1859. The face was not cut in a series other than a Gothic Tuscan X Condensed Outlined by Knox, and a curious Gothic Tuscan Condensed Italian by Wells and Webb in 1854; the latter could well qualify as one of the earliest Semi-Ornamental faces. Gothic Tuscan was engraved in a series of sizes for L. Johnson and Company by Julius Herriet, who is believed to have finished this work about 1857.

12 LINE PICA GOTHIC CONDENSED SHADE AND RAY

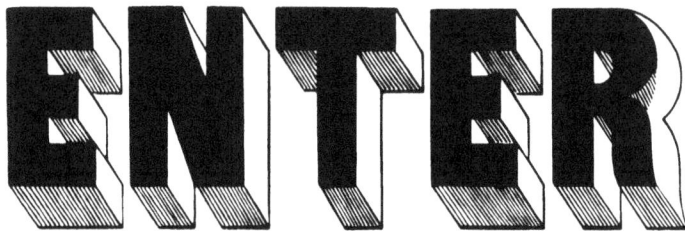

ENTER

14 LINE PICA GOTHIC, SHADE AND RAY

HUM

12 LINE PICA GOTHIC, SHADE AND DOWN-LINED

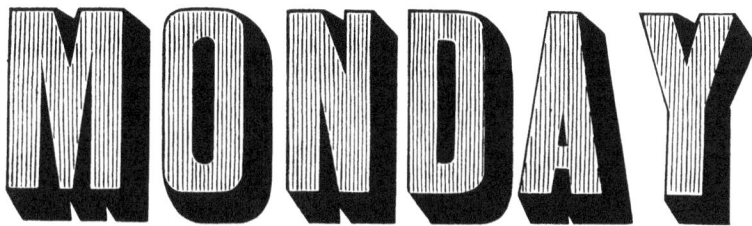

MONDAY

16 LINE PICA OCTAGON

HAD

18 LINE PICA GOTHIC, DIAMOND

HAD

14 LINE PICA GOTHIC CONDENSED SHADE, OPEN ROUNDED

HOUSE

Nesbitt, 1838.

24 AND 20 LINE CONDENSED GOTHIC

HIO
OUR
rose

20, 16 AND 12 LINE GOTHIC

CO
EOL
LIFEL

12 LINE GOTHIC NO. 2

OIED

12 AND 6 LINE CONDENSED GOTHIC NOS. 1 & 2

HIRAMAPO
GOHTIC CONDENSED

Debow, c. 1837.

10, 8 AND 6 LINE CLOSE CONDENSED GOTHIC ITALIC

MERCHANT
23567823

10 AND 6 LINE CLOSE CONDENSED GOTHIC

COLUMBUS

12 LINE CONDENSED GOTHIC OPEN MERIDIAN SHADE

FEONDAH

12 LINE CONDENSED GOTHIC ORNAMENTED NO. 1

HENDRIES

LEAVENWORTH'S   PATENT.

Debow, c. 1837.

14 LINE PICA ITALIC GOTHIC CONDENSED

USTER
hunder

20 LINE PICA GOTHIC CONDENSED BACK SLOPE

RED

Wells & Webb, 1840.

SPECIMEN

OF

Plain and Ornamental

WOOD TYPE,

CUT BY MACHINERY,

BY

WELLS & WEBB,

(LATE D. WELLS & CO.)

NO. 38 ANN-STREET,

NEW-YORK.

1840.

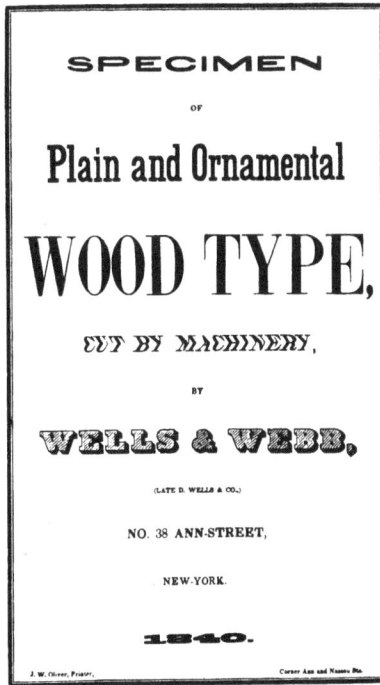

6 LINE PICA EXTENDED GOTHIC

END

6 LINE ROUND GOTHIC OPEN

TRADE.

7 LINE PICA GOTHIC ITALIAN

BONAPRE

6 LINE PICA GOTHIC ORNAMENTED

RACE

Wells & Webb, 1840.

5 LINE PICA GOTHIC

PUNISHMEN
Town Council

Bill, Stark & Co., 1853.

24 LINE PICA EXTRA CONDENSED GOTHIC

SHARE

16 LINE PICA CONDENSED GOTHIC NO. 2

HONE

18 LINE PICA GOTHIC ORNAMENTED

MEN

16 LINE PICA GOTHIC CONDENSED MERIDIAN SHADE NO. 2

MINDEN

15 LINE PICA GOTHIC CONDENSED SHADE NO. 2

READS

6 LINE PICA ROUND GOTHIC OPEN

MORTISINE

20 LINE PICA GOTHIC TUSCAN

HOSE

Wells & Webb, 1849.

105

14 LINE PICA ANTIQUE EXTRA ORNAMENTED

RISE

24 LINE PICA VENETIAN

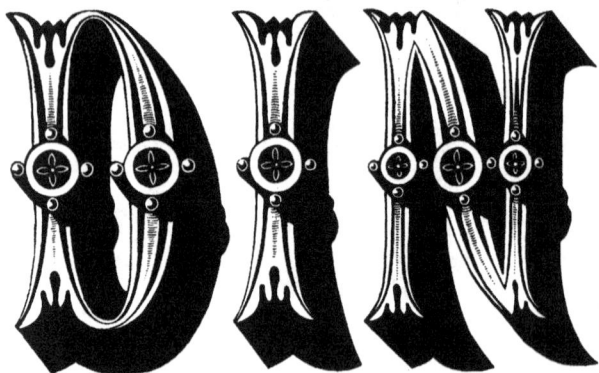

DIN

6 LINE PICA TUSCAN ORNAMENTAL

WORTH

8 LINE PICA TUSCAN SHADED

HOUSE

10 LINE PICA COMIC

ABCE

15 LINE PICA GOTHIC CONDENSED, ACORN

KALEM

11 LINE PICA GOTHIC, CHARACTERS

NESBITT

Nesbitt, 1838.

The Ornamentals

Most of the American Ornamental faces from this period are representative of European models, and it is thought that more of these found production in wood than in metal in this country. The small Tuscan Shaded, widely used by American typefounders, was illustrated by Nesbitt in 1838. In the large sizes it is a striking display face. The design called Venetian by Nesbitt, and simply called Tuscan by Blake and Stephenson in their showing from circa 1841, is believed to have originated in the French foundries. It was shown in wood only by Nesbitt, Page, and Wells & Webb in America.

The outlandish human caricature alphabet shown by Bruce, among others, was also sold by Nesbitt. Some elaborate Tuscans, such as Parisian Fancy, were among the Nesbitt specimens. Nesbitt may also have been the first to show a curious Gothic Perspective with an acorn motif, as well as a Cornered Gothic with figures worked around the letterforms holding signs advertising "Nesbitts First Premium Wood Types." This was probably only an advertising device, showing that a customer could order this face with his own advertising message on the bills.

On the basis of available wood type specimens, there appears to have been little change in Ornamental letters from those found in the 1838 Nesbitt catalogue until the 1849 Wells and Webb specimens. The Zebra faces of Figgins, circa 1849 (Wells and Webb, 1849), found interpretation as Open Shade, Outlined Shade and Outlined with Wells by 1849. Tuscan Open which was very popular in English typography during the 1840's was first shown as a metal type in America by Robb in 1844, and by Wells and Webb in 1849 as a wood type. There were a few additional French Ornamentals, but in the same vein as earlier designs, and devices applied to primary faces were now shown in conjunction with the Condensed and Extra Condensed faces. Antique Condensed Outlined would be shown with Antique Outlined, etc.

The solid letter with an open shade was adapted to most of the primary faces, and the Double Outline was being applied to a greater variety of designs. A few newspaper heads were advertised at the head of the Wells and Webb catalogue for 1849, with ten pages of trade cuts shown at the end of the book. There was also a small selection of borders among which the Greek Fret and a flowered motif were the most common. In 1838 Nesbitt showed one European Reverse with the paling effect, and in 1841 he advertised chromatic types for decorative printing: " . . . when it is understood that, with almost every specimen annexed, the body and shade form separate and distinct letters, perfect in themselves and capable of being used as such, it will be seen that they are as cheap as the ordinary styles of ornamental types."

While the wood type manufacturers were never extensively engaged in the production of historiated letters except during the 1830's when Nesbitt showed several and Wells illustrated a few letters with elaborate interior shading, the typefounders continued to show historiated type faces regularly up into the 1860's. In 1854 Hagar was to show a wide variety of metal types original with Bower and Bacon, Woods and Sharwood, and other English styles from the 1830's. The typefounders seem to have clung to these designs for a longer time than wood type manufacturers, who developed their own ideas of embellishment in the 1850's and 1860's.

6 LINE PICA ANTIQUE, ENGLISH ORNAMENTAL

RANCH

6 LINE ROMAN CONDENSED, ENGLISH ORNAMENTAL

EDINBURG

10 LINE PICA ROMAN, SPEAR AND SHADE

LARK

anthe

12 LINE ROMAN FRENCH LINED AND SHADED

ABD

10 LINE ROMAN CONDENSED AMALGAMATION LINED

ABCDF

Nesbitt, 1838.

9 LINE PICA ORNAMENTED NO. 2

TUNED

musica

10 LINE PICA ORNAMENTED

SORE

threa

D. WELLS & CO.

Wells & Webb, 1840.

7 LINE PICA SHADE, NO. 2 ORNAMENTED

HOLDEN

8 LINE PICA TUSCAN ORNAMENTED

DUNHAM

Wells & Webb, 1840.

12 LINE PICA ANTIQUE AMALGAMATION SHADED (TWO COLORS)

PET

12 LINE PICA CORINTHIAN (TWO COLORS)

LEND

12 LINE PICA GOTHIC CONDENSED OPEN SHADED (TWO COLORS)

RATE

Nesbitt, 1841 (Chromatics).

16 LINE PICA CONDENSED ANTIQUE SHADE ORNAMENTED

BOIL

14 LINE PICA TUSCAN OPEN

GRIST

Wells & Webb, 1849.

10 LINE PICA TUSCAN CONDENSED SHADE NO. 4

ADVOCATE

8 LINE PICA TUSCAN CONDENSED SHADE NO. 2

GENERALLY

8 LINE PICA TUSCAN CONDENSED SHADE NO. 3

THE CHART

10 LINE PICA TUSCAN CONDENSED SHADE NO. 1

FISNOSAY

10 LINE PICA TUSCAN CONDENSED SHADE NO. 2

SIRUPINE

10 LINE PICA TUSCAN CONDENSED SHADE NO. 3

PRISONER

8 LINE PICA ORNAMENTED

BUNDLE

7 LINE PICA ORNAMENTED

COMINS

7 LINE PICA TUSCAN OPEN SHADE

BURNEY

8 LINE PICA GOTHIC CONDENSED SHADE NO. 4

HAMILTON

7 LINE PICA ROMAN SHADE ORNAMENTED

HERMO

Wells & Webb, 1849.

1850 Through 1865

The tremendous increase of job printing during these 15 years is well demonstrated by the great number of job presses advertised and used in this period. The most famous were those of George P. Gordon, whose introduction of the Franklin press was to expand the field and make a fortune for himself. Numerous jobbing presses on the market were manufactured for only a few years and were almost as obscure in their own time as now. However, this industry reflected a market potential which gave great incentive to invention, and the patent registrar was flooded in these years with not only applications for new presses and improvements on older presses, but also for patents within the entire field of printing.

Although the process for electrotyping matrices had been perfected near the end of the last period, it was between 1850 and 1865 that the effects of the invention were really felt and seen. Because duplicate matrices could be made economically from any font of type, the pages of the American specimen books blossomed with designs stolen from competitors in this country or from foundries abroad. It is difficult to tell whether duplicating matrices created the demand for novelty which was so characteristic throughout the balance of the century, or whether it was only an instrument of this demand.

Near the end of the period, power lithographic presses were successfully brought into the trade, and there was an equal expansion of lithographic printing. The first successful experiments in using photography to enlarge or reduce images onto plates, wood, or stone had been accomplished. This was also the golden age of wood engraving. Papers were more improved in these years than any time previously, and by 1856, Americans were using more paper per year than England and France combined. The first coated paper was produced by William Waldon of New Jersey in 1852, after which there were numerous patents for improved calendering of papers—coinciding with the rise of wood engravings being used commercially.

The Civil War, which began and expended itself in this era, brought many women into the trade, particularly in the New England states, and in a number of instances, their performance warranted their continued participation after the war. The end of this period was marked by the strike of New York typographic compositors, caused by an exceedingly bitter dispute with abuses on the part of both management and workers. The strike culminated in the formation of a typographers' union which not only effected many changes in the trade but gave American compositors the highest salaries and the best working conditions in the world. The advantages won by the workmen during these years placed the typefounder at a perilous disadvantage when advertising interests in the 1870's tried to have protective tariffs eliminated on types. American labor costs were so high in comparison with the European that if Congress had eliminated the tariffs, all of the American printing trades would have suffered greatly.

Since Leavenworth had been absorbed by Wells and Webb in 1839, and Allen had ceased to manufacture wood type around 1850, only the Wells' firm and the Day brothers continued into the second period. Bill Brothers began manufacturing type in Lebanon, Connecticut, in 1850, and the Day brothers of Fredricksburg, Ohio, built a new factory to expand their operations in the early 1850's. John G. Cooley, after purchasing the Allen works in 1852, and building up his business, was to move his offices to New

York City in 1859, and his plant there in 1863.

William H. Page in partnership with James Bassett succeeded to the equipment of the Bill Brothers in 1856, after which they laid the ground for what was to become the largest wood type manufacturing plant in the United States during the 1870's. In 1854, E. R. Webb bought out the interests of Darius Wells and was to operate the firm first with partners, and later under his own name until his death in 1864. The splintering of the Day Company brought on by a laborers' strike in 1855 led to the brief operations of D. Knox and Company circa 1857, in Fredricksburg, Ohio. The Day brothers moved their equipment and offices to Columbus, Ohio, where convict labor produced their types.

During this time the proliferation of styles increased dramatically through expanding the concept of "series" of sizes with the typefounder, and "series" of styles by wood type manufacturers. Letterforms tended to be lighter and taller—particularly the Romans, Gothics, and Antiques, which were carried to the extreme compression of XXX Condensed. The use of the Light Faces which had begun in the 1840's reached full bloom in the 1850's and 1860's, and the idea was applied to old as well as to new designs as they came into being. Gothics found a particular refinement as well as variety during the period, particularly the condensed and lighter full face styles. Many of the secondary faces had a lowercase for the first time. The European Ornamentals in the larger sizes slowly began to disappear, especially those based on a Roman letterform, and the ornamentation of large display letters produced as wood type began to demonstrate some sort of equation between cost and embellishment. Also, many decorative devices reflected the machinery used to make type as well as an appreciation for originality in the ornamentation of letters. There was a marked individuality in the interpretation of styles between the various wood type manufacturers, who put a number of original designs on the market—most notably the Semi-Ornamented faces.

The bulk of American Tuscans first gained an identity as a distinct classification during these years. The typefounder who continued to copy the European Ornamented designs in great quantity and mostly in the small sizes began to transfer some wood type designs into metal: e.g., Antique Tuscans, Gothic Tuscans, Antique Expanded, and a number of ornamental treatments of conventional letters which had been exploited in wood. At the end of the period, the new French styles were apparent in the works of the typefounder, as well as the results of competition with lithographic letter styles which appeared in delicately outlined or filigreed type faces, many of which were patented.

The Antiques

Antique XX Condensed in styles of No. 1 and 2 were shown by Wells & Webb in 1854, and similar designs were shown by Page in 1859. Both showed lowercase for Antique XX Condensed No. 1, but only Page showed a lowercase for the more condensed style. Antique XXX Condensed was also shown by Page in 1866 without lowercase, but with lowercase in his 1872 catalogue. Antique Light Face with lowercase was among the specimens shown by Wells and Webb in 1854, and the same design in an Extended style with lowercase was shown by Page in 1859. Consistent with the lighter styles was a Condensed Light Face Antique listed on the 1865 price page by William Page and

16 LINE PICA ANTIQUE DOUBLE EXTRA CONDENSED NO. 1

CHANTER dangerous

12 AND 20 LINE PICA ANTIQUE DOUBLE EXTRA CONDENSED NO. 2

WELLS & WEBB, 1854.
CHAIRSTORE

6 LINE PICA ANTIQUE LIGHT FACE

CHAIRMEN
for sale here

8 LINE PICA ANTIQUE LIGHT FACE

MONTHS

Wells & Webb, 1854.

15 LINE ANTIQUE EXTRA CONDENSED NO. 1

SERMONS
wound 18

Page, 1859.

CRUMBS

teamless

6 LINE ANTIQUE EXTENDED, LIGHT FACE

ENDION
beam 65

Page, 1859.

8 LINE ANTIQUE SKELETON

MOUNDGreen

Page, 1865.

12 LINE PICA CLAREDON CONDENSED

ROTE.
refuge

Bill, Stark & Co., 1853.

called Skeleton Antique; the 1872 specimens show a lowercase for this design. Light face Antiques were to be even more popular in metal than wood, especially after 1850. In their 1856 catalogue Dickinson typefoundry showed an Antique Light Face cast in metal in a series of six sizes ranging from 24 to 72 points, which would indicate a growing popularity for these styles within the trade.

One of the most important of the Antique secondary faces was Clarendon, and although the first specimens are shown in the Bill, Stark, and Company specimens in 1853, there is an Antique by Nesbitt in 1850 that was mistakenly labeled as Clarendon with a handwritten correction. This would seem to indicate that Clarendon was being cut in wood at that time.

The design called Clarendon by wood type manufacturers bore small resemblance to the Ionics and Clarendons featured by the English typefounders during the 1830's and 1840's. The wood type styles, comparable in weight to an Antique Condensed, were a bold, masculine display type. Wood type producers did not show the Clarendon styles produced by typefounders during both the nineteenth and twentieth centuries until the late 1850's when they brought out the Light Face and Extended styles. It is entirely possible that Clarendons evolved from two separate origins, one being the smaller Ionics—which in turn had probably grown out of some modification of Roman or the smaller sizes of Antique. The other may be traced to modification in the larger display sizes of Antique, such as the Antique Outlined by Figgins in 1821. As previously mentioned, the Clarendon characteristics—bracketed serifs, treatment of the tail on the R and Q, etc.—had shown up in various interpretations of the larger sizes of Antique since the 1820's. What appears to be a third group of Clarendons would be the heavy, Condensed Clarendons as shown by Hanel in 1841 which were similar to the most popular of the American wood type Clarendons.

An early if not the first showing of Clarendon in America was as foundry type by L. Johnson and Company in 1847. The specimens ranged from 28 points to 12 lines. The first size, Two Line English, was probably a metal type since there is greater refinement in rendering individual letters, but most of the others in the larger sizes closely resemble the wood types found at a slightly later date and probably were wood types. Clarendon Condensed and X Condensed appeared in the Bill, Stark and Company catalogue for 1853, both having a lowercase. In the following year, Wells and Webb added Clarendon with lowercase, which although more bold, was essentially a condensed face. In 1859 Page's specimen book showed Clarendon, Clarendon Condensed, Clarendon Light Face which was also in X and XX Condensed, all with lowercase. This same specimen book had Ionic with lowercase, probably one of the most beautifully proportioned faces of the entire Clarendon family to be shown by any wood type manufacturer in the nineteenth century. All Condensed styles of Clarendon Light Face were so well designed that a word or line of display set with them had a remarkably even color.

Page appears to be one of the first to use the Clarendon as an Ornamental letter. His 1859 catalogue presented a number of Outlined, Checkered, Striped, Shaded designs as well as some decorative effects such as diamonds, darts, etc., borrowed from the European styles. Cooley was the first to introduce a Clarendon Full Face, which was complete with lowercase. Additionally, he showed a Clarendon

Light Face Extended without a lowercase. Clarendon Italian (first listed in 1865 on the price page of the Page catalogue), along with the French Antique and other Clarendons, was to dominate most posters in the last 20 years of the century. Today these type faces are often lumped under the single designation of Playbill, even though they are dissimilar. Also, while the styles issued by typefounders as French Antique, Egyptian and French Clarendon were patterned closely after the European models, for some unexplained reason, French Antique and Clarendon were shown only in the very condensed styles by wood type manufacturers. French Antique as cut in wood approximated a XX Condensed Antique.

Grecian X Condensed was among the specimens of Wells and Webb in 1849, and did have a lowercase in the 1854 catalogue of the same company. In the preceding year, Bill, Stark and Company had shown Grecian Condensed with lowercase. In 1858 Knox had a large showing devoted to Grecians, among which were a Light Face with lowercase and a Grecian No. 2 modified by notched serifs to create a decorative effect. Additionally, there was a Grecian X Condensed Outlined, an uncommon showing of this design. Nesbitt had shown a Grecian Light Face in 1850, but it was without a lowercase, and the Knox design did approximate this cutting.

All of the Grecian Light Face designs were cut in a full face width as compared to the normally condensed styles. The first Full Face Grecian was shown circa 1859 by Cooley without a lowercase. It was intermediate in weight between earlier Condensed styles and the heavier styles that followed. The Full Faced Grecian which was to be the pattern during the balance of the century was the one listed by Page in 1859, 1865, and probably the same as the one shown in 1872. Page cut a lowercase for this design later in the century. Wood type manufacturers were marketing a lowercase for the several styles of Condensed Grecian many years before typefounders showed similar designs.

18 LINE PICA EXTRA CONDENSED CLARENDON

TONES
euhon

Bill, Stark & Co., 1853.

8 LINE PICA CLARENDON

TUESDAY
December

Wells & Webb, 1854.

7 LINE CLARENDON, LIGHT FACE

WONDERED
abundant 25

50 LINE CLARENDON DOUBLE EXTRA CONDENSED LIGHT FACE

HIME

Page, 1859.

24 LINE CLARENDON EXTRA CONDENSED, LIGHT FACE

NEDIE
tailors!

Page, 1859.

18 LINE IONIC

CIG den 520

20 LINE CLARENDON ORNAMENTED NO. 10

HEN

20 LINE CLARENDON ORNAMENTED NO. 13

HEN

20 LINE CLARENDON ORNAMENTED NO. 16

HEN

10 LINE CLARENDON ORNAMENTED NO. 15

SHADED

15 LINE CLARENDON RAY SHADE

HUET

Page, 1859.

15 LINE CLARENDON ORNAMENTED

HONE

Page, 1859.

8 LINE CLARENDON LIGHT FACE EXTENDED

BIDE

16 LINE CLARENDON FULL FACE

HIED

16 LINE CLARENDON LIGHT FACE

HIED Delhi

Cooley, c. 1859.

16 LINE PICA CONDENSED CLARENDON

THEme

Knox, 1858.

7 LINE CLARENDON ITALIAN

Shower SNARE

Page, 1865.

112

8 LINE PICA GRECIAN CONDENSED

WESTERN
world's fair

Bill, Stark & Co., 1853.

8 LINE PICA LIGHT FACE GRECIAN

A GUN!
rased

8 LINE PICA CONDENSED GRECIAN NO. 2

MBERFAND

20 LINE PICA EXTRA CONDENSED GRECIAN

NEAR
dainh

D. KNOX & CO., FREDERICKSBURG, OHIO.

8 LINE PICA CONDENSED GRECIAN SHADE

SHORT MAPS

Knox, 1858.

12 LINE PICA EXTRA CONDENSED OPEN GRECIAN

DOCTRINES !

Knox, 1858.

15 LINE GRECIAN

MOCON

Cooley, c. 1859.

7 LINE PICA ANTIQUE

HORSE

16 LINE PICA CLARENDON

MUDIC
ketchu

16 LINE PICA CLARENDON CONDENSED

CHANTER
dangerous

12 LINE PICA GRECIAN EXTRA CONDENSED

MONTGOMERY
Montmorenci 17

Wells & Webb, 1854.

113

14 LINE PICA ROMAN NO. 2

SON

Wells & Webb, 1849.

50 LINE PICA DOUBLE EXTRA CONDENSED ROMAN

ICE

BILL, STARK & CO.   WILLIMANTIC, CT.

Bill, Stark & Co., 1853.

16 LINE PICA ROMAN DOUBLE EXTRA CONDENSED

EXHIBIT of

Wells & Webb, 1854.

10 LINE PICA HALF EXTENDED ROMAN

O E.

3 LINE PICA EXTENDED ROMAN

DEPOT
ha25

Knox, 1858.

The Romans

The number of Romans sharply diminished in wood type specimen books during this period. Of the six available wood type catalogues covering this period, only Bill, Stark and Company showed a Roman Italic, and even here there was only one showing. Backslope and Italic had practically disappeared. What emphasis there was on Romans may be found only in the XX Condensed with the lowercase shown by Page in 1859, and in the Light Face styles.

Bill, Stark and Company illustrated a Roman XX Condensed in 1853, but without a lowercase. In the next year, however, Wells and Webb showed a lowercase for this design. Knox in 1858 accompanied his showing of this style with a lowercase, but the lowercase did not become the rule until the 1870's.

Knox illustrated a unique Roman called Half Extended Roman which in width fell between the Extended and the Full Face, and there was no lowercase. In 1859 William Page showed a Roman Light Face and Roman Extended Light Face, neither with lowercase. Cooley in his catalogue circa 1859 shows additionally a Roman Extended No. 1 and Roman Light Face X Condensed, both with lowercase. The No. 1 is the same as Roman Extended first shown by Nesbitt in 1838 except that the weight of the stems has been reduced. All of the Cooley designs include a lowercase. Cooley also had a one page display of Old Style with lowercase, the first showing of this group of type faces, which were to become prominent in the 1870's and 1880's. Cooley also included the first showing in a wood type book of the Roman XXX Condensed, the extreme compression of which was more than the typefounders ever attempted. This style was the last modification of the Old Fat Face Romans which had gradually been condensed and lightened through the years. During the 1870's, Roman XXX was frequently shown with a lowercase.

During this period the typefounders moved sharply to the lighter Romans, and the 1853 L. Johnson and Company metal specimens included an extensive showing of Light Face Romans in several styles, and almost all in a series. The Light Face Romans had been shown earlier, but not in this quantity. The Extra Condensed styles in metal were almost as compressed as the Double Extra Condensed styles then being cut in wood.

16 LINE PICA DOUBLE EXTRA CONDENSED ROMAN

SPANBU 28

Knox, 1858.

24 AND 12 LINE ROMAN.

M

DIM
rint

40 LINE ROMAN DOUBLE EXTRA CONDENSED

RUDE

14 LINE ROMAN LIGHT FACE

GRIN

Page, 1859.

5 LINE ROMAN EXTENDED LIGHT FACE

COMD

Page, 1859.

ROMAN TRIPLE EXTRA CONDENSED

NICE BUD

ROMAN EXTRA CONDENSED LIGHT FACE

CHESTS

ROMAN EXTENDED NO. 1

JIB
ahn

10 AND 5 LINE OLD STYLE

In days

Chief, in fact

Cooley, c. 1859.

20 LINE PICA EXTRA CONDENSED GOTHIC

NOBLE

Wells & Webb, 1854.

8 LINE PICA GOTHIC EXTRA CONDENSED

WINDHAM CT

Bill, Stark & Co., 1853.

30 LINE GOTHIC DOUBLE EXTRA CONDENSED

CHODE

15 LINE GOTHIC DOUBLE EXTRA CONDENSED

MEBOBURG

15 LINE GOTHIC EXTRA CONDENSED LIGHT FACE

COURTING

Page, 1859.

24 LINE GOTHIC EXTRA CONDENSED

Hondane

18 LINE GOTHIC EXTRA CONDENSED

Cheap Good

Cooley, c. 1859.

The Gothics

As with the Romans during these same years, the Gothic Italic and Backslope disappeared from the specimen books with the exception of one Gothic Condensed Italic shown by Bill, Stark and Company in 1853. The 1854 Wells & Webb specimen of Gothic Extra Condensed was the same as shown for 1849, but the same style shown by Bill, Stark and Company was a much lighter style. The de-emphasis of the bolder styles resulted in an increased number of medium and light styles of Gothic during this period by wood type manufacturers.

The typefounders had begun showing the lighter Gothics regularly in the early 1840's. Page in 1859 illustrated a Gothic XX Condensed without lowercase, and a Gothic X Condensed Light Face, again without lowercase. A Gothic XXX Condensed is listed by Page for 1865. The Gothic X Condensed Light Face exhibited a good color, and differed from other Gothics, especially those of the typefounders, in the design of the round letters, which were very angular.

Several varieties of Gothic Round Condensed were common to all specimen books in these years—Gothic Round Condensed Outlined or Tooled, which were popular with typefounders during the 1860's, as were the solid faced styles. Knox presented a deviation of Gothic Round which may be identified by odd bulging serifs on the S and spur of the G, and the balance of the alphabet appears to be designed along conventional lines. Knox also showed a rather clumsily drawn Gothic Light Face without lowercase. The first showing of the lowercase for the Gothic X Condensed was by Cooley, and the entire alphabet reflected a highly refined drawing of the letterforms, which would compare favorably if not surpass many similar designs from this century. Cooley also showed a Gothic Extended which was complete with lowercase and figures. The wood type manufacturers never carried the Gothics to the same degree of lightness as the founders. One of the more extreme designs by a founder was that of L. Johnson in 1849 with a Gothic called Hairline, which certainly was! In 1859 Page showed the first Runics, without a lowercase, in a wood type specimen book; however, in the 1872 specimens, lowercase was present and was to become common throughout the balance of the century. In 1860 the Boston Type Foundry presented Runic in a series of eight sizes of metal type. Although Runics had few variations, the design was in common use for a number of years. The source of the design is unknown, and according to the descriptions given by Nicolette Gray, the style does not seem to be the one called by that name in England.

Another new design from the Page catalogue was Antique or Gothic Tuscan—a design representing one of those examples of overlap where the parent letterform cannot be definitely established. It was shown with lowercase and it was to be used extensively as a poster type, but was not cast by the typefounders until late in the century. Several Gothic Italians came into the market during the 1850's. Bill, Stark and Company in 1853 showed the first one, which was essentially the same as the one shown by Marr, the English typefounders in the same year. A related design shown by Page and Cooley at the end of the decade was called Gothic Tuscan No. 4 by Cooley, and was essentially the same design that was labeled Gothic Tuscan No. 2 by Page. The designs were the same but the cuttings differed; also, Cooley's had a lowercase while Page's did

16 LINE PICA GOTHIC CONDENSED

WINES
dreims

Wells & Webb, 1854.

8 LINE PICA CONDENSED ROUND GOTHIC

RUNS OAK

16 LINE PICA CONDENSED ROUND OPEN GOTHIC NO. 2

BROI

12 LINE PICA ROUND OPEN GOTHIC NO. 1

NAE

Knox, 1858.

10 LINE GOTHIC ROUND

DIMES

Page, 1859.

20 LINE GOTHIC ROUND

MEN

20 LINE GOTHIC ORNAMENTED NO. 1

JONES

20 LINE GOTHIC ORNAMENTED

JONES

Cooley, c. 1859.

6 LINE PICA LIGHT FACE GOTHIC

FOAM JU

10 LINE PICA GOTHIC

RICH
bona

Knox, 1858.

14 LINE RUNIC

NODEM

Page, 1859.

10 LINE RUNIC

RUNIC
Keeping

Cooley, c. 1859.

12 LINE PICA EXTRA CONDENSED TUSCAN NO. 2

LUSTER

Bill, Stark & Co., 1853.

30 LINE GOTHIC TUSCAN NO. 2

EAR

Page, 1859.

18 LINE GOTHIC TUSCAN NO. 4

HEN RIB

15 LINE GOTHIC TUSCAN POINTED

The Fir King

Cooley, c. 1859.

30 LINE ANTIQUE TUSCAN NO. 9

MORNING

buttons 16

20 LINE GOTHIC TUSCAN NO. 3

TISUES

Page, 1859.

15 LINE GOTHIC TUSCAN NO. 3

Hayneo groan

12 LINE GOTHIC DOUBLE EXTRA CONDENSED

HICS RUSK

Rendit holes

Cooley, c. 1859.

25 LINE TREBLE EXTRA CONDENSED GOTHIC

BONE

Merchantable

Page, 1865.

8 LINE GOTHIC EXTENDED

MU dou

Cooley, c. 1859.

12 LINE PICA TUSCAN EXTRA CONDENSED

TUSCAN

12 LINE PICA TUSCAN EXTRA CONDENSED SHADE, NO. 1

ABCDEF

12 LINE PICA TUSCAN EXTRA CONDENSED SHADE, NO. 3

ABCDEF

Bill, Stark & Co., 1853.

10 LINE PICA CONCAVE TUSCAN

CONCAVE!

Knox, 1858.

not. The Gothic Tuscan Italian shown by Bill, and later shown by Page and Cooley, did not have a lowercase, but was to have one later in the century. Both the Gothic Tuscan Pointed and Italian were used extensively by the typefounders during the 1860's and afterward. Nicolette Gray shows only one design which in any way resembles these two faces: the one previously mentioned as being cut by Marr in 1853. Page in one of his numbered series titled Gothic Tuscans illustrated some of the first treatments of the Gothic with points at top and bottom as well as median. This device was to have many variations over the next 25 years.

The first showing of Gothic Tuscan, sometimes called Gothic Concave (which the author will use to reduce confusion), was in the 1853 catalogue of Bill, Stark and Company, but it is thought that the design did not originate with this company. It was illustrated in a solid faced style, Open Shade, and Solid with Outline Shade. Concave Tuscan (often labeled Gothic Tuscan) Concave Tuscan Extended, Concave Tuscan Condensed, and Concave Tuscan X Condensed were all listed by William Page in 1859, and the 1872 catalogue showed lowercase for all these designs. Gothic Concave was a completely separate design from the Gothic Tuscan Condensed first shown by Wells and Webb in 1849, and was really more similar in design principle to Antique Tuscan in that concave lines were substituted for straight ones. The Bill showing did not include a lowercase, which was to come later along with a range of Full Face, Extended, and Extra Condensed, all with lowercases. Gothic Concave, which can be considered a secondary face of the Gothics, was to lead to additional designs like Phanitalians, Teutonic, etc.

Gothic Concave did not find interpretation in metal until later in the century, an interpretation that had only limited popularity even though the design was very important in wood as a poster face. Connor in his 1876 catalogue showed a series of three sizes with lowercase called Curved Gothic and patented September 8, 1874, and June 22, 1875.

There were many ornamental intepretations of Gothic during this period, and often the embellishments and ornamental devices were the same as those used on earlier treatments of Roman and Antique. Open Shade, Outlined with Shade, Outlined, etc. were applied to new designs almost as soon as the new style was introduced. The Gothic Amalgamation that appeared in this same catalogue had the same treatment as had been applied to Antique as early as Nesbitt's catalogue in 1838. The most original ornamental Gothics were those of Page in 1859. Among these designs, most of which were listed in the catalogue as Chromatics, there were an original floral and modulated Outlined, Striped, Checkered, Plaid, and Diagonal Inside Shading.

10 LINE PICA GOTHIC CONDENSED-AMALGAMATION SHADE

HORNETS

16 LINE PICA GOTHIC CONDENSED OPEN

RHINO

12 LINE PICA GOTHIC CONDENSED SHADE NO. 4

DANGE

Wells & Webb, 1854.

30 LINE GOTHIC ORNAMENTED NO. 4

DIE

20 LINE GOTHIC ORNAMENTED NO. 6

LEDE

40 LINE GOTHIC ROUND SHADE

FIE

12 LINE GOTHIC CONDENSED SHADE NO. 1

HUMIE

Page, 1859.

Type Specimens

12 LINE PICA ANTIQUE TUSCAN

ROSE

brain

8 LINE PICA ANTIQUE CONDENSED TUSCAN

MORAND

12 LINE PICA ANTIQUE TUSCAN EXTRA CONDENSED

ENGLISH

4 LINE PICA EXTENDED ANTIQUE TUSCAN

CHART

7 LINE PICA ANTIQUE TUSCAN CONDENSED SHADE

REPUBLICAN

Wells & Webb, 1854.

9 LINE PICA CONDENSED ANTIQUE TUSCAN

BUSCID!

horsyz.

4 LINE PICA EXTENDED ANTIQUE TUSCAN

SCOTS!

rebels

8 LINE PICA ANTIQUE TUSCAN NO. 2

EASTON

hrcb 32

6 LINE PICA EXTENDED ANTIQUE TUSCAN NO. 2

JHIC

krbo

Knox, 1858.

Semi-Ornamental

Nicolette Gray defines Semi-Ornamental metal types as those "Which are undecorated but which introduce a new variation to the form of the letter." The following description is offered of Semi-Ornamental wood types: They are solid-faced letters, frequently derivative in design, that obtain a decorative quality from an active contour, and that generally include some visual ambiguity between letterform and counter or between adjacent letterforms. As the majority of these faces were designed and used primarily in America, they are referred to as the American Tuscans.

The first indication of these faces emerged in the Antique Tuscan introduced by Wells and Webb in 1849. In the Wells and Webb catalogue for 1854 there were an Antique Tuscan, Extended, Condensed, and Extra Condensed —only the Antique Tuscan had a lowercase; Antique Tuscan Extended and Condensed with lowercase by Knox, 1858, X and XX Condensed with lowercase by Cooley circa 1859. Page showed an Antique Tuscan XX Condensed without lowercase in 1859. And the Knox catalogue for 1858 had an Antique Tuscan Extended with lowercase, as well as ornamental styles of Antique Tuscan—a Full Face and Extended with lowercases. The ornamentation was achieved by additional scallops and points on the contour with the face solid. Knox also included an Antique Tuscan X Condensed Outlined which was merely the result of adding an old device to a new letterform. In 1859 Page showed an Antique Tuscan XX Condensed, a face so light as a result of compressing that the letterforms fit well into the trend of Light Face styles then in vogue. There was no lowercase and it was only occasionally that one was cut for it during the century.

Page was to embellish, shade, and otherwise ornament a wide variety of the Antique Tuscans, his designs for which in his 1859 catalogue represent the most extensive showing to be found in any specimen book of the era. The 1854 Wells and Webb catalogue introduced a solid-faced Gothic Tuscan Italian which greatly exaggerated the concavity of the Gothic Tuscan Condensed first shown in the 1849 catalogue. Connor was to show a similar design in metal in his 1885 specimens (not believed to be the first date for its showing). This treatment created pronounced optical illusions resulting from the combination of counters and spaces between letters. No other company was to show this particular design, but some degree of this exaggeration occurred in later Gothic Tuscans.

In 1858 David Knox and Company showed a fairly large selection of Semi-Ornamental styles, all labeled Tuscan and numbered. While some of these are the same as shown a year later by Page, several were unique to Knox. Some of these were designed to capitalize on optical illusions, but not all were that successful, since in general they lacked the total refinement associated with Page's designs. In a few examples, it seemed as if the two cuttings by Knox and Page had a common design, but they differed almost enough to make two separate designs. Knox did use decorative motifs on the medians of several styles, such as dots, teardrops, or triangles: Page stayed with a solid face. Also, Knox showed many of these designs in an Outlined version. Page's Semi-Ornamented designs were all titled either Gothic or Antique Tuscan and numbered from 1 through 11, and a few of them were complete with lowercase. None of the Knox specimens except for two Ornamented versions of the Antique Tuscan and Extended

120

16 LINE PICA CONDENSED TUSCAN OPEN

BOLDE

10 LINE PICA OPEN ANTIQUE TUSCAN

CAPSB

Knox, 1858.

20 LINE ANTIQUE TUSCAN, DOUBLE EXTRA CONDENSED

MOHGCD

15 LINE ANTIQUE TUSCAN SHADE NO. 2

SIE

15 LINE ANTIQUE TUSCAN, CHECKED

SIG

Page, 1859.

8 LINE ANTIQUE TUSCAN OPEN

Decemb

8 LINE ANTIQUE TUSCAN EXTRA CONDENSED

Instudo

14 LINE ANTIQUE TUSCAN DOUBLE CONDENSED

South Wind!

Cooley, c. 1859.

8 LINE PICA GOTHIC TUSCAN ITALIAN

MAR

Wells & Webb, 1854.

14 LINE PICA EXTRA CONDENSED ANTIQUE TUSCAN NO. 1

YEAUH

14 LINE PICA EXTRA CONDENSED ANTIQUE TUSCAN NO. 2

HUBARD

12 LINE PICA EXTRA CONDENSED ANTIQUE TUSCAN NO. 3

HP BUR

12 LINE PICA CONDENSED TUSCAN

BFOSTEG

12 LINE PICA CONDENSED TUSCAN NO. 1

BFOSTEG

24 LINE PICA IMPERIAL

DEFS

16 LINE PICA IMPERIAL (DIFFERENT FROM SPECIMEN ABOVE)

DUELPI

Knox, 1858.

30 LINE PICA DOUBLE EXTRA CONDENSED ANTIQUE TUSCAN

FRIEDG

50 LINE PICA DOUBLE EXTRA CONDENSED ANTIQUE TUSCAN

RICE

12 LINE PICA TUSCAN

BORDS

12 LINE PICA EXTRA CONDENSED CORINTHIAN

NRTP 56

12 LINE PICA EXTRA CONDENSED GOTHIC TUSCAN

BADONPH

24 LINE CONCAVE GOTHIC

PIED

Knox, 1858.

30 LINE ANTIQUE TUSCAN NO. 2

ORION

20 LINE ANTIQUE TUSCAN NO. 5

RUBI

20 LINE ANTIQUE TUSCAN NO. 3

CORD

40 LINE ANTIQUE TUSCAN NO. 8

REN

18 LINE ANTIQUE TUSCAN NO. 7

GRINS

30 LINE ANTIQUE TUSCAN NO. 4

RUG

Page, 1859.

30 LINE ANTIQUE TUSCAN NO. 1

BEAM

15 LINE ANTIQUE TUSCAN NO. 6

CODELL

6 LINE ANTIQUE TUSCAN NO. 11

SINGask

Page, 1859.

15 LINE LIGHT FACE

SHRED

24 LINE ANTIQUE NO. 2

BRE

18 LINE GOTHIC TUSCAN NO. 2

HOURI

18 LINE GOTHIC CONDENSED NO. 3

COBERD

16 LINE GOTHIC TUSCAN NO. 6

CORN!

Cooley, c. 1859.

had lowercase. A number of the Page Semi-Ornamented designs made use of serif treatments which were reminiscent of European trifurcated and bifurcated Tuscans. His Tuscans, not only the ones in the 1859 catalogue, but also those patented by him through the next 15 years, relied on a median notch, point or bulge device, and were particularly effective because of the amazing consideration between letter weight, counter, and the resulting space between letters. Invariably the styles which functioned best were the ones that were condensed and could be composed in tight groupings.

Cooley, who showed one or two designs with interior median decorative motifs which were very much like the Knox designs, also had several interesting designs which were quite different from those of Page and Knox. A different visual principle was employed, and in a true sense, the types were not part of the Semi-Ornamented classification. One of the most novel of these was a Gothic Condensed No. 3, which was an Outlined Gothic with notches at top, bottom, and median (which incidentally added little to the design). Since the top and bottom fifths of the letter were solid and the three fifths through the center were open, an illusion was created of a band in front of the letters. This design never appeared in any other wood type specimen book but did show up as a metal type later in the century. Another Cooley design was Gothic Tuscan No. 6, which was a conventional Gothic with knobs at top, bottom, and at the median. During the 1870's and 1880's there were to be several similar designs brought onto the market, and the same device was applied especially to the Antique letterform.

One of the earliest showings of a Semi-Ornamented face (Antique Tuscan No. 5), which predates Page by several years, was first seen in the specimens of L. Johnson and Company in the section showing larger types. Because of the faces accompanying it, there is a distinct possibility that it may have originated with wood letters. Hagar in 1854 was to show the same design in the same size, and it was not until another showing by Johnson in the 1857 *Typographic Advertiser* of two sizes, 24 and 36 point, that it could be definitely classified as a metal type. In 1859 James Connor showed the same design in four sizes ranging from 24 to 60 points. The design was called Antique Tuscan by Johnson, Ornamented No. 8 by Connor. The origin for this design is unknown. It does not appear to be European, and it cannot be definitely established as originating in wood. It was, however, one of the first of a group which was most representative of the American Tuscans.

20 AND 8 LINE ITALIAN

H
STEAM

Debow, c. 1837.

The Ornamentals

The Bill, Stark and Company catalogue carried only one European Tuscan, which had been shown by Nesbitt in 1838. All the other Ornamental styles were the previously shown Antique, Gothic, and secondary faces with Outline, Outlined, Shade, etc. In 1854 Wells and Webb had a large selection of Ornamental styles. Of their many European designs, the emphasis seemed to be on the Zebra Tuscans, a number of variations on the basic Zebra design, and Ornamented Doric. At the same time they illustrated a Zebra Open Shade style with lowercase—the only known instance of a lowercase for this design being found. On the basis of showings in specimen books from these years Zebra and Doric seem to have been the most important designs of the period.

Ornamented Doric was outlined with the top half of the interior letter solid and the bottom half open. There were graduated dots inside the stem and typical Tuscan serifs. The design, believed to have originated in France, was produced by Stephenson and Blake in England about 1849. The American typefounders made it shortly afterwards, as did the wood type manufacturers in the 1850's. Among the number of interpretations of the design, some solid faced styles in several weights were popular with wood type producers during the next few years. Wells and Webb illustrated one such face in their 1854 catalogue which was called Doric, and Cooley showed a light face version of the same design. To the author's knowledge, a lowercase was never cut for this type face in any of its styles.

The Octagon faces of Gothic and Antique as shown by Wells and Webb had been modified to Octagon Shade, with the shade on the *inside* of the letterform. The Octagon Antique with interior shade had been shown as a metal type in 1845 by the Boston Type Foundry. There were three or four Roman Ornamentals, probably French in origin and quite similar to those popular in the late 1820's and 1830's. Again, there was the usual Outline, Outlined, Double Outlined, Shade, etc. treatment of the primary and secondary faces. Knox in 1858 advertised the Doric Ornamented, but had no other Ornamentals other than some Outlined Antiques and Gothic Tuscans. There were not even the Roman and Antique Open Shades. Page in 1859 had a wide selection of Ornamental letters, but no Romans. The majority of Page's ornamented faces were based on Clarendon, Gothic, Antique and Gothic Tuscan, and a few Zebra faces. Other than the Zebra, there were only a few faces betraying European influences.

Cooley illustrated several Ornamentals which appear to be unique with his specimen book of c. 1859. Appearing European in origin, they are comparable to faces from the early 1840's shown by typefounders. At least two of these designs were solid with shade and had fine reversed lines making patterns either by interlacing or tracing the outline of the letter several times. Each tracing was in reduced scale to the next one on the interior of the letterform. One other unusual face, which only resembles several English styles, has a squared terminal notched. An outlined letter, it tapers to the middle from top and bottom and meets in a horizontal knob-like protuberance at the median.

Bill, Stark and Company showed no borders, but Wells and Webb illustrated several sizes of Grecian Fret plus one Outline Shaded geometric border. Also shown were hands representative of the penman's flourish work. Knox showed a few sizes of wood rule, but no borders. William Page framed most of his Ornamental designs and all of his Chromatics with the largest selection of borders yet seen in any wood type specimen book. The great variety of designs—lacy, floral, star, etc.—with the price for each marked at the bottom of the page, were all certainly original with Page, who in this particular field was to have no rival for as long as he remained in the wood type business. Cooley showed two designs which seem to have been original with him, and one series of border designs obviously copied from Page.

12 LINE PICA DORIC ORNAMENTED

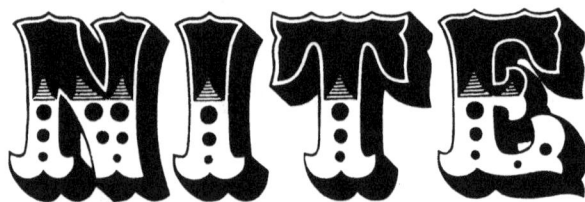

12 LINE PICA DORIC SHADE NO. 1

10 LINE PICA DORIC

24 LINE PICA TUSCAN CONDENSED ORNAMENTED NO. 1

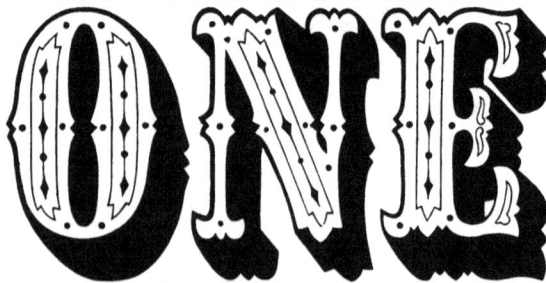

30 LINE PICA TUSCAN CONDENSED ORNAMENTED NO. 2

Wells & Webb, 1854.

7 LINE PICA TUSCAN ORNAMENTED

PEOPL

8 LINE PICA ORNAMENTED NO. 2

AILY SUN

7 LINE PERSPECTIVE CONDENSED

NEW YORK MIRR

7 LINE PICA TUSCAN CONDENSED SHADE NO. 1

AIR Lines 2

6 LINE PICA DORIC SHADE NO. 1

ORNAMENTS

28 LINE PICA ROMAN CONDENSED AND ORNAMENTED

HE

16 LINE PICA ANTIQUE OCTAGON SHADE

MUN

14 LINE PICA GOTHIC CONDENSED OCTAGON SHADE

TIMBER

Wells & Webb, 1854.

12 LINE PICA TUSCAN SHADE NO. 1

EFBODI

Knox, 1858.

12 LINE PICA DORIC SHADE NO. 2

IN BUD

Knox, 1858.

30 LINE TUSCAN CONDENSED NO. 2

HIE

30 LINE GOTHIC TUSCAN EXTRA ORNAMENTED

REND

16 LINE TUSCAN OPEN SHADE NO. 2

HEFI

24 LINE TUSCAN CONDENSED ORNAMENTED NO. 3

HIRI

16 LINE TUSCAN OUTLINE SHADE NO. 2

HEFI

20 LINE IONIC ORNAMENTED

IONI

12 LINE ORNAMENTED SHADE

CLOUD!

12 LINE GOTHIC TUSCAN SHADE NO. 1

HIDEN

Cooley, c. 1850.

30 LINE ANTIQUE TUSCAN EXTRA CONDENSED NO. 8 OPEN

RIDE

20 LINE TUSCAN OPEN ORNAMENTAL NO. 3

RENO

16 LINE TUSCAN OUTLINE SHADE

MUR

16 LINE TUSCAN SHADE

MUR

Cooley, c. 1859.

30 LINE TUSCAN CONDENSED SHADE

BET

40 LINE TUSCAN CONDENSED RAY SHADE NO. 2

BE

Page, 1859.

40 LINE TUSCAN CONDENSED ORNAMENTED

BE

Page, 1859.

12 LINE PICA TUSCAN CONDENSED NO. 2

RANGE

Bill, Stark & Co., 1853.

16 LINE PICA GOTHIC TUSCAN SHADE

MARE

Wells & Webb, 1854.

18 LINE PICA EXTRA CONDENSED OPEN GOTHIC TUSCAN

NEFAU

Knox, 1858.

15 LINE GOTHIC CONDENSED RAY SHADE NO. 1

HIRN

20 LINE GOTHIC TUSCAN DOUBLE SHADE

JER

15 LINE GOTHIC CONDENSED TUSCAN ORNAMENTED

HIRN

Page, 1859.

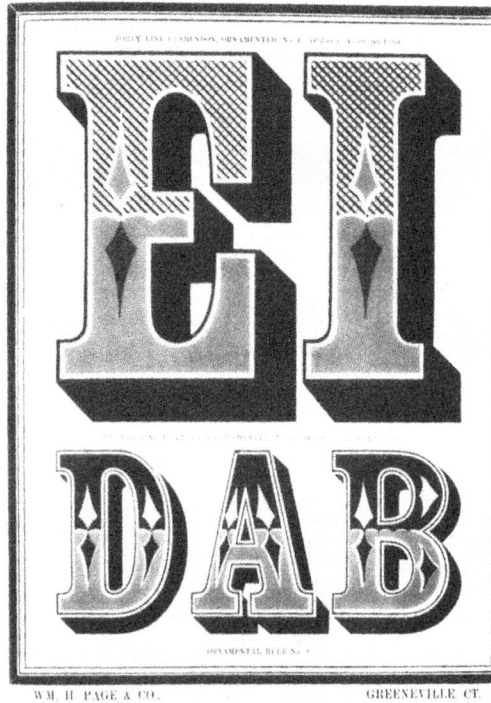

Page, 1859. Sample of chromatic types and borders shown by William Page at the back of his 1859 specimens.

The Scripts

In 1854 Wells and Webb at the front of their specimen book in a section devoted to newspaper heads showed one of the best scripts ever cut in wood, which was untitled. It was noted in handwriting that it was 14 cents per letter. Cooley showed two scripts—one being Madisonian, which had been designed and engraved by David Bruce, Jr., circa 1859, supposedly after the handwriting of Dolly Madison. The second was not a true script, and again, was first designed and engraved by David Bruce, Jr. Often called Bulletin Script, it was a backslope letter thin at the top and graduating to heavy at the base. It had a brush-like quality, but was not a true script in that letters did not connect. In the 1870's, the wood interpretations of this design, which was cut in several styles, gained a considerable following.

The Germans

In 1854 Wells and Webb showed ten pages of Germans, and William Page in 1859 illustrated several sizes of similar German designs on the first page of his specimens. Within 4 or 5 years, Page was to have greatly expanded the German series, in which many of the designs were patented. In 1870 William Page was to issue a small but handsome catalogue devoted entirely to German faces. Many of the German styles shown by Page were patented by him, and these designs date mostly from the 1860's.

12 LINE PICA TITLE SCRIPT

August.

E. R. Webb, 1854.

14 LINE MADISONIAN

Maryed

Six Lines Madisonian

Madisonian.

Four Lines Madisonian

A new style of letter, which we call Madisonian, is herewith presented to the craft. Nothing more beautiful has been in a long time invented. Heavier faces than those here shown can be cut, when desired, and any other size as well.

J. G. COOLEY & CO.   Five Lines Border. No. Five. $1.00 a foot.   South Windham, Conn.

Cooley, c. 1859.

16 LINE BRUSH SCRIPT

Chestesr

12 LINE BRUSH SCRIPT

Pr Steamr

Cooley, c. 1859.

12 LINE GERMAN

Ch. Albert

Wells & Webb, 1854.

20 LINE GERMAN

Giw

16 LINE GERMAN

Curdi

14 LINE GERMAN

Astou

6 LINE GERMAN

German Stowb 145

Page, 1859.

6 LINE PICA BLACK

Brest Toulo

Nesbitt, 1838.

12 LINE PICA CONDENSED BLACK

Hartford

Bill, Stark & Co., 1853.

1866 Through 1878

Advertising had advanced since its orgins in the late 1840's to a tremendous force in the trades by the late 1860's and early 1870's. It not only increased competition among the typefounders, but brought about significant changes in the role of the printer through the introduction of the advertising agent and volume printing. Advertising unquestionably moved job printing into the forefront as the largest single category of printing in this country, and its importance was to affect all the sister industries, correspondingly. The nature of advertising demanded "newness," a quality that was most felt in the design of typefaces in both metal and wood. It is possible that only now are we as professional designers regaining our equilibrum from the impact of advertising impetuses begun in the last quarter of the nineteenth century.

The productions of the metal typefounders were given a boost in this period through a new trend toward the use of ornamental display types in newspapers. The French newspapers had been using large display types since 1850, but in America, it had been extremely difficult to break the tradition of the "penny" paper and its agate advertisements. Undoubtedly the influence of the advertising agents who were now beginning to achieve importance was a factor behind the increasing use of display type in newspaper advertising.

The lithographic presses had been developed to produce tremendous qualities of color (chromolithography) work for an exceedingly low cost. Photo-mechanical engravings were made and used, thus sounding the first knell for the art of wood engraving, which nevertheless lingered on for another 30 or 40 years. Railroads crossed the country with spur lines being attached with great rapidity. Following the Homestead Act of 1862 and the Civil War, immigrants were moving west in waves as each new contingent of Europeans migrated to this country. Printing followed the settlers westward and in a surprisingly short time regional markets created sufficient demand for founders and manufacturers of printing equipment to build substantial operations far removed from traditional locations on the East Coast. The end of the period was marked by a financial crisis with a momentary depression of trades all over the country.

William Page, who had become the largest single producer of wood type and borders in the world, created the finest wood types ever manufactured. The firm of Vanderburgh, Wells and Company was the prime competitor of Page during these 12 years. After the fire of 1867 which destroyed the Paterson works, Vanderburgh and Wells expanded their wood type production at a new location in New York City, and while it is doubtful that the firm ever reached the peak it had attained under Darius Wells and Ebenezer Webb, it nevertheless knew a period of prosperity. In 1866, Cooley took Theodore Dauchy into partnership, thus forming the firm of Cooley and Dauchy. During these years Cooley and Dauchy exploited the new field of advertising, and they enlarged their printers' warehouse with more diligence than their wood type manufacture and marketing, so that by the time of the fire which destroyed their firm in 1868, wood type was only a minor branch of their activities. After the fire, Cooley sold his wood type business to William Page, who incorporated it into his already extensive operations.

On a limited scale, William T. Morgans began to produce wood type in Napanoch, New York in 1876, and in 1878, Charles Tubbs and his partners founded the American Wood Type Company in South Windham, Connecticut. It is believed that these two companies were only small competitors for the established firms of Page and Vanderburgh, and Wells and Company. Also, the two newcomers contributed few, if any original type designs to the wood type industry during these years.

Even though new methods for manufacturing wood type and greater quantities of new designs were to be marketed in the following years, wood type design reached a high point between 1866 and 1878. The quality of new designs issued during these years was consistently good—both for the ornamental and the plain faces. The primary families of Roman, Gothic, and Antique had run the gauntlet of being expanded and condensed by the end of the last period, so that the emphasis in this era was on the development of the secondary faces. Perhaps the most significant type designs of the period were the French Clarendons and Antiques, with all their derivative designs. While hints of the French Antique had been forecast many years earlier, such as in the treatment of weights and serifs in Caslon's Grotesque Italian, these new designs were to come out of France sometime during the early 1860's, after which they were quickly assimilated into the repertories of typefounders and wood type manufacturers all over the Western world, especially in America. These were translated into a host of new interpretations and families, and lowercase was almost always designed for each new style.

It was between 1866 and 1878 that typefounders and wood type manufacturers went their separate ways in the design of letterforms. The typefounders, committed to their competition with lithographers, also were expanding on the lighter styles of the French founders which were very popular. Most of these faces were either exceedingly fragile or delicately embellished and while not impossible for cutting in wood, they did not meet the display requirements for poster printing. The wood type manufacturers therefore began to design their own faces on a greater scale than at any previous time. Also, during these years both the founder and wood type producer began an extensive practice of patenting their original designs. In the 1874 Chromatic wood type catalogue, for example, Page had patented no fewer than 36 of the specimens.

Most design modifications took place within the Antique family, and the importance of Roman as a display type continued to dwindle. A number of Antique and Gothic "Specials," usually numbered, came onto the market, but aside from these, there were not any important variations in the primary families. The European Ornamentals had disappeared completely from the wood type specimen books, and American typefounders were less dependent on European sources and began to produce their own designs. Wood type manufacturers began showing in quantity a variety of hands, stars, ornaments, catch words, and borders. Vanderburgh, Wells and Company were to illustrate a number of bag ornaments, logotypes, and newspaper heads. Most of these items had been advertised, and occasionally illustrated previously, but not in as great a quantity. Page began marketing tint blocks, which because they were designed to print in color, were shown only with his Chromatic specimens.

The Antiques

This period belongs mainly to the French Clarendons and French Antiques along with their many derivative styles.

20 LINE FRENCH CLARENDON

REN

10 LINE FRENCH CLARENDON

Conducts

30 LINE FRENCH ANTIQUE

RING

Beautiful 35

10 LINE CLARENDON NO. 1

Human
ROME

Page, 1872.

While French Clarendon had been marketed as a wood letter in 1865 by Page, it was not until 1869 that Page showed French Antique in the *Typographic Messenger*. The French Clarendons were heavy, condensed, and had elongated serifs with distinct bracketing. The Americans, particularly the wood type manufacturers, were partial to the more condensed versions of these designs, so that both French Antique and Clarendon were to be XXX Condensed with lowercase by the early 1870's. The designs most similar to the French Antique as issued by the French and English were not cut in wood until the 1870's, when they were labeled Egyptian, or numbered as an Antique Special.

The main difference between the first display Clarendons, slightly condensed and extremely heavy in color, and the derivative faces such as French and Italian Clarendon, may be found primarily in the serif treatments. The derivative styles had serifs which constituted from one half to two thirds the total height of the letter. Clarendon No. 1 and Clarendon Italian may be distinguished mainly by these heavier serifs. The French Clarendons were heavy, but more condensed than Clarendon. Egyptian, Belgian, and Parisian are characterized by thin stems and heavy serifs, the contrast being most pronounced in the Belgian.

James Connor's Sons, one of the first typefounders to have an extensive showing of these new designs, had nine sizes of Egyptian ranging from 6 to 48 points in his 1870 specimen book. Their designs were not unlike the European models except somewhat lighter in weight and slightly more compressed. The majority of faces in this category to be brought out by American founders in succeeding years closely resembled the Connor designs. In 1867, Mc-Kellar, in his first specimen book, after taking over L. Johnson and Company, showed four sizes of French Clarendon ranging from 24 to 48 points. The design, however, identical to the face called Egyptian by Connor, was not at all a typical French Clarendon. In 1871 the Boston Type Foundry illustrated a style called French Clarendon, but it was actually the same Egyptian by Connor. Egyptian No. 4, which was like the Connor Egyptian, an Egyptian Extended, a French Clarendon Shaded (which again was not a Clarendon but an Antique), and an Egyptian Extra Condensed were also issued by the Boston Type Foundry.

It is interesting to note the inconsistency in titling, as both the face called French Clarendon and Egyptian Extra Condensed are unbracketed. In this respect, the wood type manufacturers were amazingly consistent. Derivative faces of Clarendon that were bracketed usually incuded Clarendon in the titling, and the same consistency was maintained with Antique and the unbracketed styles. Wood type Egyptians were based on Clarendons, except for unbracketed Egyptians that were always designated as specials by being numbered. Perhaps more significant than these two designs was the host of derivative faces that followed them in rapid succession. The Ornamented Egyptians (as titled by wood type manufacturers) were first shown during 1870 as Egyptian, Egyptian Tuscan, Condensed, Ornamented, and numbered. These designs, the majority of which had a lowercase and figures, were created by adding points at the median and by bifurcating serifs of a letterform that was essentially a French Antique condensed with an exaggerated difference in weights between stems and serifs. In 1876 Connor patented a novelty face based on Egyptian which was called Crescent. The top line of the top serif and bottom line of the bottom serif curved like a rocker. Another odd interpretation, called Indian, was designed in wood by Page and shown in the *Typographic Messenger* during 1874. It corresponded in every respect to the Egyptian No. 2 cut by Page except that there was not a straight line in the alphabet! Serifs were rockers and even the stems tapered to the center. A curious face related to this group was shown by Page in 1870. It was as light as Skeleton Antique except for the bottom serifs which were heavy and the font which was kept consistent by thickening the lower parts of the round letters to correspond with the heavy serifs. The face was called "Mowry Antique" in honor of Page's partner, Samuel Mowry. Heber Wells was to show the same design under the same title at a later date.

Another important classification having its origin in this period is the Aldine. In his 1870 specimen book, Connor patented an Egyptian Extended in several sizes in 1868 that reflected most of the qualities to be associated with Aldine as cut by the wood type manufacturers. Since Page patented his Aldine circa 1870, it is not known whether he or Connor originated the design. The two men had been close friends and had worked together for a number of years previously. The design had the bracketed serifs of the Clarendons, a block-like quality in the round letters and serifs that were considerably heavier than stems. Aldine Expanded was introduced by Page in 1872, along with a light style called Norwich Aldine. Both designs had a lowercase. Vanderburgh, Wells and Company in 1877 showed a York Aldine, which was more compressed than the Norwich Aldine, as well as a York Aldine No. 2. Page patented the only Ornamented Aldine—for some unknown reason, the Aldines did not receive the same ornamental effects given to other Clarendons. The Aldine faces were extremely prominent in poster printing throughout the remainder of the century, and at a later date, there were a number of Aldine styles cast by typefounders.

A variation of the Clarendon (full face style), called "Columbian," was first listed by William Page in his 1870 specimens. It was only slightly more condensed than the full faced Clarendons, and there were minor variations in the designing of individual letters. There were a great number of designs based on the Clarendon letterform which came onto the market between 1866 and 1875. These designs would correspond to the numerous Semi-Ornamented faces of the previous period, except that they do not have the same figure-ground ambivalence as the earlier designs. One reason for this may be that Page, who created a considerable number of these designs, wanted them to serve a dual function, e.g., an ornamented plain faced letter and a basic letterform which could be printed in two colors as a Chromatic. Arcadian, Celtic, Unique, Caxton, Renaissance, Expanded No. 2, Armenian, American, Ionian, Corinthian, plus a number of Clarendons, Gothics, Romans, and one Antique Tuscan Expanded were designed for color printing by Page in the comparatively short period between 1870 and 1876. Although Page had a number of Chromatic designs in his 1859 specimens, he had never before been so prolific in producing Chromatic designs as he was between 1870-74.

Some of the most popular new styles, many of which were semi-ornamented, were: Arcadian, a French Clarendon with dots as median and on the serifs in 1870; Celtic, basically a Belgian with open rectilinear ornaments at the median in 1870; Unique, a similar design to Celtic, but with different median treatment; Castilian by Wells in

15 LINE CLARENDON ITALIAN

MB

8 LINE MOWRY ANTIQUE

Central 53 EXPRESS

15 LINE EGYPTIAN ORNAMENTED

ROSE Demented

Page, 1872.

6 LINE FRENCH CLARENDON NO. 2

Establish 2 PRESS ON

Page, 1878.

UNIQUE (PATENTED)

Home 2 TINER

ION

CELTIC NO. 2 (PATENTED)

RIOTS

CELTIC (PATENTED)

ROSE

CELTIC ORNAMENTED (PATENTED)

COE

ARCADIAN NO. 1

LINE Beloveds

ARCADIAN (PATENTED)

SON

Page, 1872.

READ

Democratic

Neck
GUN

Cure 12
RODES

Trades
HARD

Sledges
WORK

Page, 1872.

1877; and Caxton No. 7 with curious knobby serifs by Page in 1872. Additionally, there were Ionian and Ionian No. 1 by Page in 1870, which were based on Antique and Mansard Ornamented and Virginian by Wells, and Armenian, a curious light Tuscan shown in the *Typographic Messenger* by Page in 1869.

Vanderburgh, Wells and Company in 1877 illustrated an Old Style Antique which retained a close relationship in weight between serif and stem. While this design had qualities suggestive of Romans, there was small resemblance between this letterform and that of Roman Old Style. In color, it was similar to the Jensen designed for and produced by the typefounders at the end of the century. There was little new in the Grecian family other than a Grecian XX Condensed with lowercase shown by Page in 1872.

The Antique Tuscan No. 9, first shown by William Page in 1859, was interpreted by Wells in 1877 as a face called Eureka. It did not have a lowercase and was much like the Page design except that it had been expanded. A popular display face, Eureka was often ornamented by adding a median dot, sometimes an open diamond. Eventually, Eureka was cut with lowercase. Similar, but lighter designs had been imported by the founder from Europe around the middle of the century, but it is not known whether Eureka was arrived at independently by Americans or was a modification of the European models.

Serif treatments such as notching, trifurcating, or adding dots, points, or notches were very characteristic of this period. These serifs may be compared to the fish-tail serifs of the preceding period as being representative design devices. The notched serifs had been characteristic of European types imported to America in great numbers from the 1830's through the 1840's. Between 1867 and 1876 the Bruce typefoundry patented a number of dotted designs.

In 1872 Page exhibited an Antique XX Condensed with lowercase, which he had already shown in 1859 but without lowercase. Also, in the 1872 specimens Page included an Antique Tuscan XX Condensed No. 1, which was only slightly less condensed than the unnumbered design. Tuscan Extended had been listed by Page in 1870 with lowercase. Although the trifurcated squared serifs with bars bisecting at the median created a busy look to the design, it was eventually cast by founders and was used for display printing during the last quarter of the century.

18 & 10 LINE BELGIAN

BEND

Reconstruct

15 LINE CAXTON NO. 7 (PATENTED)

BM

15 LINE ARMENIAN

CISE

6 LINE TUSCAN EXTENDED

lost

SXE

15 LINE ANTIQUE TUSCAN X CONDENSED NO. 5

HID

20 LINE IONIC

RIGT

Page, 1872.

12 LINE TUSCAN EGYPTIAN NO. 2

NEIGH!

12 LINE TUSCAN EGYPTIAN CONDENSED

ELGIN Watches 213

8 & 12 LINE CASTILIAN

OLD CASTILIAN

SONG BIRD1

24 LINE MANSARD ORNAMENTED

GEM

24 LINE MALTESE

HAD

12 LINE VIRGINIAN

URBANE

12 LINE CASTILIAN CONDENSED

HYDROPHOBY

Vanderburgh, Wells & Co., 1877.

HIM

Gifts

VANDERBURGH, WELLS & CO., 110 Fulton and 16 & 18 Dutch Streets, New York.

HOUND

HOME!

DAYine

Vanderburgh, Wells & Co., 1877.

134

Mind6
DINES

HOP
vine

GRADuated 3

Histories
GOLDEN

RENail 1

LONG Branch

CAN Rest 234

Vanderburgh, Wells & Co., 1877.

10 LINE EGYPTIAN X CONDENSED

SILVER Threads

12 LINE PARISIAN

All kinds of GOLD PEN

Vanderburgh, Wells & Co., 1877.

COLUMBIAN

M

Fates BIDE

8 LINE CLARENDON LIGHT FACE ITALIC

BEVEL Great Towe

5 LINE CLARENDON EXTENDED

HER PENT Inse

Page, 1872.

8 LINE ALDINE

Lech NED

4 LINE ALDINE EXPANDED

Enert RUM

8 LINE NORWICH ALDINE

DICE

6 LINE GRECIAN (FULL FACE)

NOT

10 LINE GRECIAN XX CONDENSED

Clownish 25 BOUNTIFUL

10 LINE ANTIQUE XX CONDENSED NO. 1

Democrat ROUTINE

Page, 1872.

12 LINE ATHABASCAN

BET

12 LINE MODOC

MULE

6 LINE NO. 52

DIME

Page, 1878.

4 LINE EXPANDED NO. 4

RINE

5 LINE EXPANDED NO. 3

TIN

6 LINE EXPANDED NO. 2

DE

12 LINE FRENCH CLARENDON ORNAMENTED

DICE

8 LINE AMERICAN

NAG

12 LINE ARCADIAN SHADED NO. 1

BRED

Page, 1872.

10 LINE ANTIQUE CONDENSED ORNAMENTED

DIRE

8 LINE ALDINE ORNAMENTED

ABC

Page, 1872.

60 LINE CHROMATIC IONIAN NO. 4

IIS

IIS

30 LINE CAXTON NO. 3

SIZE

30 LINE CHROMATIC FLORENTINE

MS

40 LINE CLARENDON ORNAMENTED

M

Page, 1874.

24 LINE CELTIC NO. 1 OPEN

PERT

18 LINE NO. 96

ODD

12 LINE ARCADIAN NO. 1 OPEN

SERL

12 LINE ARCADIAN OPEN

ALSO

12 LINE MARTONIAN

FARM

Page, 1878.

24 LINE MALTESE SHADED

FACE

16 LINE CASTILIAN ORNAMENTED

GENDE

Vanderburgh, Wells & Co., 1877.

20 LINE ANTIQUE TUSCAN X CONDENSED, NO. 6 OPEN

HERD

18 LINE VIRGINIAN OPEN

HIDE

20 LINE FRENCH CLARENDON SHADED NO. 6

LD15

15 LINE EGYPTIAN SHADE

BAKER!

15 LINE EGYPTIAN SHADE NO. 1

BAKER

Vanderburgh, Wells & Co., 1877.

137

20 LINE ROMAN XXX CONDENSED

FRAUDS

10 LINE ROMAN XX CONDENSED

Graduates

SHIRKING

6 LINE ROMAN X CONDENSED LIGHT FACE

Harmonize

MENTIONS

4 LINE ROMAN EXTENDED LIGHT FACE

India
RUN

4 LINE ROMAN EXTENDED

Hat
LID

Page, 1872.

The Romans

All specimen books of this period featured the double and treble Condensed Romans, even though these designs were steadily declining in favor with the trade. It is thought that the fragility inherent in their design was a factor in their loss of popularity. The printer needed a display Roman which could withstand rough handling, be highly legible, and be heavy enough for display. The designs which best filled these demands were Aetna by Page, and Painters' Roman by Wells. The first record of Aetna is a listing in the Page 1870 specimens. There is a distinct possibility that Page originated the face since he patented a number of the ornamental Chromatics based on Aetna. The nearest design to Aetna cast by the typefounders may be found in Rimmed or Ray Shaded Romans which typefounders devised to compete with letterforms created by lithographic artists. Aetna was cut in XX, X, Condensed No. 1, Condensed, and full face styles, all with lowercase. Aetna was really a design distinct from the Painters' Roman of Wells, and Bolivian by Morgans and Wilcox, even though all three had similarities. Page was to cut a design numbered 110 around 1880 that more closely resembled these last two faces than did Aetna. Painters' Roman No. 110 and Bolivian had a more pronounced curve of the stems resulting in greater concavity to the letter, while Aetna had more of a drawn out bracket and gradual tapering of stems. Wells did cut a Painters' Roman No. 1 that was based on Page's Aetna. Although these designs were prominent in poster printing in the succeeding years, they are not known to have been cast by the typefounders.

The Old Styles shown by Cooley c. 1859 were gaining ground steadily, and Page showed Old Style Condensed with lowercase in 1872, which along with the Light Face Romans was to dominate the older Fat-Face Romans. Roman Light Face Extended was shown with lowercase by Page in 1872, and like the Ionic of the same catalogue, it is a beautifully proportioned and drawn display face which found regular service throughout the balance of the century.

18 LINE AETNA ORNAMENTED NO. 2

BITS

24 LINE AETNA ORNAMENTED NO. 3

SIN

Page, 1874.

Joyous 2
SHERG

R
Cash
DUN

Page, 1872.

RE Steal

HORMarch

ARMTrades

STONED Sketches

Page, 1878.

Great
RIDE
Ingrain 14

NUPontia

DUMB founded

Neck
TIES

Vanderburgh, Wells & Co., 1877.

FOLD Stand

Page, 1878.

GOTHIC BACK SLOPE

RENACDGSTY

6 LINE GOTHIC CONDENSED NO. 2

Granite
MART

10 LINE GOTHIC CONDENSED NO. 4

LIME

7 LINE GOTHIC ROUND LIGHT FACE

CRASH

5 LINE GOTHIC ROUND NO. 1

WORD

6 LINE GOTHIC TUSCAN

Indue
MICE

10 LINE GOTHIC TUSCAN X CONDENSED

Helmet

Page, 1872.

12 LINE GOTHIC POINTED NO. 1

WE

6 LINE GOTHIC POINTED

DUN

12 LINE GOTHIC TUSCAN NO. 1

ROUND

7 LINE ETRUSCAN NO. 4

DOMAIN

4 LINE RUNIC EXPANDED

Native
HEAD

5 LINE TEUTONIC

Prescribe
BARING

Page, 1872.

10 LINE GOTHIC, X CONDENSED LIGHT FACE

WHITE Rosebud

Vanderburgh, Wells & Co., 1877.

The Gothics

A Gothic Backslope was revived and shown by Page in the *Typographic Messenger* during 1869, but the slope was not as pronounced as earlier designs. Also, the Gothic was more condensed and lighter than the styles shown during the 1830's. It is not believed that the face was accepted too readily by the trade, for in a few years Page no longer showed the design. Page had a similar experience with a face called Curved Gothic shown in 1867. The straight lines were translated as undulating lines, and while there was a novelty effect, the face does not seem to have been popular with the trade.

Runic, which first appeared in 1859, was shown by Page in 1872 as Expanded, with a lowercase. The same year Page brought out Gothic (Concave) Tuscan Extra Condensed with lowercase. A number of Gothic secondary faces first exhibited in this period were to establish new trends which were not to materialize fully until the following period. The Phanitalian shown by Vanderburgh, Wells and Company in their 1877 catalogue seems to have been a continuation of the Concave Tuscans. The concavities were more exaggerated, there were straight lines at top and bottom of the letter, and the round letters did not have the angular qualities of the Concave Tuscans. (A similar design titled Ornamented No. 10, outlined and shaded, was shown by Bruce in 1865.) Gothic (Concave) Tuscan Extended listed in the 1865 Page catalogue was probably the transitional style, as it is the first example of that family to eliminate the older treatment (the points) of round letters. A comparative showing of Gothic Tuscan Extended and the later designs of Teutonic and Phanitalians illustrates the obvious relationships between these letter styles. Teutonic with lowercase, shown in the Page 1872 specimens, was similar to the previously mentioned Phanitalian of Wells, and there were a considerable number of other styles in these years that could be traced to the Concave Tuscans. Farmers, Little and Company, typefounders, cut a design similar to Teutonic in 1874 called Arcadian, and in 1878 their specimens show patents on other related styles. Wells did show in 1877 a Phanitalian Ornamented which was unique with his company.

During this period Page presented the only real Semi-Ornamental designs which were derivative of the Gothics. Arabian was perhaps the most outstanding of these styles. First shown in the *Typographic Messenger* in 1869, it had a strong median treatment with round letters and terminals angled, and the basic letterform was most like a face called Beveled, issued at a later date. Vanderburgh, Wells and Company brought out an almost identical style called Alaskan in the same year. Page issued his design in two styles, both with lowercase: Arabian and Arabian No. 1, the latter being less condensed than the first.

In 1872 Page showed an Etruscan No. 4, which also would fall into the Semi-Ornamented classification. Terminals were rounded and had bulbous endings with a notched median treatment. Etruscan No. 5 was a Chromatic version of the same design. Another similar rounded face was the Gothic Tuscan No. 1 with a pointed bulge at the median. A Chromatic interpretation of this design was called Double Gothic, which was the same face with a shade. Aside from Gothic Chromatics already listed, Page was to utilize the Concave Tuscan in several styles, of which Ornate was the most elaborately embellished. These designs were found only in the Page specimens.

Gothic Condensed No. 4, shown by Page in 1872, was

10 LINE GOTHIC CONDENSED NO. 3

VERmont

24 LINE GOTHIC CONDENSED ITALIC

COURAGE

10 LINE CURVED X CONDENSED GOTHIC

BRAVE Girls 19

10 LINE GOTHIC ROUND X CONDENSED LIGHT FACE

PRESENTable 157

10 LINE GOTHIC TUSCAN EXPANDED

HIM

10 & 12 LINE PHANITALIAN

REServe

BENDS

10 LINE PHANITALIAN ORNAMENTED

BINDER

12 LINE PERSIAN

TO MY Heart 8

Vanderburgh, Wells & Co., 1877.

141

16 LINE ARABIAN (PATENTED)

Editions!

CHARME

10 LINE ARABIAN NO. 1

OMINOcal

Page, 1872.

10 LINE GOTHIC CONDENSED NO. 4

CURE

Shine

10 LINE NO. 51

PORK

10 LINE NO. 50

DOGats

Page, 1878.

10 LINE GOTHIC TUSCAN NO. 8

HORNE

10 LINE GOTHIC POINTED

HORNE

10 LINE GOTHIC TUSCAN CONDENSED

ITALIA Opera

7 LINE GOTHIC TUSCAN CONDENSED (LOWERCASE)

STANdard 25

20 LINE ALASKAN

ROSPECT!

Splendid

30 LINE LIGHT GOTHIC ORNAMENTED SHADE

LID

Vanderburgh, Wells & Co., 1877.

another first showing of a device to be exploited further at a later date. It was a heavy Gothic, with the weight at top and bottom of the letter slightly heavier than found in conventional display Gothics, and with the corner of each terminal drawn out into fine points. The Runics of the preceding period employed a like device. This treatment of Gothics was to expand in the next period into a great variety of styles. One practical advantage to this device was that even a crude printing would leave the corners of the letter sharp, or that the visual reading of a letter with corners pulled out slightly would lend crispness to the letter-form.

A distribution of weight similar to the Page Gothic Condensed No. 4 but following a more conventional Gothic pattern was found in Wells' Gothic Condensed Italic shown in 1877 without a lowercase. Even though the color of the type was uncomfortably ragged, the design for the most part was reasonably strong. The Gothic Condensed Light Face by the same company cut with lowercase was an exceptionally good rendering of this style. In fact, many of the condensed and light face Gothics from this period appear to have been new cuttings rather than the result of an evolutionary process from earlier bolder styles, and most of the new designs were vast improvements over the old. A number of pointed Gothics produced in these years had both the point and the knob used at the median, top, and bottom of the letter. William Page's Gothic Tuscan No. 3 of 1859 had been a forerunner of these new styles. The same knob and point treatment was applied to the Antiques as much as to the Gothics, and the knob device (often referred to as a "dot") showed up regularly in the productions of typefounders, usually combined with the fine detailing associated with lithographic styles of these same years.

20 LINE CHROMATIC GOTHIC PANELED NO. 2

RIND

32 LINE ORNAMENTED

RED

24 LINE ETRUSCAN NO. 2

MOSAIC

Page, 1874.

6 LINE GOTHIC ORNAMENTED

RENT

9 LINE CORINTHIAN NO. 2

ABCD

6 LINE GOTHIC STAR ORNAMENTED

GAMIN

6 LINE ORNATE NO. 1

RONE

8 LINE GOTHIC ORNAMENTED NO. 2

SIE

10 LINE GOTHIC CURVED SHADED

RAIN

9 LINE ORNATE NO. 2

RIDE

Page, 1872.

14 LINE PANELED CONDENSED

HIS

Page, 1878.

143

24 LINE GERMAN FULL FACE

Ku

24 LINE MUNICH

Ry

14 LINE GERMAN

Fenster

16 LINE BAVARIAN

Boston

24 LINE GERMAN CONDENSED

Numb!

18 LINE PRUSSIAN

Dienstag

24 LINE GERMAN X CONDENSED

Orations!

18 LINE COMPOSITE CONDENSED

Prozeßbes

Page, 1870.

24 LINE POSTER TEXT

Burlington

10 LINE MUNICH

Outa

Vanderburgh, Wells & Co., 1877.

Page, 1870.

36 LINE OLD ENGLISH ORNAMENTED NO. 6 (PATENTED)

If

20 LINE OLD ENGLISH ORNAMENTED NO. 5 (PATENTED)

Fair

36 LINE OLD ENGLISH ORNAMENTED NO. 7 (PATENTED)

Bi

12 LINE OLD ENGLISH ORNAMENTED

Wander

15 LINE OLD ENGLISH OPEN

Unbid

Page, 1870.

8 LINE GERMAN NO. 2

Stoffe

Vanderburgh, Wells & Co., 1877.

10 LINE BULLETIN SCRIPT

Stensil

5 LINE ARABESQUE

STEAMS

6 LINE PAGE'S BULLETIN

Printe TRAIN

Page, 1872.

6 LINE BULLETIN CONDENSED

BULletin

Vanderburgh, Wells & Co., 1877.

145

Chart showing type sizes in points and corresponding name designations of sizes, which were used in America until the adoption of a standardized point system in 1886.

1	American	14	English	40	Dbl. Paragon
1½	German	16	Columbian	44	Canon
2	Saxon	18	Great Primer	48	Four-Line Pica
2½	Norse	20	Paragon	60	Five-Line Pica
3	Brilliant	22	Dbl. Small Pica	72	Six-Line Pica
3½	Ruby	24	Double Pica		
4	Excelsior	28	Double English		
4½	Diamond	32	Dbl. Columbian		
5	Pearl	36	Dbl. Grt. Primer		
5½	Agate				
6	Nonpareil				
7	Minion				
8	Brevier				
9	Bourgeois				
10	Long Primer				
11	Small Pica				
12	Pica				

Chart illustrating the seventeen styles of die-cut type sold by William Page.
First row: Nos. 500, 501, 502, 503.
Second row: Nos. 504, 505, 506.
Third row: Nos. 507, 508, 509.
Fourth row: Nos. 510, 511, 512.
Fifth row: Nos. 513, 514, 515, 516.

1879 Through 1892

Soon after the Panic of 1879 the printing trades were deep in the most competitive turmoil they had ever known. As both wood and metal type producers existed in numbers greater than the market could support and cut-throat business practices were a natural consequence, the inevitable consolidation of both industries took place before 1900. In 1891 the typefounders united into one corporation known as the American Type Founders Company, Inc. Its very existence was remarkable because there was great public sentiment against trusts at that time, and the corporation was constantly under attack at the time of its formation as a "type trust."

More significant developments took place in this era which were to bury irrevocably many practices and artifacts of the printing trades of the past. The first commercially coated paper, produced by the Warren Mills for Theodore De Vinne in 1881, was to advance the art of half-tone printing rapidly, and to eliminate wood engraving at an equal rate. The invention of Benton's punch cutting machinery led immediately to the invention of the Linotype machine; then hard on the heels of this amazingly successful automatic composing and type making machine came the Monotype caster. The inroads on the typefoundry were both quick and devastating.

In 1886, a committee of the United States Type Founders Association recommended the adoption of the present uniform point system for type measurements to replace the older system of sizes by name. This action standardized the entire industry in one stroke.

The era began with J. E. Hamilton founding his one-man wood type manufactory and introducing veneer types to the trade in Two Rivers, Wisconsin, during 1880. In the following year, William T. Morgans built his new plant, Morgans and Wilcox Manufacturing Company, at Middletown, New York, to manufacture wood types and deal in printers' equipment and supplies. After 1883 Charles Tubbs operated the American Wood Type Company as sole owner. Vanderburgh, Wells and Company continued to prosper until the keen competition from Hamilton, especially in the field of printers' furniture, finally reduced their business.

In or about 1887, the National Printers' Materials Company began selling enameled wood type in quantities. Although there is reason to believe that celluloid types had been marketed, perhaps by the same people, at an earlier date, it was not until the "enameling" process had been patented in 1885 that it became practical to produce large quantities of celluloid type. William Page continued his operations at Norwich, but was gradually to expand his business interests into areas other than wood type. It is thought that the scale of his operation was somewhat reduced in these years even though he devised a means for die-stamping wood types in 1887. Altogether, there were six different wood type producers operating in these years, and the competition was fierce. In the end, of course, it was Hamilton who won. He purchased the entire inventory of William H. Page in 1891, of Heber Wells in 1898, of Morgans and Wilcox in 1899 (only the wood type end of the business); and eventually of the Tubbs Company in 1918.

Markets had been expanded, and each major wood type producer had outlets at several locations around the country. During the 1870's Page had begun to explore the overseas markets. Later Hamilton was successful when he traveled abroad to extend his selling domain.

The increased markets, competitive practices, and cheaper methods for producing wood type led to its general use in all print shops, large or small. The designs of this period, for the most part, reflected the frenetic market activity. Novelty superseded design, designs were pirated, and refinements characteristic of the earlier periods were lost in the need to outsell to survive. In 1879 after Page had announced that thereafter the company would number instead of name its new faces, most other wood type producers followed suit.

The typefounders suffered from most of the same problems that plagued the wood type producers: too much competition and other conditions that resulted in price-cutting and the saturation of markers. Typefounders, who created Art Nouveau styles during these years, produced one "quaint" face after another. There were 30 odd foundries operating from San Francisco, Kansas City, St. Louis, Cleveland, Chicago, to Cincinnati, in addition to the older centers of Boston, New York City, and Philadelphia.

During the earlier periods, there generally had been a pattern to the development of new designs. Either a series or families of type would be created, or else the source of derivation would be apparent. After 1879 with the more random approach to design, both wood and metal type producers often marketed "one shot" styles, which today are difficult to identify as to sequence or as to their relationship with other designs from this era. In addition, there was widespread inconsistency in the titling of new designs. The variety of names for one design reflected a condition in which the producer often disguised a pirated style with a new name. Also, perhaps some of the romanticism which was a part of the Art Nouveau period was expressed in the titling. There were a few excellent designs accomplished in the midst of this confusion. Trenton, Teniers, some of the French Antiques, Phanitalians, etc., would compare favorably with many of the earlier plain faces. However, the degeneration which was manifested so strongly in this period never reversed itself.

The Antiques

One of the few designs from this period which was expanded into a series were the Latins, occasionally called Keystone, Peerless, or Old Style Antique. As cut in wood, the design was essentially an Antique Light Face Condensed with a wedge serif. Miller and Richard, English typefounders, had illustrated a similar design called Antique No. 5 without lowercase in their 1865 specimens, but the design was lighter and the serifs less pronounced than in the wood specimens. They did, however, show a style of the same weight and similar to the wood letter Latins in 1878 as Antique No. 8 Old Style. According to Nicolette Gray, the Latins did not become common in England until about 1876.

In America the first wood specimens were shown in Page's Wood Type Album for October of 1879, in two styles of Full Face and Condensed—the latter without lowercase. In a comparatively short time, the design had been expanded to XX Condensed, X Condensed, Condensed, Full Face, Extended and Expanded, with some designs in several weights. Two heavy styles of Full Face and Expanded, both with lowercase, were introduced to the market by Page in 1883. A curious version of Latin (in the lighter styles) was Octagon Condensed made by Morgans and Wilcox circa 1890 which could be distinguished by the

PAGE'S WOOD TYPE ALBUM

18 LINE 126 (PATENTED)

PRICE
Norwich 8

NO. 120 (PATENTED)

M
SIE
Finest

16 LINE NO. 117

BOSTON & ALBANY

Page, April, 1879.

6 LINE NO. 121 (PATENTED)

Clinkers

6 LINE NO. 122 (PATENTED)

STRONG
Animal

Page, July, 1879.

6 LINE NO. 123 (PATENTED)

DERK

Page, July, 1879.

14 LINE NO. 132

Patented 7

SPRING

18 LINE NO. 127

WEST

10 LINE NO. 131 (LATIN)

BONDS

MOST Excited

18 LINE NO. 129 (LATIN CONDENSED)

MAKERS

7 LINE 130 (LATIN)

NEon

Page, October, 1879.

3 LINE NO. 96 (LATIN EXTENDED)

BID

Hamilton, 1887.

10 LINE NO. 154

EXCURSION

Page, 1883.

40 LINE EGYPTIAN ORNAMENTED

NER

6 LINE EGYPTIAN ANTIQUE

**Prudent Times
FRESH BRIDE**

10 LINE EGYPTIAN ORNAMENTED NO. 1

BRINES1

American Wood Type, 1879.

16 LINE FRENCH CLARENDON ORNAMENTED

Hearts 4

CLARENDON LIGHT FACE ORNAMENTED

Blazes 7

Morgans, Wilcox Mfg. Co., 1881.

8 LINE NO. 128

FINES

Connect 3

8 LINE NO. 145

FINES

Connect 3

8 LINE NO. 138

ROD

8 LINE NO. 139

SIZE

8 LINE NO. 141

SIZE

8 LINE NO. 147

ROD

12 LINE NO. 149

BRISTOL

Rhode Island

10 LINE NO. 151

CALENDER

Page, 1882.

9 LINE NO. 152

PRICE

4 LINE NO. 153

BID

Extend

12 LINE NO. 155

BRICK

Page, 1883.

10 LINE EGYPTIAN ORNAMENTED NO. 1

BEND

10 LINE EGYPTIAN ORNAMENTED NO. 2

RENT

10 LINE EGYPTIAN ORNAMENTED NO. 3

HEAD

10 LINE EGYPTIAN ORNAMENTED NO. 5

HEAD

10 LINE EGYPTIAN NO. 10

BAND

American Wood Type, 1883.

12 LINE TUSCAN CONDENSED

ROD

10 LINE FRENCH CLARENDON NO. 2

HOPES

American Wood Type, 1883.

12 LINE ANTIQUE NO. 1

PERT

12 LINE ANTIQUE NO. 2

HERT

12 LINE ANTIQUE NO. 4

MAILED.

12 LINE ANTIQUE NO. 5

BAY!

15 LINE ANTIQUE POINTED

HEARD

Boarders

12 LINE TUSCAN EGYPTIAN

HASP

wound

National Printers' Materials, 1887.

149

angular treatment afforded all round letters. The design was cut with a lowercase as well as in a full face style with lowercase. All of the Morgans and Wilcox Latins may be identified by a cap on the capital A. Another similar design, which appears to have been shown only by National Printers' Materials, was Antique Pointed and had no lowercase. While the general color and wedge serifs were like the Latin, the bars of the A and H were angled.

In 1871, the Boston Type Foundry illustrated both a Latin Rimmed and a plain face style, both of which were condensed and had a lowercase. Latins were cast by Connor in 1876 and Farmer, Little and Company in 1878, these dates corresponding to the renewed interest in the design in Europe. The 1880 specimens of the Boston Type Foundry exhibited an entire series of this family, all in the light style first shown by Miller, Richard in 1865.

The first Latin cut by the typefounder in a weight comparable to the wood letter styles was a design by Farmer, Little and Company in their 1884 specimens, which was complete with lowercase. Afterwards, Latin had extensive use as a metal type, and was found regularly in printing well up into the twentieth century in a variety of styles. It was used particularly by bookbinders in stamping book covers. Skeleton Antique gained in prominence during these years, both in metal and wood. In 1878 Page introduced a No. 52, a slightly expanded style complete with lowercase, and in the early 1880's No. 128, a design with splayed serifs and angular emphasis given to all the round letters. Another grouping of designs more loosely related than the Latins was a series of faces having a variety of names, but perhaps best described as the Mansards. The name is derived from the handling of serifs that resemble the characteristic Mansard roofs of the nineteenth century. European founders showed several Ornamentals employing the Mansard serif during the 1850's and 1860's. Many of the Mansard designs were ornamented by Americans, who added dots or points, or, who, while retaining the Mansard qualities, rounded the serifs and sometimes played them into a bulbous, bone-like terminal. Most of these designs, which had a lowercase, were quite well conceived and drawn as display types.

Modoc and Athabascan, introduced by Page during the 1860's, would appear to be predecessors for many of the Mansard designs, as the serif weights and ornamented effects were closely related to the designs in the 1880's. Within this group of letterforms the parent letterform is not always easy to determine—whether it was arrived at by rounding the serifs of the Antique or by swelling the terminals of the Gothic. A few designs, such as Octagon, were based on inverting the Mansard serif, angles of which turned in rather than out. The weight of all these styles, which varied, would be comparable to a range between Aldine and Egyptian, and all the serifs were heavier than the stems. The majority of the Mansards seem to have come onto the market between 1879 and 1887, after which they did not long retain their popularity.

It is undoubtedly more than a coincidence that Connor, the typefounder, and Page, the wood letter manufacturer, were both responsible for introducing a number of the Mansard designs in their respective fields at about the same time. It is believed that after 1859, when Connor first became Page's agent, the two men maintained a close personal relationship, during which they both patented similar designs. The specimen books indicate that Connor had patented a face called Mansard some time between 1872 and 1874 and a Mansard Shaded in 1875. Page had also patented several of his Mansard designs, Numbers 120, 121, 127, etc. at a slightly later date.

A number of the dotted Antiques which were popular as wood letters were patented by Connor around 1872. In the same year he also patented some decorative faces based on the Clarendon styles of Belgian, Parisian, etc. Again, while these styles differed in detail from many of the numbered designs produced by Page at the end of that decade, the basic letterforms were very much alike. In these same years, there were to be quite a few new styles of French Antique and French Clarendon which were usually numbered or labeled or Specials. One particularly handsome face was an ultra-condensed French Clarendon numbered 117 by Page in 1879. It did not have a lowercase. The 1881 specimens of the Morgans and Wilcox Company included a unique Clarendon Light Face Condensed Ornamented with median points and bifurcated Antique serifs. Also in the same catalogue was a French Clarendon Ornamented with the same serif treatment as the previous design. All terminals were notched, and the effect was somewhat like the Egyptian Tuscans. American Wood Type Company between 1881 and 1883 introduced a series titled Egyptian, Egyptian No. 1, 2, 3, 5 (it would be assumed that a 4 had been designed but was not shown), and also an Egyptian No. 10, the latter being somewhat distinct from the first four styles which were variations of the same basic letterform.

Little was done in the way of new Tuscans in this period. The American Wood Type Company in 1880 made a Tuscan Condensed which was patterned after the numbered Tuscans shown by Page in 1859. Even though these Tuscans were cut by several companies, only Heber Wells had a lowercase for his design. National Printers' Materials Company in 1887 illustrated a face called Chaldean which had a comparable weight, and nearly the same design as Parisian, but with a median treatment of diamonds and protruding knobs. The lowercase was similarly designed. In the same specimens was a design called Maltese. There were a number of Antique derivative faces in this catalogue, identified only by number, that were among the oddest, and worst designs of the century. Since this specimen book was the first major publication of the company, it is thought there was an attempt to influence the trade through novelty. After all, it was a period when novelty was being sought for its own sake. Much in the same vein, the specimen book for Morgans and Wilcox in 1891 included a number of designs, several derivative of Antique, which exhibited the same tastelessness of design. Of these, Ellsworth, in keeping with fashions of that period, is probably the worst. More like the earlier faces were Egyptian Antique No. 1, which had inverted Mansard serifs cornered much like the French treatment of Antique around 1835, and Lyric, which had the stem-serif relationship of the Parisians, with round letters flattened at top and bottom and concave lines for the sides.

While the Clarendon family and its secondary faces furnished the greatest number of letterforms for innovation during these years, many devices from the earlier periods were adapted to the newer letterforms. The notched serif, pinched waist, and median treatment dated back into the 1840's and 1850's. Even though many of these designs were more exaggerated and extreme than earlier models, a few of them made effective display faces in terms of color and letter combinations.

8 LINE CLARENDON OPEN SHADE

COLE

8 LINE CLARENDON SHADE NO. 1

COLE

8·LINE ANTIQUE CONDENSED SHADE NO. 1

HER

Page, 1890.

ALDINE EXTENDED

MET

EGYPTIAN ANTIQUE NO. 1

RICE1

ELLSWORTH

CHUB

FRENCH OCTAGON

FRAME

LYRIC

Artists4

DUM

Morgans, Wilcox Mfg. Co., 1891.

18 LINE NO. 124

PRINTER

Page, July, 1879.

10 LINE NO. 133

CIRCULAR

10 LINE NO. 116

MOREN

Birds 5

Page, October, 1879.

12 LINE GOTHIC TUSCAN NO. 5

RENT

10 LINE GOTHIC TUSCAN NO. 5 CONDENSED

HINDERED

8 LINE GOTHIC TUSCAN NO. 5 OPEN

SUBSCRIBE

15 LINE GOTHIC TUSCAN OPEN

IMPROVE

American Wood Type, 1879.

The Gothics

In these years the Gothics produced by typefounders moved steadily toward the grotesque style of Art Nouveau, and fanciful as they might have been, they were unfortunate aberrations of earlier styles. Terminals were extended above and below the lines, or curly-cued. Cross bars were broken, or moved diagonally, as opposed to the conventional horizontal stresses. Capital M, N and H were splayed with cross-bars raised, and the A's had capping bars. Curved lines were straightened and straight lines were curved. The result could only be hectic, unstable letterforms. Even though William Morris had begun his revivalistic styles in England at the end of this period, it was to be another 20 to 30 years before their full effect was felt in America, as typified by the Roycroft publications. The influence of Morris on works in this country was of philosophical interest, but represented little aesthetic improvement in type design or in typographic styling.

In terms of new designs this period belongs to the Gothics and its secondary faces. Most of the previous styles of Gothic Round, Gothic Round Light Face, and Gothic Pointed, and the Gothic in all styles of Light Face and Condensed remained popular through these years. Many styles of Gothic, especially the very condensed and Light Face styles, were recut, and there were more italics and backslopes than had been seen in some time. The new interpretations of Gothic, most of which had lowercase, were exceptionally even in color and consistent in the letterform design. Again, like the Antiques, the new styles were often numbered or labeled as Specials. Hamilton and Wells were to add Gothic Thin Face (without lowercase) to their repertories, which, as the name implies, was exceedingly light. Gothic Round was also cut in the extremely light styles at this time. A few Gothic Specials, for the most part poorly designed, were issued late in the period and had almost the same relationship between thicks and thins as found in Romans.

An important design device applied to Gothics which formed new families of related letterforms were the finely pointed Gothics. The corners of terminals were drawn out into miniscule serifs as had been done with Runics at an earlier date. Another device was a treatment of terminals equivalent to that of Mansard on the Antiques, with a thickening at the top and bottom of the letter and angles combined with curves.

Examples of finely pointed Gothics would be Trenton Unique and Teniers, some styles of Latin Antique, Gothic Specials, some numbered designs, Gothic Condensed No. 4, Excelsior cut in three styles by Morgans and Wilcox, Art Gothic by Wells and Morgans, and a similar design called Bradbury by the same company. These are representative of the extreme styles in fashion around 1890, most of which made use of the fine serifs.

The "Mansard" Gothics, some were called Mansard, numbered (Wells), or Octic (Morgans and Wilcox), often had dots or median treatments added to the design, like the Antiques. Though many designs falling into this grouping are numbered, "Phanitalian" is the most important classification. There are several of these faces, such as Phanitalian Ornamented by Wells and Page's Modoc (grouped under Antiques), which are extremely difficult to label as being either Antique or Gothic in origin.

No. 133, an angled Gothic, first shown by Page in October of 1879, did not have a lowercase for 2 or 3 years. During the 1880's, the design was exhibited by all wood type manufacturers with several ornamental styles of shade and outline also included. This design was in principle the same as the one shown by Leavenworth in the Debow Specimens during the 1830's.

The previously mentioned evolution of Teutonic Concave Gothics continued in this period. Some styles of Concave Gothic were ornamented through the use of points at top and bottom of the letter. Wells' Gothic Tuscan Condensed No. 9 had such a treatment; Concave Condensed by Morgans and Wilcox had median points; Wells had a splayed terminal and scallop treatment of a letter with flat tops and bottoms called Phanitalian Ornamented. One letter which was unusual in that it went from an ornamental to a plain face rather than the reverse was Beveled, No. 142, shown in 1882 by Page, Morgans and Wilcox, and eventually by Hamilton. It had the same basic design as Arabian or Alaskan, but without the decorative treatment, and it also had a lowercase.

Gothic Tuscan No. 5 by the American Wood Type Company is a good example of the heavy Concave Gothics that gained prominence in this period. It may be distinguished from the earlier Concave Gothics by its heavier weight distribution at the top and bottom of the letter. The design was offered to the market by most wood type producers but only the Hamilton Company provided a lowercase. William Page showed a number of styles with lowercase based on Concave Gothics among the new designs for die-cut types in his 1890 catalogue. These differed from earlier styles in that a number of them were quite condensed.

A unique design called Monhagen by Morgans and Wilcox in 1881 is somewhat like the Mansard Gothics except that the stems are much lighter and the serifs not as exaggerated. This design never had a lowercase. Another type in the same catalogue was the Gothic Condensed Ornamented, and a bolder version titled Gothic Condensed No. 4 without a lowercase. This face had the fine points on the terminals, was more condensed, and somewhat lighter than other similar designs (e.g., the Gothic Condensed No. 4 of Wells).

Hamilton and Baker in 1889 showed the Angled Gothic in an Expanded style with lowercase. The only other company to cut this design was Morgans and Wilcox, who did not include a lowercase. American Wood Type Company in 1883 illustrated a well-designed new cutting of Gothic Light Face in both an Italic and Backslope with lowercase. There were a number of other singular Gothics that reflected the Art Nouveau styles, e.g., Artistic by Hamilton in 1889, a very irregular design capitalizing on concave stems and exaggerated curves. About the same time, Hamilton was the only firm to bring out Gothic Bold, which is most interesting because of its similarity to the Gothic shown by Wells and Webb in 1840. The Gothic appeared to have the same weight relationships as the Grotesque Italian, and the Hamilton face is heavier than the earlier design, with an extremely heavy top and bottom emphasis. It was cut with a lowercase.

In 1887 National Printers' Materials illustrated the same extremity of design with the Gothics that they demonstrated with the Antiques. Their Number 21 had an undulating stem treatment and curious half serif on some letters which resulted in an incomprehensible alphabet. No. 23 illustrates some qualities of the Runic but is quite irregular in the treatment of different letters. Another unique design is Algerian, which is an angled Gothic

10 LINE GOTHIC CONDENSED ORNAMENTED

Limb 3

10 LINE MONHAGEN

GONE 2

12 LINE GOTHIC TUSCAN CONDENSED NO. 2

COMET 135

Morgans, Wilcox Mfg. Co., 1881.

10 LINE NO. 72

CINDER Alarm 3

Hamilton & Katz, 1881.

8 LINE NO. 144

Bond MUD

10 LINE NO. 124 (SHOWS LOWERCASE)

MARCH Steams 18

Page, 1882.

15 LINE NO. 142

SHINE

Establish

8 LINE NO. 51

PORK

10 LINE NO. 97

RAIL

Page, 1882.

8 LINE GOTHIC ITALIC

DREAD

8 LINE GOTHIC BACK SLOPE

DREAD

American Wood Type, 1883.

15 LINE EXCELSIOR JOB

Point!

15 LINE EXCELSIOR JOB CONDENSED

Manor1

12 LINE EXCELSIOR JOB X CONDENSED

Beautiful

National Printers' Materials, 1887.

12 LINE NO. 21

Belief

12 LINE NO. 23

BETHEL

12 LINE PHANITALIAN

ART

15 LINE BLOCK GOTHIC

CODE!

Deicate

12 LINE NO. 20

Choice BALS

12 LINE NO. 22

Boads Hotel

10 LINE ORNAMENTED NO. 16

FRED CELT

5 LINE NO. 40

D B R P J

10 LINE GOTHIC CONDENSED LIGHT FACE

Sidewalk 6

National Printers' Materials, 1887.

with pointed serifs and a median treatment of rectangular bars. Ornamented No. 16 is a strange Phanitalian letter with Tuscan serifs, protruding knobs at top and bottom, and a dotted median treatment. The basis of these designs can only be explained as an unbelievable attempt at novelty. However, a new cutting of Gothic Condensed Light Face with lowercase by National Printers' Materials is a handsome Gothic style.

Morgans and Wilcox in 1891 showed many Gothics which were almost as extreme as those of the National Printers' Materials Company, but a number of these were through permission of typefounders, such as the Boston Type Foundry, Johnson Type Foundry (sic. Author's Note: Identification of "Johnson Type Foundry" is not clear—whether there was a Johnson Type Foundry at that time even though it cannot be found in listings, or whether it was reference to MacKellar, Jordans & Smith who succeeded to the L. Johnson & Co.), Phelps, Dalton and Company, and American Type Founders. Most of the designs from this specimen book, those borrowed from the founders as well as their own, are reflective of the styles then in fashion. Of the more conventional designs, Latin Antique No. 1 is new—an even colored Gothic with some shading between thicks and thins and a slight concavity to the stems. Buffalo falls into the grouping of Gothics with fine pointed serifs. The handling of the middle bar of the capital B and R is diagonal rather than horizontal, and the serif on the crossbar of the capital G has a bulbous terminal, almost as if the alphabet were designed by putting together elements from several different styles. Gotham and Haubert are best described as typographic atrocities, even though the former had many counterparts in this period.

At the end of this era there appears to have been a flurry of ornamental Gothics, to which many devices from the earliest years of wood type production were applied. Page was responsible for a number of these designs. There was a Gothic Solid Faced with Shade that differed from earlier styles in that there was no Outline. No. 91, the same as No. 7 except that the diamonds were added, had a reversed two way arrow at the median and small diamonds horizontally placed at the top and bottom of the letter. The Gothic Condensed No. 4 of 1872 had been ornamented by outlining and using a stylized floral motif on the sides of the letter. Although the face was numbered, it was also called Corinthian No. 1, the reverse of which was known as Corinthian No. 2 (No. 1 had been shown in 1872; No. 2 was in the 1882 specimens).

In 1892, Hamilton included two styles of Ornamented Trenton: one with a solid diamond at the median and another with an open diamond at the median. Both styles were restrained and handsome. He also presented a Gothic Light Face Open Shade with an undulating diamond at the median, a Gothic with Shade Open decorated with a ball and dart motif at the median, and a Cornered Gothic in an Outlined style. Wells was to issue his Curved Gothic as an Open Shade with median decoration. As seen in the previous description, the use of the diamond as a decorative motif was widespread during these years. Page had shown some of the first examples of this device in his 1859 specimens, particularly in the decoration of certain Clarendon faces. Another peculiar device, particularly for wood types, was the use of nail or screw heads near the top and bottom of the letterform. Page employed this feature extensively in his Mansards, Bulletins, Clarendons, etc. Typefounders

had occasionally used the same device during the late 1860's.

15 LINE NO. 121

HOME

15 LINE NO. 123

HOG

10 LINE NO. 120

Ch

BIDE

NO. 122

DO

CONGO

6 LINE NO. 201

KING

8 LINE NO. 202

ROAD

Hamlets

Hamilton, 1889.

155

15 LINE NO. 168 (TRENTON)

BORDER

10 LINE NO. 187

ROSIN

12 LINE NO. 169

ROMEN

8 LINE NO. 237 (TENIERS)

REFORM the Ballot

6 LINE NO. 186

MIGE

8 LINE NO. 232

CASH Register

5 LINE NO. 208

NEW THEATRE

8 LINE NO. 228

GOLD Mine 6

10 LINE NO. 227

NeatEnds

Hamilton, 1892.

8 LINE NO. 183

MOURNS

10 LINE NO. 238 (GOTHIC BOLD)

ROSE

18 LINE NO. 194 (TRENTON ORNAMENTED)

RAZOR

18 LINE NO. 193 (TRENTON ORNAMENTED)

GREEN

12 LINE NO. 473

ICE

Hamilton, 1892.

16 LINE GOTHIC POINTED ITALIC

ENABCD

Wells, c. 1890.

10 LINE ALGERIAN

Imported.
CAPTOL

National Printers' Materials, 1887.

6 LINE GOTHAM

PRIM

Morgans, Wilcox Mfg. Co., 1891.

CULDEE (JOHNSON TYPE FOUNDRY)

Trade
BIG

CONCAVE CONDENSED

BARGAIN
HOUR

HAUBERT

BOUGH

HARRISON

ICE!

FACADE X CONDENSED

RACE

NEWTON

TIMES

TENIERS NO. 1

RICE

Morgans, Wilcox Mfg. Co., 1891.

KITCAT (JOHNSON TYPE FOUNDRY)

Maker
DUE

COMUS

Ruins
DIC

LONDON

SPORT
FUN

POSTER

LAKE

COURIER

Shades
Pose

POETIC

Mode
FIE

Morgans, Wilcox Mfg. Co., 1891.

LATIN ANTIQUE NO. 1

Friends
NEL

QUAINT (PATENTED)

DUKE

FACADE CONDENSED

BALE

LATIN ANTIQUE

Game
BEN

OLD STYLE ANTIQUE

Form
AID

BUFFALO

BANG

DUERER (JOHNSON TYPE FOUNDRY)

KINGS

ART GOTHIC (PATENTED)

Race

Morgans, Wilcox Mfg. Co., 1891.

8 LINE NO. 119

DOG

8 LINE NO. 110

ICE LOW

Page, April, 1879.

12 LINE NO. 118

PAC

Page, July, 1879.

15 LINE BOLIVIAN

Tice 3

Morgans, Wilcox Mfg. Co., 1881.

4 LINE AETNA X CONDENSED NO. 1

Merchant 25
BEAUTIFUL

6 LINE AETNA XX CONDENSED

Established
FOUNTAIN

Page, 1883.

15 LINE BOLIVIAN

SIG

American Wood Type, 1883.

The Romans

The further development of the Roman styles by the wood type manufacturer was practically negligible in this period. In no way is this fact better demonstrated than by the Hamilton Company's not showing any of the older Roman fat faces in any style, until after it purchased the Page Company in 1891, when they then used the Page patterns. Some Old Style designs continued to be shown, but for the most part, Aetna, Painters' Roman, Bolivian, Latins, and Light Face Clarendons took over the position formerly held by the fat face Romans, both in the full face and condensed styles.

A few Romans were advanced which incorporated the same Art Nouveau treatments applied to the Gothics, such as raised cross-bars, and exaggerated terminals. The antiquing of the letterform—ragged edges in imitation of a heavy impression on soft paper and ink fuzzing as occurred in older methods of printing—resulted in several variations of the Roman designs. Examples were Ben Franklin, Plymouth, Blanchard, and Pabst in both wood and metal.

After 1890, wood type manufacturers regularly acknowledged the patents of the typefounders and cut a variety of the new styles of Roman in wood. The catalogue for the Morgans and Wilcox Company in 1891 illustrated faces by De Vinne of American Type Founders (in 1895, Hamilton issued an entire catalogue of De Vinne designs cut in wood). Columbus by the same foundry, Childs by the Johnson Type Foundry, and Cosmopolitan, an Italic semi-script, by Inland Type Foundry, were also included.

BEN FRANKLIN

REN *To*

PLYMOUTH

RENd

BLANCHARD

RE d

PABST

RENda

All styles by Hamilton Mfg. Co.

4 LINE NO. 164

WORKING
Auction 49

Page, 1890.

6 LINE NO. 235

PRICE

8 LINE NO. 235

Stock

Page, 1892.

ROMAN HEADING NO. 1

HERAL

ROMAN HEADING NO. 2

BEACO

COLUMBUS (ATF)

Problem

CHILDS (JOHNSON TYPE FOUNDRY)

Imported Coa

CORONET

Sports

FLOURISH

THE PAN

DEVINNE

Numer

Morgans, Wilcox Mfg. Co., 1891.

10 LINE NO. 111

Bluster

6 LINE NO. 113

Newton

Page, April, 1879.

10 LINE NO. 112

Blank6

Page, July, 1879.

8 LINE NO. 125

Mandrake 7
PRINTERS1

Page, October, 1879.

10 LINE AMERICAN BULLETIN

Rector

American Wood Type, 1879.

8 LINE NO. 156

ONE 5

Page, 1883.

5 LINE NO. 118

Elevation

Hamilton, 1889.

6 LINE NO. 225

Yacht Racers 7

12 LINE NO. 226

Old Bank

Page, 1892.

8 LINE NO. 236

Destroy

Hamilton, 1892.

CASLON

Moderation

BELMONT

Charming

ALMAH (PATENTED)

Correct Sty

LEGHORN SCRIPT

Leghorn Script

COSMOPOLITAN

Ramblers

Morgans, Wilcox Mfg. Co., 1891.

ALLIED WOOD TYPE MFG. COMPANY

NO. 285 MODE—FUTURA MEDIUM CLASS O

15 Line 4A Cap font $24.38   No. 1 fig. font $5.98

TRIP

12 Line 4A Cap font $21.20   No. 1 fig. font $5.20

EAGLE

NO. 287 MODE—FUTURA BOLD CLASS O

15 Line 4A Cap font $29.68   4a l.c. $24.08   No. 1 fig. font $7.28

RIG1

12 Line 4A Cap font $25.44   4a l.c. $20.64   No. 1 fig. font $6.24

DAY5

1893 and Afterwards

At the end of the century America was mightily transformed from its position of 1828. The country was now settled and linked by a network of railroads, enormous industrial complexes lay along the East Coast, and new population centers with growing industrial potential had developed inland. A series of wars, financial crises, labor unrest, and other adverse conditions had served to temper and unite the nation, which entered the twentieth century as both a political and an industrial world power.

Hallmarks of American Victoriana were fading because of the tremendous changes brought on by nineteenth-century technical accomplishments and the demands of a new age. In printing, wood engraving waned as the half-tone processes improved, ornamental effects were reluctantly eliminated as structure was emphasized over decoration, hand-set types were used less and less as the Linotype and Monotype took over the bulk of text composition, and the once powerful typefounders fell into general decline. Coated papers became stock items in every printery, and magazine publication increased enormously during the first 25 years of the century. Lithography, which had dropped to a million dollars annually in 1900, was revived by Rubel's invention of the offset press in 1904, and as the processes connected with this new medium improved in the ensuing years, lithography has undergone a resurgence which has not yet halted. In typography, the eccentric styles of Art Nouveau were replaced by a dull period of neo-classicism in text types, and display types moved slowly toward the "modern" look, mostly through some variation of the Gothic faces.

Advertising, as we know it today, was firmly established. The effects that it was to have on the general economy in America later in the century had their origins in these years around the turn of the century. Its growth was strongly interwoven with the expansion of printing, particularly in the field of magazine publication.

The first man to concentrate effectively on magazine advertising had been J. Walter Thompson around 1880. *Scribner's Monthly* (after 1881 called *Century*) was the first of the literary magazines to actively solicit advertising, and in doing so, it broke with the older traditions. *Harper's* had refused to accept any outside advertising for the first fourteen years of its existence (1850-1864). *Cosmopolitan,* founded in 1889, was carrying as many as 103 pages of advertising by 1897. *Youth's Companion,* founded in 1827, was to be a pace-setter for other journals during the last thirty years of the nineteenth century. It was one of the first to lay-out ads, and was widely copied in this respect. It was the first to regularly use photographic illustrations, and it ran the first full page color advertisement—a reproduction of a painting by Perrault for Mellin's Food. *Ladies' Home Journal* and *Everybody's* were other popular journals from this period around 1900.

On the American typographical scene during the early twentieth century were men like Cooper, Goudy, Rogers, Updike, Rollins, and others, who created the styles and produced the new designs. In Europe, the Bauhaus, which advanced its typographical concepts based on lowercase sans serifs and severe styling, eventually began to influence American design and advertising during the 1930's.

During the first 30 years of the twentieth century, there were some new cuttings of nineteenth-century styles like Ultra-Bodoni, Onyx, Memphis, Karnak, Stymie, etc. Since the new designs were almost always clumsy as compared to their prototypes, it is difficult to understand why the earlier and better designs did not survive. New display letters such as Cooper Black and Cheltenham were grossly inferior to the earlier designs, yet they became workhorse types. It can only be concluded that these years were very bad for American typography.

The wood type era ended with the purchase of the William Page Wood Type Company by the Hamilton Manufacturing Company in 1891. Although Hamilton, after diligently cultivating the trade, had a few good years, ironically he found that the times had changed, and when he had finally monopolized the market, the use of wood type was rapidly declining. The end was hastened by the perfection of the offset printing process after the turn of the century.

After the purchase of the Page Company, Hamilton reissued copies of the die-cut type catalogues in his own name in which these types were advertised as the most reasonable wood types ever manufactured.

The last Hamilton specimen book of die types was dated 1906, after which die-cut manufacture is believed to have been curtailed.

Although the wood type styles typical of the nineteenth century continued to appear in specimens for a while, they were dropped from catalogues by 1920. They had been replaced by a large variety of Gothic styles, all of which were greatly inferior in design to the best Gothic designs from the preceding century. The wood type era had ended.

ALLIED WOOD TYPE MFG. COMPANY

NO. 290 REX-STYMIE CLASS P

6 Line 4A Cap font $12.72   4a l.c. $10.32   No. I fig. font $3.12

ABCD abc

8 Line 4A Cap font $14.84   4a l.c. $12.04   No. I fig. font $3.64

DESIGN

10 Line 4A Cap font $16.96   4a l.c. $13.76   No. I fig. font $4.16

RANG

NO. 205 FASHION GOTHIC CLASS L

6 Line 4A Cap font $12.72   4a l.c. $10.32   No. I fig. font $3.12

ABCE abc

NO. 210 CORVINUS SKYLINE CLASS P

8 Line 4A Cap font $19.00   4a l.c. $15.48   No. I fig. font $4.68

TRAIN

10 Line 4A Cap font $21.20   4a l.c. $17.20   No. I fig. font $5.20

FARE

Rugged
(Class O)

6 Line RUGGED—7¢ per character in fonts
3A Cap Font $5.25; 4A Cap Font $7.42; No. I Figure Font $1.82

RECOVERIES 24

8 Line RUGGED—9¢ per character in fonts
3A Cap Font $6.75; 4A Cap Font $9.54; No. I Figure Font $2.34

DESIGNER 8

10 Line RUGGED—11¢ per character in fonts
3A Cap Font $8.25; 4A Cap Font $11.66; No. I Figure Font $2.86

BEGUN 15

12 Line RUGGED—14¢ per character in fonts
3A Cap Font $10.50; 4A Cap Font $14.84; No. I Figure Font $3.64

HERDS3

15 Line RUGGED—17¢ per character in fonts
3A Cap Font $12.75; 4A Cap Font $18.02; No. I Figure Font $4.42

SOLE5

Rugged Inline
(Class R)

6 Line RUGGED INLINE—12¢ per character in fonts
3A Cap Font $9.00; 4A Cap Font $12.72; No. I Figure Font $3.12

8 Line RUGGED INLINE—14¢ per character in fonts
3A Cap Font $10.50; 4A Cap Font $14.84; No. I Figure Font $3.64

10 Line RUGGED INLINE—17¢ per character in fonts
3A Cap Font $12.75; 4A Cap Font $18.02; No. I Figure Font $4.42

12 Line RUGGED INLINE—20¢ per character in fonts
3A Cap Font $15.00; 4A Cap Font $21.20; No. I Figure Font $5.20

15 Line RUGGED INLINE—26¢ per character in fonts
3A Cap Font $19.50; 4A Cap Font $27.56; No. I Figure Font $6.76

Cheltenham Bold
(Class O)

6 Line CHELTENHAM BOLD—7¢ per character in fonts
3A Cap Font $5.25; 4A Cap Font $7.42; No. I Figure Font $1.82

HERD2

8 Line CHELTENHAM BOLD—9¢ per character in fonts
3A Cap Font $6.75; 4A Cap Font $9.54; No. I Figure Font $2.34

SUE8

10 Line CHELTENHAM BOLD—11¢ per character in fonts
3A Cap Font $8.25; 4A Cap Font $11.66; No. I Figure Font $2.86

ED4

12 Line CHELTENHAM BOLD—14¢ per character in fonts
3A Cap Font $10.50; 4A Cap Font $14.84; No. I Figure Font $3.64

BID

Cheltenham Condensed
(Class O)

6 Line CHELTENHAM CONDENSED—7¢ per character in fonts
3A Cap Font $5.25; 4A Cap Font $7.42; No. I Figure Font $1.82

BUDGE4

8 Line CHELTENHAM CONDENSED—9¢ per character in fonts
3A Cap Font $6.75; 4A Cap Font $9.54; No. I Figure Font $2.34

BEDS 6

10 Line CHELTENHAM CONDENSED—11¢ per character in fonts
3A Cap Font $8.25; 4A Cap Font $11.66; No. I Figure Font $2.86

RIG 2

12 Line CHELTENHAM CONDENSED—14¢ per character in fonts
3A Cap Font $10.50; 4A Cap Font $14.84; No. I Figure Font $3.64

ICES

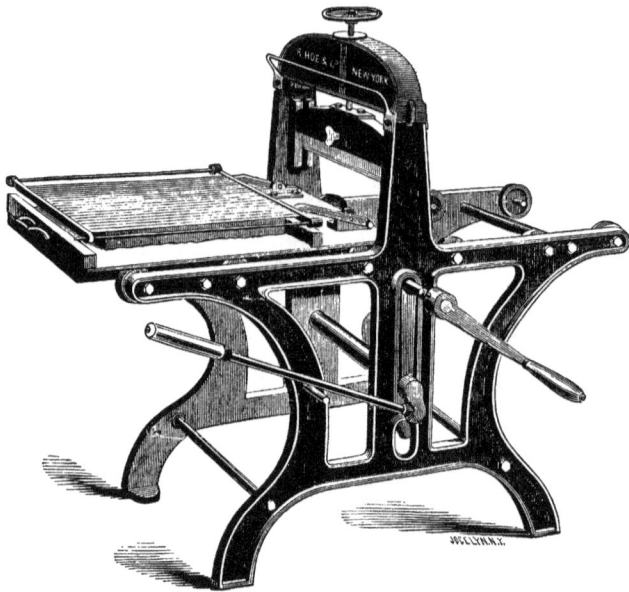

Lithographic Hand Press, circa 1870. Manufactured by R. Hoe & Co.

The first power lithographic press manufactured by Hoe in the 1860's.

Hughes & Kimber's Steam Lithographic Press.

During the first half of the nineteenth century, since the sources for most type designs could be found in Europe, American founders concentrated only on keeping abreast of the new styles. However, in the second half of the century, competitive printing conditions and improved printing technology helped to turn the founder and wood type producer away from an exclusive dependence on foreign sources. As the products of the founder found a market with the printer, the rivalry between the various printing mediums was to have a definite effect on type design, perhaps more so than usually believed.

One of the most spirited commercial contests of the day may be found in the efforts of the typefounder and lithographic draughtsman to outdo one another in the design of letterforms between 1860 and 1875. This contest was to align the wood engraver, letterpress printer, and typefounder against the lithographic printer and artist. Photography had limited use by both sides, and there were important influences by the metal plate printer, writing masters, and sign painters.

Lithography

Lithography, as the most flexible of all printing mediums, could reproduce the works of the engraver, typefounder, wood engraver, and artist. The transfer process allowed for ease in making multiple copies. In detail, it could outdo the metal engraver, but up to the time of the large power presses in the last quarter of the century, it was a slow method of production. A hand press could make about 400 impressions per day whereas the power press would give up to 5,000 impressions per day. The preparation of plates, as was also true for metal plate engraving, took a great deal of time and the cost was correspondingly high. The metal plate printer, who could get an average of 300 impressions a day from his press, confined most of his works to short run and quality work such as stamps, fine book illustration, banknotes, etc. On the other hand, the letterpress printer could produce a tremendous volume of printing in a short time, his types were re-usable, and the initial cost of preparing a form was considerably less than for either lithography or engraving. He could not, however, produce as elaborate an image as his competitors. Therefore the founder created a fantastic variety of devices so that the printer could compete aesthetically with the other mediums. At no time in this century did lithography ever produce the volume of work put out by letterpress, but with an improved technology and equipment, and after the perfection of the chromo-lithographic presses, color could be printed much more cheaply than by letterpress.

Not until 1828 was the first commercial lithography introduced in the United States by the Pendleton brothers, plate makers and stationers of Boston. The next 3 years found lithographic printing taking hold in Philadelphia, New York City, and Baltimore. Lithographic and copperplate printing plants together totaled 26 in 1850; there were 53 lithographic plants in 1860, and 55 by 1872.

Up to 1850, all lithographic presses were hand operated, and the basic machine used was similar to what is now found in the printmaking departments of most art schools. The prototype of this press had been the copperplate printing press with a sturdier frame, a scraper bar instead of a pressure cylinder, a lever to set the pressure, and a crank in place of the wheel to move the bed. Steam as a power source had been used on letterpress machinery since

1811, but it was not until 1850 that Eugues of Paris took out patents for a powered lithographic press. He sold his patents to a press-building firm in London, Hughes and Kimber, who were to improve on the original patents and to construct a number of machines. This press was introduced in America in 1866, but it was not long before the firm of Hoe and Company began producing American steam-powered machinery.

For some printing needs, lithography was better than all other methods. Illustrations, title pages, stock certificates, checks, labels, portraits, maps, etc., lent themselves to the medium. Also, posters in one or more colors for billboards and other large display work were suited for lithography because large work could be reproduced less expensively than with other processes.

Living in a photo-mechanical age today, we tend to forget the technical accomplishments of the nineteenth-century craftsmen, which even in retrospect are remarkable. Hulmandel established a lithographic house in London circa 1810. Examples of his work dating from 1819 can be seen in a small book called *Some New Improvements in Lithography*. A needle-through ground technique, after the manner of the etcher, was used that produced such fidelity of detail that it would be difficult to surpass it today with modern technology. Marvelously detailed lithographic letters were delineated by a variety of means; very small letters could be engraved directly on the stone either by hand or with a pantograph-engraving machine or transferred from types proofed on special paper with a gelatin coating. In the latter instance, a few faces of type, such as the smaller sizes of Gothic, were made to be used especially in offset work. The letters were made in reverse, for when conventional types were used, a transfer of the transfer was necessary to face the type properly for printing. Large letters, illustrations, or billheads were engraved directly on stone. This was done by coating the stone with a thin solution of gum arabic which when washed off left a thin film of gum in, rather than on the stone. The design was usually traced from a sketch to the stone and then engraved in the film of gum by means of sharp pointed steel tools.

Engraving was a tedious process as practically all the work had to be done under a magnifying glass with great care. The engraved lines were made very shallow—the aim being to cut only through the prepared surface. In this way the stone, which could absorb ink, was uncovered at those points. A small illustration or an elaborate line of lettering might take several days to complete, since the work was painstakingly slow.

Any copy of this nature was done on small stones, and proofs of it were transferred to the large printing stones at the time of printing. The small stones could be stored easily as compared to the "printing stones," which ranged up to 44 by 62 inches in size. Illustrations, type, borders, etc., might be proofed from a variety of sources and registered on the large printing stone so that all transfers were made at one time. On such items as labels, enough transfers could be made from the small stone to cover the large printing stone entirely, and through this step and repeat process great quantities could be printed cheaply. Additionally, proofs could be taken from copper or steel plates, wood engravings, or drawings made with crayon or tusche, and transferred to the lithographic stone where they could be faithfully reproduced.

All lithographers accumulated a number of engraved head-

Small transfer stone illustrating variety of material stored on a single stone.

Lettering and illustration photographed from a stone which shows the lithographic engraving techniques.

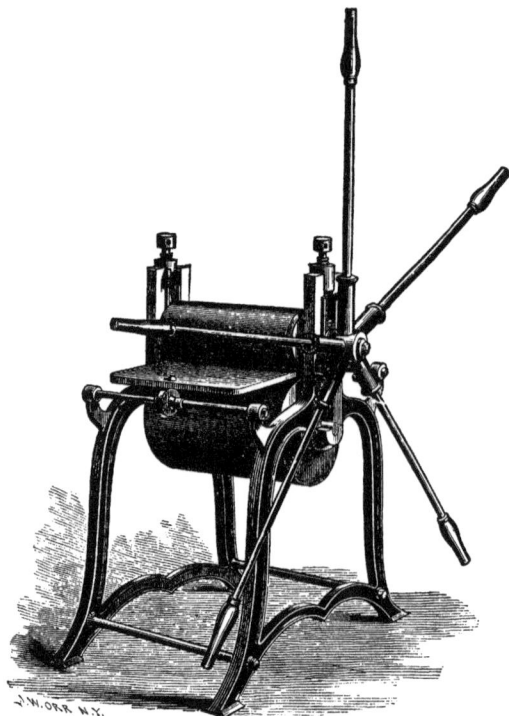

American copperplate hand press, circa 1870.

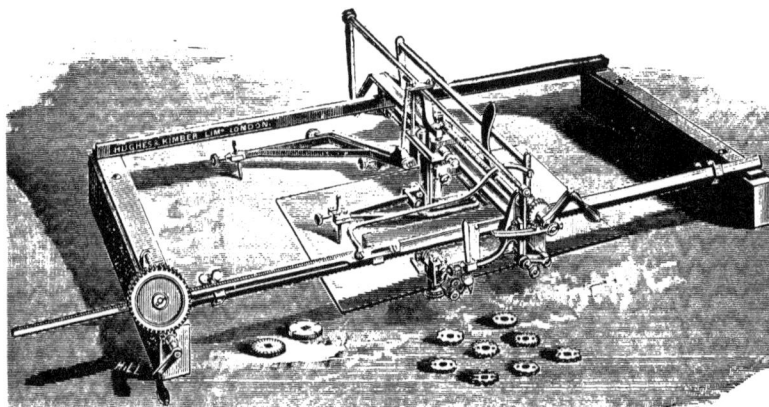

Engravers' ruling machine, circa 1880.

Metal table used by metal plate engravers for engraving circles and curves.

ings, borders, corner pieces, decorative designs, date lines, etc., which could be suitable for numerous jobs. By using stock engravings in combination with a newly engraved design, they could fill orders at reduced prices without sacrificing the detail so dear to all Victorian businessmen. The delicate shaded backgrounds, vignetted edges, and shaded letterforms were done mechanically with a ruling machine, and there were a number of other devices for producing stippling, dotted or coupon lines, and other special effects.

The lithographic artist had in common with the metal and wood engravers a freedom to make changes in the drawing of letterforms from one job to the next. As a medium, lithography lent itself to elaborating since its inherent soft, delicate qualities could be exploited by the artist. Because the artist was not bound by the horizontal and vertical stress of letterpress printing, lettering could curve, undulate, or move along any predetermined line. Letters could interweave or overlap, as opposed to type, which by necessity had to butt one another. Also, letters could easily be drawn into illustrations instead of being inset or double printed by letterpress. With all of its advantages, lithography was a formidable competitor of letterpress and the typefounder.

Metal Plate Engraving

During the few years of respite that the typefounder enjoyed in the contest with lithographers, he had to compete with the metal engravers. The competition was never based on production, but rather on prestige. Copper and steel engravings, representing quality, had traditionally been used for title pages of fine books, certificates, writing manuals, stationeries, labels, etc. The shaded letters of the engraver before and after 1800 inspired the efforts of the typefounder in the production of delicately shaded and embellished decorated display types.

Steel engraving, invented in America by Jacob Perkins circa 1814, was similar to copperplate, but the steel plates were more durable, and had the added advantage that new plates were easily made when the old ones wore down. The engraving process was as follows: soft steel was lighly etched with acid, engraved out in the same manner as on copper, and the completed plate then hardened. Unlike copper engraving, the hardened steel plate was faced with a soft steel blank and run through a press under sufficient pressure to create a male mold, which was then hardened. When the original plate was too worn to print, the male plate was run through the press with a soft blank producing an exact replica of the original plate.

Because engraving and printing by an intaglio process do not favor printing solids of any dimension, engraved letterforms were characteristically light, with fine lines and flourishes giving them distinctiveness. The work of the engraver was closely allied to that of the writing masters in that the medium was excellent for scripts. For the larger letters, it was necessary to shade the bold part of the letters, such as the stems, with lines or decorative embellishments. The engravers made extensive use of the ruling machine, essentially the same tool employed by lithographers and wood engravers; and shaded shadows, as well as the delicate horizontal or diagonal shading on the letter stems were hallmarks of engraved ornamental letterforms. This ruling machine, generally ignored as a factor in type design, is in reality an excellent example of how design may grow out of technical means. It was certainly important in the shaping of Victorian typographic imagery.

Lithography replaced metal plate printing to such a great extent that by 1870 very few metal plate establishments were still in operation. There was, however, a resurgence of interest in intaglio printing with the perfection of rotogravure in 1895.

Wood Engraving

Wood engraving never posed any serious competition to the typefounder. This medium was especially popular for illustrations, magazine covers, views of buildings, landscapes, pictures of machinery, portraits, seals and insignias, labels, bill heads, check and envelope plates, tobacco and other stamps, and posters. In competing with lithographers and metal plate engravers, the wood engraver was the ally of the letterpress printer. Some of their work included carved ornate bill heads, illustrations combined with type, custom designed letters, etc. The engravers' work was multiplied many times over through the typefounders' practice of selling first stereotypes, and later electros from the original engravings of trade cuts, ornaments, and emblems. American type books in the 1820's and 1830's would often have half their space devoted to pictures of cuts and ornaments. Newspaper cuts portraying runaway slaves, steamships, locomotives, etc., were used in classified sections to aid the reader in identifying subject matter at a glance. Early specimens included cuts of famous race horses, some of which folded out of specimen books to 24 inches. The noble redskin or female allegorical figures were favorite subjects for check-ends. Trade cuts illustrated practically every form of business of the day, from that of the artist to the undertaker. There were lodge emblems, trademarks, patriotic or political ornaments such as eagles or flags, and after 1880, a wide selection of exceedingly handsome wood cuts of livestock and poultry. Directed to the agricultural Midwest, these represent the last body of work of this kind to demonstrate the best qualities of American commercial wood engraving. Most of the engravers of these materials for the typefounder were anonymous, but Bullen, in the catalogue of American Type Founders Library duplicate sale, did describe a Mr. Boiler who was engaged by Thomas MacKellar for engraving trade cuts. Bullen went on to say that MacKellar specimens were all originals, in excess of twelve hundred, and that they had been a constant source of supply for his competitors since few founders ever produced original designs. A number of Bewick vignettes that regularly appeared in American specimen books seem to have been popular through the period. For the small printer at a distance from the services of an engraver, trade cuts were a blessing, as they eliminated the time and cost required to engrave each illustration new.

Most of the cuts were general enough to function for a variety of situations. Some provision could also be made for personalizing a cut with a scroll, tablet, or frame so that the printer could insert the message or name of the client.

The decline in quality of these items began in the 1890's and by 1900 was almost complete. It was partly caused by an increased use of half-tones for illustrations, and by the fact that the caliber of drawing previously attached to the craft had disappeared.

In 1840 there were scarcely 20 professional wood engravers in America, and another 20 years passed before the best

Exemplar CARTARUM LATINA, quam HIBERNICA

Two typical examples of how the metal engraver decorated the Roman letter in titling plates, maps, trade-cards and title pages.

Advertisement for John Hall carried in the specimen book of the Albany Type Foundry, 1826.

Initials by Thomas Bewick.

1,591. 35c. 649. 60c. 1,309. 60c.

1,321. 45c. 1,585. $1.25.

363. 75c. 470. 35c. 460. 35c.

1,320. 60c. 1,752. 35c. 358. 60c.

3,455. 25c. 3,456. 25c. 3,457. 25c. 3,458. 30c. 3,459. 25c.

Type metal ornaments electrotyped from wood engravings.

3,500. Agriculture. 3,501. Agricultural Implts. 3,502. Apothecary.

 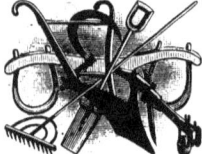 

3,505. Baker. 3,506. Billiards. 3,507. Blacksmith.

 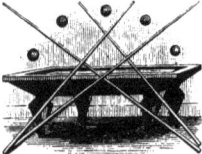 

3,510. Book-binder. 3,511. Bookstore. 3,512. Boot-maker. (Gent's)

3,515. Brewer. 3,516. Bric-a-brac. 3,517. Brush-dealer.

  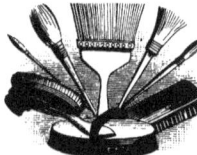

Electrotyped trade cuts made from wood engravings.

Stock cuts on animal and poultry husbandry electrotyped from wood engravings and sold by the typefounder.

166

wood engraving was done here. In 1870 there were more than 400 engravers, and some houses such as that of Edward Sears of New York City employed more than 100 men. It is strange that America and England which won such renown in wood engraving during the nineteenth century should have been so lacking in the tradition of wood engraving. With the exception of John Day in the sixteenth century, England could not boast a tradition until the time of Thomas Bewick beginning in the 1770's. The first American wood engraver was Alexander Anderson, whose earliest work dates from about 1793, but he did not work exclusively with wood until after 1812. Anderson instructed three pupils: Lansing, Morgan and Hall, and he himself continued engraving until he was 94 years old. Also around 1812 Abel Bowen began engraving in Boston, and shortly afterwards, A. J. Mason, a skilled English engraver migrated to this country and practiced his profession. J. A. Adams, perhaps better known for his pioneering work with electro-typing, was a wood engraver working in New York City in 1826.

The contribution of wood engravers to letter or type design is difficult to assess, since very little is known about how much of the engravers' work with the letterform was creative and how much was imitative. Nicolette Gray mentions that some three-dimensional ornate letters on lottery bills from about 1808 in London were presumably engraved on wood in imitation of type. From her description, these faces would appear to have been forerunners of the open face shade designs so extremely popular with typefounders 10 to 20 years afterwards. Wood engravers continued to engrave fancy initials, and undoubtedly they originated some of the letter designs on bill heads and title pages. There is no evidence, however, that any of these works had a significant influence on typefounders.

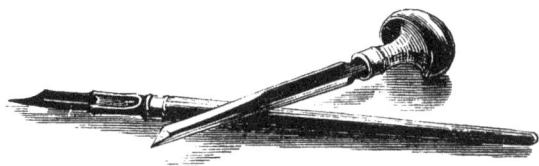

Sign Painters & Penmen

The profession as it was practised in the nineteenth century was quite different from what we consider it to be today. It included a rigorous apprentice system, which required great skill and knowledge of letterforms. Some of the lettering manuals published in this period were directed exclusively to the sign painter. Also many writing books devoted a section to ornamental letters, which were advertised as being of great service to artists, draughtsmen, sign painters, and clerks. The earlier books were mostly printed from metal engravings and occasionally from wood. Later in the century, a number were produced through photo-lithography. The range of letterforms shown was quite diverse—some obviously based on historical sources, particularly the manuscript initials, and others patterned after the designs of the founder, usually with some alterations.

Sign painting, which has origins considerably older than those of printing, can be traced as a profession back to the Egyptians and Greeks. After the invention of printing and the introduction of types, the sign painter generally borrowed the designs of the printer for his letters. Ruari

Wood engraved ad for magazine, c. 1890.

Billhead, custom engraved.

Wood engraved illustrations for variety show broadside.

Two lines used in bag work.

The nineteenth century American writing master plied his trade through correspondence schools, business schools, institutes, etc. One of the most telling testimonials to his skills are these stylized drawings rendered with elaborate flourishes of the steel pen. It is said that the itinerant writing masters would pin their most impressive drawings on the walls of local barbershops as a means of advertising, and in this manner they would gather enough students to establish a writing class. Also, in the numerous writing and lettering books from the period, these drawings were interspersed with lessons and examples as a means of demonstrating the author's abilities.

Penmen's manuals were widely distributed and copied during the century. The earliest manuals were printed from wood engravings, later by lithography and a number from steel engravings. A few manuals were published exclusively for signpainters—both professional and amateur—and it was increasingly common for the penmen to devote a section of their books to lettering.

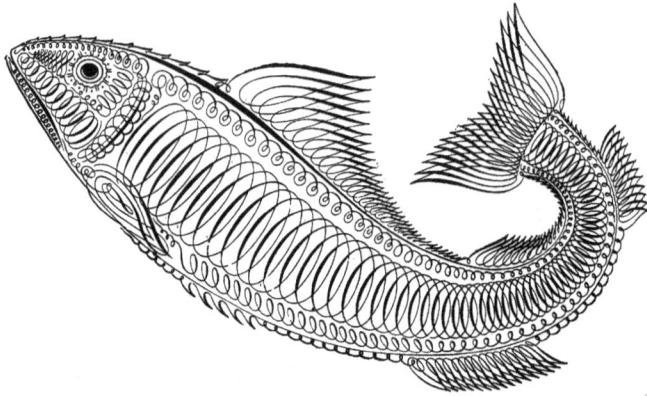

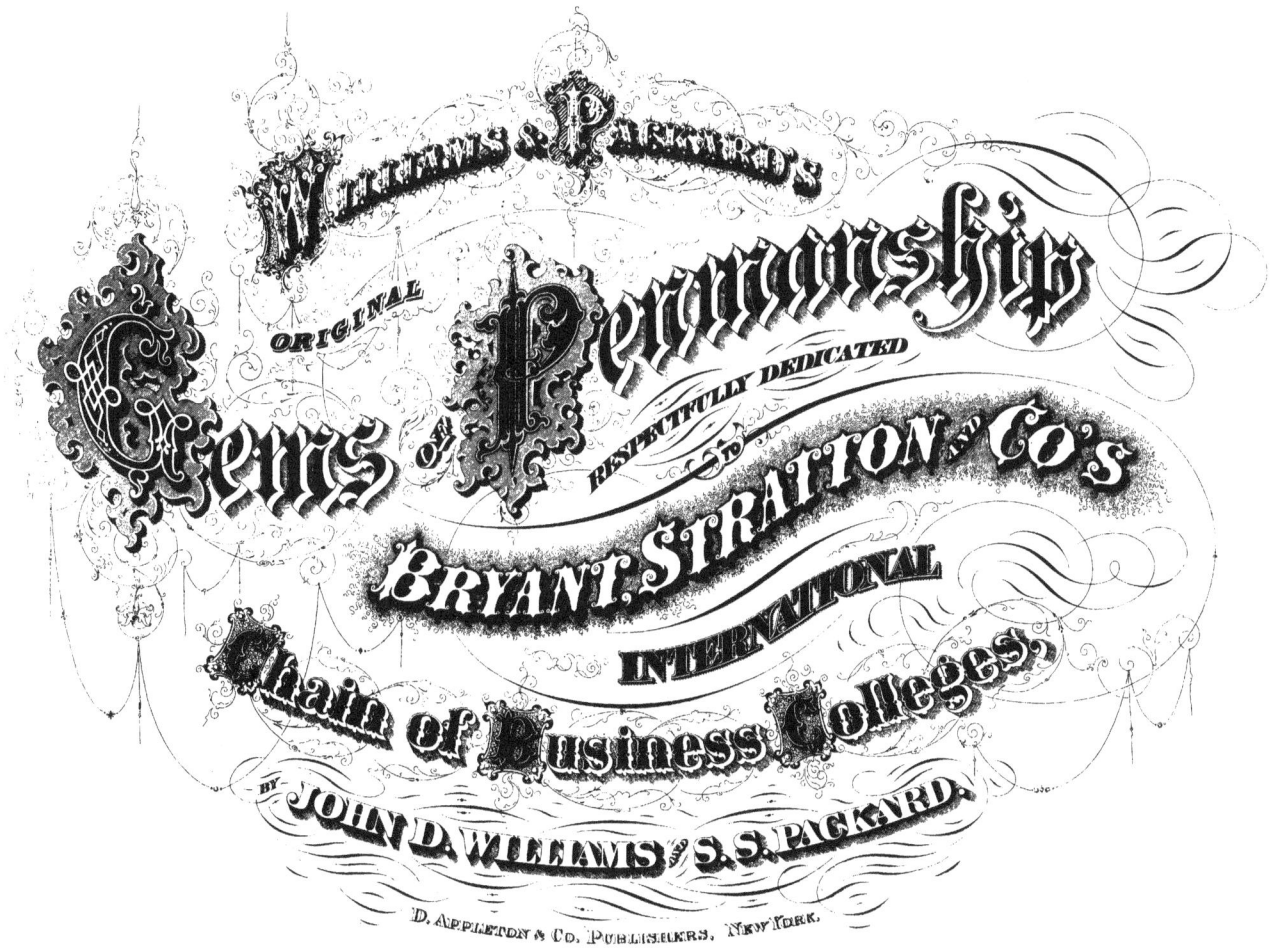

Williams and Packard, 1866.

Esser, 1877.

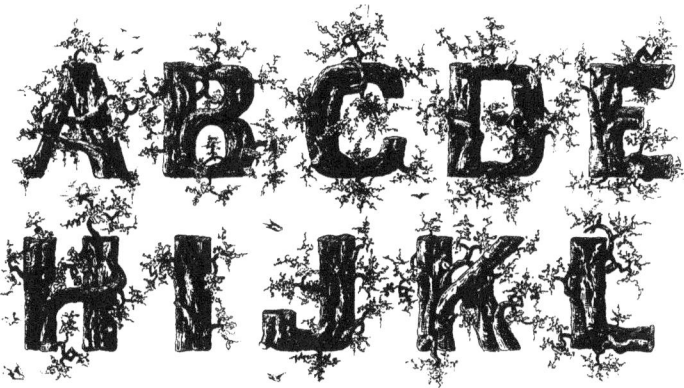

Ames, 1879.

Dearborn, 1873.

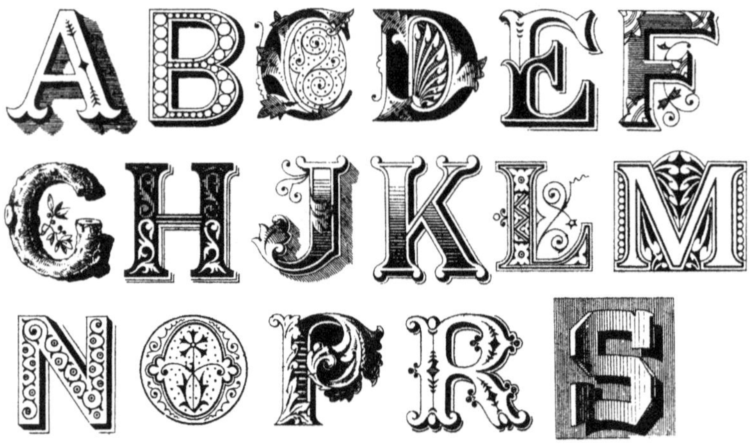

ABCDEF
GHJKLM
NOPRS

Esser, 1877.

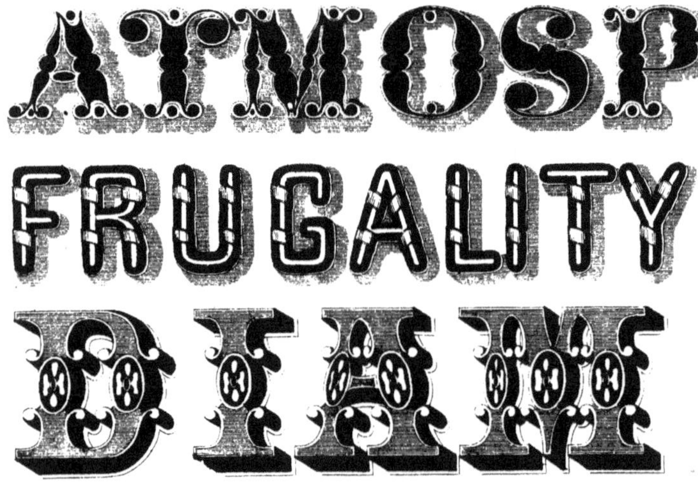

ATMOSP
FRUGALITY
DIAM

VARIOUSLY SHADED ROMAN PRINT.

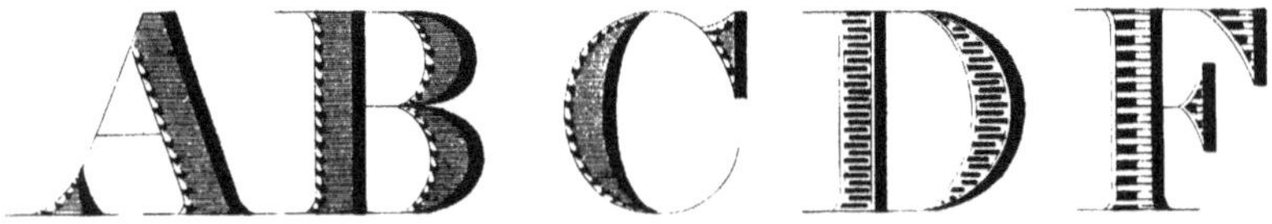

ABCDF

Becker, 1854.

Roman Shaded, barious.

ACDEFG

Delamotte, 14th edition, 1906.

Illuminated Capitals, designed for Lower Case, Elizabethian.

ABCDF

abcdefghijklmnopqrstuv

Dearborn, 1873.

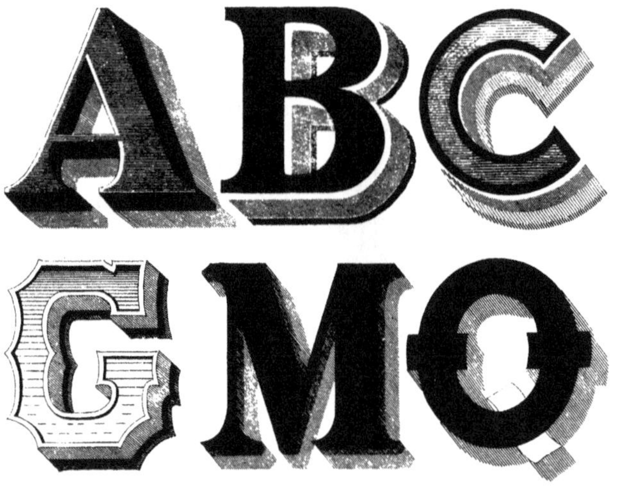

ABC

GMO

Marking Alphabet.

ABCDEFGH

SPURED ALPHABETS

ABCDEFG
abcdefghijkl

Ames, 1879.

BOSTON OCTAGON EGYPTIAN.

ABCDE

NEW YORK ROMAN.

ABCD

BOSTON OCTAGON FULL BLOCK.

GHDE

MPQRS

Boyce, 1878.

McLean, in his article, "An examination of Egyptians," states: "Until late in the eighteenth century signwriters had usually based their letter-forms upon available type designs. We see the typographical influence of Van Dyck, Caslon and Baskerville upon fascias, signboards and other lettered announcements now preserved in town halls, churches, museums and other buildings. During the early nineteenth century, however, signwriters began to break away from these models and to become more adventurous, particularly in the employment of decorative alphabets." In Europe, the early history of the sign painter was associated more with the illustrative arts than with the rendering of letterforms, as most signs depended on a picture to carry a message. Also, the sign painter was frequently expected to carve his designs into wood in the making of sign boards.

The works of the sign painters were so profuse by the middle of the eighteenth century that the size and the placing of signs were regulated by the governments of both France and England, and in the mid-1800's, in America. In this same period, the sign painter doubled as a decorator of carriages, since it was extremely fashionable to paint the carriage panels with brightly colored scenes or other decorative motifs. The art of carriage painting carried over into the next century, and was practiced by the sign painter in America during the first years of the nineteenth century. During this period, outdoor sign painting increased at a much faster rate than poster printing. Used mainly by agents for patent medicines, merchants, tobacco firms, etc., ads were painted on rocks, buildings, fences and barns. In all probability, the sign-painting industry was larger during the nineteenth century than it is now. Sign painters often advertised themselves as "Sign and Ornamental" painters, and after 1850, often doubled as house painters "with a variety of accompanying skills in interior decoration and knowledge of the latest marbling effects." In America, almost every town, even though modest in size, listed in the city directory several sign painters, and also, then as now, there were a number of itinerant sign painters.

Interestingly enough, even the sign painters suffered loss through competition with lithography, as by 1870 lithographers had devised a means for mass producing gilded signs. The most elaborate designs could be transferred to a special thin Russian sheet iron, gilded, and japanned, and when produced in quantities such as for insurance companies, fire-alarms, etc., they were one-twentieth of the cost charged by a sign painter.

It is curious, but the sign painter continued to keep alive the old type styles long after the printer and typographer had discarded them in favor of changing fashions. This was particularly true for signs in building identification. Today, a person may visit almost any commercial area of a city and find excellent examples of nineteenth-century letterforms—perhaps faded and peeling on the older buildings but also freshly painted signs for smart new shops, both having the same Victorian letterforms. Many of the plain letters such as Antiques, Gothic Extended, and Clarendons lend themselves to the scale required for lettering on buildings. British designers successfully revived these same letterforms for pavilion identification at the Festival of Britain in 1951, and these applications lent great impetus to the succeeding revival of Victorian letters.

Some of the more fanciful designs for sign letters appear

to have been borrowed from the penman, especially the decorated Romans in which each letter of the alphabet has a unique embellishment. Other designs reflect the same qualities associated with the decorated letters done by engravers at the end of the eighteenth century. It seems strange that many books recommended to the sign painter contained letterforms based on engraving techniques, since they do not seem particularly suited for the brush, paint and gold-leaf techniques of the sign painter. One instance where the sign painter may lay claim to invention is in the Antique or Egyptian letterform. The slab serif can be more logically associated with the brush than the graver, and the design is appropriate to the needs of the sign painter. While the claim cannot be positively confirmed, it is still a reasonable assumption and generally supported.

Much as with the work of the wood engraver, the inventiveness of sign painters will probably never be entirely known, as the profession had few historical exponents, and the trade has been traditionally looked down upon by letter or type historians. However, a surprising number of recognized artists, such as Holbein, Correggio, Watteau, Vernet, and Gericault, have left records of having at one time or another painted signs, either as a lark, or to pay a tavern bill.

Photography

In commercial work, photography had quite a different role from its present one. M. Poitivin of Paris, a trade photographer, published a paper in the *Bulletin of Inventions* in 1850 which outlined a means of putting an image on the lithographic stone through photo-mechanical means. Five years later he experimented with an albumen process on grained stone. Within 10 years photography was in general if not extensive use in lithography. With the transfer process perfected, however, there was not that much incentive for the photographic processes to be pushed in lithography, particularly in line work. *American Encyclopaedia of Printing* states in 1871 that "there have been introduced lately two different methods, which are also patented, for producing photographs on plate-glass to be printed in the usual lithographic manner. The impressions produced by these processes compare favorably with those of the best photographs, and there is no doubt that they will at some not so distant day make an important addition to the art of printing." (Believed to be the Heliotype process, based on Poitivin's principles, patented by Ernest Edwards of Boston.)

Photography was used in wood engraving in the 1860's, and one engraving house of the time was to advertise, "We have facilities for photographing on wood, thereby rendering the picture as correct as nature can make it." With the photographic process, the image could be affixed to the block, but the engraver still had to translate the tonal qualities into the dots, lines, and cross-hatch of wood engraving. From contemporary comments, specifically

those of W. J. Linton in 1879, it would seem that not all engravers hastened to embrace the new process, feeling that abolishing drawing would eventually lead to lowering of standards in the craft, and that distortion often existed in photography whereas a drawing could be made to illustrate more effectively the wishes of the client. The chief advantage of photography for both lithographers and wood engravers was the speed and ease with which a picture could be made to any size on the block or stone. The enlarging and reducing by photographic means were the particular aspects of photography that found the greatest application in commercial work up to the time when the halftone screen was perfected by Frederick Ives in 1878.

The American Printer

The American printer, assisted by the ingenuity of the typefounder, had at his disposal many novel ways to match his handiwork against that of the engravers and lithographers. There were brass rules, circular and oval quadrats, serpentines, and numerous patented devices which allowed him to duplicate the freedom of his competitors' typographic styling. Indeed, the detail of lithography and engraving could be achieved in combination borders (which provided a versatile means for framing, decorating or separating copy), flourishes, scrolls, ornaments, elegant initial letters, and cartouches—but with considerably more work! With quadrats and serpentines, the compositor could set type in circles, ovals, or he could undulate it across the page. In this brand of job work, Americans surpassed the Europeans for many years. Also, poster printers could place type almost as freely as lithographers by setting it in gypsum or plaster on jobs requiring no previous proofs.

At the beginning of the century, the few borders appearing in American specimen books seemed to have originated with wood engravers. However, Caslon in England and the French printers were producing wide ornate borders made from metal engravings which were exceedingly opulent and beautifully executed. Bullen maintains that, with few exceptions, all countries depended on France for borders until the mid 1870's. Certainly American typefounders borrowed freely from European sources. In fact, except for a few men like David Bruce, Jr., the founders did not attempt to design original borders in the United States until well into the second half of the century. In his 1853 specimen book, Bruce showed a number of chromatic borders printed in two colors, and while similar ones were shown by other founders, they all disappeared from the specimen books in a few years.

Perhaps the most unusual, if not the most fanciful, borders of the century were the Chinese and Japanese ones designed and cut by William Jackson for McKellar, Smiths and Jordan, and the Egyptian, Japanese, and Assyrian designed and cut by Harrison Lounsbury for Bruce, all of which were marketed about 1880. These exotic borders were compete with a variety of corner pieces, ornaments, illustrations, and related pieces, and unlike previous and subsequent borders, the general effect was more illustrative than decorative.

After 1850 most ornamental borders were engraved on type metals, and electrotype matrices made from the originals. With the ease of manufacture, borders became even more plentiful and intricate. The border styles would change with typographical fashions—from ornate to plain and light to heavy—throughout the century. Ornamental

Egyptian Combination Border, George Bruce's Sons & Co.

COMBINATION BORDER, No. 57.

Japanese Combination Border, George Bruce's Sons & Co.

COMBINATION BORDER, No. 3.

George Bruce's Sons & Co.

Mortised label borders.

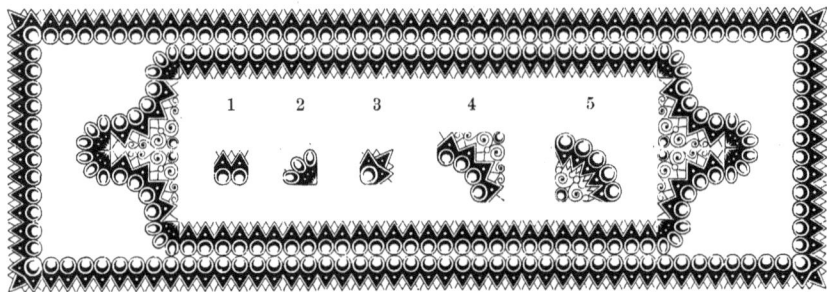

Circular Quadrats. Made in various sizes to form circles or parts of circles from one to 24 inches in diameter. Also, the quadrats can be arranged in serpentine and eccentric curves.

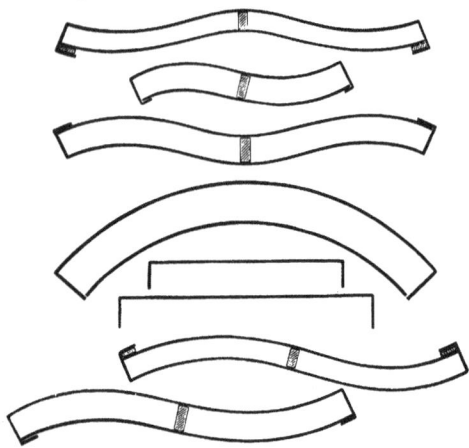

Labor-saving curvatures. Morris's adjustable line formers were supposed to do away with bent leads, plaster, wax, and other methods of making curved lines.

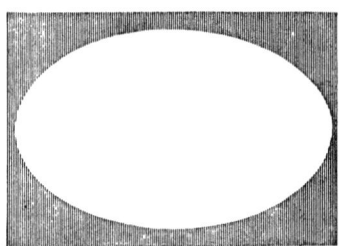

Hollow Quadrat. Useful as frames or miniature chases for circular or oval jobs. Cast in various sizes and graduated to pica ems.

Curving machine. A tool for curving leads for eccentric composition of type.

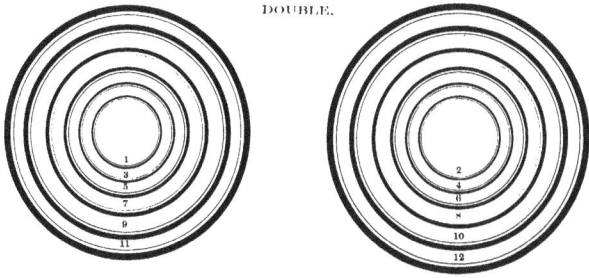

Brass circles.

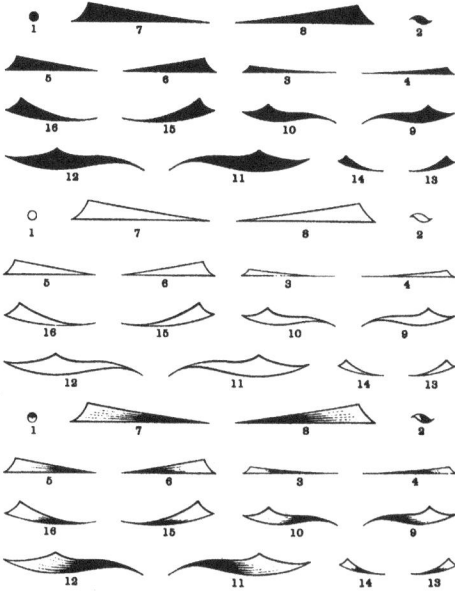

Pointers—solid, contour, and shaded.

Logotypes. In the last quarter of the century every specimen book showed at least a page of these logotypes which could be purchased in several sizes. They too reflect the letterpress printers' efforts to compete with lithography and engraving.

CURVES & TWISTS

CHOICE   HANDSOME   UNIQUE

DESIGNS

D. & G. BRUCE,

TYPE AND STEREOTYPE-FOUNDERS,

Chambers-Street, near Chatham-Street,

1818.   NEW-YORK.

D. & G. BRUCE,

TYPE AND STEREOTYPE-FOUNDERS,

SLOTE-LANE,

1813.   NEW-YORK.

Every compositor had at his disposal a number of ornamental units which could be used to create effects similar to those of the engraver or lithographer.

Twelfth-century initial letters from the British Museum.
*(*The Handbook of Mediaeval Alphabets and Devices,
Henry Shaw, 1856.)

*English brass inscription letters, fifteenth and sixteenth
century. Alphabet taken from the monument of Henry
VII and other brasses. Words were separated through use
of the flowers at the bottom. The notch as a decorative
motif, which is quite characteristic of these brass letters,
was to find wide application in type styles around the
mid-nineteenth century.*

Wood engravings from Shaw's Handbook of Mediaeval
Alphabets. *Based on letters from the Missle Traijectense,
1515.*

units were cast so they might be combined into a variety
of shapes and were identified as combination borders.
These units were used to form ornamental vignettes,
boxes, or groundwork, as well as to frame the page. Corner
pieces were offered in alternate patterns; and there were
many styles and sizes of ornamental dashes, scrolls, colo-
phons for chapter endings, and pen dashes.

The wood borders enjoyed a small revival when wood type
manufacturers discovered in 1879 a process for stamping
designs into the wood cheaply. For the most part, the
wood designs were quite different from those produced
by the typefounders.

Flourishes cast in type metal provided the swish and flair
commonly identified only with the engraving and writing
masters, and no small elegance could be accomplished by
a competent compositor using the range of sizes and variations supplied by typefounders. After the middle of the
century, there was a decided increase in the number and
styles of initial letters. Certain of these, designed to. be
printed in more than one color, came with intricate tail
pieces, and the combined effect of color, initial, and tail
piece was reminiscent of the illuminator's art after which
they had been modeled.

Pierced initials—i.e., decorative shapes with an opening to
insert a capital of the printer's choice—were a favorite of
the printer in the early years of the century. Facsimile initials—consisting of small ornamental flowers arranged
into a variety of frames or fields for initial letters—gained
only limited popularity because of the time and labor required for composition. More common were cast backgrounds in a square or rectangle with minute patterns
usually printed in pale colors over which a capital, or
ornamental letter would be imprinted in a dark color.

In the last quarter of the century, the use of filigreed initials became extremely popular. Many of these had letter
and filigree on separate bodies so that they could be
printed in either one or two colors, or the letters could
be printed separately. The Boston Type and Stereotype
Foundry was the first American company to show these
faces in 1845. Texts, Uncials, and Romans were the most
frequently used letterforms, with revivals from both the
illuminators' and engravers' historiated and decorative
styles abundantly in evidence. During the 1880's, some of
the novelty faces were also adapted as initial letters.

In the design of intial letters, the nineteenth-century
founder clung to the historical traditions more closely
than he did in either text or display types. There was really
little invention other than mechanical ingenuity in their
manufacture. However, the skill of the nineteenth-century
compositor in fitting, piecing, and composing all these
elements—borders, flourishes, flowers, initials, rules, and
serpentines—cannot be found today. Probably we shall
never again see this craftsmanship in printing and typographic composition.

The following initials were taken from Type of the
De Vinne Press, *Theodore De Vinne, 1907.*

Initials with trails.

Pierced initials.

Medieval.

No. 14   No. 15

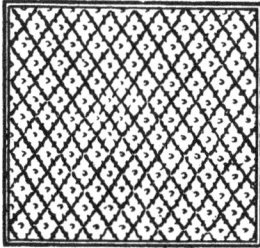 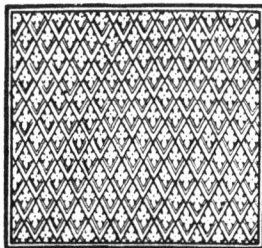

No. 16   No. 18

 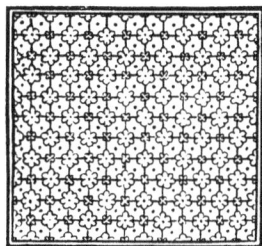

Backgrounds for initials. To be overprinted with type of the printer's choice.

Silhouette, Italian Renaissance.

Chromatic initials.

Initials with trails.

Filigreed initials.

Single letters.

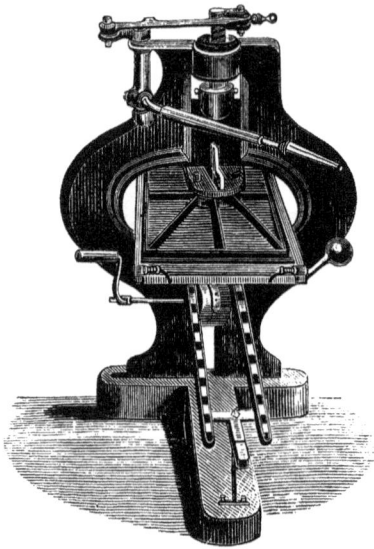

The Stanhope Press. The first all-metal press, which was built by Lord Stanhope in England during 1800.

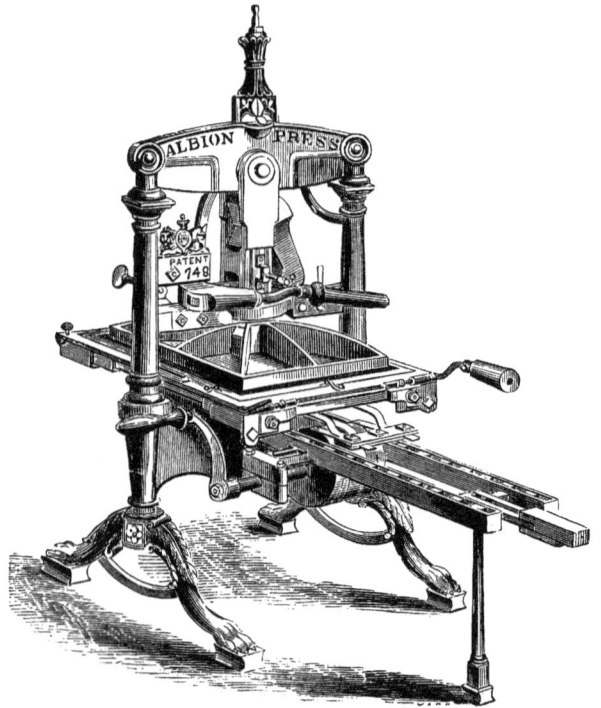

The Albion Press, 1823. Invented by Mr. R. W. Cope, London.

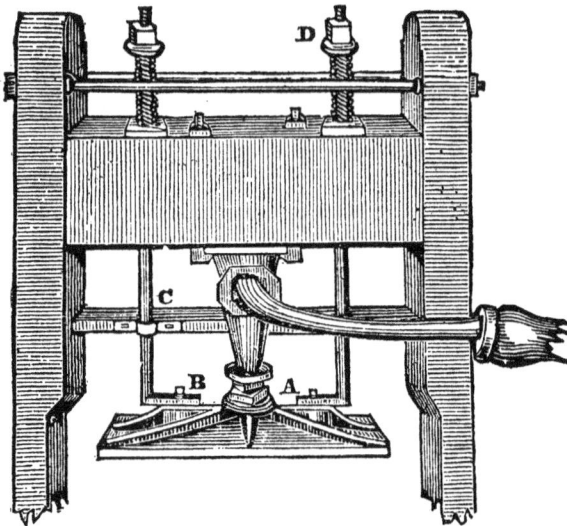

The Ramage Press. First American press manufactured with an iron bed—after 1800.

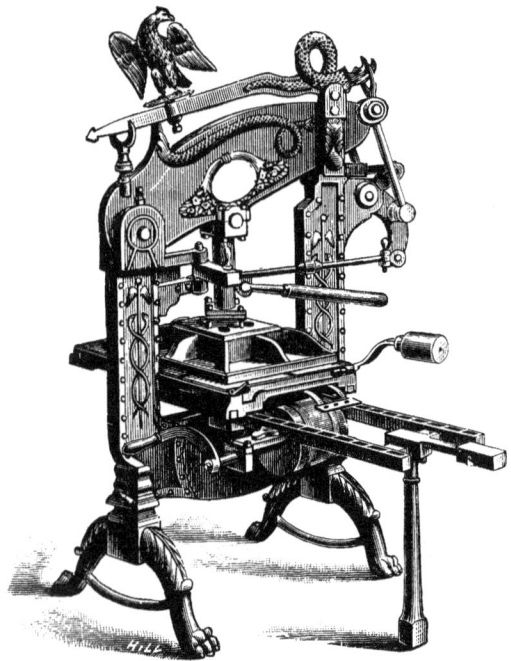

The Columbian, circa 1813. Invented in Philadelphia by an American, George Clymer.

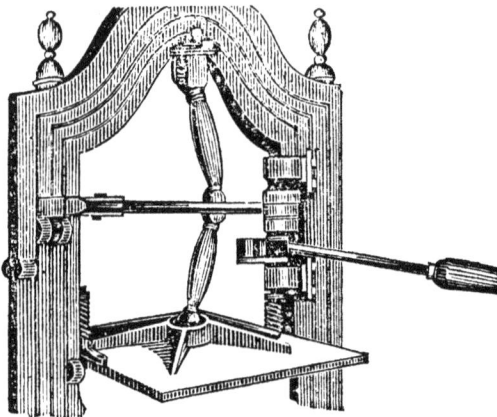

The Wells Press, circa 1819. Invented by John J. Wells.

This showing of presses illustrates only a few of the multitude of new presses produced in America during the nineteenth century. However, it does show some of the more prominent models of country and clam presses which produced the bulk of job printing during the century, and there can be no question that the inventiveness of American press manufacturers contributed much to the advance of the printing trades in this period.

Campbell Country Press. Andrew Campbell was the first American to engage in country-press manufacturing.

The Washington Press. Manufactured by Shniedewend & Lee of Chicago, 1884-93. Original Washington press invented by Samuel Rust in 1829.

Potter Improved country press, c. 1870.

Adams Platen Power Press, patents for 1830 and 1836 by Seth Adams of Boston.

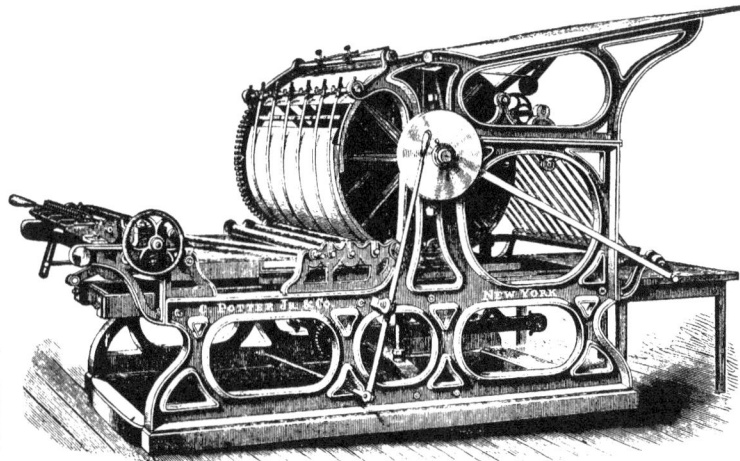

The Newbury Country Press. Manufactured by A. & B. Newbury, Coxsackie, New York.

Taylor Country Press. A. B. Taylor established himself in press manufacturing in New York City during 1842.

179

The Henry Cylinder Press.

"Franklin" 1855-72. Patented by George P. Gordon in 1855 and perfected by 1858.

The Babcock Printing Press, 1880's.

Nonpareil Press, 1868-85. Distributed by the Cincinnati Type Foundry.

Taylor Drum Cylinder.

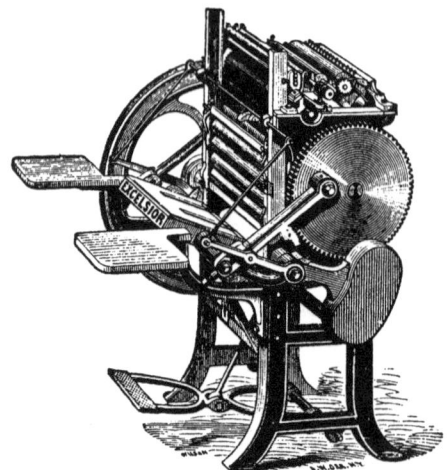
Excelsior Press, 1868-70. Patented and manufactured by William Braidwood of New York City.

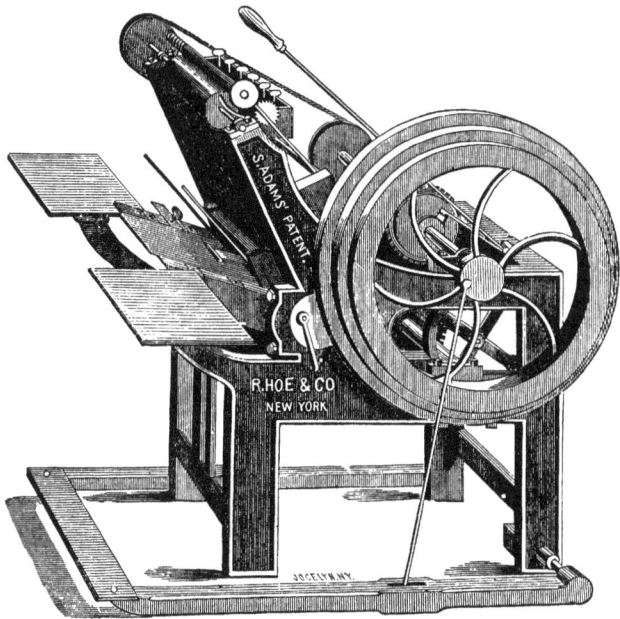

Hoe Double Cylinder, circa 1842.

Bed and Platen Job Press, 1853-59 (1859-73, Hoe).
Patented and marketed by S. Adams between 1853-59.
Afterwards it was manufactured by R. Hoe & Company,
New York City.

"Liberty," circa 1860. Patented by Frederick Degener.
After 1877, manufactured by F. M. Weiler, New York City.

Hoe Three Revolution, circa 1844.

Taylor Double Cylinder. A. B. Taylor Printing Press &
Machine Co., established in New York City, 1842.

"Peerless-Gordon," 1891-1900. Manufactured by Peerless
Printing Press Company, Palmyra, New York.

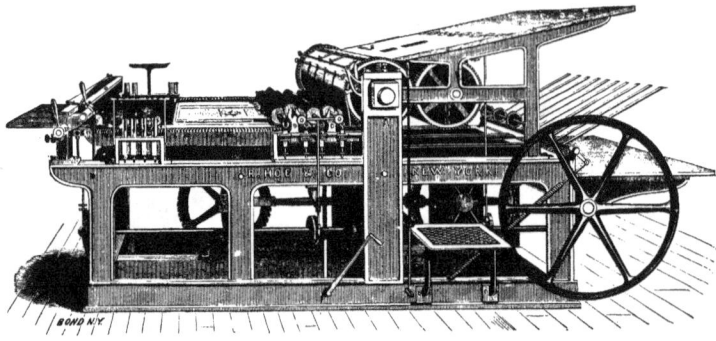

Stop-cylinder wood cut press. Manufactured by R. Hoe &
Company and especially designed for fine printing of
wood cuts.

Acme Newspaper and Job Press, circa 1870. Invented by
C. W. S. Montague. Run by either hand or steam and
manufactured in Boston.

"Pearl," 1876-1927. Manufactured by Golding Mfg. Co.,
Boston, Mass.

Rapid Cylinder Press, George W. Prouty & Co. in business
circa 1878-1926, Boston, Mass., Chicago, Ill. and
Madison, Wis.

"Clipper," 1881-89. Manufactured originally by the
Globe Manufacturing Company, Palmyra, New York,
later by Jones Manufacturing Company of the same city.

"Reliable," 1886-89. Manufactured by Palmer & Rey, San Francisco, California.

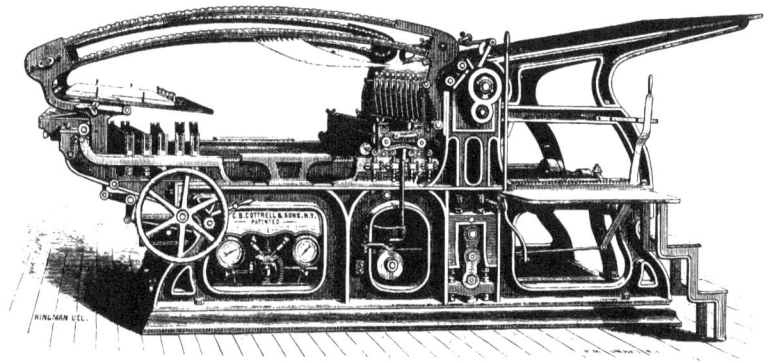

Cottrell Front Delivery Press, circa 1886. Delivers the sheet printed side up in full view of the pressman, lays sheets straight, with no flys, strings, tapes or obstructions of any kind. Manufactured by G. B. Cottrell & Sons, New York City and Chicago.

Chromatic Printing Press, 1871-73. A press designed to print three colors in one impression. Invented and marketed by Suitterlin, Claussen & Company of Chicago.

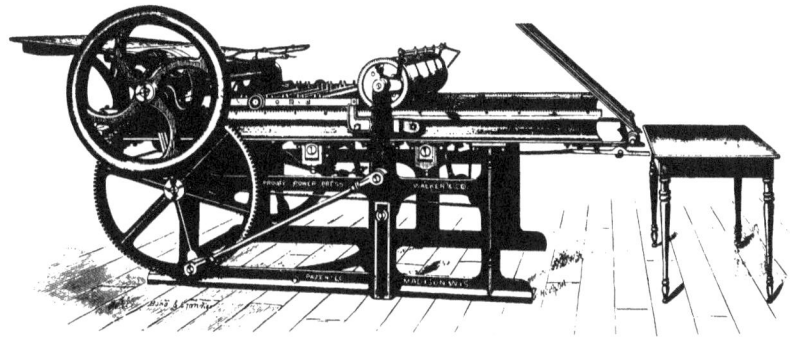

Prouty Combination Book, News and Job Press, new series, 1886.

Gally Press, 1880's. Patented in 1863 by Merritt Gally.

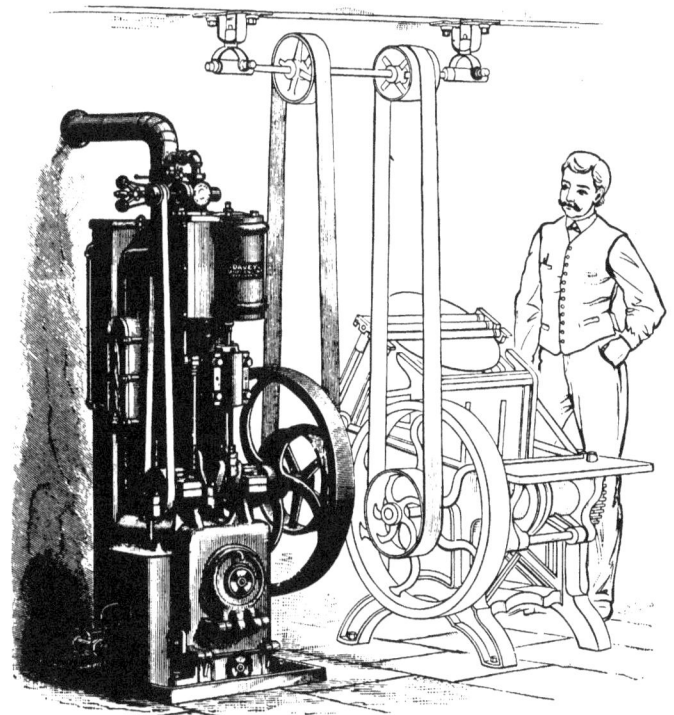

Steam boilers used to power printing machinery.

THE GREAT
STONE AND MURRAY
CIRCUS!

SPECIAL NOTICE!

Messrs. STONE & MURRAY, grateful for the generous patronage of past years, have endeavored this season to fulfill the many obligations they owe to the Public by increasing the attractiveness of their Circus, and elevating it above its former excellence, by congregating a Troupe of

STAR PERFORMERS!

ABSOLUTELY UNPARALLELED!
WHICH WILL RENDER THE

Varied Exhibitions of Skill and Intrepidity

Wonderfully captivating and greatly superior in style and finish to any similar performances ever given in this country. Nothing has been omitted to make this Circus attractive and popular, and eminently beyond competition. The Entertainments will comprise many characteristics quite new in this Continent, and inimitable in style.

PICTURESQUE GRANDEUR AND RADIANT BEAUTY
THE
BRILLIANT SCENES

In the Arena will be moulded to DELIGHT THE VOTARIES OF PLEASURE, and to form FESTIVALS OF ENJOYMENT and FASCINATING PASTIMES for 'Old and Young, Grave and Gay.'

In order to gratify the popular taste for Sensational Wonders, Stone & Murray will introduce, GRATUITOUSLY,

TWO NEW SPECTACULAR SCENES

Which, for effective skill and insensibility to danger, have no parallels in the annals of amusements.

THE FIRST SENSATION will be presented on the Morning of Exhibition Day, and is the rarest Display of Splendor ever exhibited in America. The Chief Attraction of this Grand Pageant will be the ELEGANT

BAND CHARIOT

Containing Prof. O. P. PERRY'S Unequaled Orchestra,

Drawn by 16 Horses!
SUPERBLY DECORATED WITH COSTLY TRAPPINGS, AND
DRIVEN BY ONE MAN, MONS. J. H. PAUL,
The Wonderful Maitre du Cheval.

The pictorial view of this surprising Exhibition, on the border of this bill, will convey a partial idea of its immense broadside, and the entire outfit necessary to give effect to the scene will be in keeping with the lavish outlay of money so freely expended in making the interior performances of STONE & MURRAY'S CIRCUS.

CONSPICUOUS FOR SPLENDOR, AND UNEQUALED IN MAGNITUDE!

This TRIUMPHAL PARADE will pass through the principal streets of each place the GREAT CIRCUS is announced to visit, and will prove a gratifying and satisfactory Exhibition.

THE SECOND SENSATION WILL BE A FREE OFFERING OF

PHENOMENAL FEATS OF DARING!

And will be given at ONE OCLOCK, P. M., by the distinguished Tight Rope Danseuse,

MADEMOISELLE JEANETTE ELLSLER,
Who will Walk from the Ground to the Apex of the Pavilion and return, ON A SLENDER WIRE.

THIS THRILLING
FREE EXHIBITION!

Will afford the lovers of MARVELOUS FEATS OF SKILL a rare opportunity of viewing a

CULMINATING GLORY OF FUNAMBULISTIC ART!
THIS INTENSELY FASCINATING DISPLAY OF COURAGE AND SKILL

UP - IN - THE - AIR!

Will naturally inspire in the beholder a tremor of fear for the safety of the brave Lady while executing this

WALK FOR LIFE!

But her perfect skill banishes danger, and her freedom from thought of peril, renders an accident almost impossible, as the termination of this

GRAND ÆRIAL PROMENADE

Brings the just and ENTHUSIASTIC PLAUDITS of the DELIGHTED SPECTATORS, who will always remember the Scene as one of the MOST EXCITING AND IMPRESSIVE EVER BEHELD, and Transcending in Startling Features all prior Acts of Sensational Interest.

The Poster Houses

Poster is an abbreviation of "posting bill," which is said to have originated in the fact that several centuries ago it became a custom to attach notices to posts on the sidewalks of Fleet Street in London.

During the eighteenth century in America, the promiscuous posting of bills on trees, fences, walls and abandoned buildings was done mostly to promote lotteries, much the same as in England at an earlier date. Among the first truly commercial bills were those for auctions and stagecoach timetables, and after the mid-eighteenth century, posters were hung for theatrical groups. These posters were often tacked to boards in country inns, and it was quite natural that as other commercial notices were printed, they too would be posted in the same places. The country inn remained one of the most popular spots for hanging bills until about 1835. Circuses had been among the foremost exponents of broadside advertising, most often using the eighteen-inch bill, and their posters dominated the scene for the first quarter of the nineteenth century. As the number of posters increased and the inn could no longer accommodate the numbers and sizes of bills, there was an increased use of outdoor signs and posters. After 1835, printed clothing-store posters were common on main roads leading into the larger cities as well as on buildings and fences. Men carrying large posters on sandwich boards could be found along lower Broadway in New York City during the 1820's, and they were found in even greater numbers during the 1840's. Larger posters were displayed from horse-drawn wagons beginning in the 1830's. It was at this time that billsticking (the act of pasting up posters) could be identified as a distinct profession, and their main support came from museums, theatres, patent medicines, clothing stores and hatters.

By the 1860's it is estimated that there were at least 275 professional billsticking and board and rock painting firms —each employing 2 to 20 men. Kissam & Allen of New York City are believed to be the first firm to erect their own boards, this being in 1872, and from this date on leasing of outdoor advertising space became a regular practice.

Although P. T. Barnum had published many bills for his various enterprises before he took over the American Museum in New York City in 1842, it was after this date that he exploited the handbill and poster in the greatest quantities and to the best advantage. Barnum, as perhaps no other single man, gave impetus to the entire field of advertising, and particularly to the development of the hand bill and poster, and in doing so, helped to further popularize the large ornate display types. Also, he was greatly responsible for the increased use of wood cuts in advertising—especially the large pine-wood cuts which were used for outdoor posters. Some of the finest broadside printing from this century was the circus posters produced for Barnum during the 1870's.

During the Civil War, the government was one of the most substantial users of outdoor advertising, having issued thousands of recruitment posters which were displayed in many locations previously inaccessible to commercial advertisers. The use of outdoor posters by the government at this time added to an already expanding use of painted signs and outdoor posters, and by the late 1860's the first legislation in America was passed which limited outdoor advertising. Although there had been a growing reaction to the indiscriminate posting of bills and painting

ACADEMY OF MUSIC
FOURTEENTH STREET,
THURSDAY, APRIL 27, 1876
TONY PASTOR'S
GRAND
JUBILEE FESTIVAL

☞ TWO GRAND PERFORMANCES
Will be given the same Evening, one at

TONY PASTOR'S NEW THEATRE and one at the ACADEMY OF MUSIC

TONY PASTOR, GUS WILLIAMS, HARRY KERNELL & JENNIE MORGAN
TONY PASTOR APPEARING AT BOTH ENTERTAINMENTS.

THE LARGEST COMBINATION OF

SPECIALTY ARTISTS in the WORLD

Under the personal superintendence of TONY PASTOR, SOLE PROPRIETOR, who will appear at each and every performance given by his unrivalled organization. Mr. PASTOR takes pleasure in announcing his Company for the season of 1876 in this Mammoth Programme.

OVERTURE .... H. T. DYRING and ORCHESTRA

The Entertainment will commence with the Laughable Sketch, called

THE DAYS OF '76
OR, THE FOURTH OF JULY ORATION.
DEMOSTHENES BLACK .... CHAS. WORLEY | PROF. WHITE .... FRANK GIRARD

BABY BINDLEY
The precocious Musical Genius, Character Artist, Vocalist and Dancer, performing difficult Solos on innumerable Instruments.

Miss JENNIE MORGAN
The distinguished Operatic Soprano, in her repertoire of Cavatinas and Home Ballads.

LURLINE, THE WATER QUEEN
WATSON, THE MAN FISH
In which they perform the WONDROUS FEATS of EATING, DRINKING, SMOKING, WRITING, SLEEPING, CARD-PLAYING, SOMERSAULTS, and FLEXIBILITIES UNDER WATER, in a commodious ILLUMINATED GLASS TANK, surpassing all aquatic feats ever before accomplished by others, and introducing many never attempted by any other man or woman.

TONY PASTOR
Who will appear at every performance in a New and Original Catalogue of HUMOROUS, MOTTO, DESCRIPTIVE and LOCAL SONGS.

THE BRAHAMS
Musical, Sketch and Dialect Artists, introducing their Specialty, THE DANCING QUAKERS.

THE CANNON BALL TOSSER
JIM, the Ball-Tosser .... CHAS. WORLEY
ROSCIUS DUMONT, (the American Barry Sullivan) .... FRANK GIRARD
MR. CALMER, Dramatic Manager .... MR. H. BRAHAM

GUS WILLIAMS
The Dutch Momus, surnamed "Earl of Pretzel," and Heir Apparent to the throne of King Gambrinus, the King William of America, and Monarch of all German Comedians. Mr. Williams will appear in his Famous and Original Songs, Stories, Anecdotes, &c.

KARL LIND
The Stockholm Wonder and Antipodean phenomenon, balancing himself upon his head on a pyramid of parlor furniture, such as tables, sofas, chairs, hat racks, and ninety Champagne bottles, until he reaches the dome of the theatre, and while in this seemingly perilous position, playing upon Musical Instruments, such as the Banjo, Drum, Cornet, Violin, Guitar, and the English Concertina, and discharging Fire-Arms while balancing himself upon his head.

HARRY KERNELL
The North of Ireland Comedian, Vocalist and Dancer. Mr. Kernell is the leading representative of this peculiar, pleasing and popular style of Celtic Comedy, and will present his most amusing Sketches, for which he has become so justly famed.

CROSSLEY AND ELDER
Field Athletes, in their Caledonian Sports, such as High Leaps, putting Heavy Weights, Exhibitions of Strength with the Teeth, lifting enormous objects at arm's length, and all the sports of and for which the Scotch are so fond and famous.

MISS MARIE WHITTINGHAM
AND
MASTER NEWMAN
POPULAR PRICES.
General Admission .... 50 Cents | Boxes, seating four $6.00
Reserved Seats .... $1.00 | Boxes, seating eight $10.00
Gallery .... 25 Cents | Seats in Boxes $1 50
Box Office open daily.   Seats can also be secured at 114 Broadway.
D. B. HODGES, Business Manager
Boston Job Print, Alden Street.

Example of the side-grain technique which was peculiar to American poster houses after 1870. Carved in soft basswood, a woodcut for each color, and printed on large flat-bed presses, these posters were usually simple in concept but gaudy in color. This particular example (7' 9" x 40", fragment of a billboard) was engraved and printed by Harold Thompson (c. 1930) of Minneapolis, Minnesota. He learned the art from his father, who operated a poster printing business in Minneapolis during the later part of the 19th century.

LARGE AUCTION SALE.

Thursday, July 14.

WILL be sold at the Auction Store, by order of the mortgagee of a bankrupt, a large lot of

TABLE CUTLERY,
GLASS LAMPS,
CROCKERY, CHINA,
BRITANNIA WARE, &c.

150 sets fine table and tea Knives and Folks, **14** sets of Carvers, butchers and bread Knives, **100** pair glass Lamps **120** Waiters, **50** pair Britannia Lamps, Britannia Tea and Coffee Pots, **3** doz. printed and painted Chambers, **20** doz. vegetable Dishes, **22** doz. Bakers, **30** doz. printed Plates, **68** Bowls and Pitchers, **20** doz. Coffee and Tea Sets, **100** printed Pitchers, **6** China Tea Sets.

Also, **15** patent Matrasses.

Sales commence at **9** o'clock, A. M. *Every article must be sold.*

B. & W. HUDSON, Auct'rs.

If the weather is stormy sale first fair day after.

T H E

MARTHA WASHINGTON
TEMPERANCE
FAIR,

AT UNION HALL:

Will be continued **THIS** afternoon and evening, and to-morrow, and will be terminated to-morrow evening.

This Evening the
GLEE CLUB,

Will sing several *Glees, Songs, &c.* Admittance 12½ cents.

October 6th, 1842.

---

of signs, it was an advertisement for Jacob's Oil painted on a rock at Niagara Falls which finally brought about prohibitive legislation.

Up until the 1880's most posters had been printed letterpress using engravings and wood or metal types. The largest posters which could be produced by lithography up to this date were 28 by 44 inches, but in 1880, the Courier Company of Buffalo lithographed some four foot posters for *Uncle Tom's Cabin* showing the bloodhounds pursuing Eliza across the ice. These large colorful lithographic posters advertising the circus, burlesque and drama were to become so popular that eventually the lithographic establishments replaced the older poster houses.

As the nineteenth century had progressed, the printing trades tended to specialize more and more in the specific needs of their clientele. The poster houses, one of the results of this specialization, are believed to have started operating about 1840. Concentrated in New York City in the early years, they had an enormous investment in jobbing and poster types. During the 1870's, one prominent New York establishment, Clarry and Reilly, in addition to a great store of types, carried a $150,000 inventory of stock cuts.

As printers entered into this phase of poster specialization, it was natural that their employees would do likewise. One firm of the day was to note, "Every man has become by intuition formed for his allotted task." Also, it was quite customary for skilled workers in poster houses to stay for years in one establishment as compared to men in other branches of the trade, who were generally more transient. In addition to the skilled compositors and pressmen, these poster house workers consisted of a number of engravers and artists, usually at the ratio of one artist to every three engravers.

Ringwalt in his *American Encyclopaedia of Printing* observed that the art of engraving poster cuts on large slabs of basswood or pine was for a long time peculiarly American. Also, several blocks were carved for multicolored posters, and the use of color in show bills was an American innovation. The first four color bill, credited to Thaddeus Anderson circa 1839, was a poster for Raymond and Weeks, managers of Herr Dreisbach Menagerie. Joe Morse was the engraver, and the bill was printed on an old Smith Hand Press in Boston.

In the poster houses, larger posters were done on a number of separate sheets, large letters and illustrations were printed in sections. When the printing was completed, the sheets were frequently assembled and pasted together before delivery, or they were assembled by the bill hanger at the time of posting. Any wood letters over 120 line were almost always hand carved by an engraver, after which the larger letters were saved to be used on other jobs. The engraver would carve sorts as needed until in time a major part of the font would accumulate. Many of these letters, which were 3 and 4 feet high, have become curiosities as out of date today as the ink ball! Vast quantities of stock items, such as ornamental borders, cuts, panels, and rules were kept on hand. These could always be drawn upon for fast jobs, or to supplement the original work of the engravers.

The handbill compositor of the day was an eminently practical man whose approach to a job is well exemplified by his remaining works. For an abundance of copy and short measure he required a proportionately condensed face; wide measure and limited copy called for an ex-

panded letter style. Since each of the major type families was cut in a wide range of weights and widths, the compositor might choose from as many as ten variations of a single design. Emphasis was given to key words by either weight, size, or ornamentation. Separation of thought was achieved by change of design of rules and ornamented dashes. Wood and metal type faces were mixed freely and often the block of type was topped with an engraved wood pictorial image or an ornate logotype.

Color was used sparsely, but ornamented dashes, heavy rules, engraved wood illustrations or stock ornaments were profusely employed. The result was often a coarse, textural block containing a great variety of type faces. Impact came from boldness and rich textures. Letterpress imposed an essentially vertical and horizontal stress, whereas the lithographic posters were drawn with elements of type and illustration intertwined in amorphous combinations.

Handbills had no designer as we know him today. The printer in consultation with the client was responsible for the appearance of the bill. Not only was there an amazing variety of types, but also a great store of ornaments, stars, borders, hands, and trade cuts. Thus, the bulk of handbill design in the nineteenth century was accomplished by selecting and organizing stock elements. In spite of the fact that practicality overruled aesthetics in composition, there were many handsome bills. Theodore De Vinne, in a left-handed compliment, could say in 1883 that a "greater improvement has taken place in the printing of handbills than of books."

Directness of typographic poster designs during the first half of the nineteenth century began to wane after 1870 and by 1880 the first symptoms of degeneration in both letter design and poster format were self-evident. Novelty replaced sensitivity in letter design, quantity was substi-

A large Kelly flat-bed press similar to those used for printing wood type in the nineteenth-century poster houses.

Large wood letters were commonly stored on their sides or ends in racks to prevent warpage.

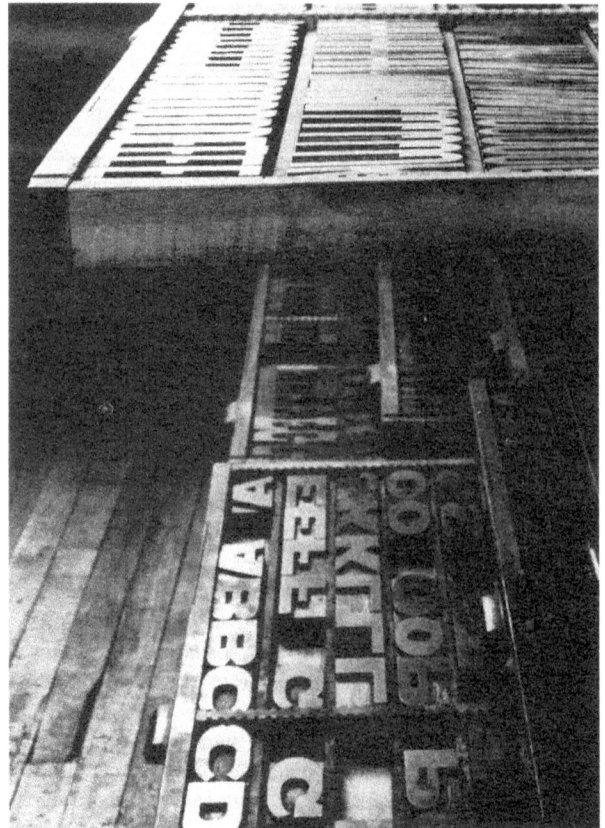

Smaller sizes of wood type are stored in wood type cabinets which were built expressly for this purpose, and cases were much larger than standard type cases.

tuted for quality in borders and ornaments, and the total effect was more decorative than communicative. Pictorial means were emphasized over typographic in this same period, and this undoubtedly is linked to the increased popularity of chromo-lithography and the comparative ease of illustration connected with this process.

Some contemporary advice of the period to would-be poster printers which can be considered somewhat humorously today pointed out, "They need much capital and they must be good judges of men, for theatrical and show managers who are their best customers, are not sound risks in the same sense as publishers or merchants." Each company had a great variety of printing executed before the beginning of the season, supplemented by some as it was going on, and the requisite amount was sent to the manager from time to time as he directed or according to an itinerary he proposed at the beginning. Besides this, wherever certain productions enjoyed such widespread popularity that a number of troupes performed the same play, the printer would print quantities of a bill leaving blank spaces for cast, time, place, etc. Then this information could be imprinted on separate order.

By 1890, there were only 30 of these old poster houses still operating in the United States. It is not entirely known what brought on their gradual demise, other than that conditions changed for their clientele—i.e., the great days of vaudeville and the traveling entertainment troupes were passing, and magazine-newspaper advertising had replaced much of the poster notices.

For all practical purposes, the old poster houses have now disappeared, replaced by offset and silk screen. In 1955, however, one such house in its third generation was still in existence in the upper midwest. Walking through the shop one could easily conjure an image of what these establishments must have been like in their hey-day. Huge flat-bed presses capable of printing 50-inch-wide sheets occupied the back central space; the walls were lined alternately with bulky wood type cabinets and compartmented racks for storing the larger sizes of wood type and cuts. The types were stored resting on either their sides or ends to reduce warpage. Imposition tables stood between the type and presses, and an 8-foot partition enclosed a rolltop desk at the front entrance. Stacks of unprinted stock and wrapped packages ready for delivery were piled near the back entrance where an ancient elevator still provided access and egress for freight. Locked up forms stood along the walls and next to cabinets resting at wild angles. Across one wall a narrow bench was color splattered with inks remaining from a thousand mixings. Helter-skelter on the walls hung the momentary objects of the pressman's pride, posters yellow and faded with age or pristine white, and there they hung until they fell and were swept out with the trash. The proprietor had entered the poster business just before 1900, and was still active in the business when the author first visited the plant in 1955. He still carved large letters by hand, and replaced missing or damaged letters. Each year a new Shrine Circus poster illustration was carved showing big, bold lions, elephants and ringmasters, and invariably, a small awe-struck youngster in *knickers*.

A related group of poster printers specialized in needs of the railroad companies, since much of this printing required unique machinery such as that used in printing tickets, coupons, time-tables, etc. Also there was frequently a time limit for supplying printed materials that only a specialized shop could hope to meet. Later the

Ornamental wood engravings found in the loft of an old bag company.

railroad printer extended his facilities to include the printing of advertising bills and cards, and therefore kept a great variety of wood and jobbing types on hand. Railroad posters were among the most representative ephemera from the period. Broadside advertisements announcing special excursions, and propaganda encouraging citizens and immigrants alike to move west and homestead were typical Americana.

Bag companies required huge inventories of wood type in their business well into the first 20 or 30 years of the twentieth century. Because printing coarse bag fabrics directly from wood type reduced the life of the type substantially, late in the nineteenth century most companies would lock up the form of wood type and make a mat from which they cast a rubber plate to print from. The resilience of the rubber afforded a better imprint than would have been possible with either wood or metal. Many of the colorful flour and feed bags of several generations ago were printed in some part with wood type supplemented by the work of the wood engraver.

Besides the poster and bag houses, there were a host of job printers ranging from the cubby-hole big city jobber to the country shops. From orations, bills, cards, pamphlets, certificates, tickets, to newspapers, they would print any job within their means, and work that has become some of our richest heritage from the period was accomplished in these small shops. The frontier printer, because of the distance from suppliers, was usually a man of great ingenuity and many skills, whose output was extremely diversified. His equipment was kept in working order through the local blacksmith's and his own efforts. Often he was reporter, editor, compositor, and printer. When occasion demanded, he could carve sorts or larger letters on the side of a plank, and while his posters lacked the finesse of the city printer, he still managed to get out a bold and effective broadside for auctions, land sales, stage bills, or a country dance.

A fringe benefit to finding old wood type today is discovering examples of crude but effective illustrations by the country printer on the reverse side of his wood type. If short a letter, he chose another block of the same set and carved the needed letter on the reverse side. Almost always this could be done without impairing the printability of the type. Even today, it is difficult to persuade most country printers to part company with their wood type, as it is useful for many kinds of notices which are no longer common in metropolitan areas, or which would have to be printed by other means in more specialized or progressive city shops.

A font of type found in Iowa had these crude illustrations carved on the back of the wood letters. They were probably used in a country newspaper to enhance a local story or advertisement.

Typefounding

Typefounding as a commercial enterprise in America dates back to 1798 when Binny and Ronaldson started their foundry in Philadelphia. If the first tools and equipment were not made in Europe, they were at least designed by Europeans, and American founders were dependent on imported European strikes for the means of casting types. The type styles of England, France, and Germany, the chief sources for these imports, were to dominate American printing for several decades. However, reliance on strikes from abroad at a time when demand was increasing daily for new and more types could only lead to the production of punches by native engravers, since the long intervals between order and receipt were impractical for an expanding industry.

One of the first American punch cutters was Edwin Starr, who in an announcement of the Boston Type and Stereotype Foundry for 1826 boasted that in the past 15 years, at least one half of all types cast in the United States were from punches cut by his own hand. His brothers Richard and Henry Starr were also punch cutters of some reputation. William F. Hill, who died circa 1820, was a skillful punch cutter, best known in his day for the cutting of ornamental effects. At somewhat later dates, George Bruce and his nephew, David Bruce, Jr., and George Lothian were to become recognized letter designers and engravers, whose works were dispersed among all the foundries. As the industry was small during these years, it constituted a close fraternity, within which personnel, strikes, etc., were exchanged. James Connor, Lyman, Starr, Pelouze, Phelps, Dalton, and Bruce, for example, all worked in the Boston Type and Stereotype Foundry at one time or another, before eventually operating foundries of their own.

At first the typefounding industry in America was dependent on immigrants who brought the requisite skills from the more advanced trades in Europe. Many skilled workmen came from Scotland and Germany, and often channels were kept open between the American establishments and those in these countries so that advances in craft as well as new styles could travel rapidly. The introduction of Scotch faces in America came through James Connor in this manner. In 1858, George Bruce was to declare through the pages of the *Printer* "that in all things they (typefoundries) were American." When Americanization of the trade did finally take place, large numbers of young boys and women were hired, the latter most often used in the dressing of type after casting and preparatory to wrapping. In 1812 there were but three typefoundries in this country, but the numbers increased to sixteen in 1839, twenty-one in 1858 and thirty-two in 1860, a number which was to stay fairly constant for another 10 years. In these later years, it was estimated that there were 20 punch cutters, as many as then employed in Europe. (*Typographic Messenger*, Vol. VII, No. 4, October 1872).

The assortment of display shown by American typefounders in the first quarter of the century was minimal, because of their limited means for keeping up with the rash of novelty faces which were rapidly increasing in favor abroad. The greatest single problem seems to have been the lack of workmen with requisite skills, or the traditions of many years in the trade which served the foreign foundries so well. When one stops to think of the primitive equipment in use at that time, one realizes that skills were the main compensating factors. The hand mold was the prime tool, and as it pertains to the casting of ornamented types, De Vinne was to comment at a later date, "—ornamental letters were slow to engrave, and the fine lines were liable to breakage in making the strike, and not one type caster in a dozen could reproduce in the cast type all the fine detail." This situation was not to change drastically until the force pump was adapted to the mold in 1834.

An examination of the production of American typefounders during their early period seems to indicate that they were too busy keeping abreast of the Europeans to introduce any styles of their own. One exception might be the lowercase letters not shown by the Europeans but included in American specimens for many of the ornamental, or very large styles. The Americans did master in a comparatively short time the art of casting large letters, and their specimens include a substantial number of these in various styles. It is thought that the engraved brass matrices of the American founders for the larger sizes were not in use in Europe at the same time, and therefore peculiarly American.

In discussing the evolution of display types in the United States, almost a constant reference is made to Nicolette Gray. In her book, *Nineteenth Century Ornamented Type Faces and Title Pages,* she has accomplished the most thorough work yet done on Victorian types. The dates for specific designs that she gives are used as pivot points for discussing the introduction of these same faces onto the American scene. Also, types excluded from her listings might be a basis for isolating American typographic contributions, since her charts are quite complete, and as she does include a substantial number of the French and German styles.

In the following digest of American type styles, other than a brief reference to the initial specimen book of Binny and Ronaldson of 1812, the catalogue of the Albany foundry for 1826 has been chosen as a starting point because it was the first specimen book to carry a substantial number of display types. From this point on, there was to be a rapid increase in the production of ornamented and large letters by American founders.

Many American specimen books issued before 1850 devoted a great deal of space, often over half the book, to illustrations of cuts, borders, and sundry ornamental or illustrative materials. In 1831 Bruce had 21 pages of borders exclusive of the other ornamental works; the Baltimore specimens of 1832 gave over half the book to ornamental effects. After the middle of the century the showing of letter specimens increased, and a ratio of approximately one third ornamental to two thirds type specimens became the rule.

In the 1812 Binny and Ronaldson specimen book the ornamental types shown were one 2 line tooled Roman and three sizes and styles of ornamented Romans, similar to the light Dutch and French engraved faces. In 1815, Bruce showed only body types; in 1816 he illustrated 8 sizes and styles of flowers, and in 1818 there were 43 styles of flowers, and no ornamental designs. Bruce exhibited an 8 line Antique Outline, 10 line Antique, some large Grotesque lottery figures, Roman Tooled and Double Shade, and a 7 line Italian in 1824.

In view of its continued use and relevance to American typographic styles during the succeeding years, Italian is perhaps the most interesting of these designs. The Italian Grotesque had been first shown by Caslon in 1821, but Nicolette Gray writes that it had been used at an ear-

FOURTEEN LINE PICA.

Min

TEN LINE PICA ANTIQUE.

TON

Albany, 1826.

TWELVE LINE PICA GOTHIC CONDENSED.

MERIT
Min
manifes

Bruce, 1837.

lier date in France, and that its name, "Italian," could conceivably suggest an even earlier origin. Although a number of writing manuals include this same style, which is fairly consistently labeled "Italian Print," its exact relationship with the penman's profession is not known. A provocative reference to Italian is found in Frank Presbrey's "The History and Development of Advertising" on page 64 in a quote from (Joseph) Addison, English engraver, writer and bookseller of the eighteenth century. The quote (from 1710) relates: "Of late Years, the N.B. has been much in Fafhion: as alfo little Cuts and Figures, the Invention of which we muft afcribe to the Author of Spring Truffes. I muft not here omit the blind *Italian* Character, which being fcarce legible, always fixes and detains the Eye, and gives the curious Reader fomething like the Satisfaction of prying into a secret." *If* Addison is indeed referring to the same Italian first shown as a type by Caslon in 1821, this would mean that this design had been cast and used in England over a hundred years before Caslon's specimen. Of added interest is Addison's description of the letters which indicates both recognition and a perceptive insight into semi-ornamental letters which surpasses anything published during Victorian times when the semi-ornamented letters found their greatest application.

When Italian Grotesque was first marketed by Caslon it was the subject of tirades by typographical authorities, and deservedly so, as it was an awkward and inconsistent design. However, other than the decorated and tooled Romans, it was one of the first display designs used in America and continued to be found in American specimens regularly up to the end of the nineteenth century, which was much later than it was used in Europe. Borrowed literally from the English, this Italian in 1837 was produced by the Boston Type and Stereotype Foundry in a 12 line style which was considerably modified in comparison to the earlier designs. During the mid-1850's, both Connor and Johnson showed additional variations. Connor issued a series of Italian including Italic, Backslope, and Extended. His designs had an elegance not found in the original designs. The types were small, ranging from 6 to 18 point. The thins had been reduced to hairlines, retaining only the horizontal emphasis of the serifs, and eliminating many of the inconsistencies of the earlier designs. All of these new faces were complete with lowercase.

Another aspect of the Italian which has been generally overlooked is that the original design incorporated many characteristics of the French Antiques and Egyptians, which did not arrive on the scene until the 1860's. The fact that there may have been a direct relationship between the Italian and these later faces is supported to a degree by a design patented by Bruce in 1872 called Italian Antique, which is a style of French Antique that is clearly derived from the Italians. The weight of serifs to stems, a horizontal block-like counter to curvilinear letters, and the handling of certain features such as the tail of the capital R, link the Italians closely to many of the designs published in the 1860's and 1870's in America as well as in Europe.

In 1826 Richard Starr of Albany issued the largest selection of display types yet seen in the United States. The Romans were shown in Open, Double and Meridian Shade in sizes not exceeding 16 points. Outlined Antique and Italic were displayed in conjunction with a Tooled Antique and Italic, none of which were more than 5 line.

ENGLISH TWO LINE LETTERS, ORNAMENTED.

LONG PRIMER TWO LINE LETTERS, ORNAMENTED.

BREVIER TWO LINE LETTERS, ORNAMENTED.

NONPAREIL TWO LINE LETTERS, ORNAMENTED.

Decorated types from Binny & Ronaldson, 1812.

Grotesque Italian, Caslon, 1832 (first shown by Caslon in 1821).

Italian, Albany, 1826.

Antique Open, Albany, 1826.

Antique Open, Albany, 1826.

Black Open, Albany, 1826.

Antique Italic No. 1, Albany, 1826.

ALBA

No. 2.

TROY

No. 3.

ONEID

Tuscan Open, Bruce, 1831.

THE NEW

Ornamented, Bruce, 1831.

SOD

wat

Lottery figures, Bruce, 1831.

$35

Open, Bruce, 1831.

CHRON

They included lowercase for both Outlined and Tooled, but not the Italics. The large plain letters went in size to 10 line Antiques and a 14 line Roman which was the largest specimen in the book. A few ornamental borders based on grapes, medallions and floral motifs appear to have originated as wood cuts. They came in large sizes of 4 to 6 lines.

The only styles from this specimen that have a questionable origin are the Antiques. The style shown by Starr is lighter in weight than those shown in succeeding years and similar in weight to the first models printed by Figgins in 1815, although it had a different treatment from Figgin's models for the middle bar on the capital E and in the tail of the R. The Antique Outlined with lowercase does not fit into Nicolette Gray's charts as she indicates that Bower and Bacon first published the design in 1830 with no lowercase. Also, she shows no record for the Antique Outlined Italic nor a lowercase for the Antique Tooled (indicated only as Open by Gray).

Starr included a 6 line Ornamented Roman, which was the first of its kind to be shown in an American specimen book. This style and its italic were frequently among the specimens of all American founders up to mid-century. This design, which had originated in France, was reinforced with a variety of new French designs that had the fat face Roman as the basic letterform. Baker and Greeley, Boston printers, had shown the same design in the previous year. The Boston Type and Stereotype Foundry gave a lowercase to the italic version of this Ornamented Roman, but curiously enough a lowercase was not designed for the Roman style. In 1831 Bruce exhibited a very similar design, in all probability a modification of the original, which did include a lowercase for the Roman. The two designs differ only in the interior shading. A series of (English) Black, both solid and tooled in sizes from 10 to 24 point along with the previously mentioned Italian rounded out the display specimens of Starr.

The Boston Type and Stereotype Foundry specimens for 1828 duplicated many of Starr's designs, but had a greater variety of sizes, some going up to 20 line. A 16 line set of lottery numerals were included, which were shown by Bruce again in 1831. A Clarendon Fluted (Outlined) appeared in an 8 line without lowercase. The Capital T and R had a Clarendon treatment of tail and serifs, the middle bar of the E had rounded brackets, and the serifs of the N and M were clearly bracketed even if serifs on other letters retained the right angles of the Antiques. Nicolette Gray has identified this design as a Clarendon, attributed to Figgins in 1821. The design was without lowercase.

It is believed that the Americans and Germans accomplished more in the modifying of the large display Clarendon than either the French or the English. While the English may lay claim to the smaller styles of Ionic and the Full Faced Clarendon, apparently they did not do much in the way of ornamenting this design or in adding to the condensed, heavy styles which evolved in America in the second half of the century, or to the heavy, slightly condensed styles shown in Germany in the early 1840's. Oak Leaf, an ornamented design which would fall into the same category as the Roman Ornamented shown by Starr in 1826, was shown in an 8 line without lowercase. It had also been exhibited by Baker and Greeley in 1825. Borders shown in this specimen were identical to those of the Starr catalogue.

Another design included in the Starr specimen book, which had only limited exposure at later dates, was an English Roman Backslope. It had been popular in England and often in the larger display sizes. Called Contra Italic by Nicolette Gray, it is credited to Figgins in 1815 for capitals and in 1821 for lowercase. The English Roman Backslope was in capitals only, as was a 2 line Pearl shown by White in 1829. It is believed that both of these backslopes had been originally cut for the Philadelphia foundry of Johnson and Smith (originally cut in three sizes: Great Primer in addition to these two) and that no other punches were made for this design in America.

Another curiosity is a solid version of the Fluted Antique which also exists in an 8 line size. At a slightly later date, wood type manufacturers would often cut a solid and ornamented or outlined style from the same pattern. It is not known if there is significance between these two specimens of solid and outlined Antique, but the solid style shows up only once again even though it closely resembles the full faced Clarendons brought out in the late 1860's. The same design was included in 1834 specimens of Johnson and Smith.

E. White of New York City in 1829 showed in addition to the usual shade, double and Meridian Shade Romans, a Brevier Antique Open Shade. Nicolette Gray assigns this design to Thorowgood in 1824 (as well as an italic style in 1824 of the same). The larger sizes of Roman Open Shade in America had originated with Figgins in 1815. A slightly condensed style of Roman Open Shade had been illustrated in 1808 by Caslon. White also shows a series of three sizes of Roman Tooled with two corresponding italics of the same design (Binny and Ronaldson had shown a 12 point Roman Tooled in 1812), and these designs may be traced back to Fournier and Rosart in the eighteenth century.

George Bruce of New York City in 1831 exhibited the previously mentioned Antique Open Shade in three sizes as well as one size of the italic. A 10 line Roman Open Shade similar to the one first shown by Caslon in 1808 is illustrated with lowercase and numbers. Three sizes of a Tooled Roman are included which differ from the previously described Tooled Romans of White in that their style is full fat face, without lowercase. A new Tuscan Shaded shown in a 2 line small pica was to remain popular for many years. Although cut in large sizes in wood by Nesbitt, it was most often found in small sizes. This type was cast in 1825 by Thorowgood, who, according to Bullen, most likely got the design from France. A number of grotesque ornamental dashes appear to have come from either Holland or Germany. Related to these dashes in style are a set of 16 line lottery numerals formed of the human figure, which, with an entire alphabet of the same style, were regularly found in American specimens until the late 1840's. Nicolette Gray claims the use of human caricature in letterforms was peculiar to German and Dutch founders, and the practice was never adopted by English founders. Twenty-one pages of borders as well as some new designs appeared also to have come from Holland or Germany as they were quite heavy in color and coarse in line.

The 1834 specimen book of Johnson and Smith of Philadelphia, one of the most important of its time, is reputed to have contained almost every design produced by all founders in the United States at that time. These specimens included the first showing of the large, 10 line

Oak Leaf, Baltimore T.F., 1832.

Fluted, Baltimore T.F., 1832.

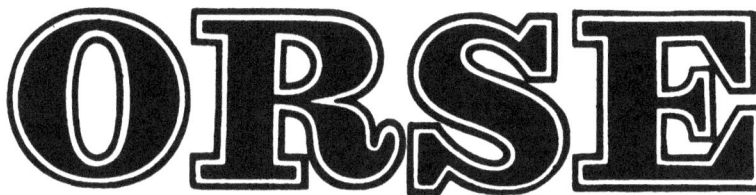

Antique, Baltimore T.F., 1832.

Ornamented, Baltimore T.F., 1832.

Ornamented, Baltimore T.F., 1832.

Lottery figures, New England T.F., 1834.

BAN

LOUI

Ornamented, Johnson & Smith, 1834.

Me

Ornamented No. 1, Johnson & Smith, 1834.

BEA

pati

Double Shade, Johnson & Smith, 1834.

ABCDEFG

Ornamented, Johnson & Smith, 1834.

TEL

Italic Antique Shaded, Johnson & Smith,

LIN

Antique Open Shade and Italic in capitals only. Small French styles shown by Binny and Ronaldson in 1812 were repeated with one additional similar style. Perhaps one of the most significant inclusions in this book were the heavy Gothics, composed of Gothic, Gothic Condensed, a Gothic Open Shade, and a Gothic Open Shade with a Line Shade on the Shade. The largest Gothic is 12 line and the smallest the 4 line Open Shade. These designs are curious for several reasons, among which are the crudeness of manufacture—apparent in the spacing, the unevenness in weight, and the poor quality of draughtsmanship. It is difficult to rationalize these qualities of the founders' performance with the large sizes of Roman and Antique.

There was a lowercase for the Gothic Condensed and the design of counters in such letters as "c" and "e" was very unusual. Nicolette Gray credits Figgins with designing the first heavy Gothics in 1832 but with no lowercase. Thorowgood brought out a more condensed style in 1834 which was most similar to the condensed design shown in the 1834 Johnson and Smith catalogue. There are, however, distinct differences in the drawing of the British and American styles. An 8 line Roman Condensed new to American specimens came complete with lowercase. Nicolette Gray credits both Thorowgood and Figgins with this style for 1832 and Figgins with its lowercase in 1833. There was also a curious 14 line Roman with lowercase which was considerably lighter in the stems than the previous fat faced Romans. The serifs were rounded at the ends rather than squared, and the handling of the middle bar of the capital E was also different from fat face styles. A 7 line Roman Shade with interior horizontal shading was presented for the first time, without a lowercase. A number of European Tuscans, most with some form of interior decoration or shading, were shown in sizes approximating 4 to 6 line. One page of this Johnson & Smith catalogue showed these Tuscans which were advertised as patterns for heads to be engraved on order (these types were sold as cast types by American founders at a later date).

The White, Hagar and Company 1835 specimen book included a heavy Gothic that was an improvement over those of Johnson and Smith. The capital S particularly was drawn with more even weight and there was improved spacing between letters. The largest sizes of Antique, Roman, and Gothic yet seen were in this catalogue along with many wood type designs going up to 24 line. A style called Tuscan, the same as Italian Tuscan No. 16 cast by Thorowgood in 1825, was a first showing in American specimens. The first outline faces to be presented by the founders were an English Outline (an Antique but looked a great deal like a Clarendon in weight and serifs) and a Black Outline.

Robb and Ecklin of Philadelphia showed in their 1836 catalogue an outline Gothic in a 10 point size—all of these outline styles were introduced in small sizes. The Gothic and Antique outlined originated with Blake and Stephenson in 1833 and 1834. An interesting face from these specimens is the Gothic Condensed in three sizes—12, 16, and 20 point—without lowercase or numerals. This face is amazingly modern and could be compared to a modern Alternate Gothic in weight and color. Nicolette Gray credits Wilson in 1843 with a similar style. Although it is probable that the American design was imported, its exact origins are not known to the author. The

Robb and Ecklin book included many specimens previously shown by Johnson and Smith in 1834 and by White, Hagar and Company in 1835. Very often the pages are identical to those shown earlier by other founders.

In 1836 Connor and Cooke of New York City exhibited few new designs. There was a 7 line Ornamented Roman with a variation of the interior embellishment, which would fall into the broad category of Ornamented Romans imported from France. Another ornamental style, a line shaded Tuscan studded with star disks is shown in a double paragon size which appears to have originated in Germany. In fact, the title page announced a large import of German borders and decorative pieces which would tend to support the supposition regarding the origins for the display type.

The 1837 specimens of George Bruce introduce Skeleton, a small outline Roman which was a companion to the earlier outline Gothics, and Antiques. Skeleton was shown in 10, 8 and 6 point size without lowercase or figures. Nicolette Gray gives Stephenson and Blake credit for this design and dates it circa 1838. Bruce introduced a number of new ornamentals in this edition, among which were German Perspective, and French and English ornamental types in the smaller sizes. The first ornamented Antiques by American founders were included in these new showings: an Antique Open Shade with interior shading on a horizontal, and one with a floral motif suggestive of German designs. In the heavy Gothics, Bruce exhibited a specimen that finally replaced the eccentric lowercase "e" of the Johnson and Smith showing, and the design seems much more refined than earlier specimens. There was a new Ornamented Roman and a 12 line Gothic Outlined, the latter credited by Nicolette Gray to Thorowgood in 1832. Also, there was a good display of the lighter styles of ornamental borders. (The copy of this specimen book in the Columbia Library collection contains some pages that have been tipped in, among which are one from an 1848 George Bruce and Company catalogue, and one price page from what appears to be the same 1848 specimen.) The 1837 catalogue of the Boston Type and Stereotype Foundry added only a few new styles of ornamental letter—four based on the Roman and one 12 line Tuscan. No lowercase or figures were shown for these designs. The John White specimens for 1839 introduced a 12, 10, 8, and 6 point full faced Gothic in a light style. This showing, which had no lowercase or figures, included an R and Q, the latter with a curiously drawn tail. Extended Shade (Antique) in 10 point style was illustrated complete with lowercase and figures. At a glance, the parent letterforms seems to be Roman, as the serifs have been greatly reduced. The design also had Clarendon characteristics in that all the serifs had a slight bracket. Roman Extra Condensed without lowercase or figures was a first showing as well. The Gothic Condensed first shown by Robb in 1836 appeared in a series of four sizes by White, but there was still no lowercase or figures.

In 1841 Johnson and Smith presented the first showing of Grecian by an American founder in two sizes of Canon and 2 line Great Primer. Nicolette Gray lists an Elongated (the equivalent of Grecian Extra Condensed) for Wood and Sharwood circa 1841 and for Thorowgood in same year, but the date 1839 was given in the American showing. She also lists a Condensed for Thorowgood in 1842. The Johnson and Smith specimens were somewhat more condensed than the British styles shown by Gray.

Gothic Condensed, Johnson & Smith, 1834.

FURN prices

Gothic, Johnson & Smith, 1834.

MAN

Gothic Shaded Open   *Gothic Shaded, Johnson & Smith, 1834.*

MORE

Four line Tuscan (same as Thorowgood's Italian Tuscan shown in 1825), White, Hagar & Co., 1835.

KL

English Outline (Stephenson & Blake show this design in 1833), White, Hagar & Co., 1835.

ABCDEFGHIJ

Black Outlined, White, Hagar & Co., 1835.

Few men, my friends

Ornamental No. 1, Connor & Cooke, 1836.

NE

Ornamented No. 2, Bruce, 1837.

Lottery figures (also in 1831 specimens), Bruce, 1837.

Twelve line pica Gothic Condensed Open (Nicolette Gray lists this design for Thorowgood in 1832), Bruce, 1837.

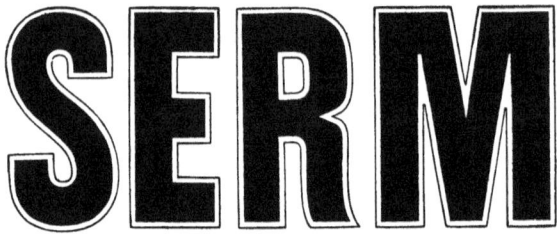

Gothic Condensed, Bruce, 1837.

Antique Ornamented, Bruce, 1837.

Ornamented, Bruce, 1837.

Ornamented, Bruce, 1837.

Skeleton, Bruce, 1837.

There were a number of new ornamentals, one of which originated with Caslon in 1830, a splayed Tuscan with pearls at the median. Most of the others demonstrated a French influence in ornamentation. Italian, Antique Expanded, and a Roman appeared as small reverses: 2 line English, and 2 line Nonpareil. A Roman No. 1 reminiscent of the intermediate Romans immediately preceding the fat face styles was shown in capitals only and without figures. A great number of wood types were included, both plain faced and ornamental.

In 1842, George Bruce illustrated the first American Roman Extended as metal type in three sizes of 10, 8, and 6 point. The date 1839 included in the sampling may refer to the Roman Extended's first showing. In England this same style was shown by Caslon in 1835. Nesbitt had exhibited it in 1838 as a wood type complete with lowercase and figures. The Bruce specimen did not include a lowercase, and the Caslon design was not listed as having a lowercase. Bruce showed a Roman Extra Condensed which was more condensed than that shown by John White in 1839. It was most like a style initiated by Thorowgood circa 1838. Three sizes of 10, 8, and 6 point Gothic, full faced and a light style, were displayed that were similar to those described for White in 1839, but the irregularities had been eliminated and the drawing of the letterforms was generally better than the White designs. Again, there was no lowercase or figures. In the larger ornamental faces there was a new style of Gothic Shade in perspective—with shade to the left, a Gothic Double Outlined Shade with a Ray Shading around the conventional shade, an Antique Shade, and a Line Shade with interior shading with horizontal emphasis. The designs seem to have been printed from wood letters.

Specimens of Robb for 1844 demonstrated an increasing fascination with the "phantom" look in type design. Figgins had published one of the first of these styles in 1843, which consisted only of parallel ruled lines. Since there was no linear definition of the letter contours, the effect was a light, ghost-like color. Gothic and Antique both were given the same treatment. Also, Ray Shades were found in sufficient numbers to become characteristic of the 1840's. Gothic Condensed of earlier specimens was given a line shade, and the series expanded to include a 22 point size. Many new European ornamented faces displayed for the first time in these specimens incorporated the Ray Shade, or a graded (graduated) interior shading, such as the Zebra of Figgins. Antique Condensed with lowercase was featured in a text arrangement in an 18 point size.

L. Johnson and Company of Philadelphia in its 1844 specimens included a 6 line Roman Light Faced Condensed without lowercase. It was during the 1840's that light face styles began to replace the heavy fat face Romans in the founder's specimen books. They were accompanied by the extremely condensed styles in all three primary families—Gothic, Antique, and Roman, and the overall color of these new styles was light as compared to the boxy, black designs prevailing during the 1820's and 1830's. Some of the first Germans were illustrated in these 1844 specimens, after which they were to be found regularly in all metal and wood specimens until near the end of the century.

John White in 1845 exhibited some recently imported styles of Tuscan, most of which were in outline. Also, a 2 line Small Pica Outline Gothic with two weights of line created an illusion of slight dimension. There were figures, but no lowercase for this design, and it was reasonably well drawn except for the capital G and figures 6 and 9 which were inferior to the others. A substantial number of wood types were included in these specimens. Johnson in 1847 presented the largest number of new styles yet to be introduced at one time. A majority of these were based on the European Tuscans and many were "phantom" designs. Doric Ornamented from France made its first appearance. This design in both metal and wood was to be used extensively from this date through the next 10 years. The first Rustic, with tree limbs or bark as a decorative motif, was shown in a 24 point size, and in the 1880's Page was to cut a like style in wood. This example was somewhat unusual in that the motif had been adapted to a letterform which retained a structure based on type. Most Rustics, formed by arranging boughs into the shape of a letter, were quite irregular. There was a curious Gothic Condensed with Line Shade. Curves were treated as straight lines and counters were mostly angular. In general, it was a clumsy design.

There were seven sizes of Clarendon, the smallest size being Two Line English and the largest 12 pica. It is interesting to note the number of discrepancies in design between the different sizes. The capital E will have a serif on the middle arm on some sizes and not on others; some terminals such as the lowercase a and e will have a slightly bulbous ending and others will be squared off; the dot on the lowercase i will be square in some instances, round in others. It is thought that the larger sizes were printed from wood letters.

Gothic Condensed Round and Tooled was first shown in an American specimen book in a 2 line Great Primer. Nicolette Gray assigns this design, as well as ornamented version of it, to Caslon in 1844.

Up until 1845, almost all specimens were common property among the major American typefounders, and finding a design in one catalogue would almost assure that it could be found in half a dozen other books. Also, as the introduction of new designs was gradual, it is comparatively simple to approximate the dates of their introduction into the American repertory of display designs.

However, by mid-century, when the American typefounder had the machinery, trained workmen, and markets to expand his operations into new levels of production, new designs are increasingly difficult to trace. The quantities of display letters being produced fairly well eliminated the practice of every founder producing the same designs, since it was easier for a founder to take the order and fill it at an agreed price from another founder owning the matrices. One type house advertised that it could fill orders for other founders' designs almost as quickly as for its own. The 1840's and early 1850's saw tremendous numbers of European designs being produced in this country.

One of the first important American typefounding inventions was introduced by David Bruce, Jr. of New York City in 1834. It was a device known then as a squirt machine, a hand force pump attachment for forcing the lead into the mold under pressure. The machine was devised to better cast the ornamental designs, which, according to Theodore De Vinne, owed their popularity to this contrivance. Another invention of Bruce incorporating the force pump was the first successful automatic type caster, initially patented in 1836 but further improved in 1838

Italian, Boston T. & S. F., 1837.

Ornamented, Boston T. & S. F., 1837.

Ornamented, Boston T. & S. F., 1837.

Ornamented, Boston T. & S. F., 1837.

Ornamented No. 2, Boston T. & S. F., 1837.

HA A

Ornamented No. 3, Boston T. & S. F., 1837.

DI N

Ornamented No. 4, Boston T. & S. F., 1837.

NET

Test.

Gothic, Boston T. & S. F., 1837.

UNITED STATES

Ornamented, New England T.F., 1838.

TURE

Extended Shade, White, Hagar & Co., 1839.

ABCDEFGHIJKL

in truth it would be

Gothic White, Hagar & Co. in 1839.

ABCDEFGHIJKLMNOPQRS

Gothic, White, Hagar & Co., 1839.

ABCDEFGHIJKLMPQR

Gothic Shade, White, Hagar & Co., 1839.

ABCDEFGHIJKLMN

Ornamented No. 2, Johnson & Smith, 1841.

W

No. 1, Johnson & Smith, 1841.

ABCDEFG

Ornamented, Johnson & Smith, 1841.

WILL 78

French Shaded, Johnson & Smith, 1841.

DELAWARE,

Ornamented No. 3, Johnson & Smith, 1841.

LONDON,

Grecian, Johnson & Smith, 1841.

ASSEMBLY

Gothic Outline, Johnson & Smith, 1841.

VIRGINIA, NORTH CAROLINA,

Perspective, Johnson & Smith, 1841.

ABCDEFGHIJKLMNOPQRST

Gothic Condensed, Bruce, 1842.

Boston &

Gothic Perspective, Bruce, 1842.

CHARLE

Extended, Bruce, 1842.

YORK 1839

200

Extra Condensed, Bruce, 1842.

ABCDEFGHIJ

Gothic, Bruce, 1842.

A B C D E F G H I J K L Q R S

Antique Condensed, Robb, 1844.

ABCDEFGHIJK

We hold these truths to
that all Men are created
are endowed by their

Backslope Shaded, Robb, 1844.

THE NORTH

Ornamented, Robb, 1844.

STANDARD

Tuscan Shade, Robb, 1844.

A B C D E F G H I J K L

Line Ground, Robb, 1844.

PHILADELPHIA

Gothic Condensed Shaded, Robb, 1844.

ABCDEFGHIJKLMNOPQ

Ornamented No. 2, Robb, 1844.

C B Y O

Ornamented No. 3, Robb, 1844.

BARD

Ornamented No. 2, Robb, 1844.

MANT

Phantom, Robb, 1844.

STUVWXYZ&,;.

Tuscan Ornamented, Robb, 1844.

ABCDEFGHIJ

Gothic Shaded, Robb, 1844.

ABCDEFGHIJKLMNOP

Ornamented No. 5, Boston T. & S. F., 1845.

BAN

Ornamented No. 2, Boston T. & S. F., 1845.

RANCE.

Light Face, Boston T. & S. F., 1845.

THEM

Shade, White, 1845.

BALTIMORE

Open Shade, White, 1845.

TELEGRAPH. $12

English Tuscan shown by White in 1843

NEW-YORK AND

Gothic Shade, White, 1845.

ABCDEFGHIJKLM

Ornamented, L. Johnson, 1844.

YOUNG LAD

Ornamented, L. Johnson, 1844.

MASSACHUSETTS,

Light Faced Condensed, L. Johnson, 1844.

FORE

Grecian Shade, White, 1849.

HARDWARE

Grecian Shade, White, 1849.

PASSENGER

Ornamented No. 1, White, 1849.

ILLUSTRATED

Ornamented, White, 1849.

INDEP

Gothic Shade, White, 1849.

GEORGE

Condensed Open Gothic, White, 1849.

JOURNAL.

Ornamented No. 1, White, 1849.

SUPERIOR

Ornamented No. 2, White, 1849.

MAGAZINE OF LITERA

ABCDEFGH

EXAMPLE 24.

ABCDEFGKLMM

EXAMPLE 25.

ABCDEFGHIK

EXAMPLE 26.

ABCDEGHJIK

EXAMPLE 27.

ABCDEFGHIJKLM

EXAMPLE 28.

ABCDEFGHI

EXAMPLE 29.

Ornamental types used in British and American typography from 1850 to 1860 and after. These types are mainly French in origin.

ABCD abcdefghijklmof

ABCD abcdefghijkln

ABCD abcdefghijklmrs

Some of the most popular European ornamental designs from 1870.

ABCD abcdefghp   ABCD efghiklmno

Clarendon.   French Clarendon.

ABCD efghjklmn   **ABCabcdefgk**

Antique.

Four European typographic inventions.

AABCDENNORW   ABCDEG

ABC DE GG KK

Variations of a French invention of the 1860's which was revived and extended in America during the period between 1880 and 1885.

ABCabcdefg
Example 1.—Philadelphian.

ABCabcfeing
Example 2.

ABCDEFGHIJP
Example 3.

ABCDE
Example 4.

ABCDabcefghn
Example 5.

ABCDEK
Example 6.

ABCDE
Example 7.

ABCabcdg
Example 8.

ABCDEGHJKLNQR
Example 9.—Made by Bruce.

1870 to 1875. All except number 9 originated with MacKellar, Smiths & Jordan.

1875 to 1880. All except number 17 originated with MacKellar, Smiths & Jordan.

ABCabcdefghr
Example 10.

ABCEHGKM
Example 11.

ABCDabeimg
Example 12.

ABCDEGHIJKR
Example 13.

ABCDEGHKQN
Example 14.

ABCDEFGHJLKN
Example 15.

ABCDEIKN
Example 16.

ABCDEFGN
Example 17.—Bruce.

ABCDEGM
Example 18.

ABCDEGH:JKLMRSP
Example 19.

ABCDEGHJNQS
Example 20.

ABC·DEHINP
Example 21.

ABCDabcdeg
Example 22.

ABCDEGHMRS
Example 23.

ABCabcdefghijklnopt
Example 24.

ABCDABCEJK
Example 25.

ABCDabcefghijklnps
Example 26.

ABCefgD
Example 27.

1875 to 1885. All originated with MacKellar, Smiths & Jordan.

Ornamental dashes, Bruce, 1831.

ABCDAbcDEFGHIJKLS

Example 28.—Dickinson. J. W. Phinney's first design, and the first American letter of its class.

ABCABcabcdefghjklnp

Example 29.—Dickinson.

ABCDabcdefghijklmnos

Example 30.—Dickinson.

ABCDEFGHMPRS

Example 31.—Dickinson.

ÆBCDEGHJKLMNORS

Example 32.

ABCDabcdefgo

Example 33.—The first success of the Central Type Foundry.

ABCDEFabcdefghijklmnopqw

Example 34.—Central.

ABCabcDdefghijklmnopqrsw

Example 35.—Central.

ABCDEGH✳MQRSW

Example 36.—MacKellar.

ABCabcd✳Metafghjks

Example 37.—MacKellar.

1880 to 1885. Not all are of this period, but all are representative.

ABCDabcdefghjkms

Example 38.—MacKellar.

ABCDABCD✳GHIJKNR

Example 39.—Dickinson.

ABCabdefghjo

Example 40.—Dickinson.

ABCabcdefghkjn

Example 41.—MacKellar.

ABCabcdefghpq

Example 42.—Central.

ABCDabcdefghjklmu

Example 43.—Central.

ABCDEFGM

Example 44.—Central.

ABCDabcdefghijklmopqrt

Example 45.—Boston.

ABCacdegikno

Example 46.—Central.

ABCDEGHR

Example 47.—MacKellar.

1885 to 1890. During this period, the Central, Dickinson, and Cleveland Type Foundries were the leaders.

CBCDabcesuhijkr

Example 48.—Central.

ABCabcfghilnp

Example 49.—Boston.

ABDacfeghinops

Example 50.—Central.

ABBCDE AND GHN

Example 51.—Dickinson.

ABCDEFGR✳O

Example 52.—Dickinson.

ABCaabcdefg

Example 53.—Dickinson.

ABbCDacdefghiklmno

Example 54.—Dickinson.

ABCacdefghijk The

Example 55.—Boston.

ABaCcihSkg

Example 56.—MacKellar.

(These charts are from "Discursions of a Retired Printer," *by Henry Lewis Bullen, in* Inland Printer, *March and May, 1907.)*

Ornamental border, New England T.F., 1834.

and 1843. First used commercially in 1844 at the Boston Type and Stereotype Foundry, in a few years the type caster was found in every important foundry in America and in many European foundries. (Legros and Grant are not prepared to give Bruce credit for a new invention. They maintain that his machine was basically the same as the English pivotal caster and that patents had been taken out for it previous to those of Bruce.)

Although there were constant experiments throughout the century to find improved equipment, it was the Bruce machine which gave the most service in America until the Barth type caster in 1888. On an ordinary type, it could cast at the rate of 175 characters per minute, and would average at least 100 per minute, as opposed to the 15 per minute of the hand mold. George Bruce was to point out in 1858 that the automatic caster made possible a higher grade of ornamental work than had been possible with the hand mold—for the same reasons as the squirt machine. Another factor which could not be lightly dismissed in its day was that there was an approximate 25 percent reduction in cost for the customer brought about through automatic casting of types.

Others had preceded David Bruce, Jr. in the search for a satisfactory means of automatically casting types. Perhaps the most notable was William Johnson, who built machinery for Elihu White. Advertising in the 1829 specimen book, Johnson wrote: "Having brought my Patent Type Casting machine to a high degree of perfection, I herewith present you with a specimen of the type cast therein, and beg leave to remark, that a number of founts cast in the machine, have been in use from one to two years, and have proved to be in no respect inferior to the best hand cast letter, and to possess some important advantages over hand cast type. By the aid of a forcing pump, applied to the metal at the moment of casting, much harder metal is used than can conveniently be cast in a hand mould, thereby increasing the durability of the machine type."

At the same time, Starr and Sturdevant of Boston and Lothian of New York were working on the idea for machine-cast type. The Boston Type and Stereotype Foundry carried the experiments of Starr and Sturdevant into building and operating several machines, but finally the project was abandoned. The Baltimore Type Foundry advertised in its 1832 specimen book, "The type cast by machinery being found superior to that cast by hand, the proprietors have introduced into their Foundry the machine invented and made by Edwin Starr, who has the superintendence of the Foundry..." It remained for David Bruce, however, to perfect his casters before machine-cast type became general, and for this invention, Bruce received a silver medal in 1844 from the Franklin Institute. Another pivotal invention, patented in the name of Thomas Starr in Philadelphia August 4, 1845, was a process by which matrices could be electrotyped from punches, engravings, or cast types (Edwin Starr's name has been attached to this invention by De Vinne as well as others; and also, at least one account credits James Connor with the discovery, but the name of Thomas Starr was on the patent). In the card file of his ATF Library, Bullen had made the notation, on the card listing the patent, "Appears to be the beginning of the use of electrotype matrices, an invention of great importance to the pirates of type faces, otherwise a grave calamity to the type making industry." When the invention was first

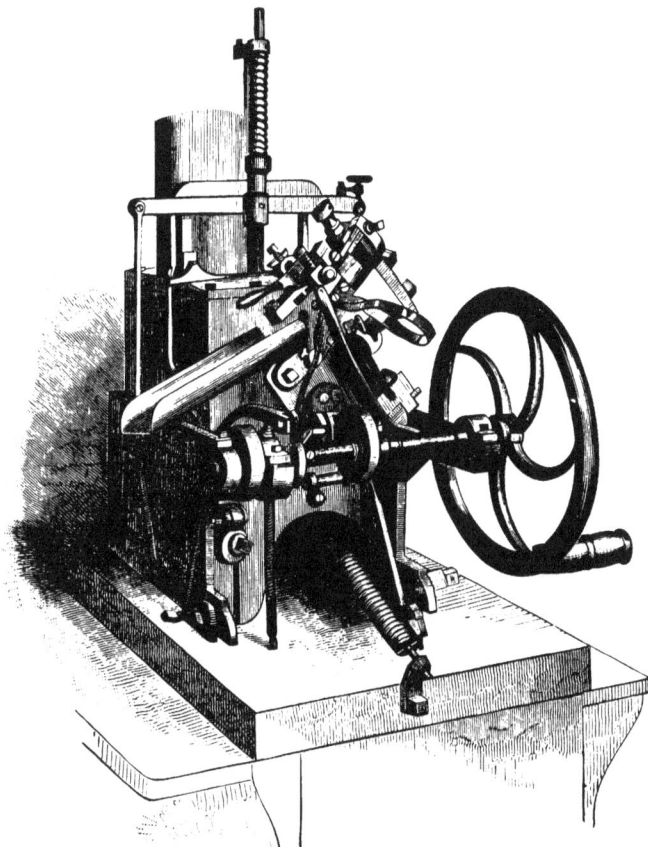

Bruce type-casting machine. Patents in 1838 and 1843, by David Bruce, Jr.

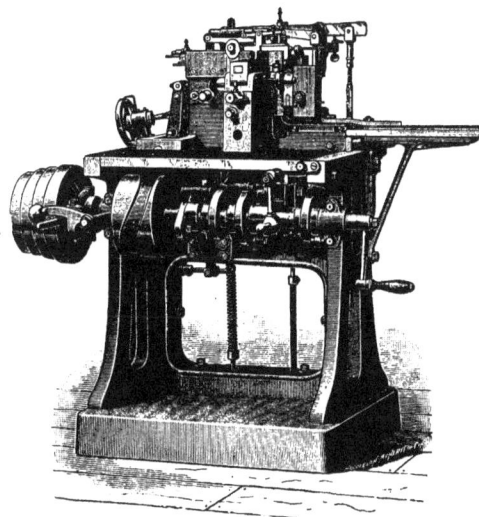

Barth Type Caster. Patented January 24th, 1888. This machine would produce more than half again what older machines could do. In addition, it broke off the jet, ploughed a groove between the feet, and rubbed down the feather edges at the angles.

Ornamental borders, Baltimore T.F., 1832.

Flowers and borders, White, Hagar & Co., 1835.

Minionette, L. Johnson, 1844.

made public, it was not well received, but within 5 or 6 years became popular. The type or engraved design, fitted from the back into square or rectangular openings in a metal plate, left the face of the letter slightly recessed when one looked at the face of the plate. After the design was secured, the plate and type underwent an electro process until enough copper had been deposited to fill the space over the face of type flush with the surface of the metal plate. The copper matrix was then removed, reinforced with brass, and fitted for conventional molds. The full importance of this invention may be realized when one considers that, before, making a set of punches would take a skilled cutter up to 1 year—especially with an ornamental type. The cost to the founder for even a simple Roman was not less than $1,200, and an ornamental design would cost in the neighborhood of $1,600 to produce. After the introduction of the electrotype matrix, it was customary to engrave new designs on type metal, particularly the ornamental faces, and also the large types; the engravings were electrotyped and matrices made and fitted. This process considerably expedited the making of new designs. The process was slow but very inexpensive.

The electrotype matrix, more than anything else, was responsible for the fantastic number of display and ornamented faces in the United States. Not only were the productions of the American foundries exploited, but also all the designs of European founders were added to the American inventories. The extensiveness of this activity is best demonstrated by the huge specimen books and the infinite variety of styles found in printing from that period. The full impact of electrotype matrices was felt as a dual effect: one was that new designs could be produced with ease, and the other was that parties having no special skills could enter the typefounding business as easily as they could purchase a font of type and electrotype their own matrices; e.g., small foundries could build an inventory as comprehensive as that of the major founders, and. cheaply! Whereas a legitimate founder might spend a year in preparing a new design, within weeks of the time it was marketed, both American and European competitors could be selling the same design. Attempts were made to patent original designs, but then, as now, they were mostly a losing proposition. It is interesting, however, that many of the extremely complicated ornate faces of the 1860's that were patented seem to have been better protected than the plain faces which came out in the late 1880's and 1890's. Rubens, brought out by Dickenson, was pirated in a year by at least four foundries who made small alterations in the design. In The *Printer* Bruce wrote an article in 1858 in which he alluded to legislation before Congress to outlaw the electrotyping process. It was also mentioned that the copyright law passed in the previous session "for some reason, as passed, is perfectly inapplicable to our wants."

Typefounders were probably hardest hit by the process during the early 1870's when they engaged in an all-out struggle with a new, but burgeoning advertising business. During the 1860's agents began the practice of buying advertising space, mostly in the small but numerous country newspapers, through bartering type for space. Sometimes the agencies actually operated captive typefoundries, but more frequently they operated side-street shops where by using the electrotype matrices, they could produce quantities of type, usually much inferior to that

Steam-powered type caster shown by MacKellar & Jordan at the Centennial Exposition in Philadelphia, 1876. Basic machine is the Bruce type caster.

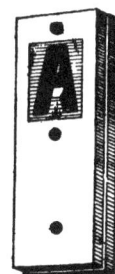

Electrotype matrix system patented by Thomas Starr. A square was sunk in a plate of copper. A hole was made in the sunken square; the head of the original type was fitted snugly to protrude through this hole. Enough copper was deposited to fill the sunken square flush with the surface of the plate.

The copper plate containing the square copper intaglio electrotype of the original letter has been riveted to a heavier copper plate.

The finished matrix, fitted up in line, set, position and height, ready for the casting machine.

This process was slow, but relatively inexpensive. (From an article by Dr. Ralph Eckman in Printing Impressions, *October, 1965.)*

TWO LINE PICA BORDER, No. 92.

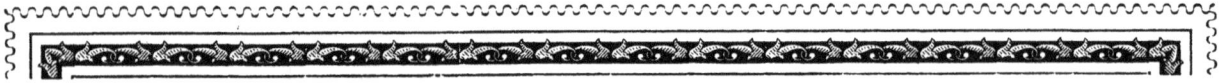

TWO LINE ENGLISH BORDER, No. 28.

THREE LINE SMALL PICA BORDER, No. 7.

THREE LINE SMALL PICA BORDER, No. 8.

THREE LINE SMALL PICA BORDER, No. 9.

THREE LINE SMALL PICA BORDER, No. 10.

FOUR LINE BOURGEOIS BORDER, No. 1.

FOUR LINE LONG PRIMER BORDER, No. 3.

FOUR LINE SMALL PICA BORDER, No. 13.

Borders shown by Hagar in his 1860 specimen book which reflect the lighter styles of ornamental border that were becoming increasingly fashionable. Undoubtedly a number of these designs were imported from France or England.

sold by typefounders, but sufficiently printable to serve their purposes for trading, or for selling to printers at reduced rates. The ill-feeling between typefounders and advertising agents was apparent to everyone by the 1870's, and no opportunity was lost for either side to blast their opponents. Through the pages of his *Typographic Messenger,* James Connor in 1873 was to write, "The collector (the duties of this "collector" were to collect bills owing the journal on which he was employed and procure new advertisements or the renewal of old ones) was generally a wanderer from some obscure village who had been taken on by his own assertion of being an experienced clerk or skillful compositor; but proving, on trial, woefully deficient and too illiterate or thick-headed to improve, was made porter, carrier, drudge or collector. Having a tongue of guile, a cheek of brass, inordinate conceit and remarkable imperviousness to contempt or insult, the collector frequently succeeded in procuring advertisements under circumstances where a gentlemen would have failed, and thus became a useful although despised adjunct of the paper. Mainly through lack of vigilance on the part of publishers, the collector of the past has welled into the 'agent' of today; and now, by reason of his ill-gotten means, he wields a power undreamed of by his former self." (*Typographic Messenger,* Vol. VIII, No. 2, April 1873, "Advertising Agents in Conclave.")

In the 1870's the festering situation based on conflicts of interest between agents, printers, typefounders, publishers, and editors burst into the open. The controversy had many sources, but the price cutting among agents was near the root of the problem. It is believed also that printers and publishers resented the commissions, ranging from 25 to 40 percent, taken by agents, because beforehand the former had received the full amount. Agents countered by pointing out that the vast increase in business brought into the shops more than offset the loss through commissions. In these same years, several state editorial conventions set aside time to discuss means for policing advertising practices within their states, and, in 1870, the Pennsylvania editors presented a bill to the State legislature to establish a "Bureau of Advertising." Needless to say, all parties joined the battle with great vigor, during which there were charges and counter-charges that echo even in present-day attitudes and expressions.

The main contest between agents and typefounders began when agencies thought that there should be a rebate from the founder on types used in advertisements created through the agents. Under the leadership of George P. Rowell, the agencies harrassed the founders unmercifully, and went so far as to bring before Congress a petition to drop the protective tariff on imported types. Since this tariff was 25 percent, and since European prices were much lower than those of the American typefounders, many native companies would have folded, or at least been in serious difficulties. Advertising charged the American founders with a monopoly from which they ruthlessly exploited the printers by extorting unreasonable prices for their products, etc.

The pressures continued until about 1885 when a number of firms broke the uniform scale of prices and began giving substantial discounts covertly. Finally one Chicago firm published a price list of reduced prices. From this first step, all foundries entered into such a cut-throat competition among themselves that prices were reduced as

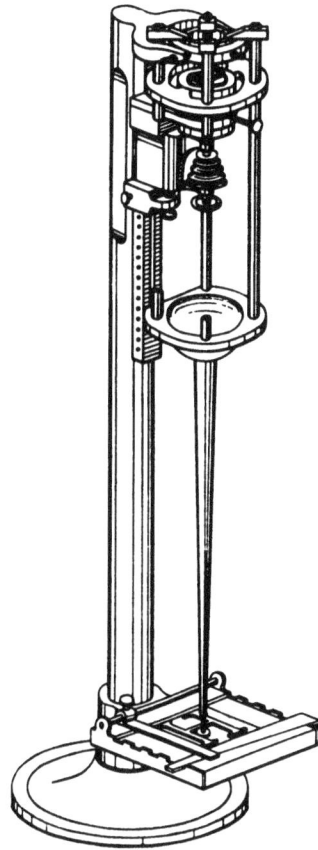

Benton Punch Cutting machine. (From patent drawings of Linn Boyd Benton, 1885.)

much as 40 and 50 percent. As this situation could not continue for long without bringing ruin to the entire industry, a large trust was founded consisting of two houses in Boston, one in New York, one in Philadelphia, two in Cincinnati, one in St. Louis, and one in Chicago, plus a dozen smaller foundries. In 1892, this trust operated under the name "American Type Founders Association," which paid extremely high prices, partly in cash and partly in stock for all companies brought into the trust. Even though the problems of typefounders were the result of complex conditions arising from changing social patterns, improved technology, and new economic conditions, the invention of the electrotype matrix had generally raised havoc in the industry. It made possible an undercutting competition by the advertising interests, allowed competing foundries to become established with small capital, and destroyed any trade advantage from original works—all of which tended to saturate the markets and lower prices. The blow that was to further deteriorate the founders' position was the invention of the punch-cutting machine patented by Linn Boyd Benton of Milwaukee, Wisconsin, in 1885. Legros and Grant say that this machine, originally used to engrave master type patterns in type metal to produce matrices by electro deposition, was patterned in principal after the wood type machinery that had been in use since 1834 to cut wood types. The Benton machine was improved and used for engraving steel matrices with great precision. The success in 1886 of the Linotype machine, which marked the beginning of the end for the great typefounding era in America, was largely due to the Benton punch cutter. It had been the competition between lithography and

GREAT PRIMER GOTHIC ORNAMENTED.

EVERY ARTICLE NECESSARY FOR A PRINTING OFFICE. 1853

GREAT PRIMER ORNAMENTED. No. 1.

$5478. A FAT KITCHEN MAKES A LEAN WILL. £2986

GREAT PRIMER ORNAMENTED, No. 2.

IF YOU WOULD HAVE BUSINESS DONE; GO, IF NOT, SEND

GREAT PRIMER ORNAMENTED, No. 3.

AS POOR RICHARD SAYS, "A STITCH IN TIME SAVES 9"

TWO LINE BOURGEOIS SKELETON ANTIQUE.

WE HOLD THESE TRUTHS TO BE SELF-EVIDENT, THAT ALL MEN ARE CREATED

PARAGON PERSPECTIVE.

MANY HANDS MAKE LIGHT WORK, TOO MANY COOKS SPOIL A BROTH

TWO LINE LONG PRIMER CONDENSED SHADED.

THE GOOD PAYMASTER IS LORD OF ANOTHER MAN'S PURSE. $900

TWO LINE LONG PRIMER GOTHIC DOUBLE SHADED.

CREDITORS ARE A SUPERSTITIOUS SECT

TWO LINE LONG PRIMER ORNAMENTED, No. 1.

LYING RIDES UPON DEBT'S BACK

TWO LINE LONG PRIMER ORNAMENTED, No. 2.

REMEMBER THAT CREDIT IS MONEY

TWO LINE SMALL PICA ORNAMENTED, No. 1.

BUFFALO AND ROCHESTER RAIL ROAD

TWO LINE SMALL PICA ORNAMENTED, No. 2.

A BORROWER IS SLAVE TO THE LENDER

TWO LINE SMALL PICA ORNAMENTED, No. 3.

DIVISION AVENUE OMNIBUS

TWO LINE SMALL PICA ORNAMENTED, No. 4.

A CAMP MEETING WILL BE HELD HERE IN 2453

TWO LINE SMALL PICA ORNAMENTED, No. 5.

$25,00 FOR A VERY GOOD LEVER WATCH

TWO LINE SMALL PICA ORNAMENTED. No. 6.

A PENNY A DAY IS $3,65 A YEAR

Page from 1860 specimen book of W. Hagar. There were 30 pages of ornamental types ranging from 6 points to 12 line. (Half of these pages illustrate sizes and styles that could easily be wood type.) Over half of the total book is devoted to ornamental borders, ornaments and other decorative effects.

letterpress which prodded the typefounders to their greatest achievements. Connor was to say in 1872, "The enterprise of many of our founders, in the production of fancy styles of type, having been at once appreciated by the printer (as opening a channel for his closer competition with lithographers, who had been steadily encroaching upon his most profitable departments) and the liberal encouragement the founders have received in this direction, has stimulated them to considerable in the origin and production of many new faces that have never paid the cost of getting up the matrices. Compare the specimen books of the present day with those of thirty years ago, then but few types of the ornamental school were in existence, and the range of fancy printing was of the most limited character."

In retrospect, Bullen commented in 1907, "Philadelphian broke the spell. It is not inventive, but it easily surpassed all previous ornamental shaded letters of its class, and was a revelation of what could be done to impart the softness and delicacy of lithography to a heavy design. It was the aim of American designers to rival the effects obtained on the lithographic stone, and in this they succeeded."

The designs of MacKellar, Smiths and Jordan, and of Bruce, brought about the shift of emphasis from Europe to America in the art of letter design and typefounding during the 1870's. In reference to that period of American dominance, Bullen was to remark, "The old world idea was to elaborate and ornament the conventional alphabet. The American idea of design is inventive—characterized by novelty of form rather than ornament, although the latter feature has not been neglected." The point is apt when the European imports from the first half of the century are viewed. While ornamental effects were still prominent in the competitive race with lithography, the invention in form reflected by the designs leading up and into the Art Nouveau were almost entirely dependent on shape for their decorative qualities as opposed to embellishment within the letter form. In the United States the wood type manufacturers were the first to recognize the advantages of innovating with the shape instead of searching for new decorative devices. They also were more prone to invent freely on the basis of function, both in terms of display design and of the equipment used to produce the type. The typefounders were tied to a competitive situation during the 1860's and to a revival during the balance of the century for their letter design sources, and both practices hindered a more functional approach to letter design.

Fat Face Romans, Antiques, Gothics, along with the Clarendons were the results of English ingenuity, but found amplification by Americans at the same time. Bullen credits the French with creating the best Ornamental styles, which were slavishly copied and imitated by both American and English typefounders up to the 1870's. It is thought that Germans contributed more in this period than they have been given credit for, for many of their large Perspective and Ornamented designs found wide application. Beginning in 1867 and continuing through the century, American typefounders surpassed European founders in both the number and quality of jobbing faces they produced. During this period, there were in the neighborhood of 30 American typefounders producing type in a sometimes bitterly competitive market. The styles would change about every 5 years, and around every 10 years the entire fashion would become different.

Without going into detail, we must acknowledge that many styles of type associated with the nineteenth century would never have come into being had there not been corresponding advances in other branches of the trade during those years. The introduction of composition rollers by Booth of New York City in 1826 made possible the printing of delicate ornamental types in a manner which could not have been achieved with an inking ball or the crude rollers previously used. The development of presses, particularly the high speed platen machines of the early 1850's, contributed immeasurably to the entire field of printing. Names such as Hoe, Gordon, Taylor, Bullock, and a host of others were to revolutionize printing in this hundred years, and they provided American printers and typefounders with the best equipment possible to display their talents. An interesting machine of rather short popularity was the chromatic press marketed in the 1870's. Working from a split fountain, printers turned out multi-colored sheets with one impression. Also, improvements in paper and card stocks were a major factor in the design of letters. For example, the calendared papers developed for better printing of wood engravings encouraged fine types. It is said that the rapid development of colored printing used mostly in the production of show bills gained impetus from the improved manufacturing techniques in the production of colored inks.

Francis Picabia, Dadaist, 1922.

Filippo Tommaso Marinetti, Futurist movement, Milan, 1915.

Filippo Tommaso Marinetti, Chair.

Although the wood type manufacturers ceased to produce the older styles, tremendous stocks of these types can still be found in a variety of printing establishments around the country. In shops located in rural areas and in smaller towns, the old styles of wood type continue to be used almost daily for the printing of outdoor bills, newspaper heads, political banners, state or county fair posters, etc. In small Midwestern towns, a visit to the local restaurant, post office, or town newspaper will uncover printing from these old wood types. Even though the designs are out of style, many printers refuse to part with them under any circumstances.

It was undoubtedly among the ranks of amateur printers that the revival of Victorian types first began. The frugality of the country printer had kept many of the old faces around and in some use, and probably this was the source that first exposed the possibilities of wood type to the amateur printers, who in addition to their dedication to the craft of printing, were frequently avid collectors with all the instincts of a pack-rat! By the 1930's, the interest in nineteenth century types had developed into considerable proportions among the English hobby printers. With a few notable exceptions, the revival began somewhat later in this country. Elrie Robinson, a Southern country-printer, spent much of his life collecting types and ornaments from the preceding century with which he printed limited editions of catalogues illustrating typographic Americana of the 1800's. His collection undoubtedly helped to focus attention on these styles in America and eventually ended up in the New York Public Library as the Robinson-Pforzheimer Collection. It still serves students and interested parties as one of the most accessible and complete collections of its kind.

There would seem to be a direct connection between the interests of the English amateur printer who rediscovered in the 1930's the delights of the Victorian type faces and the application of these same type faces by designers for pavilion identification, exhibits, and promotion for the Festival of Britain in 1951. The use of the Victorian letters for this event best marked the beginning of the revival of nineteenth-century type faces on a scale exceeding the interest of the amateur groups. During the next 15 years, designers in both Europe and America found many applications for the large wood letters which were far beyond those uses intended by the originators.

It is thought that this revival might be attributed in part to a reaction brought on by the severity of Bauhaus styles, which in turn had been a reaction to the Victorian styles. Also, there was a general lack of display types other than those produced in the previous century, at a time when an enormous variety of styles was demanded for the constantly expanding advertising business. Perhaps another factor was that most of the ornate letter designs, being extremely individualistic, served to give some humanism to a period dominated by science and technology.

Underlying what was largely a commercial application of Victorian faces during the late 1940's, 1950's and 1960's was a period beginning around 1915 and running up through the 1930's, which had its origins in Europe, and to a varying degree, utilized both the smaller type-forms and the large wood letters as vehicles of visual expression. The work was done within a variety of art movements, such as the Dada, Futurist, and Constructivist. Letters appearing in collage construction were used abstractly and were quite outside the traditional use of type as a means of conveying word messages. The poetry of Guill-aume Apollinaire, a poet and spokesman for the Cubists, is an immediate precursor to much of the advertising typography of today, as would be the sensitively composed collages of Kurt Schwitters.

There were similarities in the work produced in the various movements, undoubtedly because many overlapped one another in time and because the groups were close geographically. The letter compositions of Marinetti, a Futurist poet, are for example, difficult to distinguish from similar compositions by some Dadaists. In their use of type styles, these artists limited themselves to the plain faces such as Gothic, Antique, and some French Clarendons or French Antiques. Wood types found a place in many of their posters and collages, although a few artists preferred to draw the letters, which they would usually render in direct, plain-faced styles. This aspect may be contrasted with the mid-twentieth century fascination for the ornamented and semi-ornamented styles. For most of the early works, color was subservient to organization—ranging from the free organization of the Dadaists to the severely formal typography of the Bauhaus.

Later, during the 1930's and early 1940's, several European publishers went to the provincial typographic styles as a guise for political commentary. Leo Longanesi used many of the wood types and ornaments in his *L'Italiano*. Typographically a classicist, Longanesi saw the Victorian types as the "irrecoverable Paradise Garden of Italy's golden age." Maccari in his publication, *Il Selvaggio*, espoused the cause of "etrapaese," a literary, artistic, anti-internationalist, anti-cosmopolitan, back-to-the-cultural-farm movement. He strove for the provincial image by mixing nineteenth-century type faces, after the manner of the country printer, as a means of visually underscoring his cause. These two publications began a trend that was further perpetuated by *L'Europea* and *Il Mondo*, both produced by Domus Publishing in the 1940's and 1950's. One of the prime examples from this school of imagery in political publications is the American magazine *Monocle*, which has afforded some of the most imaginative use of wood letters in support of editorial comment.

Victorian wood letters were extremely "visual"—having pronounced positive-negative qualities combined with active contours. The scale of most letters provided a dimension unknown to text typography and created a new typographic context of oversized letters which eventually led to "typographic illustration." Letterforms ceased to function as type but were used only as design elements; used out of context in color, scale, and arrangement, these older letterforms found entirely new interpretations. This trend, although not limited to America, found its greatest exploitation here.

While amateur printers in both England and the United States had revived many of the old styles, they usually restricted themselves to substituting a few lines of ornate type for prevailing styles. It was the designer who actually created the new applications. During the 1950's Robert Jones, a designer who also is a printing enthusiast, published some of the most entertaining of the earliest works using nineteenth-century types and ornaments through his Glad Hand Press. The trend grew and inevitably infiltrated advertising, so that it was to be found quite regularly during the 1950's and at its peak during the early 1960's. Some designers, such as John Alcorn, Lionel Kal-

Mecano, Dadaist, 1922.

Cover design of L'Italiano, *edited by Leo Longanesi, June, 1931. Original in black and orange.*

Fat Faces

Advertising and publishing typographers will be interested to know that Stephenson Blake have recently been examining some original matrices which they have in their archives of nineteenth-century Fat Faces, and hope, at a later date, to reissue a range of sizes of these types, particularly the vigorous early specimen shown here.

Stephenson Blake Caslon

THE CASLON LETTER FOUNDRY SHEFFIELD

93

Two advertisements from Alphabet & Image No. 5 *(September, 1947).*

THE SOUTH

EDITOR'S NOTE: *Unlike some of the conversations reprinted in Monocle, the one below actually took place. It was taped in the studio of WMCA, a New York radio station, and—except for the deletion of some sections because of space limitations and the addition of some explanatory notes in parentheses—it is reproduced as it was spoken. As soon becomes apparent, it was spontaneous and unrehearsed.*

All of the participants have reported race stories from the South. Gene Grove is a reporter for the New York Post, whose most recent experiences in the states of the Aging Confederacy were in Americus, Georgia, and Birmingham, Alabama. Peter Goldman, an Associate Editor in the National Affairs section of Newsweek, specialized in civil rights stories and had the bad judgement to leave the comfortable New York end of the teletype machine to visit such places as Oxford, Mississippi in person. Philip Benjamin of The New York Times, who was also in Birmingham when many of the citizens were in the streets, claims the most extreme southern assignment of covering the International Geophysical Year expedition to Antarctica, an experience upon which he based a recently published novel Quick Before It Melts (he has a parallel claim to the most far-fetched book plug). Fred Powledge is also with The New York Times, for which he covers race stories both in New York and the South, and he formerly had what is known as the "seg beat" at the Atlanta Journal. He is from North Carolina and speaks with an accent that some people find unattractive but he rather likes. The Moderator is Calvin Trillin, who once covered the South for Time and has gone back two or three times for The New Yorker, for which he is a staff writer.

The panelists have a variety of approaches to their jobs, and they seem to be united mainly by a common desire not to be injured in the line of duty.

61

THE GREAT WALL STREET JOURNAL OF MARVIN KITMAN

For years I have been reading in the newspapers that Chiang Kai-shek will be retaking the Mainland soon. The way my State Department's China Policy hasn't changed significantly since 1950, they obviously still believe in Chiang. It occurred to me that as a loyal American I should do something to show that I believed in Chiang, too. By studying the market, I finally found something in the China Policy for me.

An account executive at Merrill Lynch, Pierce, Fenner & Smith, the nation's largest securities dealers, had been calling me for a long time to handle my brokerage account. I decided to give him the business. "This is the first time I'm going into the market," I warned him in the crowded board room at Merrill Lynch's Madison Avenue branch. "So I want to begin my portfolio with government bonds."

"That's sound," my customer's man said.

"Buy Imperial Chinese Government Hukuang Railways 5% Sinking Fund Gold Loan of 1911," I ordered.

My customer's man's face started sinking even before I had finished telling him the name of the bond. "It's a real yellow chip," I tried to assure him. "The Chinese really know how to build railroads. That's why we let them build all our railroads.

I didn't think it was my business to tell him that an American President had once recommended Hukuang as a solid investment to J. P. Morgan. *The Collected Letters of Theodore Roosevelt, Volume*

18

John Gregory Dunne's THE ORANGE OUTRAGE OR

HOW I LEARNED TO STOP LOVING THE JAPS AND HATE THE CHINESE

"HOW TO TELL YOUR FRIENDS FROM THE JAPS:

"Virtually all Japanese are short.

"Japanese are seldom fat; they often dry up as they age.

"Most Chinese avoid horn-rimmed spectacles.

"Japanese walk stiffly erect, hard-heeled. Chinese more relaxed, have an easy gait.

"The Chinese expression is likely to be more kindly, placid, open;

53

Three story heads from Monocle, VI, No. 1 *(Summer, 1964).*

ish, and Milton Glaser, developed illustration techniques which beautifully complemented the revival styles. Under Louis Dorfsman's direction, old display types found excellent use for CBS, both in promotion, and as TV titles. More recently, Mo Lebowitz, using the press as a creative tool and wood letters as elements, has produced promotional pieces which combine a high degree of imagination with superior technical abilities and a great sense of humor. Although it is easier to associate a style with a particular professional, such as the previously named three designers, larger letters in advertising and promotion should be considered on a much wider scale. The practice of printing with large letters has been very extensive for a number of years, and some of the finest individual works have been created behind professional anonymity by persons using these elements only occasionally, or by relatively unknown designers and hobby printers. Many artists, both painters and designers, incorporated the large letter into a variety of subjective statements which comprise a significant form of artistic expression. Norman Ives worked for a number of years with collages made up of letterforms cut into segments and rearranged within a grid. At least one of these was translated into a large mural for the Paul Randolph Arts Building at Yale University. From his early collages, Ives has now moved to silk-screen, painted canvas, and three-dimensional cubes as vehicles for working with these letterforms. Robert Indiana, Jasper Johns, and many other painters have found the visual qualities of the large letters exciting elements, and their paintings have frequently overlapped the work of designers in the exploitation of these letters. Recent trends in Op Art are not unrelated to nineteenth-century considerations in the design of semi-ornamental faces, but the optical complexities of designing so as to accommodate the possible letter combinations within 26 letters, figures, and signs is far more complex than the one-image productions of today's "Op" artist!

Love, Robert Indiana. Dayton's Gallery 12.

Letter collage, Norman Ives, c. 1958.

Die, Robert Indiana. Walker Art Center.

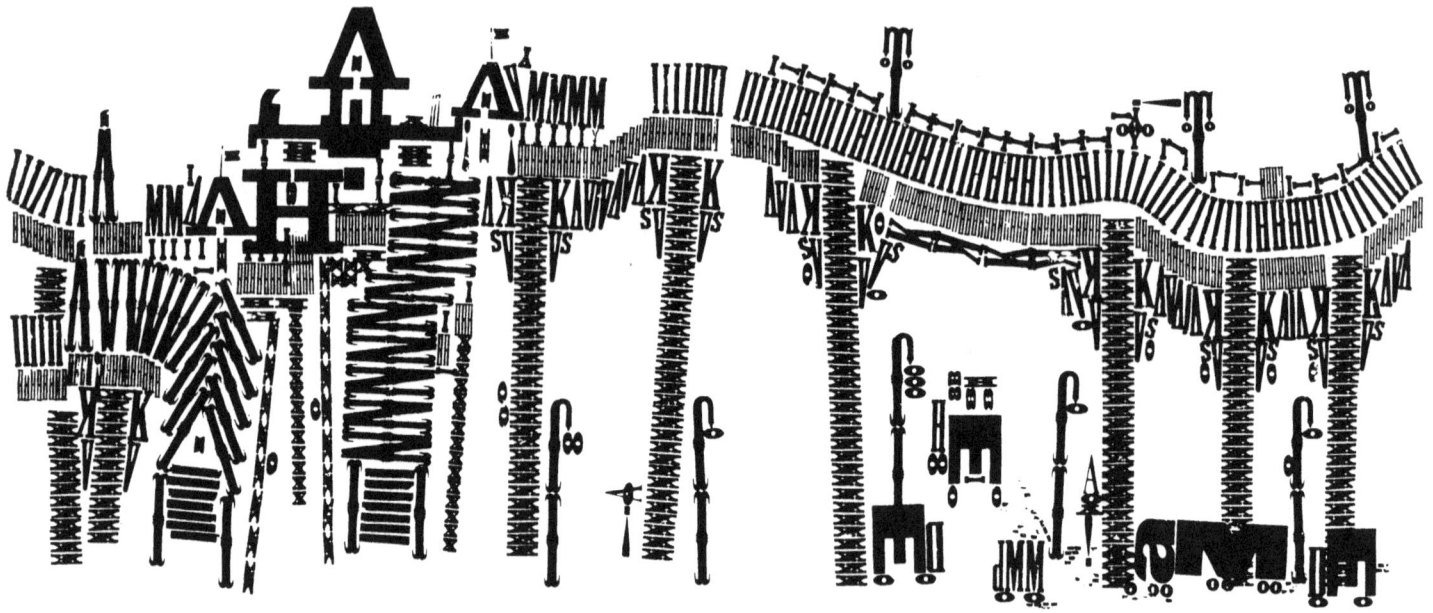

Third Avenue El, Norman Gorbaty, Yale University, 1955.

Movie poster, John Vandover, Kansas City Art Institute, 1964.

Visual Poetry, *Josua Reichert, 1962. First part of a four-part poem by Ludwig Greve.*

Mo Lebowitz, Antique Press. Taken from an announcement.

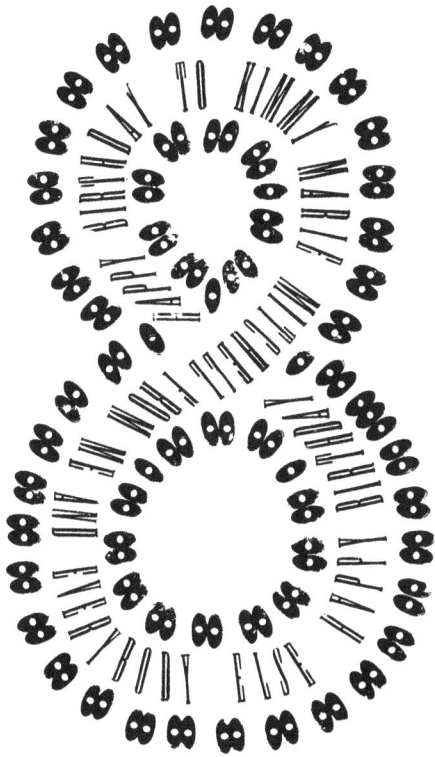

Letter Z, Jerry Poppenhouse, Kansas City Art Institute, 1965.

Letter T, Ray Bales, Kansas City Art Institute, 1965.

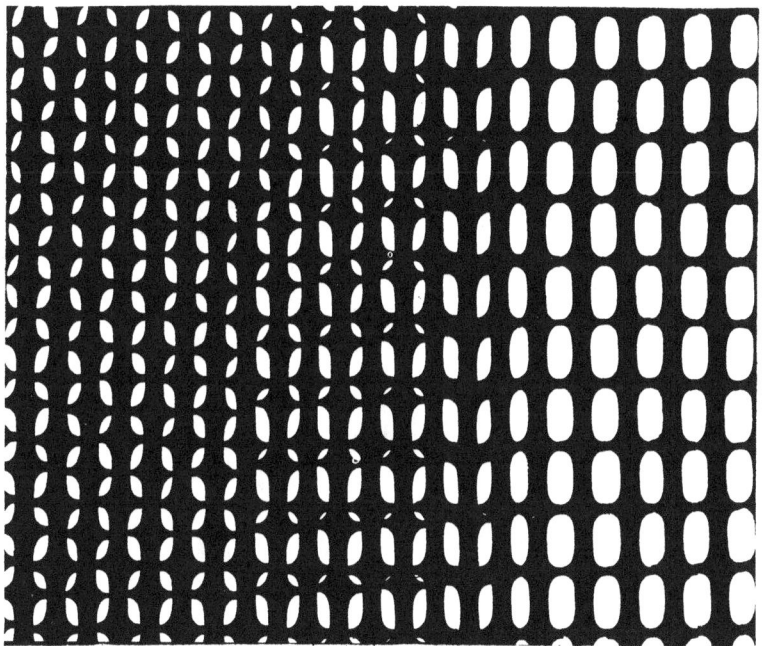

Letter I, Bill Philyaw, Kansas City Art Institute, 1965.

Top. Birthday greeting to a little girl. Below. Hoot poster. Joe Lucca

Geofroy Tory, Itinerarium Antonini, *1512.*

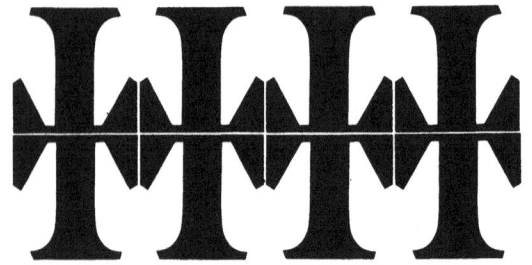

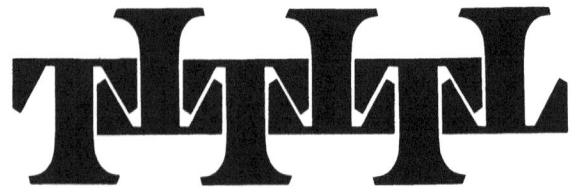

Werner Pfeiffer, circa 1963.

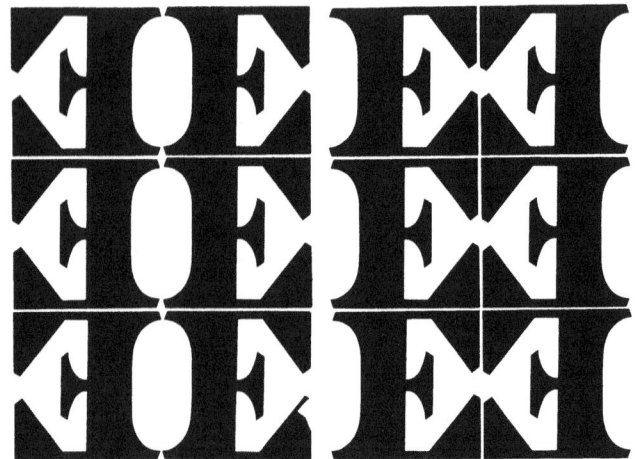

Mark by Giulio Confalonieri for a publisher.

Visual exercises with wood letterforms by Carl Miller, Yale University, 1962.

218

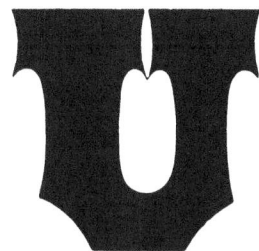

Visual exercises with wood letterforms by Carl Miller, Yale University, 1962.

Demonstration of figure-ground relationships which appear to have been more consciously developed in the design of wood type than with metal types.

6-3=◎2

Excerpted from a CBS announcement.

GILDED CAGE

A ROSE IS A ROSE IS A ROSE IS A ROSE IS A ROSE IS A ROSE

SUMMER

*Walker Art Center Summer Classes brochure,
Rob Roy Kelly.*

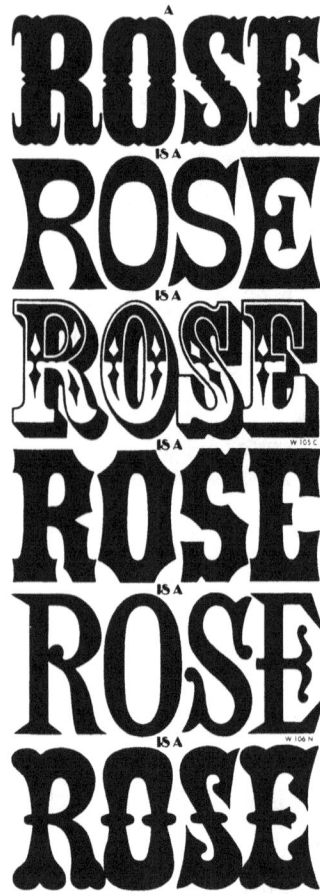

FROM THE CHICKEN HOUSE TO YOU

*Three illustrations by John Alcorn from Headliners
Catalogue.*

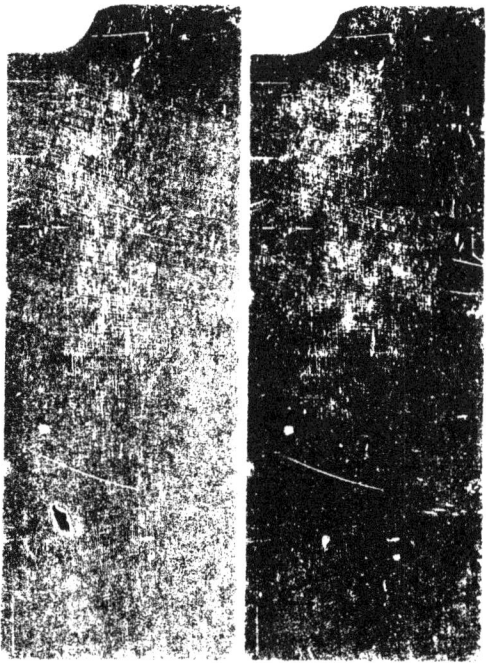

The Prop. and wife have stood side-by-side for eleven
years of wedded bliss. The only other bliss of which the
Prop. has knowledge is ignorance. Mo Lebowitz: Prop.

Announcement by Mo Lebowitz.

*Artone
Studio India
Ink*

Trademark by Seymour Chwast.

Hand lettering and decorative effects using 19th-century
wood letters as models. Lettering by Tom Carnase,
Herb Lubalin, Inc.

Flower Show
Parish House
Pound Ridge
Community Church

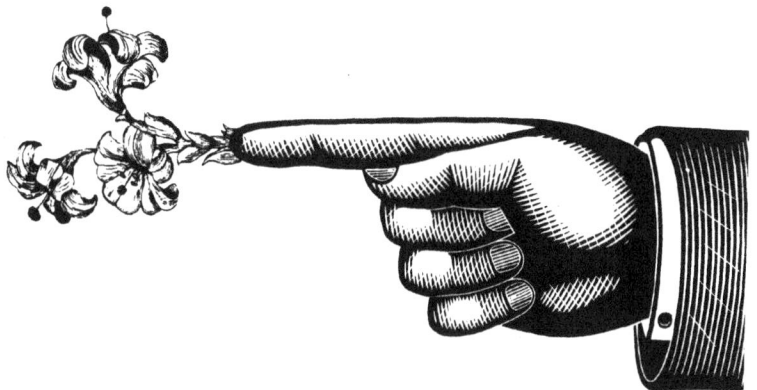

Poster from the Glad Hand Press by Robert Jones.

WARNING

750,000,000
BARRELS OF WHISKEY

☞ CONSUMED IN THE ☜

U.S.A. DURING

THE PAST 2 MONTHS

(DRINK UP, THEY'RE GAINING ON US!)

FAMOUS SAYINGS
FROM HISTORY

"KEEP YO
COTTON PICKIN'
HANDS OFFA
MA GIN"

ELI WHITNEY 1793

NOTICE

BEWARE the EVILS
❋ OF THE ❋
DEMON RUM

THERE IS NO JOY IN
THE CONSUMING OF
ALCOHOLIC BEVERAGES
!!!!!!!!!!!!!!!!!!
UNLESS YOU HAVE A VERY LARGE GLASS

VOTE

FOR THE TWO
PARTY
SYSTEM

❈ ONE ON FRIDAY AND ❈
||||ONE ON SATURDAY!||||

Robert Nix for Hallmark Cards, Inc., 1965.
All typefaces have been hand-rendered even though based
on Victorian types.

Sheldon Rose, 1967.

Sheldon Rose, 1965.

Wall-piece, Peter Cooper Galleries. Sheldon Rose, 1967.

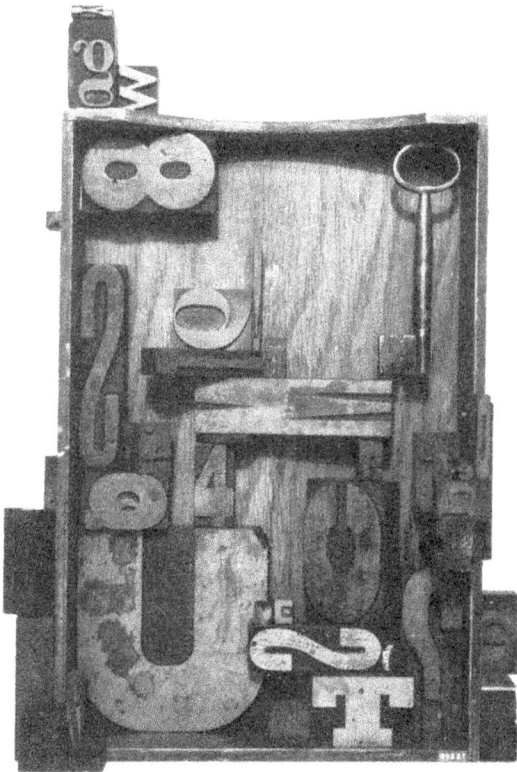

Quest. Sheldon Rose & Gloria Gentile, 1967.

In 1965, Mr. Rose located a poster printing plant for sale, and through a hasty partnership was able to raise funds sufficient to obtain the complete inventory of wood type. The partnership was soon dissolved, and Rose, retaining most of the wood types, began construction of dimensional and flat decorative pieces utilizing the wood type itself. It may be said that his flair combined with the inherent qualities of the wood letters has resulted in rich and handsome works.

Wall-piece, Bruce Freidlich Advertising. Sheldon Rose, Stuart Scherr, and Steve Goodman, 1966.

The wood letters are continually used for concrete poetry, and configurational imagery. There may well be a direct relationship between a renewed interest in large letters and the current popularity of letter combinations as trademarks. Wood types have found their way into school workshops, where they have proved a highly effective tool in teaching as a means of implementing perceptual exercises. Some of the finest configurational works done with letterforms has been accomplished by students around the country, and it is unfortunate that this work has not had a larger audience.

Willard Morgan, a New York printer and publisher, an avid collector of equipment and memorabilia connected with printing, has, with his two sons, Lloyd and Douglas, accumulated the largest collection of wood types in the United States. They have distributed a number of colorful catalogues of wood letters, and sold reproduction proofs from the types. Under an arrangement with Headliners, Inc., a number of their wood type designs have been put on film and sold through the numerous Headliner franchises. In addition to the many styles available on film, added variety was introduced through photo-flexing. Perhaps the single greatest market for these designs has been in newspaper advertising. This has been an interesting trend as it so closely approximates the original uses for the large wood letters, and it is believed these letter styles have been particularly successful in this field of advertising. It could be noted at this point, that in addition to the nineteenth-century wood letter designs used for newspaper advertisements, there have been a tremendous number of letters drawn "in the style of" the nineteenth century which have little relationship to any previous styles. While not particularly well done, they are nevertheless interesting since newspaper advertising is probably one of the last remaining outposts for this kind of letter design.

The great popularity of the Victorian wood letter now seems almost to be in the past again. The interlude represented by the revival has been both entertaining and interesting when compared to a conjectural projection of the incredibly dull trade typography predominant during the period between 1920 and 1950. Likewise, the inventiveness in using the decorated types and ornaments probably supersedes what would have evolved from the poor taste in commercial illustration from the same years. Recent attempts to strengthen the revival by moving to Art Nouveau influences have not been particularly successful, rightly so in the face of the magnificent Victorians. It is time now to move out of this past and begin to build beyond our own traditions.

ART TONE BLACK BOTTOM (SEYMOUR CHWAST)

WEST DR. DOLITTLE

MANSARD POINTED A

WEST CASA BLANCA

BABYFAT (MILT GLASER)

STANDLE GEMUTLICH B

WEST GOTHAM BLOCKSHADOW

Twentieth century lettering in the "spirit of" Victorian types. Examples taken from Photo-Lettering Inc.

Lettering for an SH & L ad by Gerry Gersten.

ST. PAUL CIVIC OPERA

PRESENTS

TOSCA

ST. PAUL AUDITORIUM

THEATRE

OCT. 5, 6, 7, · 8:30 P.M.

A recently printed wood type poster which indicates how barren poster printing has become in this century.

FOODTOWN'S PRICES GOOD ALL WEEK — MONDAY THRU SATURDAY
Strictly Fresh - Pan Ready - Whole

fryers

Lb. **23**c

CUT UP FRYERS 27c

·Buy Several at This Low Price·

Lean — Fresh
Ground BEEF Lb. **39**c

HORMEL'S BONELESS RIB EYE
STEAKS Lb. **79**c

HORMEL'S RANGE THICK SLICED
BACON 2 Lb. Pkg. **99**c

Peters DELICIOUS MEAT PRODUCTS "PICK THE PACK WITH THE PINE CONE LABEL"

TRUCKLOAD SALE

HORMEL'S THURINGER
Summer Sausage **69**c Lb.

HORMEL'S
Little Sizzlers **39**c Pkg.

Peters SKINLESS WIENERS	Lb. 1½ Lb. Bag 69c	PETERS PORKETTES	Pkg. 59c
Peters RING BOLOGNA	2 10-oz. Rings 79c	Peters PORK SAUSAGE ROLLS	Lb. 39c
Peters SMOKED LIVER SAUSAGE	Lb 49c	Peters And SLICED LUNCHEON MEATS	3 Pkgs. $1
Peters ECONOMY SALAMI	Each 89c	Peters SKIN-ON WIENERS	Lb Pkg 69c
Peters Large SLICING BOLOGNA	Lb. 49c	CHIPPED BEEF or HAM	Pkg. 39c
Peters SMOKY CHUBS	Each 69c	Peters Sliced Luncheon Meat ROAST BEEF LOAF or BOILED HAM	Pkg. 59c

Hormel's "Ready to Eat" CANNED BONELESS
HAMS 5 Lb. Can **$3**.39

SERVICE COURTESY FRIENDLINESS DEPENDABILITY LOW PRICES

FREEDOM FOODTOWN

U.S.D.A. GRADED CHOICE
CHUCK STEAKS Lb. **49**c

FOODTOWN SUPER MARKETS
THE STORES WHERE PRICES ARE ALWAYS LOWER

Peters—Fresh Frozen **BEEF STEAK** Lge. 18-oz. Pkg. **59**c

LIMIT RIGHTS RESERVED

A handbill which is similar to those distributed from house to house. Printed by a multilith and on cheap paper, they perform much the same service as the nineteenth-century handbill or broadside. But the combination of type and hand lettering clearly reveals how much the art of the broadside has degenerated in seventy-five years.

DAY!

SPRING SIZZLER

Early Bird Tackle

SALE

BUY-OUT

ONE LOW PRICE

FREE

FAMOUS BURPEE SEEDS

new   FREE!   SAV-ON

BALLS

TOMORROW
IS
DOWNTOWN DAY
GREAT

Current newspaper advertising utilizes great numbers of Victorian styles. In the daily newspaper you may find the Fat Face Romans, Antiques, and Gothics in the same profusion as in the nineteenth century. A few faces have been taken directly from the older types, but the majority by far are current innovations by hand letterers using Victorian concepts of decoration and display.

This sign now stands in South Windham, Connecticut, at the foot of the road that once led to the wood type mill built by Edwin Allen in 1850 and used by John G. Cooley and later by Charles H. Tubbs. Today, residents of South Windham are puzzled by this odd street name, not realizing that it is perhaps the only commemoration of a once-thriving industry.

WOOD TYPE SPECIMENS

The following wood type specimens are grouped into three primary families—Roman, Antique, and Gothic. They have been arranged into a sequence that accentuates both the gradual modification of a basic design into several designs, and the feasibility of placing most nineteenth century wood type designs in one of the three primary families. The main exceptions are a number of Tuscan designs and some of the Art Nouveau faces that came onto the market near the end of the century.

Most of these specimens are shown as they were proofed, with all the rounded corners, nicks, and other irregularities resulting from years of use. In a few instances, specimens have been enlarged to fit the format, but to the detriment of the design. However, the basic letterform structure may be identified. With the exception of a few specimens, which are noted in the captions, these types were collected and proofed by the author, and for the most part were found in the Midwest.

The dates given in the captions for first showing may not be the earliest date that the design was marketed, but it is indicative of the period when that particular face was in general use. Identification of the company that cut each specimen was made on the basis of a manufacturer's stamp on the type itself.

It is unfortunate that the specimens are not more complete, but as the printer often purchased wood type in capitals only (especially large letters), these specimens are fairly representative of how a printer might stock wood letters: capitals only, with or without figures, and usually a lowercase only in smaller sizes. The best single reference to nineteenth century wood type styles is the previously mentioned 1906 Hamilton Wood Type Catalogue.

A B C D E
F G H I J;
K L M N O
P Q R S T
U V W X Y
Z & Æ Œ -,

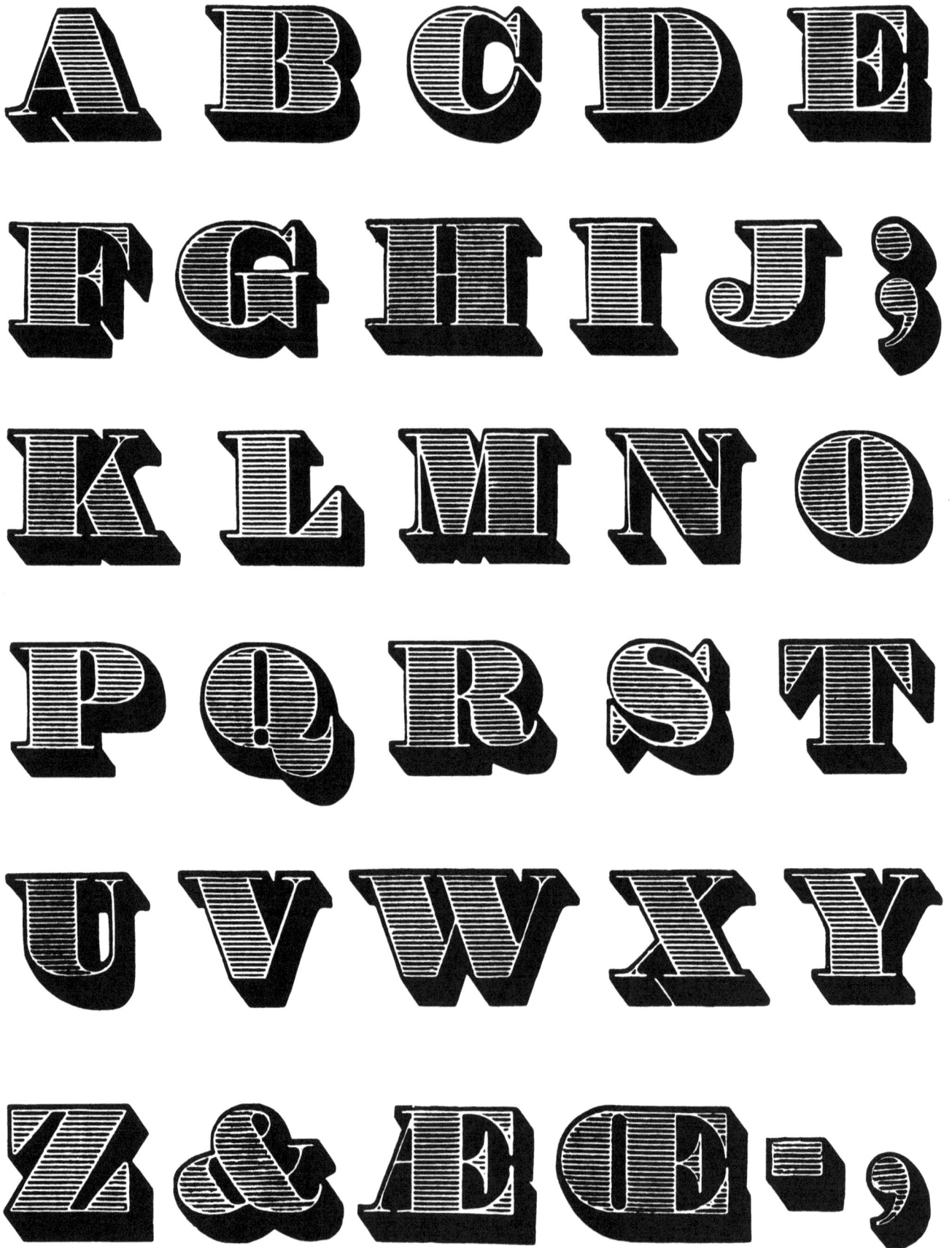

Roman Ornamented. First shown by George F. Nesbitt in his 1838 specimens. This specimen is printed from types in the Robinson-Pforzheimer Collection of the New York Public Library. This design may have come from France, since this style of decoration was popular there at that time. The American models usually had a lowercase and figures. The interior line shading is representative of letter decoration by the metal plate engraver, and is a carryover from the previous century. The same line shading—horizontal, diagonal and vertical—was applied to Gothic and Antique styles a short time after this Roman evolved; however, all line-shaded faces began to fade from specimen books by 1850.

A B C D
E F G H
I J K L
M N O P
Q R S T
U V W !
X Y Z &

Roman Extended. First shown by George Nesbitt in his 1838 specimens. This design was cut by the Page Company. Lowercase and figures are missing. This design was most popular during the first half of the century. The earliest specimens were more extended than the one shown here, and they did include a lowercase which is believed to have originated as wood type. Caslon cast an expanded Roman in 1835 which did not have a lowercase.

ABCDEFG
HIJKLMN
OPQRSTU
VWXYZ&
abcdefgh
iïjklmno!
pqrstuvw
xyzœæ-,;:
ffffffffffffÆ

Roman. First shown by Darius Wells in his 1828
specimens. This specimen is printed from types at
Rochester Institute of Technology, Rochester, New York.
Figures are missing. One of the oldest of the large display
letters used in this country, this style gradually fell into
disuse after 1850.

ABCDEF
GHIJKL
MNOPQ!
RSTUV.;
WXYZ&,

*Roman Condensed. First shown by George Nesbitt in his
1838 specimens. This specimen is printed from types at
Rochester Institute of Technology, Rochester, New York.
Lowercase and figures are missing.*

ABCDEFGHIJK
LMNOPQRSTU
VWXYZ & 1234
567890$ abcd
efghijklmno
pqrstuvwxyz
&&&& fi ffi ffi ffi ff fl

Roman X Condensed. First shown by George Nesbitt in
his 1838 specimens. Representative of the trend toward
lighter styles which began in the late thirties and
continued through the forties. Roman was to be further
condensed into XX and XXX styles.

ABCDEF
GHIJK
LMNOP
QRSTU
VWXYZ
123456
7 8 0 & $ $

Aetna (similar to designs called Painter's Roman by Heber Wells and Doric by Morgans & Wilcox). First listed by William Page in his 1870 specimens. Lowercase is missing. Design is typical of those that replaced the older Fat Face Romans during the second half of the century. Retaining a Roman quality, but sturdier because of the treatment of thins, the face was exceedingly well received by job printers.

ABCDEFGHIJ
KLMNOPQRS
TUVWXYZa
bcdefghikl
mnopqrstu
vwxyz 1234
567890 &!.'-$

Doric Condensed. This specimen is printed from types at Rochester Institute of Technology, Rochester, New York. This design would have been issued by Morgans & Wilcox during the 1880's.

ABCDEF
GHIJKL
MNOPQ!
RSTUV-
WXYZ&.

Painter's Roman (frequently numbered marking it as a Special). Cut by both Page and Wells. This specimen is printed from types at Rochester Institute of Technology, Rochester, New York. It came onto the market during the 1870's. Lowercase and figures are missing.

ABCDEF
GHIJKL
MNOPQS
RSTU&&&
VWXYZ
1234567890

Caslon. This design was cut by Hamilton and put on the market after 1900. It appears to be patterned after the metal types of the founder. Lowercase is missing.

ABCDEFGH
IJKLMNOP
QRSTUVW
XYZ123456
7890&&&$
&$ abcdefg
hijklmnopq
rstuvwxyz

De Vinne. Cut by Hamilton circa 1895. Another cutting in wood of a popular metal type.

ABCDE
FGHIJK
LMNOP
QRSTU
VWXY
Z12345
67890&

Unique (No. 203 by Hamilton). First shown by Hamilton
in his 1889 specimens. Lowercase is missing. Fairly typical
of Roman designs from this period.

ABCDEFG
HIJKLMN
OPQRSTU
VWXYZ&
I34567890$
& & abcdef
ghijklmnop
qrstuvwxyz

Ben Franklin. Cut by Hamilton and shown near the end of the century. Design copied from metal type design of the founders.

ABCDEFG
HIJKLMNO
PQRSTUV
WXYZ1234
567890&$ab
cdefghijklmno
pqrstuvwxyz

Jenson Old Style. Cut by Hamilton with permission of
ATF in 1906.

A B C D E
F G H I J
K L M N
O P Q R S
T U V W
X Y Z & !
¡ ', ., ? ! '& &

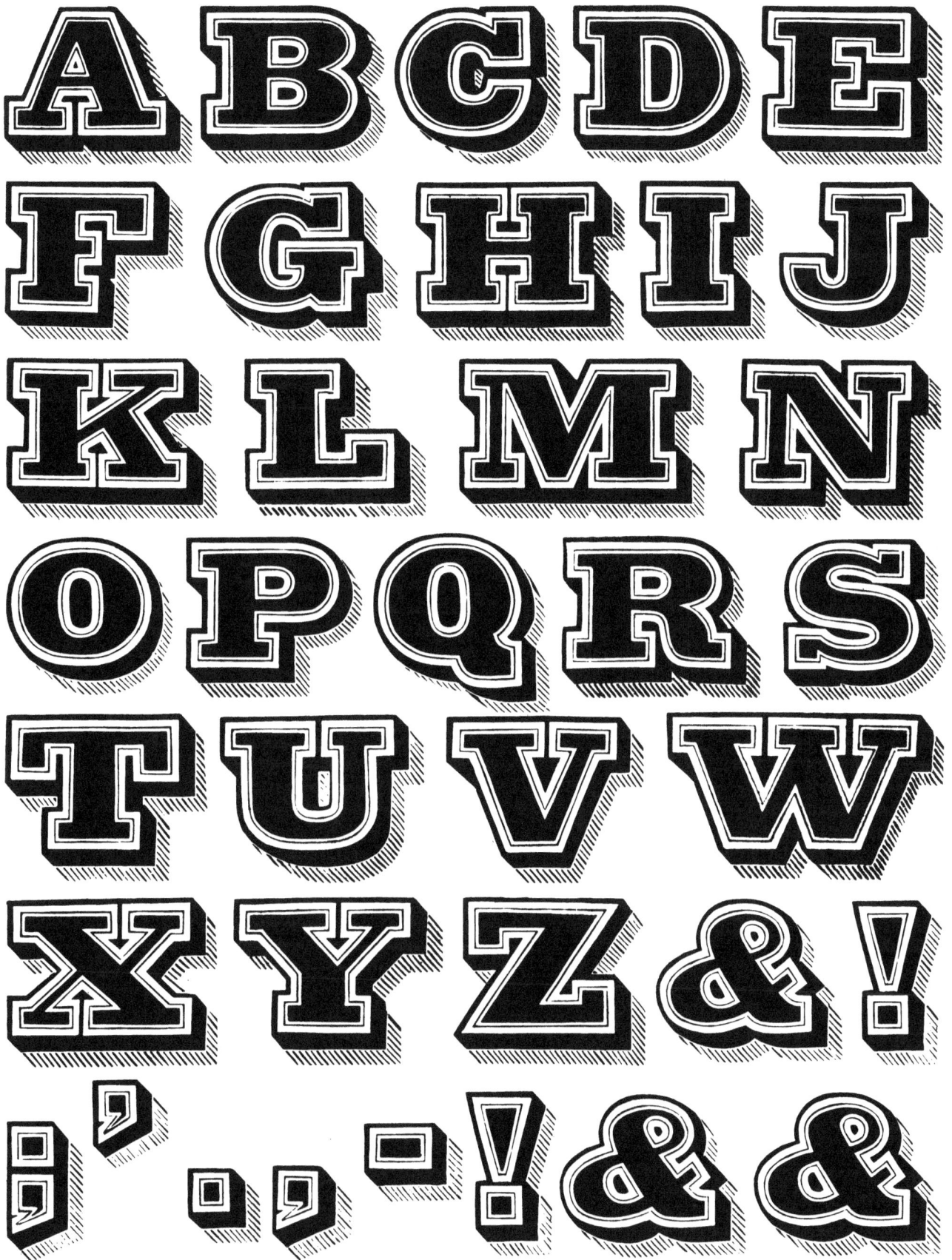

Antique Double Outlined Shade—half ray and half solid shade. Called Antique Ornamented by Wells & Webb and shown in their 1849 specimens. This specimen is printed from types at Rochester Institute of Technology, Rochester, New York. No lowercase or figures were designed for this face. The same decorative treatment, outlined, half solid and half ray shade, had been applied to the Gothic at an earlier date. These styles were most common in America in the 1840's.

ABCDE
FGHIJ!
KLMNO
PQRST
UVWXS
YZ&123
4567890

Antique. First shown by Darius Wells in his 1828
specimens. This design cut by the Page Company.
Lowercase is missing. American styles of Antique were
much heavier than those shown by Figgins in 1815.
Wells also showed Antique Italic and Backslope, neither
with a lowercase.

ABCD!
EFGHI
JKLM
NOPQ!!
RSTU!
VWXY
Z Æ Œ $
123456
7890 $!

Antique Extended. First shown by George Nesbitt in his 1838 specimens. This design cut by the Hamilton Company. Lowercase is missing. Antique Extended may have originated, as a wood type as it shows regularly in wood type catalogues some fifteen years before the typefounders included it in their specimens. (Nicolette Gray dates the design 1841 and believes it is American in origin.)

ABCDEF
GHIJKL
MNOPQ
RSTUV
WXYZ&

Antique Condensed. First shown by George Nesbitt in his 1838 specimens. This design cut by the Page Company. Lowercase and figures are missing.

ABCDEFGHIJKL
MNOPQRSTUVW
XYZ&&&&abcdef
ghijklmnopqrst
uvwxyzoooooo

Antique X Condensed. First shown by Wells & Webb in
their 1840 specimens. Figures are missing. This cutting
is not identified by imprint, but it is believed to be more
representative of the style as cut during the latter part
of the century.

ABCDEFGHIJKLM

NOPQRSTUVWXY

Z1234567890$&

Antique XX Condensed. First shown by William Page in his 1859 specimens. Lowercase is missing.

ABCDEFGHIJKLM
NOPQRSTUVWXY
Z1234567890&$

*Antique XXX Condensed. First shown by William Page
in his 1859 specimens. Lowercase is missing.*

ABCDEFGH
IJKLMNOP
QRSTUVW
XYZ& abcde
fghijklmnop
qrstuvwxyz
1234567890

Antique Light Face. First shown by Wells & Webb in
their 1854 specimens. This particular font of type differs
from other versions—the blocks are very old, and the type
appears crudely manufactured, perhaps entirely handmade.

ABCD EFGHI JKLM NOPQ RSTU VWXY Z&&&

Antique Light Face Extended. First shown by Wells &
Webb in their 1854 specimens. This design cut by the
Hamilton Company. Lowercase and figures are missing.

ABCDEFGHIJK
LMNOPQRSTU
VWXYZO&&&
abcdefghijklmno
pqrstuvwxyzooo
1234567890O$

Skeleton Antique. First listed by William Page in his 1865 specimens. These light styles of Antique were very popular with the typefounders during the last quarter of the century.

ABCDEFGHI
JKLMNOPQ!
RSTUVWXY
Z&123456789
Oabcdefghijkl
mnopqrstuvw
xyz$ffifflffflfifi

Egyptian No. 2. First shown by William Page in his 1878 specimens. This design was sometimes called Egyptian Antique (serifs are unbracketed). The design was much used by typefounders.

ABCDEFGHIJKL
MNOPQRSTUV!
WXYZ&1234567
890$abcdefghijkl
mnopqrstuvwxyz

Antique No. 7. First listed by William Page in his 1870 specimens. This design cut by the Hamilton Company around 1889.

ABCDEFGHIJKLMNO

PQRSTUVWXYZ&S!

1234567890abcdefgh

ijklmnopqrstuvwxyz

French Antique. First listed by William Page in the
Typographic Messenger *during 1869. This interpretation
is peculiarly American, and originated with the wood type
producers. The European French Antiques were not so
condensed and had a different serif to letter-height ratio.*

ABCDEFGHIJ

KLMNOPQRS

TUVWXYZ &

Celtic Ornamented (Chromatic). This design patented by William Page circa 1870. No lowercase or figures were designed for this style. Only one block is printed here, but a second block meant to print in a second color was included with the font. The design is based on a French Clarendon.

ABCDEFG
HIJKLMN
OPQRSTU
VWXYZ&1
234567890

Clarendon No. 1. First shown by William Page in
Typographic Messenger during 1867. Lowercase is
missing.

ABCDEFGHIJK
LMNOPQRSTU
VWXYZ&&&&
1234567890$

French Clarendon. First shown by William Page in Typographic Messenger *during 1865. Lowercase is missing. Notice bracketed serifs. The two styles of French Clarendon and Antique were extremely popular* in poster printing during the last thirty years of the century. Of all wood types remaining, these styles and their variations probably constitute the largest bulk.

ABCDEFGHIJKLMN

OPQRSTUVWXYZ&

French Clarendon XXX Condensed, No. 117 (Page).
First shown by William Page in his Page's Wood Type
Album, July, 1879. Lowercase and figures are missing.

ABCDEFGHIJK
LMNOPQRSTU
VWXYZ&1245
67890$ abcdefg
hijklmnopqrst
uvwxyzßffiffifflfflffl

Egyptian. First listing by William Page in his 1870 specimens.

ABCDEF$
GHIJKL!
MNOPQR
STUVW!
XYZ&12
34567890

Norwich Aldine. First shown by William Page in his 1872 specimens. This design originated with the Page Company. Lowercase is missing. Heber Wells cut a style patterned after Page's, and these were the only two companies to market this design under this title.

ABCDEFGH
IJKLMNOP
QRSTUVW
XYZ&&&&12
34567890$!

French Clarendon No. 2. First shown as a wood type during the 1870's. This cutting by the Hamilton Company. Lowercase is missing. There were a number of variations of this style, but each modification was given a separate name or number. The cap on the capital "A" is a distinguishing trait for this group of letterforms.

ABCDEFGHIJ
KLMNOPQRS
TUVWXYZ&
&1234567890

Belgian. First listed by William Page in his 1870
specimens. Lowercase is missing.

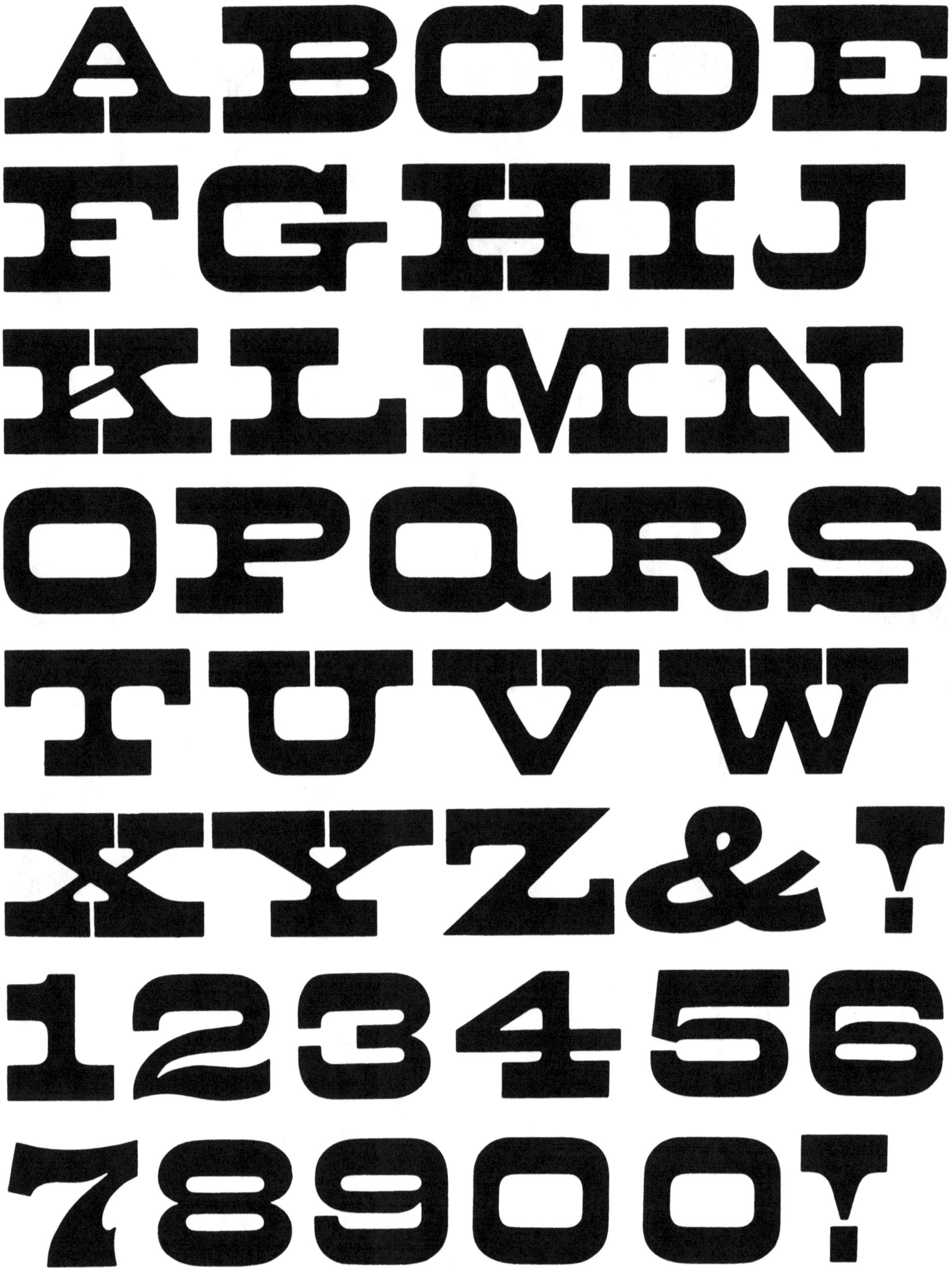

ABCDE
FGHIJ
KLMN O
OPQRS
TUVW
XYZ&!
123456
789 00!

Aldine Expanded. First shown by William Page in his 1872 specimens. This cutting by the Hamilton Company. Lowercase is missing. An even more extended style of this face was shown by Morgans & Wilcox during the 1880's.

ABCDEF
GHIJKL
MNOPQ!
RSTUV?
WXYZ&

Aldine. First listed by William Page in his 1870 specimens. Lowercase and figures are missing. A prominent display face from these years which probably originated as a wood type and with the Page Company.

ABCDEFG

HIJKLM !

NOPQRST

UVWXYZ

&1234567

890000$

Aldine Ornamented. First listed by William Page in his 1870 specimens. Lowercase not designed for this face. The design was patented by William Page, and it is the only known ornamented style of Aldine.

ABCDEFG
HIJKLMN
OPQRSTU
VWXYZ&a
bcdefghijkl
mnopqrstu
vwxyz fi ffl

Clarendon Extended. First shown by William Page in his
1859 specimens. This cutting by the Page Company.
Figures are missing.

ABCDE
FGHIJK
LMNOP
QRSTU
VWXYZ

Columbian. First listed by William Page in his 1870
specimens. Lowercase and figures are missing.

ABCDEF
GHIJK&
LMNOP
QRSTU
VWXYZ

Ionic. First shown by William Page in his 1859 specimens.
Lowercase and figures are missing. This design is one of
the most beautifully proportioned display faces from
the period.

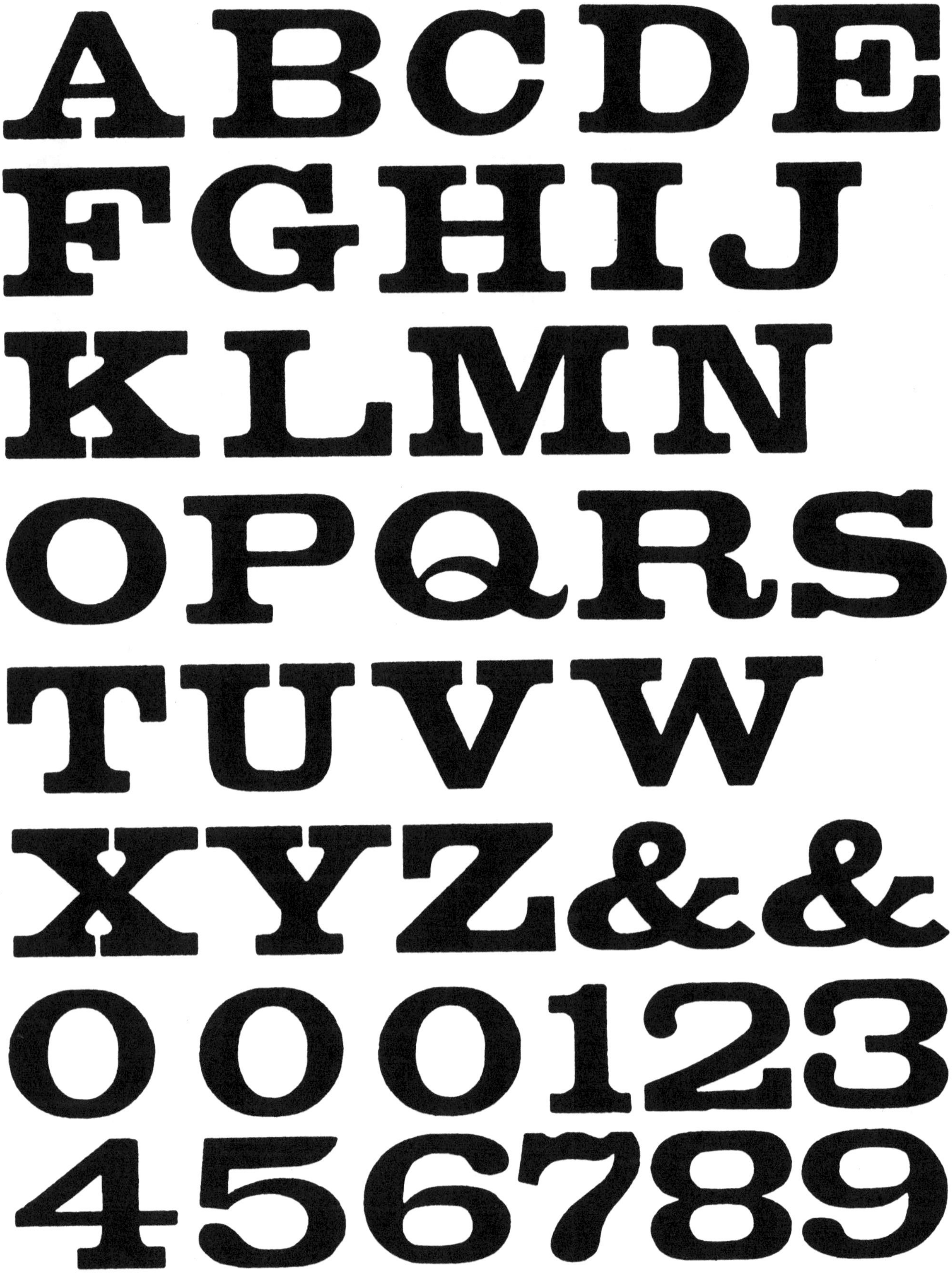

ABCDE
FGHIJ
KLMN
OPQRS
TUVW
XYZ&&&
OOO123
456789

Clarendon Extended. First shown by William Page in his
1859 specimens. This cutting by Hamilton Mfg. Company
(compare with Page specimen on page 267). Lowercase
is missing.

ABCDEF
GHIJKL
MNOPQR
STUVW
XYZ&Æ

Ionic Condensed. First listed by William Page in his 1865 specimens. This cutting by the Page Company. Lowercase and figures are missing.

ABCDEFG
HIJKLMN
OPQRSTU
VWXYZ&

Grecian Condensed. First shown by Wells & Webb in the
L. Johnson specimens for 1846. Lowercase and figures
are missing.

ABCDEFG
HIJKLMN!
OPQRSTUV
WXYZOOO

Grecian X Condensed. Lowercase and figures are missing. This cutting came from a country newspaper office in central Nebraska. The owner remembered his father telling of purchasing the type from salvage of a well-established newspaper shop in South Dakota that had burned in 1885. This type appears to have been carved entirely by hand. The Roman Extended shown was also purchased from the same source, but it was a machine-made type.

The heavy serifs on the middle arm of the capital "E" and "F" are characteristic of designs from early in the century; later, these serifs were minimized or, in some instances, eliminated.

ABCDEFGHIJKLMNO!

PQRSTUVWXYZ&1234

567890$abcdefghijklm

nopqrstuvwxyzﬀﬃﬄﬁﬀﬁ

*Clarendon XX Condensed. First shown by William Page
in his 1859 specimens. This cutting by the Page Company.
It is believed that this design originated as a wood type,
and with the Page Company.*

ABCDE
FGHIJ
KLMN
OPQRS
TUVW
XYZO

Full Faced Grecian. First listed by William Page in his 1859 specimens. This cutting by the Page Company. Lowercase and figures are missing. (Heber Wells never cut a lowercase for this design.) The Condensed styles of Grecian preceded by some fifteen years this full faced design. The Full Faced Grecian is believed to have originated as a wood type.

ABCDEFGHIJ

KLMNOPQRS

TUVWXYZ&1

234567890$

Grecian X Condensed. First shown by Wells & Webb in the L. Johnson specimens for 1846. Lowercase is missing.

ABCDEFGHIJ
KLMNOPQRS
TUVWXYZ&

Grecian XX Condensed. First shown by John Cooley in
his 1859 specimens. Lowercase and figures are missing.

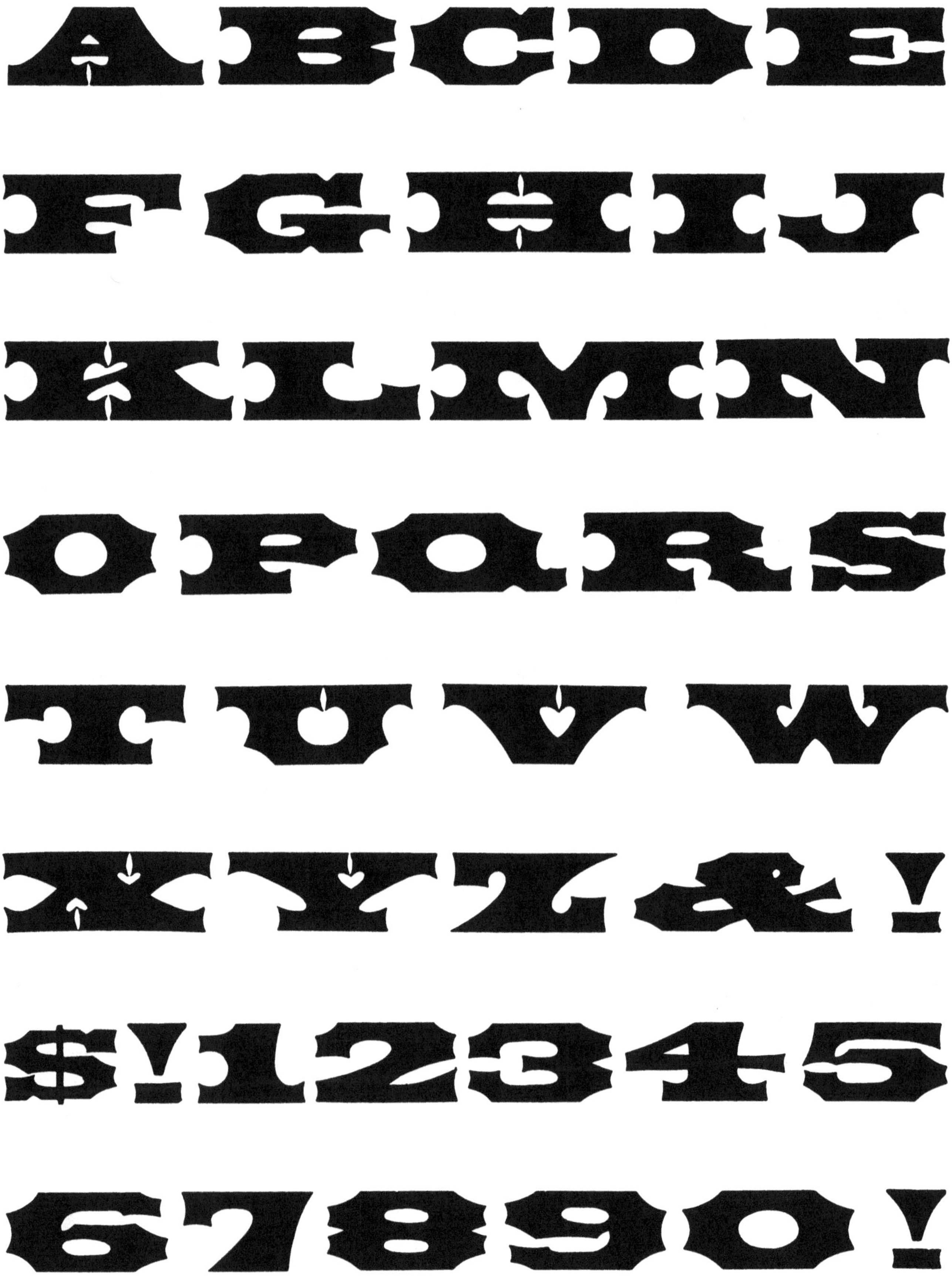

ABCDE
FGHIJ
KLMN
OPQRS
TUVW
XYZ&!
$¥12345
67890!

Antique Tuscan Expanded. First shown by Wells & Webb in their 1854 specimens. Lowercase is missing. This Expanded style did precede the Extended style shown on the opposite page.

ABCDE
FGHIJ
KLMN!
OPORS
TUVW
XYZ&!

Antique Tuscan Extended. First shown by Wells & Webb in their 1854 specimens. This cutting by the Hamilton Company. Lowercase and figures are missing. When this font of type was found, the capital "W" still had glued to its side a paper wrapper indicating the type was manufactured in 1881, the first year Hamilton was in business. This specimen is printed from a veneer type.

279

A B C D E
F G H I J
K L M N !
O P Q R S
T U V W !
X Y Z & &

Antique Tuscan. First shown by Wells & Webb in their 1849 specimens, without lowercase. Lowercase was first shown in their 1854 catalogue. Lowercase and figures are missing. This design was important in American typographic styling during the nineteenth century. It was especially popular with typefounders from 1860 to the end of the century. It is almost certain that the design originated as a wood type and with the Wells Company.

ABCDEFG
HIJKLM
NOPQRS
TUVWXY
Z&0123 4
567890$

Antique Tuscan Condensed. First shown by Wells &
Webb in their 1854 specimens. This cutting by the Page
Company. Lowercase is missing.

ABCDEFGH
IJKLMNOP
QRSTUVW
XYZÆ&&&

Antique Tuscan XX Condensed. First shown by John Cooley in his 1859 specimens. Lowercase was not always designed for this face.

ABCDE!
FGHIJK
LMNOP
QRSTU!
VWXYZ
&OOOO123
4567890

Antique Tuscan Outlined. First shown by William Page in his 1859 specimens. This cutting by Vanderburgh, Wells & Company. No lowercase was designed for this face. A six and eight line specimen of this design was shown by W. & H. **Hagar** *foundry in 1854. The price list carried a wood type font scheme, and it is thought they sold Wells' type, so this could easily be a wood type.*

A B C D E
F G H I J !
K L M N
O P Q R S
T U V W
X Y Z & 1
2 3 4 5 6 !
7 8 9 ! 0 $

Latin Extended. First shown by Hamilton in his 1888
specimens. This cutting by the Hamilton Company.
Lowercase is missing. Latin Extended may have originated
as a wood type even though the lighter styles came from
England and France during the 1860's.

ABCDEF
GHIJKL!
MNOPQR
STUVW$
XYZ1234
567890&

Peerless Condensed, Old Style Antique, No. 131 (Page).
First shown by William Page in Page's Wood Type
Album, October, 1879. Lowercase was not always
designed for this face.

ABCDEFG
HIJKLMN
OPQRSTU
VWXYZ&!

Latin, Peerless, Old Style Antique (this particular style, No. 129, is by Page). First shown by William Page in Page's Wood Type Album, *October, 1879. Lowercase and figures are missing.*

ABCDEF
GHIJKL$
MNOPQ!
RSTUVW
XYZ&123
4567890

No. 154. Patented by William Page in 1887. Lowercase
is missing. This is one of the seventeen styles designed
for the die-cut types of Page and Setchell.

ABCDEF
GHIJKL
MNOPQ
RSTUV!
WXYZ&

Tuscan Outlined. First shown by Wells & Webb in their
1849 specimens. Figures are missing, and no lowercase
was designed for this face. This design originated in
Europe and was very popular in England during the 1840's.

ABCDEFG
HIJKLMN
OPQRSTU
VWXYZ&!

Phanitalian, No. 132 (Page). First shown by William Page in Page's Wood Type Album, *October, 1879. Lowercase and figures are missing.*

ABCDEF
GHIJKL
MNOOO
PQRSTU
VWXYZ

No. 515. Patented by William Page in 1887. No lowercase
was designed for this face, and figures are missing. This
is one of the seventeen styles designed for the die-cut
types of Page and Setchell.

ABCDEFG
HIJKLMN
OPQRSTU
VWXYZ&!

Kurilian, Eureka. First shown as a wood type during the
1880's. Lowercase and figures are missing. The basic
design for this style came from Europe and was shown by
American typefounders during the mid-1850's.

ABCDEFGHIJ

KLMNOPQRS

TUVWXYZ&

1234567890$

Egyptian Ornamented. First listed by William Page in his 1870 specimens. This cutting by the Tubbs Company. Lowercase is missing. This design, and the one on the facing page, were widely used in the last twenty years of the century and are commonly associated with Frontier events—they appear on stage bills, " Wanted" posters, etc.

ABCDEFGHIJ
KLMNOPQRS
TUVWXYZ&12
34567890$ab
cdefghijklmnopq
rstuvwxyzflffffiffl

*Tuscan Egyptian. First shown during the 1880's. This
cutting is by the Hamilton Company.*

ABCDEFGHIJ

KLMNOPQRS

TUVWXYZ 12

34567890 $ $

No. 501. Patented by William Page in 1887. No lowercase
was designed for this face. This is one of the seventeen
styles designed for the die-cut types of Page and Setchell.

ABCDEFGHIJ
KLMNOPRS!
TUVWXYZ.&

Antique Tuscan No. 8. First shown by William Page in his 1859 specimens. This design was marketed only by Page and Cooley, and this particular cutting appears to be by the latter. This specimen was printed from types at Rochester Institute of Technology, Rochester, New York. No lowercase or figures were designed for this face.

ACDEFGHIJKL

MNOPQRSTU

VWXYZ&Œ'.,,,,

Antique Tuscan No. 1. First shown by William Page in his 1859 specimens. This cutting by Page and from types at Yale University. Lowercase and figures are missing.

Even though this design includes several characteristics of the European Tuscans, such as fish-tail serifs and median bulges, it is one of the American Tuscans.

ABCDE
FGHIJK
LMNO!
P&RST
UVWX
YZQ,·:

Octagon. First shown by George Nesbitt in his 1838 specimens. It is thought that a lowercase was never designed for this face, and figures are missing or were never designed. This design is probably the oldest shown here. The design is believed to have originated in France.

ABCDEF
GHIJKL
MNOPQ
RSTUV!
WXYZ&

Gothic. First shown by Leavenworth, circa 1837, in a condensed style, and shown by George Nesbitt in this style in his 1838 specimens. Lowercase and figures are missing. This heavy style of Gothic was not cast by American typefounders until very late in the nineteenth century.

ABCDE
FGHIJK
LMNOP
QRSTU
VWXYZ
&$!?&&
12345
67890

*Gothic Extended. This particular cutting made by the
Hamilton Company after 1900. Lowercase is missing.*

ABCD
EFGHI
JKLM
NOPQ
RSTU
VWXY
Z&123
4567
890$!

Gothic Extended. First shown by Wells & Webb in their
1840 specimens. Lowercase was not always designed for
this face; Allen showed first lowercase in 1850. It is
believed that this design originated as a wood type and
with the Wells Company.

ABCDEFG
HIJKLMN
OPQRST!
UVWXYZ
1234567
890 & & ?

Gothic Light Face. First shown by William Page in his 1859 specimens. This cutting is by the Hamilton Company. Lowercase is missing. Light face styles of Gothic, particularly the condensed designs, were revived in the late 1870's and used throughout the 1880's. The new light styles were well executed.

ABCDEFG
HIJKLMN
OPQRST!
UVWXYZ
12345678
90$&!OO

Gothic Condensed Outlined. First shown by Wells & Webb in their 1849 specimens. The first showings did not include a lowercase; however, later in the century a lowercase for this design was fairly common. This design was found in the specimens of George Bruce for 1837, and it is probable that he showed a wood type because of the size of the specimen. This design was cut as Comstock by the typefounders.

ABCDEF GHIJKLMNOP

QRSTUVWXYZ&1234

567890$?!abcdefgh

ijklmnopqrstuvwxyz

*Gothic Special. Designed and cut by the Hamilton
Company after 1900.*

ABCDEFGH
IJKLMNOP
QRSTUVW
XYZ&$123
4567890O

Gothic Condensed Light Face; No. 2 (Heber Wells);
Gothic Condensed No. 6 (Hamilton); No. 133 (Page).
This design first shown by Page in 1879. First example of
angling the corners on Gothic in this country by Leaven-
worth in the 1837 specimens, but the practice was not
common until the late 1870's. This design cut by American
Wood Type Company. Lowercase is missing.

ABCDEF
GHIJKL
MNOPQ
RSTUV!
WXYZ&

Gothic Round. First shown by George Nesbitt in his 1838 specimens. Lowercase and figures are missing. The Nesbitt design was an Outlined or Rimmed Gothic Round. The Caslon Foundry issued several Gothic Round designs, of which an ornamented one, in particular, came into general usage in America around mid-century.

ABCDEFGH
IJKLMNOP
QRSTUVW
XYZ & ?!! 12
34567890

Gothic Bold. First shown by Hamilton in his 1889
specimens. Lowercase is missing. Very similar to a curious
design included in the 1838 Nesbitt catalogue. The
Nesbitt design appears to have resulted from applying
the same modifications to the Gothic that had been
applied to Antique to create the Grotesque Italian.

ABCDEFGH
IJKLMNO
PQRSTUV
WXYZ&&

Modified Gothic XX Condensed. Design cut late in the
century. This cutting by the Tubbs Company. Lowercase
and figures are missing.

ABCDEFGHI
JKLMNOPQ
RSTUVWX!
YZZ&12345
67890Oabc
defghijklmn
opqrstuvwx
yzZ ffi fi ff ffi ffl

Concave Tuscan (often called Gothic Tuscan). This style
was preceded by the lighter and more condensed styles
which were first shown by Bill, Stark & Company in their
1853 specimens. This cutting by Vanderburgh, Wells &
Company.

ABCDEFG
HIJKLMN
OPQRST
UVWXYZ
&&-!!;;''

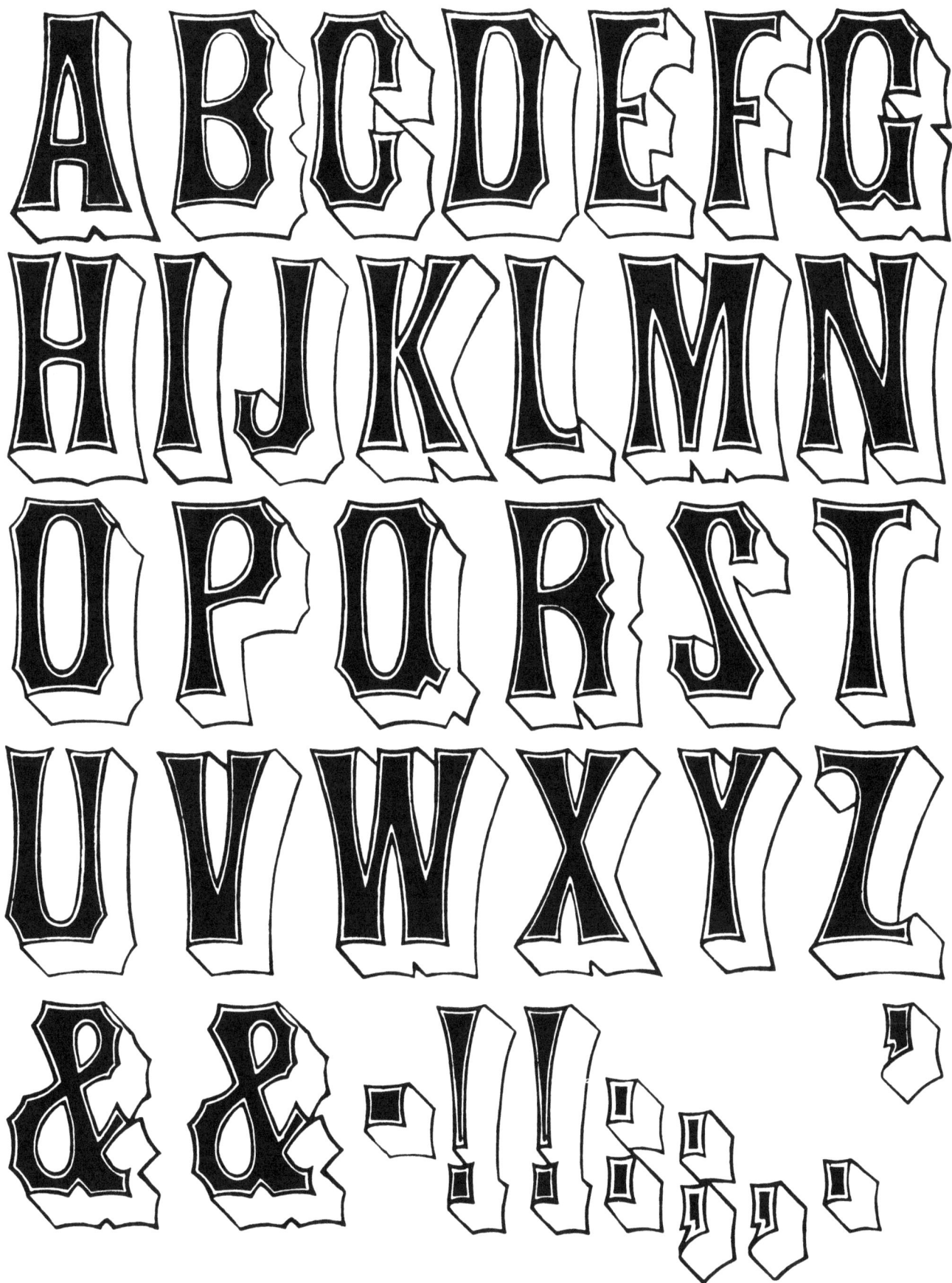

Concave Tuscan Open Shade. First shown by Bill, Stark & Company. This specimen printed from types at Rochester Institute of Technology, Rochester, New York. No lowercase was designed for this face, and figures are missing.

A B C D E F G
H I J K L M N
O P Q R S T U
V W X Y Z &
& . , ! ; : ?

Concave (Gothic) Tuscan Double Outlined Shade. First shown by William Page in his 1859 specimens in a slightly different ornamental style. This specimen printed from types in the Robinson-Pforzheimer Collection of the New York Public Library. No lowercase was designed for this face, and figures are missing. This design was shown by W. & H. Hagar in their 1854 specimens. The design was ten line, and it is thought to have been a wood type.

A B C D E F
G H I J K L
M N O P Q
R S T U V &
W X Y Z &

Concave Tuscan Condensed. First shown by Bill, Stark
& Company in their 1853 specimens. Lowercase and
figures are missing.

ABCDEFGHI
JKLMNOPQ
RSTUVWX?
YZ0S$!!&&
123456789

Concave Tuscan X Condensed. First listed by William
Page in his 1865 specimens. Lowercase is missing.

ABCDEFGH
IJKLMNOP
QRSTUVW
XYZ&123
4567890O

Concave Tuscan X Condensed Outline (Wells), No. 59
(Page). No lowercase was designed.

ABCDEFGHIJ

KLMNOPQRS

TUVWXYZ123

4567890$&!

Gothic Tuscan No. 1 (Page). First shown by William Page in his 1859 specimens. No lowercase was designed for this face.

ABCDEFGHIJ
KLMNOPQRS
TUVWXYZ&!!

Gothic Tuscan, Antique Tuscan, Antique Tuscan No. 9 (Page). First shown by William Page in his 1859 specimens. Lowercase and figures are missing.

ABCDEFG
HIJKLMN
OPQRST
UVWXYZ
&1234 56
7890$.!'•

No. 515. Patented by William Page in 1887. No lowercase
was designed for this face, and the figures are missing.
This is one of the seventeen styles designed for the
die-cut types of Page and Setchell.

ABCDEFG
HIJKLMN
OPQRSTU
VWXYZ!!
12345678
90&&&$

Gothic Tuscan Condensed. First shown by Wells & Webb in their 1849 specimens. First specimens included a Modulated Outline as well as solid face styles. A lowercase was not always designed for this face. Page cut some ornamental styles of this design for his 1859 specimens, and an Outlined, or Rimmed, design was popular in both metal and wood. Typefounders cast this design in several sizes during the 1850's. It is thought that the design originated as a wood type and with the Wells Company.

317

ABCDEF
GHIJKL
MNOPQ
RSTUV!
WXYZ&
ÆÆ.,;'-!!!

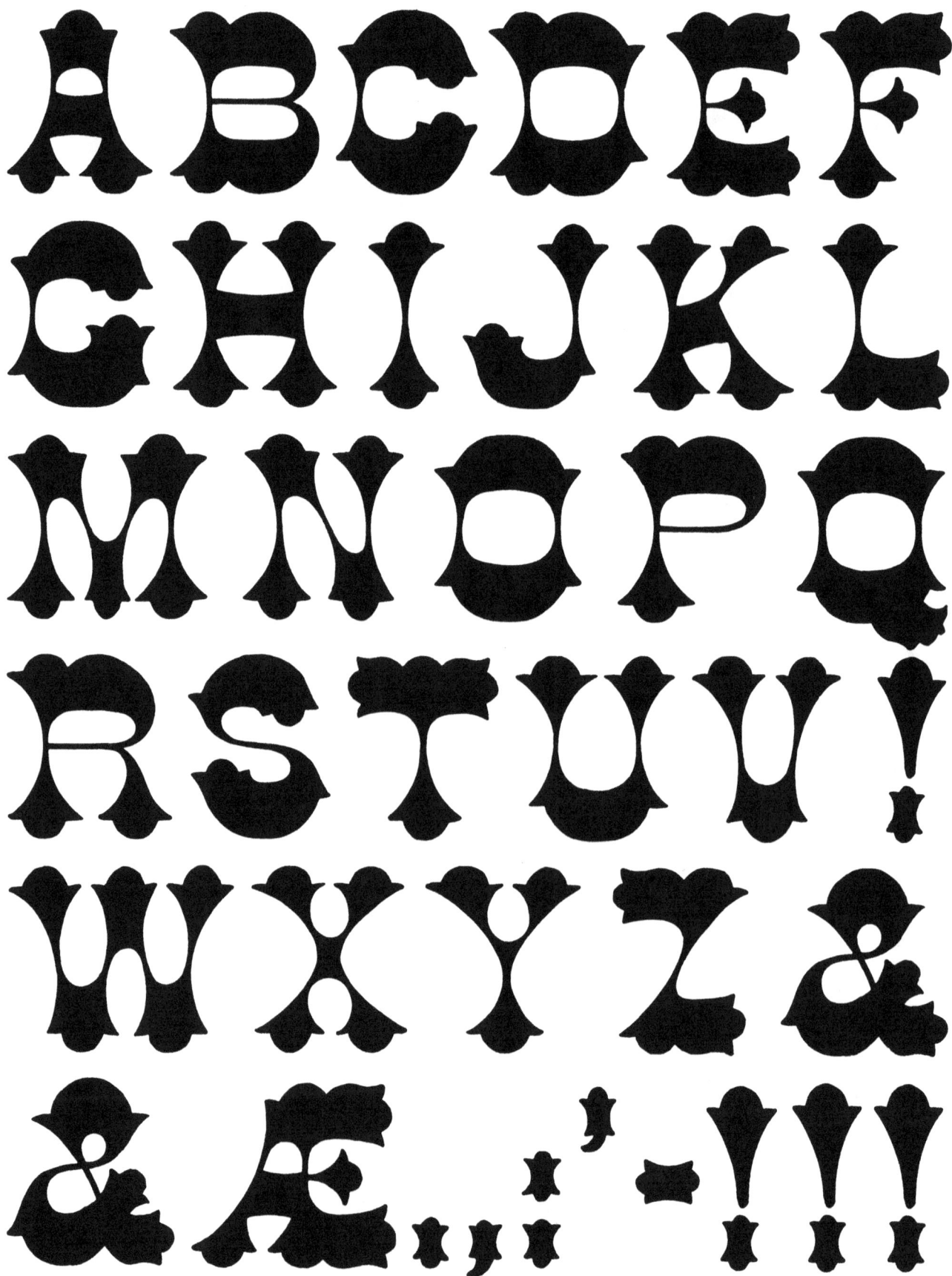

Gothic Tuscan Italian. First shown by Wells & Webb in their 1854 specimens. This specimen printed from stereotypes mounted on wood in the Robinson-Pforzheimer Collection of the New York Public Library.

It is believed that this design originated as a wood type and with the Wells Company. No lowercase was designed. This design was cast in small sizes by the typefounders.

ABCDEFGHIJ
KLMNOPQRS
TUVWXYZ&!
1234567890

Gothic Tuscan Pointed. First shown by William Page and
John Cooley in their 1859 specimens. Lowercase is
missing.

ABCDEFGH
IJKLMNOP
QRSTUVW
XYZ&1234
56789$!00

Tuscan Italian. First shown by William Page in his 1859 specimens. Lowercase was not designed for this face in every instance. This design was shown by Connor & Sons, in 1855, in a size which suggests that it was cut in wood.

ABCDEFG
HIJKLM!
NOPQRST
UVWXYZ

Gothic Tuscan Condensed No. 2 (Morgans & Wilcox),
No. 124 (Page). First shown by William Page in Page's
Wood Type Album, *July, 1879. A lowercase was not*
always designed for this face, and figures are missing.

ABCDEFGHI
JKLMNOPQ
RSTUVWXY
Z&&ffiffffifflffl
abcdefghijk
lmnopqrstuv
wxyz!!!!!!!!!!

No. 51 (Page), Mansard (Heber Wells). First shown by
William Page in his 1878 specimens. This cutting by the
Page Company. Figures are missing.

ABCDEFGHIJKL
MNOPQRSTUVW
XYZ&12345678
90$ Sabcdefghiikl
mnopqrstuvwxyz

Beveled, No. 142 (Page). First shown by William Page in
his 1882 specimens. This cutting by the Page Company.

ABCDEFG
HIJKLMN
OPQRSTU
VWXYZ&
&&&1234
567890$

No. 508. Patented by William Page in 1887. Lowercase is
missing. This is one of the seventeen styles designed for
the die-cut types of Page and Setchell.

ABCDEFGHIJ
KLMNOPQR
STUVWXYZ
!12345678
90$£2&&&

No. 510. Patented by William Page in 1887. Lowercase is missing. This is one of the seventeen styles designed for the die-cut types of Page and Setchell.

ABCDEF
GHIJKL
MNOPQ
RSTUV
WXYZ&

Gothic Tuscan Condensed No. 3 (Heber Wells), Antique
Tuscan No. 11 (Page), Antique Tuscan Condensed No. 11
(Morgans & Wilcox). First shown by William Page in his
1859 specimens. Lowercase and figures are missing.

ABCDEFG
HIJKLMN
OPQRSTUV
WXYZ&12
34567890

Runic. First shown by William Page in his 1859
specimens. Lowercase is missing.

ABCDEFGHIJ
KMNOPQRST
UVWYXZ&123
4567890abcd
efghijklmnooo
opqrstuvwxyz

No. 506. Patented by William Page in 1887. This is one
of the seventeen styles designed for the die-cut types of
Page and Setchell.

ABCDEFGH
IJKLMNOP
QRSTUVW
XYZ&&&12
34567890$

No. 500. Patented by William Page in 1887. Lowercase
is missing. This is one of the seventeen styles designed
for the die-cut types of Page and Setchell.

ABCDEF
GHIJKLM
NOPQRS
TUVWX
YZ&123
4567890

Courier. This design was cut only by Morgans & Wilcox,
so it must be dated after 1881. Lowercase is missing.

ABCDEFGHIJ
KLMNOPQRS
TUVWXYZ&$
1234567890abc
defghijklmnopq
rstuvwxyzflflffffi

Teutonic. First shown by William Page in his 1872 specimens.

ABCDEFGHIJKL
MNOPQRSTUV!
WXYZ&123456
7800000$abcd
efghijklmnopqr
stuvwxyzmmm

*Teniers, Unique (Heber Wells), No. 165 (Page). First
shown by Hamilton in his 1888 specimens.*

ABCDEFGHIJKLMN
OPQRSTUVWXYZ!
$&1234567890 abc
defghijklmnopqrs
tuvwxyzᴧᴧᴧᴧᴧᴧᴧ

Trenton. First shown by Hamilton in his 1889 specimens.
Hamilton cut one ornamental style of this face with an
open diamond and points at the median, and it was a
handsome design.

A B C D E F

G H I J K L

M N O P Q R

S T U V W

X Y Z & O !

Doric Chromatic. First shown in the 1850's as a wood type. Design was imported from Europe, most likely France, during the late 1840's. Lowercase and figures were not cut for this style.

ABCDEFG
HIJKLM!
NOPQRS?
TUVWX
YZ.,:;&

Venetian. First shown by George Nesbitt in his 1838
specimens. The design is believed to have originated in
France during the 1830's, and it quickly spread to
England (Blake & Stevenson, c. 1841) and America. No
lowercase or figures were designed for this face.

During 1959 when I first began researching wood types, there was no sense on my part for what was being sought or how to proceed. The involvement was without plan or objective. Initially, my inclination was to collect wood type for students to use in class, and later, to find answers for student questions regarding the wood types they were using. At the beginning, stimulus was clearly external rather than internal.

After a relatively short time, my "hunting instincts" were thoroughly aroused and my efforts to collect additional wood types intensified. As more fonts of wood type accumulated, I wanted to record them and began the process of printing 17 x 22 inch specimen sheets. I do not recall why, but from the beginning, the sheets were numbered. As pages were printed, I needed to find additional designs in order to print more pages.

After a period of time, I had acquired numerous boxes of wood type and printed a quantity of specimen pages, but I did not know the names of designs and where, when or who had made them. In short, I was printing a book regarding a subject that I knew absolutely nothing about.

As specimen sheets were printed, many factors such as duplicates, variations, completeness, condition or size of fonts among other considerations began to focus the search toward more specific objectives. In particular, some wood types carried a manufacturer's imprint, and I began to keep a careful record of imprints by different companies and variations. This raised even more questions. The interaction between collecting and recording fostered speculation and generated curiosity. It was becoming increasingly apparent that to make wood types more meaningful and to provide credibility for the collection, it was necessary to supplant speculation with fact. It was the desire to identify, describe and catalog what I had collected that channeled me into the search for information. Searching and collecting led to identifying and recording, and, for me, that was the foundation for research and everything else became elaboration.

Each of the activities involves process, and as one was refined or extended it impacted on the others. For instance, in acquiring new specimens I discovered from experience that: First, the most productive sources for wood types were small country printers or urban jobbers. It is characteristic for most printers who have storage space to never throw anything away. Next, most larger cities had firms that specialized in buying out entire shops and reselling the equipment and materials. Often it was possible to purchase quantities of type as a lot, complete with cabinets. The initial outlay was greater but unit cost would generally be low. Third, whenever on a trip, or sometimes on a nice day in the Spring, I would just take off traveling back roads going from one small town to another. My family hated to go on vacation with me because of stopping at every small town and checking printing shops while they waited in the car.

I quickly learned to know where to look for small town print shops—usually a block off main street. I always wore old clothes as I did not want to look like a "city slicker." I never parked the car in front of the shop so they could see my license plate. I always opened conversation by inquiring if they had any wood type. If the answer was affirmative, I asked to look at it. After examination, if the type was worth having, I inquired if they would be interested in *disposing* of the wood type. To ask if they would be willing to sell it created suspicion that I knew something they did not, and perhaps I was trying to take advantage of them. To ask if they were interested in *disposing* of the type left the door open for several options—to give it to me, to sell it to me or to consider trading it for another style. I had a number of duplicate fonts which were reserved just for trading.

Finally, if they would not dispose, sell, or trade for the type, I recorded the name, address and phone number of the print shop. I would contact them once or twice a year to see if they would let the type go. Sometimes it took three to five years before they would let me have it. Much of the time I could eventually persuade them to part company with the type.

The gathering of information gradually evolved into a pattern. My initial survey revealed that there were no books about wood type *per se*. Two of the most obvious sources for information were trade publications from the period and wood type specimen books. *Inland Printer* was perhaps the most useful of the trade publications. Although it was indexed, it required great patience to go through each copy year-by-year, month-by-month and page-by-page. There were some odds and ends of trade papers such as company newsletters but nothing as complete as *Inland Printer.*

To better understand wood type, it was necessary to know the evolution of metal type, printing, lettering and the use of wood in the history of printing. I was so ill at ease using libraries that I began collecting my own reference books. This was done through book dealers who specialized in out-of-print books on typography and printing such as Chiswick Book Shop and Kraus in New York City, Margaret in Detroit, Dawson in Los Angeles and a few others. By checking the bibliographies in the better reference books, I was able to make the best choices for my library.

Specimen books were especially informative—each one would reveal where the type was made, who manufactured it and what designs were available at that time. Many of the specimen books had brief introductions that gave some company history, information regarding new designs, manufacturing processes or equipment and branch offices.

I soon found that the largest number of specimen books were housed within Special Collections at Columbia University's Butler Library. On my whirlwind trips to New York City, I would always set aside a couple of hours to spend at the library going through the card catalog. I would call up a number of specimen books, examine them quickly, and if they looked good to me because of display or information, I marked them to be microfilmed. Newberry and Huntington libraries had some specimen books, and I made arrangements over the phone to have them microfilmed. On receipt of the microfilm copies, I sent them out to be printed to size and spiral bound. This gave me roughly seventy specimen books spanning the years between 1828 and 1906.

At the Hamilton Manufacturing Company, I located roughly thirty to forty old wood type specimen books from several different wood type manufacturers. I was permitted to take these catalogs to Minneapolis where I made 4 x 5 ortho negatives of all materials pertinent to the research. Arrangements were made with Hamilton to add the catalogs to the collection at Columbia which doubled the holdings of wood type specimen books.

In research, any body of concise, organized information is extremely important. Examination of specimen books provided me with the entry headings to search library catalogs, newspaper files, magazine indexes, trade directories, business records and so on. As bits and pieces of information were revealed, each provided additional avenues for search. Sometimes the information dove-tailed with other materials forming comprehensive segments. Other times information was disconnected and provocative. I found it rewarding to save every scrap of mystery information because almost always it became meaningful at some point in the future.

All my collected wood type was proofed and all the reference materials were gathered. Visual materials were recorded on 4 x 5 ortho negatives and indexed. I had photographed illustrations from microfilm, reference books, art work and reprographic copies. I had ordered photographs, retouched reprographic copies and microfilm from libraries and historical societies. I had typed a text which was regularly cut into sections so it could be rearranged. Corrections and insertions were typed on separate pieces of paper and attached to the manuscript. Periodically the entire manuscript was retyped, incorporating all the changes.

The collecting part of the research—both specimens and information—was done throughout the year. The enormous amount of photographic work was done during summer months when school photography labs were not in use. Much of the typing was done during school vacations. All in all, I spent about nine years preparing for publication, and it was another three years or so for the manuscript to go through editing and production. I also did the book design and key-lining. This was not only a labor of love, it also was hard, tedious labor—period!

Anyone who has gone through the research process has a keen appreciation for the precise and concise nature of cataloging and catalogs. When invited by staff at the *Silver Buckle Press* to write an introduction for their collection of wood types, I felt honored. It is an opportunity to express my view regarding the importance of such documentation, to me or to anyone doing research.

ROB ROY KELLY

Reprinted with permission from Specimen Book of Wood Type from the Collection of the Silver Buckle Press, *1999, courtesy of the Silver Buckle Press, University of Wisconsin-Madison.*

BIBLIOGRAPHY

Wood Type

(Allen, Edwin.) *"Description of Allen Spool Company,"* NORWICH BULLETIN (Norwich, Conn.), Jan. 21, 1881.
　"Edwin Allen, formerly of Norwich, was Wood Type Cutting Machine Inventor," NORWICH BULLETIN (Norwich, Conn.), July 25, 1922.
　"Edwin Allen," THE RED ENVELOPE (Worcester, Mass.), No. 17 (April, 1922); No. 19 (June, 1922).
　"The Allen Rotary Press," THE INLAND PRINTER (Chicago, Ill.) IV, No. 12 (Sept., 1887), 816.

Bayles, Richard M. (ed.). HISTORY OF WINDHAM COUNTY, CONNECTICUT. New York: W. W. Preston & Co., 1889. (P. 365, Horatio and Jeremiah Bill; pp. 299-301, Allen, Page and Tubbs.)

Bullen, Henry Lewis. *"Discursions of a Retired Printer: An Ideal American Citizen—the inventor of wood types and the routing machine, and his successor and competitors,"* THE INLAND PRINTER (Chicago, Ill.) XXXIX, No. 5 (Aug. 1907), 675-83.

Byers, Mark R. BIOGRAPHY OF J. E. HAMILTON. Two Rivers, Wisc.: Hamilton Manufacturing Co., 1932.

Carr, Horace. A VENERABLE FONT OF TYPE. Cleveland, Ohio: Published by the author, 1928. (Pamphlet listed in card index under DARIUS WELLS in Rare Book Room, New York Public Library.)

(Cooley, J. G.) Death of J. G. Cooley. NORWICH RECORD (Norwich, Conn.), April 7, 1909.
　Death of J. G. Cooley. NORWICH BULLETIN (Norwich, Conn.), April 8, 1909.
　"Cooley's proposed home for indigent printers," NORWICH BULLETIN (Norwich, Conn.), Aug. 13, 1874.
　"J. G. Cooley & Co.," THE PRINTER (New York), II, No. 11 (1859), 258.
　Articles by Cooley listed in card index of Connecticut Historical Society, Hartford, Conn., 1842-53.
　"New Publications," PRINTERS MONTHLY BULLETIN (Boston, Mass.), June, 1858.
　TYPOGRAPHIC MESSENGER (New York), IX, No. 3 (July, 1874).

(Day brothers manufactory.) *"First Wood Type Manufactory West of Allegheny Mountains was located in town of Fredericksburg"* (files in newspaper office, Fredericksburg, Ohio, name of paper unknown), June 14, 1919.
　"Wood Type," ROUNDS' PRINTERS' CABINET (Chicago, Ill.), May, 1857.
　First ad by W. T. & S. D. Day Co. following their purchase of J. D. Foster & Co.

DeVinne, Theodore. PLAIN PRINTING TYPES (*"The Practice of Typography"*). New York: Oswald Publishing Co., 1914. (P. 345, wood types.)

(Galvanized wood type.) THE INLAND PRINTER (Chicago, Ill.), V, No. 7 (April, 1888), 482.

GREAT INDUSTRIES OF THE UNITED STATES. Hartford, Chicago, and Cincinnati: J. B. Burr & Hyde, 1873. (Pp. 1265-71, wood type.)

(Hamilton, J. and Baker, W.) *"Dissolution of partnership between J. Hamilton and William Baker,"* THE INLAND PRINTER (Chicago, Ill.), VI, No. 24 (Jan., 1889), 351.

Hauenstein, Edward H. *"The Infancy of Wood Type West of the Alleghenies,"* THE INLAND PRINTER (Chicago, Ill.), LIV, No. 3 (Dec., 1919), 297-98 (Day Brothers).

Jacobi, C. T. PRINTER'S HANDBOOK OF TRADE RECIPES, ETC. London: The Chiswick Press, 1887. (P. 97, celluloid stereotypes.)

Kelly, Rob Roy. AMERICAN WOOD TYPES, 1828-1900. Kansas City: Published by the author, 1964. (Portfolio of specimens.)
　"American Wood Type," DESIGN QUARTERLY 56. Minneapolis, Minn.: Walker Art Center, 1963.
　"Wood Letters in the 20th Century," MATRIX 7. Rochester, N.Y.: Office of Educational Research, Rochester Institute of Technology, 1965.

Larned, Ellen D. HISTORY OF WINDHAM COUNTY, CONNECTICUT. Worcester, Mass.: Published by the author, printed by Charles Hamilton, 1880. (Pp. 516-17, 561).

Larson, Cedric. *"The Story of Wood Type,"* AMERICAN PRINTER AND LITHOGRAPHER, March, 1956, p. 28.

(Leavenworth and Webb.) *"The Old Factory on Doctor's Creek,"* ALLENTOWN MESSENGER (Allentown, N. J.), Nov. 10, 1904.

Loy, William E. *"Designers and Engravers of Type: William Page,"* THE INLAND PRINTER (Chicago, Ill.), XXII, No. 5 (Feb., 1899), 243.

Lyon, Peter. *"Isaac Singer and his Wonderful Sewing Machine,"* AMERICAN HERITAGE (New York), IX, No. 6 (Oct., 1958), 34. (Day Brothers.)

(Morgans, William T.; Morgans & Wilcox Mfg. Co.) *"A new manufacturing enterprise—Morgans & Wilcox Mfg. Co.,"* MIDDLETOWN DAILY PRESS (Middletown, N.Y.), July 28, 1880.
　Obituary notice for William T. Morgans, MIDDLETOWN DAILY PRESS (Middletown, N.Y.), April 15, 1882.
　An account of the life of William T. Morgans following his death on April 14, 1882, THE ORANGE (Middletown, N.Y.), 1882.
　"A wooden printing press," GAZETTE (Jarvis, N.Y.), n.d. (Article indicates that it was written shortly after Morgans' death, and that in addition to this article, there was a page 1 story on the death of William T. Morgans.)

(National Printers' Materials Co.; New York Celluloid Stereotype Co.) *"Gatherings,"* THE AMERICAN BOOKMAKER, April, 1886, p. 134.
　"Enameled Wood Type," Oct., 1887, p. 141.
　Enameled wood type (advertisement), THE INLAND PRINTER (Chicago, Ill.), V, No. 26 (July, 1888), 797.

(Page, William H.; Wm. H. Page & Co.; Wm. H. Page Wood Type Co.) *"Announcement of New Process Wood Type,"* THE INLAND PRINTER (Chicago, Ill.), V, No. 22 (Oct., 1887), 58.
　"Announcement of the sale of Wm. H. Page Wood Type Co. to Hamilton Mfg. Co., Two Rivers, Wisconsin," THE INLAND PRINTER (Chicago, Ill.), VIII, No. 23 (Jan., 1891), 472.
　Order for wood type whereby each letter incorporated 160 (square) feet of lumber, NORWICH BULLETIN (Norwich, Conn.), Sept. 31, 1871.
　"That font of wood type," ROUNDS' PRINTERS' CABINET (Chicago, Ill.), Nov., 1857, p. 1.
　"Page's Chinese Wood Type," NORWICH BULLETIN (Norwich, Conn.), Jan. 2, 1875.
　"Sale of William H. Page Wood Type Company to Hamilton Mfg. Co.," NORWICH BULLETIN, (Norwich, Conn.), Jan. 8, 1891.
　"Description of Wm. H. Page & Co. located at Greeneville, Conn." (reprint from Typographical Messenger), NORWICH BULLETIN, Aug. 30, 1869.
　"New Process Wood Type," THE AMERICAN BOOKMAKER, Sept., 1887, p. 93.
　"Seen and Heard," THE AMERICAN BOOKMAKER, May, 1888, p. 119.
　"Removal of a famous factory," THE AMERICAN BOOKMAKER, Jan., 1891, p. 29.
　Page's Wood Type Album (Norwich, Conn.), I, No. 1 (April, 1879); I, No. 2 (July, 1879); I, No. 3 (Oct., 1879). (After their purchase of the Page Co., Hamilton Mfg. Co. bound these three issues into a hard-cover book which was widely distributed.)
　Note: Information pertaining to Wm. H. Page's other business enterprises—Page Steam Heating, Combination Company, Page Boiler Company, etc.—is listed in NORWICH BULLETIN card files under Wm. H. Page Wood Type Co. and Page Boiler Company. Newspaper files also contain Norwich City Directories, beginning in 1857, and annually from 1861 through the wood type manufacturing period in Norwich.

Romaine, Lawrence B. A GUIDE TO AMERICAN TRADE CATALOGS: 1744-1900. New York: R. R. Bowker Co., 1960. (American Wood Type Co., p. 271; J. G. Cooley, p. 276; D. Knox, p. 281; Chesman, Nelson & Co., p. 275; William Page, p. 284; Hamilton, p. 279; Morgans & Wilcox, p. 283;

National Printer's Materials Co., p. 283; Tubbs & Co., p. 286; Wells & Webb, p. 286; Heber Wells, p. 287.)

Royle, Vernon. RETROSPECTIVE: HISTORY OF THE ROUTING MACHINE. Paterson, N. J.: Royle & Sons, 1918.

(Rubber coated wood type.) *"Improved wood type—Mr. Peter Gfroerer and his Rubber Coated Type,"* THE PRINTING TIMES AND LITHOGRAPHER, Oct., 1879, p. 223.

Trumbull, L. R. A HISTORY OF INDUSTRIAL PATERSON, NEW JERSEY. Paterson, N. J.: C. M. Herrick, 1882. (Vanderburgh, Wells & Co., Pp. 285-86.)

(Tubbs & Co.) THE INLAND PRINTER (Chicago, Ill.), XXXIX, No. 3 (June, 1907), 417.

(Vanderburgh, Wells & Co.) *"Vanderburgh, Wells & Co. move to new location at No. 8 Spruce St., New York City,"* THE AMERICAN BOOKMAKER, June, 1890, p. 161.
   "Dissolution of partnership between Mary Low, A. Vanderburgh and Heber Wells," THE INLAND PRINTER (Chicago, Ill.), IV, No. 16 (June, 1887), 637.
   "Fire in North Ward, Location Bobbin and Type Factory," newspaper identified only as "G" (Gazette?) (Paterson, N. J.), Feb. 22, 1867.

(Webb, E. R.; E. R. Webb & Co.)
"Death of E. R. Webb," THE PRINTER (New York), V, No. 7 (July, 1864) 103.
   Notice to the trade of partnership dissolvement, dated Oct. 13, 1862, TROW'S NEW YORK CITY DIRECTORY: 1863-64 (New York).
   Obituary, THE NEW YORK TIMES (New York), June 24, 1864.
   "Discursions of a Retired Printer," THE INLAND PRINTER (Chicago, Ill.), XXXIX, No. 29 (Sept., 1907).

(Wells, Darius.) PRINTER'S REVIEW (Boston, Mass.), Summer, 1888.
   "Wells and Bannan," TYPOGRAPHIC ADVERTISER (Philadelphia, Pa.), XI, Nos. 81-82 (Summer/Autumn, 1875), 1.
   "Obituary," THE TYPOGRAPHIC MESSENGER (New York), X, No. 2 (April, 1875), 14.
   "Darius Wells: Inventor of the Routing Machine," THE INLAND PRINTER (Chicago, Ill.), V, No. 26 (July, 1888), 778.

WINDHAM BI-CENTENNIAL, 1692-1892. Hartford, Conn.: The New England House Printing Co., 1893. (P. 74.)

(Wood type catalogues and publications.) CATALOGUE OF THE BOOKS IN THE LIBRARY OF THE TYPOTHETAE OF THE CITY OF NEW YORK. New York: Printed at De Vinne Press, 1896.

(Wood type manufacture.) *"The manufacture of wood type,"* THE INLAND PRINTER (Chicago, Ill.), VIII, No. 6 (March, 1891), 562-63.
   "History and Manufacture of Wood Type," THE TYPOGRAPHIC MESSENGER (New York), IV, No. 4 (July, 1869), 53-54.

Wood Type Patents

Gfroerer, P. Patent No. *217,607.* July 15, 1879, U. S. Patent Office, Washington, D. C.

McCreary, J. M. Patent No. *9454.* December 7, 1852, U. S. Patent Office, Washington, D. C.

Merritt, M. G. Patent No. *387,527.* August 7, 1888, U. S. Patent Office, Washington, D. C.

Moreau, Volney M. Patent No. *265,623.* October 10, 1882, U. S. Patent Office, Washington, D. C.

Page, William, and Setchell, G. C. Patent No. *375,008.* December 20, 1887, U. S. Patent Office, Washington, D. C.
____. Patent Nos. *402,850, 402,851,* and *402,852,* May 7, 1889, U.S. Patent Office, Washington, D. C.

Setchell, G. C. Patent No. *389,112.* September 4, 1888, U. S. Patent Office, Washington, D. C.
____. Patent No. *402,863.* May 7, 1889, U. S. Patent Office, Washington, D. C.

White, G. F. Patent No. *219,887.* September 23, 1879, U. S. Patent Office, Washington, D. C.

Wood Type Specimen Books: 1828-1918

AAS   *American Antiquarian Society, Worcester, Mass.*
ATF/CU   *Typographic Library and Museum of the American Type Founders Company, Special Collections, Columbia University, New York*
CHS   *Connecticut Historical Society, Hartford, Conn.*
HA   *Hamilton Manufacturing Company Archives, Two Rivers, Wisc.*
HLAM   *Henry E. Huntington Library & Art Museum, San Marino, Cal.*
MMA   *The Metropolitan Museum of Art, New York.*
NL   *Newberry Library, Chicago, Ill.*
NYPL   *New York Public Library, New York*

1828.   Darius Wells, 161 Broadway, New York. ATF/CU
1838.   July 1. George F. Nesbitt, Tontine Building, Wall & Water Streets, New York. ATF/CU
c. 1838. J. M. Debow, Allentown, New Jersey. NYPL (Rare Book Room)
1840.   Wells & Webb, 38 Ann Street, New York. ATF/CU
1841.   George F. Nesbitt, Tontine Building, Wall & Water Streets, New York. ATF/CU
1846.   L. Johnson, type founder, Philadelphia, Pa. (Wells & Webb specimens.) ATF/CU
1849.   April 28 (date hand inscribed). Wells & Webb, 18 Dutch Street, New York. ATF/CU
1853.   Bill, Stark & Company, Willimantic, Conn. ATF/CU
1854.   Wells & Webb, 18 Dutch Street, New York. ATF/CU; NL
1854.   E. R. Webb & Co., 18 Dutch Street, New York. (Same specimens as in the 1854 Wells & Webb catalogue.) ATF/CU
1858.   D. Knox & Co., Fredericksburg, Ohio. NL
1859.   October 1. Wm. H. Page & Co., Greeneville, Conn. ATF/CU
c. 1859-60. (dated 1850 by NL). John G. Cooley, South Windham, Conn. NL
1870.   October 1. Wm. H. Page & Co., Greenville, Conn. ATF/CU; HA
1872.   Dauchy & Co., 75 Fulton Street, New York. (Wm. H. Page & Co.) ATF/CU
1872.   August 1. Wm. H. Page & Co., Greeneville, Conn. ATF/CU; NYPL (Rare Book Room); HLAM
1873.   Wm. H. Page Co., Greeneville, Conn. ATF/CU
1874.   The Wm. H. Page Wood Type Co., Greeneville and Norwich, Conn. (Chromatic Types.) ATF/CU; NL (copy listed as c. 1875); MMA
1876.   The Wm. H. Page Wood Type Co., Norwich, Conn. ATF/CU; AAS
1877.   Vanderburgh, Wells & Co's., 110 Fulton, 16 & 18 Dutch Street, New York. ATF/CU
1878.   April 1. The Wm. H. Page Wood Type Co., Norwich, Conn. ATF/CU; HLAM
c. 1879   (dated by Huntington Library). American Wood Type Company, South Windham, Conn. HLAM
1879.   The Wm. H. Page Wood Type Co. (Page's Wood Type Album), Norwich, Conn. Book, Vol. 1, Nos. 1 & 2, ATF/CU; Nos. 1, 2 & 3, HA; Nos. 2, 3 and 4, HLAM
1881.   Morgans & Wilcox Manufacturing Co., Middletown, New York. ATF/CU
After 1881. Morgans & Wilcox Manufacturing Co., Middletown, New York. ATF/CU
c. 1881-85. Hamilton & Katz, Two Rivers, Wisc. (Holly Wood Type.) ATF/CU; NYPL (Rare Book Room)
1882.   The Wm. H. Page Wood Type Co., 108-116 Franklin Street, Norwich, Conn., and 61 Beekman Street, New York. ATF/CU
1883.   January 1. American Wood Type Co., South Windham, Conn. NL
1883.   The Wm. H. Page Wood Type Co., 200-202 Clark Street, Chicago, Illinois. (Specimens for sale by Schniedewend & Lee.) ATF/CU

1884.   Allison & Smith (dealer outlet), Cincinnati, Ohio. HLAM
1884.   Hamilton & Katz, Two Rivers, Wisc. NL
1884.   Morgans & Wilcox Manufacturing Co., Middletown, New York. ATF/CU
c. 1884-90. Morgans & Wilcox Manufacturing Co., Middletown, New York. NL
1886.   Tubbs & Company, South Windham, Conn. CHS
1887.   National Printers' Materials Co., 279 Front Street, New York, NL
1887.   Vanderburgh, Wells & Co's., 110 Fulton Street, 16 & 18 Dutch Street, New York. ATF/CU
1887.   May 1. Hamilton & Baker, Two Rivers, Wisc. (Holly Wood Type.) ATF/CU
After 1887. Nelson Chesman & Company, St. Louis, Mo. (dealer catalogue). HLAM
1888.   The Wm. H. Page Wood Type Co., 108-116 Franklin Street, Norwich, Conn. ATF/CU
1888.   Sept. 1. Hamilton & Baker, Two Rivers, Wisc. ATF/CU
1889.   March 1. The Hamilton Mfg. Co., Two Rivers, Wisc., and 259 Dearborn Street, Chicago, Ill. ATF/CU
1889.   Aug. 1. The Hamilton Mfg. Co., Two Rivers, Wisc., and 259 Dearborn Street, Chicago, Ill. ATF/CU
1890.   January. The Wm. H. Page Wood Type Co., 286-296 Franklin Street, Norwich, Conn. (New process wood type—die cut.) ATF/CU
1890.   Chesman, Nelson & Co. (National Printers' Materials Co.), Chicago, Ill. (Enameled wood type.) HLAM
1890.   Heber Wells & Co., 8 Spruce Street, New York. ATF/CU
1890.   Morgans & Wilcox Manufacturing Co., Middletown, New York. ATF/CU
1890.   The Wm. H. Page Wood Type Co. 286-296 Franklin Street, Norwich, Conn. (End cut types.) HA
1891.   Heber Wells & Co., 8 Spruce Street, New York. NL
1891.   The Hamilton Mfg. Co., Two Rivers, Wisc. AAS
After 1891. Golding & Company (dealer outlet). HLAM
1892.   Jan. 1. The Hamilton Mfg. Co., Two Rivers, Wisc.; 327-329 Dearborn Street, Chicago, Ill.; and 16, 18, & 20 Chambers Street, New York. ATF/CU
1892.   Jan. 1. The Hamilton Mfg. Co., Two Rivers, Wisc.; 327-329 Dearborn Street, Chicago, Ill.; and 16, 18, & 20 Chambers Street, New York. (Large wood type.) ATF/CU
1892.   The Hamilton Mfg. Co., Two Rivers, Wisc.; 327-329 Dearborn Street, Chicago, Ill.; and 16, 18, & 20 Chambers Street, New York. (New process wood type.) ATF/CU; NYPL (Rare Book Room) New York. ATF/CU
1895.   Heber Wells & Co., 157-59 William Street, New York. ATF/CU
1895.   The Hamilton Mfg. Co., Two Rivers, Wisc. ATF/CU
1895.   Oct. 1. The Hamilton Mfg. Co., Two Rivers, Wisc. ATF/CU
c. 1900.   Tubbs & Co. CHS
1900.   The Hamilton Mfg. Co., Two Rivers, Wisc. and Middletown, New York. ATF/CU
1901.   September. The Hamilton Mfg. Co., Two Rivers, Wisc. and Middletown, New York. ATF/CU
1906.   The Hamilton Mfg. Co., Two Rivers, Wisc. ATF/CU
1918.   The Hamilton Mfg. Co., Two Rivers, Wisc. (Tubbs Mfg. Co., Ludington, Mich., specimens.) ATF/CU

Metal Type: Manufacture and History

Berry, W., Johnson, A. F., and Jaspert, W. P. THE ENCYCLOPAEDIA OF TYPE FACES. London: Blanford Press, 1958.

Bruce, George. "Art of Type Founding," THE PRINTER (New York), I, No. 12 (April, 1859); I, No. 1 (May, 1858); IV, No. 3 (February, 1862).

Bullen, Henry Lewis. DUPLICATES OF THE TYPE SPECIMEN BOOKS, ETC., UNITED STATES AND FOREIGN FOR SALE BY THE TYPOGRAPHIC LIBRARY AND MUSEUM OF THE AMERICAN TYPE FOUNDERS COMPANY. Jersey City, N. J., October, 1934.
     "Discursions of a retired printer;—Revolution in typographical display from the ornamental to the masculine...," THE INLAND PRINTER (Chicago, Ill.), XXXIX, No. 3 (June, 1907), 353-59.
     "Discursions of a retired printer;—Illustrations of the progress of American type design from 1870-1890...," THE INLAND PRINTER (Chicago, Ill.), XXXIX, No. 2 (May, 1907), 193-98.
     "Discursions of a retired printer;—Development of body types and job or display types from 1450 to 1870 briefly sketched...," THE INLAND PRINTER (Chicago, Ill.), March, 1907.

Carter, Thomas Francis. THE INVENTION OF PRINTING IN CHINA AND ITS SPREAD WESTWARD. Revised by Carrington Goodrich. New York: The Ronald Press Co., 1955.

(Decorative typography.) "Decorative Typography," THE PRINTER (New York), IV, No. 3 (February, 1862), 35.
     "New Egyptian Border," TYPOGRAPHIC ADVERTISER (Philadelphia, Pennsylvania), XXVI, Nos. 103-104 (Spring, 1881).

Denman, Frank. THE SHAPING OF OUR ALPHABET. New York: Alfred A. Knopf, 1955.

De Vinne, Theodore. TITLE PAGES: PLAIN PRINTING TYPES ("The Practice of Typography"). New York: The Century Company, 1902.
——. THE INVENTION OF PRINTING. New York: Francis Hart & Company, 1876.
——. TYPES OF THE DE VINNE PRESS. New York: The De Vinne Press, 1907.
——. TITLE PAGES AS SEEN BY A PRINTER. New York: The Grolier Club, 1901.
——. SPECIMENS OF QUAINT TYPES. New York: The De Vinne Press, 1883.

Dowding, Geoffrey. AN INTRODUCTION TO THE HISTORY OF PRINTING TYPES. London: Wace & Company, Ltd., 1961.
(Early American typefounders.) "James Connor," THE PRINTER (New York), II, No. 1 (May, 1859).
     "David Bruce, Sr.," THE PRINTER (New York), I, No. 11 (March, 1859).
     "George Bruce," TYPOGRAPHIC ADVERTISER (Philadelphia, Pennsylvania), XII, No. 1 (October, 1866).

(Fancy rule composition.) "Contrasted Styles," AMERICAN ART PRINTER (New York), XI, No. 2 (March/April, 1888).

Fern, Alan. "Old fashioned types and new fangled typography," TYPOGRAPHICA 14. Bedford Square, London, n.d., pp. 27-31.

Grabhorn, Robert. NINETEENTH CENTURY TYPES. San Francisco: Grabhorn Press, 1959.

Gray, Nicolette. LETTERING ON BUILDINGS. New York: Reinhold, 1960.
——. XIXTH CENTURY ORNAMENTED TYPES AND TITLE PAGES. London: Faber & Faber, Ltd., 1938.

Green, Ralph. "Collectors compile list of 19th Century (American) Type Specimen Books," NEW ENGLAND PRINTER, April, 1952, pp. 74-76.

Gress, Edmond G. FASHIONS IN AMERICAN TYPOGRAPHY, 1870-1930. New York: Harper and Bros., 1931.

Hlavsa, Oldrich. A BOOK OF TYPE AND DESIGN. New York: Tudor Publishing Company, 1960.

Hutchings, R. S. ALPHABET. Birmingham, England: Kynoch Press, 1964.
——. A MANUAL OF DECORATED TYPEFACES. New York: Hastings House Publishers, 1965.

Johnson, A. F. TYPE DESIGNS, THEIR HISTORY AND DEVELOPMENT. London: Grafton & Co., 1951.
——. "Fat faces, their history, forms and use," ALPHABET & IMAGE NO. 5 (London), September, 1947, pp. 43-55.

Legros, L. A., and Grant, J. C. TYPOGRAPHICAL PRINTING-SURFACES. London: Longmans, Green & Co., 1916.

Lindegren, Erik. ABC OF LETTERING AND PRINTING TYPES. Vol. C, New York: Museum Books, Inc., 1965.

Loy, William E. *"Designers and Engravers of Type: The Early American representatives of the letter cutter's art,"* THE INLAND PRINTER (Chicago, Ill.), XXIV, No. 5 (February, 1900), 709.
____.*"Designers and Engravers of Type: John Wehrle,"* THE INLAND PRINTER (Chicago, Ill.), XXIV, No. 6 (March, 1900), 852.
____.*"Designers and Engravers of Type: Samuel Sawyer Kilburn,"* THE INLAND PRINTER (Chicago, Ill.), XXII, No. 2 (November, 1898), 185.
____. *"Designers and Engravers of Type: David Bruce,"* THE INLAND PRINTER (Chicago, Ill.), XXII, No. 6 (March, 1899), 701.
____. *"Designers and Engravers of Type: Edward Ruthven,"* THE INLAND PRINTER (Chicago, Ill.), XXIII, No. 1 (April, 1899), 64.
____. *"Designers and Engravers of Type: Julius Herriet, Sr.,"* THE INLAND PRINTER (Chicago, Ill.) XXII, No. 4 (January, 1899), 465.
____. *"Designers and Engravers of Type: T. Lounsbury,"* THE INLAND PRINTER (Chicago, Ill.), XXIII, No. 2 (May, 1899), 216.

McLean, Ruari. *"An Examination of Egyptians,"* ALPHABET & IMAGE NO. 1. London, 1946, pp. 39-51.

McMurtrie, Douglas C. THE BOOK, THE STORY OF PRINTING & BOOKMAKING, New York, London, Toronto: Oxford University Press, 1957.

Mores, Edward Rowe. A DISSERTATION UPON ENGLISH TYPOGRAPHICAL FOUNDERS AND FOUNDRIES. Edited and with introductory notes by Harry Carter and Christopher Ricks. London: Orford University Press, 1961.

Mosley, James. *"English Vernacular,"* MOTIF (Winter, 1963-64).
____. *"The Nymph and the Grot: The Revival of the Sanserif Letter,"* TYPOGRAPHICA 12 (December, 1956).

Parker, Mike. *"Punches and Matrices of the Museum Plantin-Moretus,"* PRINTING & GRAPHIC ARTS, VI, No. 3 (September, 1958).

Phillips, F. N. PHILLIPS' OLD FASHIONED TYPE BOOK. New York: Frederick Nelson Phillips, Inc., 1945.

Reed, T. B. A HISTORY OF THE OLD ENGLISH LETTER FOUNDRIES. Edited by A. F. Johnson. London: Faber & Faber, Ltd., 1952.

Ringwalt, Luther J. AMERICAN ENCYCLOPAEDIA OF PRINTING. Philadelphia: Menamin & Ringwalt, 1871. (Pp. 253-57, job letter; p. 503, wood type.)

Scarfe, Laurence. ALPHABETS. London: B. T. Batsford, 1954.

Silver, Rollo G. TYPEFOUNDING IN AMERICA, 1787-1825. Charlottesville, Virginia: University of Virginia Press, 1965.

Steinberg, S. H. FIVE HUNDRED YEARS OF PRINTING. London: Faber & Faber, Ltd., 1959.

TWO CENTURIES OF TYPEFOUNDING. London: H. W. Caslon & Co., printed by George W. Jones, 1920.

Updike, D. B. PRINTING TYPES, THEIR HISTORY AND USE. 2 vols. Cambridge, Mass.: Harvard University Press, 1951.

Wroth, Lawrence C. THE COLONIAL PRINTER. Charlottesville, Virginia: University of Virginia Press, 1938.

1. Binny and Ronaldson, 1809-1812, Philadelphia, Pa.
2. R. Starr & Co., 1826, Albany, N. Y.
3. Boston Type and Stereotype Foundry, 1828, Boston, Mass.
4. E. White, 1829, New York, N. Y.
5. George Bruce, 1831, New York, N. Y.
6. Baltimore Type Foundry, 1832, Baltimore, Md.
7. Johnson & Smith, 1834, Philadelphia, Pa.
8. New England Type Foundry, 1834, Boston, Mass.
9. White, Hagar & Co., 1835, New York, N. Y.
10. Robb & Ecklin, 1836, Philadelphia, Pa.
11. Conner & Cooke, 1836, New York, N. Y.
12. George Bruce & Co., 1837, New York, N. Y.
13. Boston Type and Stereotype Company, 1837, Boston, Mass.
14. New England Type and Stereotype Foundry, 1838, Boston, Mass.
15. John T. White, 1839, New York, N. Y.
16. Johnson & Smith, 1841, Philadelphia, Pa.
17. George Bruce & Co., 1842, New York, N. Y.
18. Samuel N. Dickinson, 1842, Boston, Mass.
19. Alexander Robb, 1844, Philadelphia, Pa.
20. L. Johnson, 1844, Philadelphia, Pa.
21. Boston Type and Stereotype Company, 1845, Boston, Mass.
22. John T. White, 1845, New York, N. Y.
23. L. Johnson & Co., 1847, Philadelphia, Pa.
24. Samuel Dickinson, 1847, Boston, Mass.
25. George Bruce & Co., 1848, New York, N. Y.
26. John T. White, 1849, New York, N. Y.
27. Lewis Pelouze, 1849, Philadelphia, Pa.
28. L. Johnson & Company, 1849, Philadelphia, Pa.
29. James Conner & Son, 1850, New York, N. Y.
30. William Hagar, 1850, New York, N. Y.
31. New England Type & Stereotype Foundry, 1851, Boston, Mass.
32. L. Johnson & Co., 1853, Philadelphia, Pa.
33. George Bruce, 1853, New York, N. Y.
34. Baltimore Type and Stereotype Foundry, 1854, Baltimore, Md.
35. W. & H. Hagar, 1854, New York, N. Y.
36. James Conner & Sons, 1855, New York, N. Y.
37. L. Johnson & Co., 1856, Philadelphia, Pa.
38. Boston Type Foundry, 1856, Boston, Mass.
39. Wm. Hagar, Jr. & Co., 1858, New York, N. Y.
40. Dickinson Type Foundry, 1859, Boston, Mass.
41. James Conner & Sons, 1859, New York, N. Y.
42. Boston Type Foundry, 1860, Boston, Mass.
43. Wm. Hagar, Jr. & Co., 1860, New York, N. Y.
44. Farmer, Little & Co., 1862, New York, N. Y.
45. Bruce's New York Type Foundry, 1865, New York, N. Y.
46. Dickinson Type Foundry, 1867, Boston, Mass.
47. Boston Type Foundry, 1867, Boston, Mass.
48. MacKellar, Smiths & Jordan, 1868, Philadelphia, Pa.
49. Farmer, Little & Company, 1868, New York, N. Y.
50. Bruce's New York Type Foundry, 1869, New York, N. Y.
51. James Conner's Sons, 1870, New York, N. Y.
52. Boston Type Foundry, 1871, Boston, Mass.
53. Farmer, Little & Co., 1874, New York, N. Y.
54. James Conner's Sons, 1876, New York, N. Y.
55. Farmer, Little & Co., 1878, New York, N. Y.
56. Bruce's New York Type Foundry, 1882, New York, N. Y.
57. Farmer, Little & Co., 1884, New York, N. Y.
58. James Conner's Sons, 1885, New York, N. Y.
59. Marder, Luse & Co. Foundry, 1893, Chicago, Ill.

Typefounder's Specimen Books: 1809-1893

The following list of type specimen books represents those catalogues consulted in detail and believed by the author to be pertinent to the text. The majority of these catalogues may be found in Special Collections, Columbia University, and a very few are in the library of the author.

Decorative and Ornamental Letters

Astle, Thomas. THE ORIGIN AND PROGRESS OF WRITING. London: Chatto and Windus, 1876.

Bernard, Auguste. GEOFROY TORY. Translated by George B. Ives. New York and Boston: Riverside Press, 1909.

Doede, Werner. THE BIBLIOGRAPHY OF GERMAN CALLIGRAPHIC BOOKS. Hamburg, Germany, 1958.

Lehmann-Haupt, Hellmut. PETER SCHOEFFER OF GERNSHEIM AND MAINZ. Rochester, N. Y.: Leo Hart, 1950. (Reference to large wood-cut and metal initials used by Gutenberg and Schoeffer.)

Morison, Stanley. *"Decorated Types,"* FLEURON NO. 6 (London), 1928.

Morison, Stanley, and Meynell, Francis. *"Printer's Flowers and Arabesques,"* FLEURON NO. 1 (London), 1923.

Nash, Ray. CALLIGRAPHY & PRINTING IN THE SIXTEENTH CENTURY. Antwerp: The Plantin-Moretus Museum, 1964.

Nesbitt, Alexander. 200 DECORATIVE TITLE PAGES. New Yorker: Dover Publications, Inc., 1964.
____. DECORATIVE ALPHABETS AND INITIALS. New York: Dover Publications, Inc. 1959.

Ryder, John. A SUITE OF FLEURONS. London: Phoenix House Ltd., 1957.

Shaw, Henry. THE HAND BOOK OF MEDIAEVAL ALPHABETS AND DEVICES. London: Henry George Bohn, 1856.

Smith, Percy. *"Initial Letters in the Printed Book,"* FLEURON NO. 1 (London), 1923.

Springer, Jaro. ALPHABETS GOTHIQUES. Paris, 1897.

Strange, Edward F. ALPHABETS. London and New York: George Bell & Sons, 1907.

Decorated Letters: Writing and Lettering Manuals

Ames, D. T. AMES' ALPHABETS. New York, 1879.
____. AMES' BOOK OF FLOURISHES. New York, 1890.
____. AMES' GUIDE TO SELF INSTRUCTION IN PRACTICAL AND ARTISTIC PENMANSHIP. New York, c. 1882.

Barbini, Carlo. ALFABETI FANTASIA. Milano, n.d. (c. 1870).

Becker, George J. BECKER'S ORNAMENTAL PENMANSHIP AND DRAUGHTSMAN'S LETTER BOOK. Philadelphia, Pa., 1854.

Boyce, A. P. THE ART OF LETTERING. Boston, Mass., 1878.

Copley, Fred S. COPLEY'S PLAIN & ORNAMENTAL STANDARD ALPHABETS. New York: George Woodward, 1877.

Dearborn, N. S. AMERICAN TEXT BOOK FOR LETTERS. Boston, 1873.

Delamotte, F. EXAMPLES OF MODERN ALPHABETS, PLAIN AND ORNAMENTAL. London: Crosby Lockwood & Son, 1906.

Fugger, Wolffgang. HANDWRITING MANUAL: A PRACTICAL AND WELL-GROUNDED FORMULARY FOR DIVERS FAIR HANDS. Nuremberg, 1553. (Facsimile by Oxford Press, London, 1960.)

Gerlach, Martin. ALPHABET ORNE. Vienna, 1898.

Keuffel and Esser Company. DRAUGHTSMAN'S ALPHABETS. New York, 1887.

Knowles & Maxim. REAL PEN WORK, SELF INSTRUCTOR IN PENMANSHIP. Pittsfield, Mass., 1881.

Leadenhall Press. BOOK OF ALPHABETS, PLAIN & ORNAMENTAL. London, n.d. (c. 1900).

Mettenleiter, Johann. SCHRIFTARTEN. Munchen, c. 1840.

Midolle, Jean. OEUVRES DE JEAN MIDOLLE: ECRITURES MODERNES. Strasbourg, 1834-35.

Petzendorfer, Ludwig. SCHRIFTEN ATLAS. Stuttgart: Hoffman, 1894.

Schwandner, Johann G. CALLIGRAPHIA LATINA. (Facsimile by Dover Publications, Inc., New York, 1958.)

Taber-Prang Art Company, PRANG'S STANDARD ALPHABETS. Springfield, Mass., 1901.

Van Thielen. NOUVEAU RECUEIL DE PRINCIPES ET DE MODELES L'ECRITURES. Bruxelles, 1840.

Williams & Packard. GEMS OF PENMANSHIP. New York, 1866.

Wyss, Urbanus. LIBELLUS VALDE DOCTUS, ELEGANS & UTILIS, MULTA & UARIA SCRIBENDUM LITERARUM GENERA COMPLECTENS. Zurich, 1549. (Fragments.)

The Trades

Adams, Thomas F. TYPOGRAPHIA. Philadelphia and Pittsburgh: James Kay, Jr. & Brothers, 1845.

AMERICAN CUT BOOK. Jersey City, N. J.: American Type Founders Co., 1900.

Ashton, John. A HISTORY OF ENGLISH LOTTERIES. London: The Leadenhall Press, Ltd., c. 1885.

Bewick, Thomas. A MEMOIR OF THOMAS BEWICK. London: Longman, Green, Longman and Roberts, 1862.

Burr, A. M. LIFE AND WORKS OF ALEXANDER ANDERSON, M.D. New York: Burr Brothers, 1893.

CATALOGUE OF MACHINERY AND MATERIALS FOR ENGRAVERS, LITHOGRAPHERS. London: Hughes & Kimber, c. 1875.

De Vinne, Theodore. PRINTING IN THE NINETEENTH CENTURY. New York: Lead Mould Electrotype Foundry, Inc., 1924.

(Disagreement between typefounders and advertising agents.) *"To the Printers of the United States,"* TYPOGRAPHIC MESSENGER (New York), VII, No. 1 (Jan. 1872), 1. *"Advertising Agents in Conclave,"* TYPOGRAPHIC MESSENGER (New York), VIII, No. 2 (April, 1873).

Eckman, Dr. Ralph. THE HERITAGE OF THE PRINTER. Vol. I. Philadelphia: North American Publishing Co., 1965.

Fowler, Nathaniel C. ABOUT ADVERTISING AND PRINTING. Boston: A. M. Thayer and Co., 1889.

Green, Ralph. A HISTORY OF THE PLATEN JOBBER. Chicago: Printing Office of Philip Reed, 1953.

Hackleman, Charles W. COMMERCIAL ENGRAVING AND PRINTING. Indianapolis: Commercial Engraving Publishing Co., 1921.

Jackson, John, and Chatto, W. A. HISTORY OF WOOD ENGRAVING. London: Henry George Bohn, 1861.

Jacobi, Charles T. THE PRINTERS' HANDBOOK OF TRADE RECIPES, HINTS AND SUGGESTIONS. London: Chiswick Press, 1887.

Kainen, Jacob. GEORGE CLYMER AND THE COLUMBIAN PRESS. New York: The Typophiles, 1950.

Kauffer, McKnight E. THE ART OF THE POSTER. London: Cecil Palmer, 1924.

Kubler, George A. A NEW HISTORY OF STEREOTYPING. New York: Published by the author, 1941.

Larwood, Jacob, and Hotten, John C. THE HISTORY OF SIGNBOARDS. London: Chatto & Windus, 1900.

Lewis, John. PRINTED EPHEMERA. Ipswich, Suffolk: W. S. Cowell, 1962.

Linton, W. J. SOME PRACTICAL HINTS ON WOOD ENGRAVING. New York: Lee & Shepard, 1879.

MacKellar, Thomas. THE AMERICAN PRINTER. 14th edition. Philadelphia: MacKellar, Smiths & Jordan, 1883.

McLean, Ruari. VICTORIAN BOOK DESIGN. New York: Oxford University Press, 1963.

Martin, Gordon. THE PLAYBILL. Chicago: Institute of Design, 1963. *"How Illuminated Show Bills are Printed,"* MIRROR OF TYPOGRAPHY (New York), III, No. 3 (Autumn, 1871), 35-36.

Munsell, Joel. TYPOGRAPHIC MISCELLANY. Albany: J. Munsell, n.d.

PAPER & PRINTING RECIPES. Chicago: Published by J. Sawtelle Ford, 1883.

Pasko, W. W. AMERICAN DICTIONARY OF PRINTING AND BOOKMAKING. New York: Howard Lockwood & Co. 1894.

PRACTICAL ENGRAVING ON METAL. London: Percival Marshall & Co., 1900.

Presbrey, Frank. THE HISTORY AND DEVELOPMENT OF ADVERTISING. Garden City, N. Y.: Doubleday, Doran & Co., Inc., 1929.

Ringwalt, Luther J. AMERICAN ENCYCLOPAEDIA OF PRINTING. Philadelphia: Menamin & Ringwalt, 1871.

Rosner, Charles. PRINTER'S PROGRESS, 1851-1951. Cambridge, Mass.: Harvard University Press, 1951.

Rowell, George Presbury. *"Forty Years an Advertising Agent,* 1865-1905," PRINTER'S INK, (New York), 1906.

Rowsome, Frank Jr. THEY LAUGHED WHEN I SAT DOWN.

New York, Toronto and London: McGraw-Hill Book Co., 1959.

Savage, William. PRACTICAL HINTS ON DECORATIVE PRINTING. London, 1822.

Senefelder, Alois. THE INVENTION OF LITHOGRAPHY. New York and London: Fuchs & Lang Manufacturing Co., 1911.

Thompson, David C. THE LIFE AND WORKS OF THOMAS BEWICK. London: The Art Journal Offices, 1882.

Twyman, Michael. JOHN SOULBY PRINTER, ULVERSTON. Museum of English Rural Life, University of Reading, 1966. (Catalogue.)

Wilson, Fred, and Grey, Douglas. MODERN PRINTING MACHINERY. London, Paris and New York: Cassell and Co., Ltd., 1888.

www.ingramcontent.com/pod-product-compliance
Lightning Source LLC
Chambersburg PA
CBHW050615290326
41929CB00063B/2909